THE PROBLEM OF INFLATION

CARNEGIE - ROCHESTER CONFERENCE SERIES ON PUBLIC POLICY

A supplementary series to the Journal of Monetary Economics

Editors

KARL BRUNNER
ALLAN H. MELTZER

Production Editor

ANGELA L. BARNES

VOLUME 8

NORTH-HOLLAND PUBLISHING COMPANY
AMSTERDAM • NEW YORK • OXFORD

THE PROBLEM OF INFLATION

Editors

KARL BRUNNER

Graduate School of Management
The University of Rochester

ALLAN H. MELTZER

Carnegie-Mellon University

1978

NORTH-HOLLAND PUBLISHING COMPANY
AMSTERDAM • NEW YORK • OXFORD

©North-Holland Publishing Company, 1978

ISBN North-Holland for this volume: 0444 85147 x

Publishers:

NORTH-HOLLAND PUBLISHING COMPANY
AMSTERDAM • NEW YORK • OXFORD

Sole distributors for the U.S.A. and Canada:
ELSEVIER NORTH-HOLLAND, INC.
52 VANDERBILT AVENUE,
NEW YORK, N.Y. 10017

Library of Congress Cataloging in Publication Data
Main entry under title:

The problem of inflation.

(Carnegie-Rochester conference series on public
policy ; v. 8)
    Includes bibliographies.
    1. Inflation (Finance)--Congresses. I. Title.
HG229.P944   332.4'1   78-772
ISBN 0-444-85147-X

PRINTED IN THE NETHERLANDS

INTRODUCTION TO THE SERIES

The Carnegie-Rochester Conference on Public Policy was initiated several years ago through the efforts of the Center for Research in Government Policy and Business at the University of Rochester and the Center for the Study of Public Policy at Carnegie-Mellon University. This book is the eighth volume in the series which presents the papers prepared for the conferences, plus the comments of discussants and participants.

Policies depend not only on theories and evidence, but on the structure of policymaking bodies and the procedures by which policies are made, implemented, and changed. The conferences direct the attention of economists to major problems of economic policy and institutional arrangements. We hope that the papers and the conferences will encourage further research on policy and on the effects of national agencies and international institutions on the choice of policies.

The Carnegie-Rochester Conference is an open forum. Participants are united by their interest in the issues discussed and by their belief that analysis, evidence, and informed discussion have lasting effects on the public and its institutions.

This eighth volume of the series, offered as a supplement to the <u>Journal of Monetary Economics</u>, contains papers presented at the April 1977 conference. Future volumes of the conference proceedings will be mailed to subscribers as a supplement to the journal. The editor of the journal will consider for publication comments on the papers published in the supplement.

We are indebted once again to Jean Morris and Jean Patterson for their assistance in the conference arrangements and proceedings. Phyllis McLaughlin typeset this and the preceding three volumes in the series; it is a pleasure to acknowledge her careful work.

K. BRUNNER
A.H. MELTZER
Editors

CONTENTS

Karl Brunner and Allan H. Meltzer:
The Problem of Inflation. 1

Pieter Korteweg:
The Economics of Inflation and Output Fluctuations
in the Netherlands, 1954-1975: A Test of Some
Implications of the Dominant Impulse-cum-Rational
Expectations Hypothesis. 17
E.J. Bomhoff:
Appendix C: Box-Jenkins Models for Inflation,
Output Growth, and Impulse Variables. 69

André Fourcans:
Inflation and Output Growth: The French
Experience, 1960-1975. 81

Michele Fratianni:
Inflation and Unanticipated Changes in Output
in Italy 141

Victor Argy:
A Comment on the Korteweg, Fratianni, and Fourcans
Papers 181

Anna J. Schwartz:
Inflation and Output Changes in France, Italy, and
the Netherlands: A Comment 193

Dean S Dutton:
The Economics of Inflation and Output Fluctuations in
the United States: 1952-1974. 203

Manfred J.M. Neumann:
The Impulse-Theoretic Explanation of Changing Inflation
and Output Growth: Evidence from Germany 233

Michael J. Hamburger:
  Inflation and Output Fluctuations in the
  United States and Germany: A Comment on the
  Dutton and Neumann Papers.   271

Bennett T. McCallum:
  Inflation and Output Fluctuations: A Comment
  on the Dutton and Neumann Papers   277

Peter D. Jonson and John C. Taylor:
  Inflation and Economic Stability in a Small
  Open Economy: A Systems Approach   289

Pieter Korteweg and Allan H. Meltzer:
  Inflation and Price Changes: Some
  Preliminary Estimates and Tests of
  Alternative Theories   325

Jerome L. Stein:
  Inflation and Stability: A Comment on
  the Jonson and Taylor and Korteweg and
  Meltzer Papers.   355

Jeremy J. Siegel:
  A Comment on the Korteweg and Meltzer and
  Dutton Papers   369

THE PROBLEM OF INFLATION

Karl Brunner
University of Rochester

and

Allan H. Meltzer
Carnegie-Mellon University

I. THE SURVIVAL OF MACRO THEORY

The Full Employment Act of 1946 expressed the hope that fiscal policy supported by a passive monetary policy would exorcise economic stagnation and deflationary gaps. But the opportunities of the new macro policy remained submerged during the Truman and Eisenhower administrations. Monetary and fiscal policy was used to contain the two bursts of moderate inflation that erupted in 1950 and 1955-56. The decade of the sixties opened with an essentially stable price level.

A new phase began with the Kennedy administration. Its economic advisors articulated the virtues of the "new economics," and expounded the rosy prospects expected to result from the government's control of the macro economy. The Kennedy administration's tax policies provided a vehicle to establish broad public awareness of the new opportunities for enlightened fiscal policies. The apparent success of the policies in increasing employment without increasing inflation fostered the belief that economists had acquired the understanding and developed the means to hold the economy on a stable course.

The world has moved fourteen years beyond this promise. A radical change has occurred in the economic climate. The U.S. economy suffers increasing inflation accompanied by higher levels of unemployment. Until the past decade, inflation was either a temporary phenomenon or an endemic regional problem (e.g., South America). Now inflation persists all over the world.

The experience of mounting economic instability, inflation, and higher unemployment cannot be reconciled with the expectations propagated during the Kennedy and early Johnson years. Ten or twelve years after fiscal policy activism was acclaimed as an instrument of macrostabilization policies, the bankruptcy of "macroeconomics" was openly discussed. One also heard Keynesians (neo- and otherwise) discuss the hope for the rise of a new Keynes who would set macroeconomics on a proper course.

1

The declaration of "intellectual bankruptcy" may have been motivated by disappointment with the results of fiscal stabilization policies and the failure of fine-tuning activism. Belief in a reliable trade-off between inflation and the rate of unemployment eroded. Observation of the coincidence of persistent inflation, falling output, and rising unemployment, a phenomenon graced with the term "stagflation," conveyed a sense of intractability. Politicians and their spokesmen do not like the (shorter-run) consequences with respect to unemployment and output of an anti-inflationary program. Even less attractive is the implication that public policy must choose between a smaller recession at a lower inflation now or a series of recessions over the future ten to fifteen years at much higher rates of inflation. Politicians' responses suggest that economists are at fault for failing to provide a macroeconomics assuring the reconciliation of anti-inflationary policies with "permanent full employment." This expectation about the duty of economists may partly explain the hope for a new Keynes.

The impact of the OPEC actions of October 1973, and subsequently, created new problems for macroeconomic policies committed to maintaining full employment at rising real wages. Economic analysis, on the other hand, had no difficulty finding the effect on the price level, the temporary effect on the rate of inflation, and the permanent effect on potential output. Careful analysis predicted that the Eurodollar market would not collapse in the absence of controls and intervention. Careful analysis also showed that the OPEC countries would not accumulate their current surpluses as financial assets but would spend for consumption and investment.

The experience of the past ten years, however, has revealed serious flaws in standard macro theory shaped by the Keynesian tradition. Keynesian theory did not present adequately the working of fiscal or monetary policy and neglected the interaction between the two sets of policies. The role of expectations was barely recognized, and important channels linking shifting policy patterns with capital markets or price behavior on output markets were neglected also. All this does not establish the bankruptcy of macroeconomics, but means that macroeconomics moves beyond the Keynesian phase of the 1950s and 1960s. Systematic attempts to subsume the experiences of the past ten years into a coherent story have yielded substantial results. The contributions of many groups of researchers have deepened our understanding of the inflation problem. This volume of the Carnegie-Rochester Conference Series participates in the ongoing stream of research seeking a useful understanding of macro events. The nature and range of questions addressed by the studies is clarified and interpreted in Section II. Section III traces the broad lines of work and summarizes the major results.

II. AN ANALYTIC BACKGROUND AND SURVEY

The price level is determined by the real (including fiscal policy) conditions and the monetary state of an economy. Many factors contribute to variations in the price level. Price movements reflect adjustments to temporary or persistent changes in real or monetary conditions. The inflation inquiry addresses the question of persistent or long-maintained increases in the price level. It is not concerned with the mass of transitory shocks operating on the price level or with once-and-for-all changes in underlying conditions affecting the price level once and for all. Both transitory shocks and once-and-for-all changes modifying the price level may occasionally reflect important economic problems deserving attention. But their analysis will not clarify the permanent drift into long-run inflation so clearly visible during the 1970s in Western countries.

The basic framework for this analysis of the inflation problem describes the interaction between asset markets and output markets in response to government budget policy and a pattern of deficit finance. The structure is presented with substantial simplification.[1] Equation (1) describes the equilibrium of the output market:

$$(1) \quad y = d + g + x$$

$$d = d \ [i - \pi, p, ap, P, ry, p^*, e] \quad d_1, d_2 < 0 < d_3, \ldots, d_7$$

$$x = x \ [p, p^*, y^*, e, B^*]. \quad x_1 < 0 < x_2, \ldots, x_5$$

Real output supplied by the private sector equals real expenditure. Expenditure consists of the domestic private sector's purchases d, the government sector's purchases g of private output, and the rest-of-the-world's purchases x of domestic output. The arguments in the function describing d and x are: i = nominal interest rate, π = anticipated rate of inflation, p = price level of output, ap = anticipated level of p, P = price level of real assets, p^* = price level of foreign output, e = exchange rate, y^* = foreign real income, B^* = foreign

[1] The reader will find a more detailed presentation of the scheme in several of our previous papers: Brunner (1976b), Brunner and Meltzer (1976a, 1976b, 1976c).

monetary base, and ry = received real income defined as the sum ry = y + $g\frac{w}{p}$ gem. The second term in the sum is the real wage bill paid by government.

Two asset markets are introduced to describe the interaction of three assets. Equation (2) describes the credit market:[2]

(2) $a\,(i,P,u)\,B = \sigma\,(i - \pi, p, ap, P, ry, S, e)$

$$a_1, a_2 > 0, \quad \sigma_1, \sigma_4 < 0 < \sigma_2, \sigma_3, \sigma_5, \ldots, \sigma_7$$

(3) $m(i,P,u)\,B = \lambda(i, p, ap, P, ry, e).$

$$m_1 > 0 > m_2, \quad \lambda_1, \lambda_3, \lambda_6 < 0 < \lambda_2, \lambda_4, \lambda_5$$

The left-hand side presents the banking system's absorption of assets as a product of an asset multiplier a and the monetary base B. The right-hand side reflects the public's stock supply of assets to banks. The outstanding stock S of government securities is among the determinants of this supply. Equation (3) is the money market. The left-hand side introduces the money stock as a product of monetary multiplier and monetary base, and the right-hand side presents the public's demand for money.

Three more equations are required for our purposes. Equation (4) describes the government sector's budget constraint:

(4a) $\Delta B_1 = \mu\,def$

(4b) $\Delta S = (1 - \mu)\,def$

$$def = pg + gw \cdot gem + I\,(i, \tau)\,S - t\,(p, ry; \tau).$$

The term def expresses the deficit; gw = money wage rate per unit of employment; gem = government sector employment; $I(i,\tau)$ measures the average net

---

[2]The symbol u   represents a vector of policy variables (rediscount rate, ceiling rate of interest, reserve requirement ratios) and other determinants of m and a.

4

cost per unit of outstanding security as a function of the (average) rate of interest i and a tax vector τ. The magnitude IS is the government sector's net interest payments. The first three items of def measure the government's total expenditures. The last item in the deficit expression makes the net tax revenues a function of price level, real income, and tax vector. A financial parameter μ describes the financing of the deficit. A portion μ of the deficit is financed with new base money by means of open-market operations and a portion $(1 - \mu)$ with issues of new securities to the banks and the public. Open-market operations change base money and securities in opposite directions and can be expressed in terms of μ.

Equations (5) and (6) relate the balance on international current account with the monetary base and specify the composition of the monetary base:

(5) $\Delta B_2 = px - imp\ (i - \pi,\ p,\ p^*,\ P,\ ry,\ e)\ p^* e,$

$$imp_1,\ imp_3 < 0 < imp_2,\ imp_4, \ldots, imp_6$$

where imp denotes the real volume of imports;

(6) $B = B_1 + B_2 + NFP.$

The monetary base is the sum of three components. B_1 and B_2 are implicitly defined by (4a) and (5). The first component reflects the past financing of the government, and the second component reveals the history of the balance of current account. The last component NFP is the public's net foreign position on domestic and foreign asset markets.[3]

The last equation introduces the private sector's price-setting behavior as a function of output, real capital K, the wage index w, the foreign price level p^*, and the exchange rate:

(7) $p = p(y,\ K,\ w,\ p^* e).$ $p_2 < 0 < p_1,\ p_3,\ p_4$

_____

[3]Brunner and Meltzer (1976b) discusses the role of NFP in the context of asset markets. The instantaneous adjustment of asset markets in contrast to the gradual adjustment of the current balance of payments means that the public's net foreign position is always adjusted to prevailing market conditions. The monetary base always reflects the fully adjusted NFP, but adjusts gradually to the underlying current account.

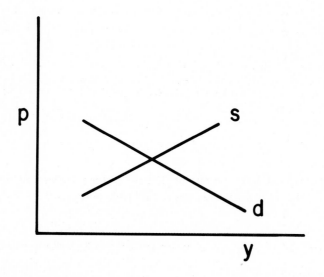

Figure 1

The wage variable provides the link with the labor market and reflects the structure of wage contracting and the expectations shaping the contracts. Expectational adjustments enter the system via π, ap, and w.

The basic analytic framework can be condensed in a diagram that gives an intuitive understanding of the interacting processes shaping the inflation problem. The exposition begins with the short-run equilibrium describing the adjustment of the economy to the inherited financial and real stocks and the prevailing expectations. Figure 1 shows the short-run equilibrium position. The supply curve s represents the price-setting function. The expenditure curve d summarizes output and asset market equations (1) - (3). Every point on d is a combination of price level p and output y that equilibrates simultaneously all asset markets and the output market. The slope of d depends on the structural properties of the three markets. Its position reflects prevailing expectations and inherited stocks.

Inflation is shown by persistent upward drift of the intersection point. Analysis of inflation seeks to determine the role of the forces--fiscal and monetary policy, expectational and foreign variables--that change the positions of the curves. In this context, we disregard the real capital stock and problems of growth.

An increase in the government's real absorption g from the private sector or of government employment gem shifts the demand curve up or to the right, raising price level and output. The rise in the price level expresses the competition between the major sectors for available output and the responsiveness of supply behavior to current market conditions. An increase of wages gw paid by the government to its employees induces a similar shift, and an increase in the base B or in outstanding securities induces, via the adjustments imposed on the asset markets, an increase in spending, with a corresponding effect on output and the price level. Thus, fiscal policy, expressed by g, gem, gw, τ, and financial policy, represented by B and S, move the short-run system to higher levels of output and prices.

The underlying analysis yields information beyond this broad qualitative result. The constraints imposed on the basic structure imply a definite order for the magnitude of the shifts induced by fiscal and financial policy variables. The shift of the d line induced by B exceeds the corresponding response to the fiscal variables by a large multiple. Moreover, the elasticity of p with respect to S is smallest, probably less than half the elasticity with respect to g.[4] The effect of S is sufficiently weak that even large increases in S exert little

[4] Brunner (1976b) develops an argument bearing on this ordering. The responses are the elasticities of p with respect to the policy variables holding output, foreign variables, wages, and anticipations constant.

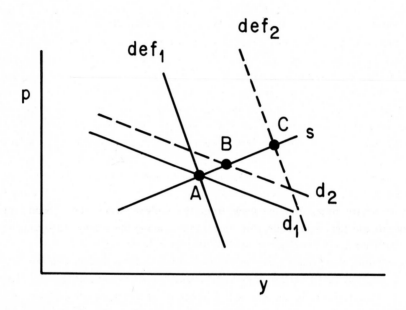

Figure 2

net influence on the price level in a growing economy. The increase in S is, therefore, most unlikely to produce inflation, and attention must be directed to the behavior of other variables.

Aggregation of equation (4a) shows the dependence of the stock of base money on the history of the budget. B_1 is the portion of the accumulated deficit financed by issuing base money. The def line in Figure 2 describes budget balance, i.e., $\Delta B_1 = \text{def} = 0$. The budget balance equation defines an implicit function in p and y. The slope of the line depends on fiscal arrangements affecting the nature of expenditure policies (nominal or real) and the responsiveness of nominal tax revenues to current or past price level and output. With sufficient responsiveness of tax revenues to current conditions, the def line has a negative slope much steeper than the slope of the expenditure curve.

The initial position of short-run equilibrium at A lies at the intersection of the lines d_1, s, and def_1. Since the equilibrium position is on the def line, there is a balanced budget under the prevailing fiscal policy. An increase in g (or gem) shifts both d and def to the right or upwards. The underlying structure implies that the (vertical or horizontal) shift of the def line is a multiple of the shift in the d line. With wages, capital stock, and foreign prices unchanged, fiscal policy moves the system along the supply curve to the new short-run position B. But this position cannot be maintained. The point B lies below the def line, so the short-run system produces a budget deficit, raising the monetary base. The feedback from the budget pushes the expenditure curve to the right. The short-run system moves along the supply curve until it settles at the point C, a position of stock-flow equilibrium.

With a fixed supply curve, the total effect of fiscal policy is the sum of two components. The first is a pure fiscal effect with invariant stock variables. This effect is shown by the movement from A to B. The second component, expressed by the system's shift from B to C, is the monetary effect of the given fiscal policy. The relative magnitude of the shift elasticities derived from the underlying structure indicates that the monetary effect dominates the pure fiscal effect. Consequently, variations in the monetary variable reflect the major persistent effect of fiscal policy on output and the price level. The pure fiscal effect adds a separate and additional effect.

Expectational adjustments are readily incorporated into the analysis. An increase in the anticipated price level (or in the anticipated rate of inflation π) shifts the expenditure curve up and reinforces the output and price effect along a given and invariant supply schedule. But, expectations underlying evolving wage contracts also adjust and modify w correspondingly. The supply curve moves up and to the left. These expectational processes do not produce a movement of ap and w with uniform magnitude and timing. The two variables involve expectations of overlapping but differently composed groups. In the case of w, they also involve contractual adjustments which are spread over time.

The budget must be balanced at every equilibrium position, so the economy reaches equilibrium only when the d and s curves intersect on the def line. The response of prices to fiscal policy depends on the position of the def line, but the rate at which prices change and the distribution of the fiscal stimulus between prices and output depend on the relative speeds and magnitudes of the various expectation adjustments. A comparatively large and rapid adjustment of w determines a correspondingly larger price and smaller output effect. The rate of price change produced during the adjustment imposed by a new def line is also larger. Eventually, all wage contracts adjust to the prevailing price and market conditions. The supply curve moves to an inter-section with the def line in the neighborhood of a vertical line, in the p, y plane, representing normal output of the private sector. The position of the expenditure curve is pushed to this intersection by changes in the underlying stocks of financial assets issued to finance the deficit.

The inflation problem may be decomposed into two stages. The first is the effect of fiscal policy on the position of the def line, the second, the relation between the short-run and longer-run price level. The def line and the fully adjusted supply schedule, corresponding to a fully adjusted w, determine jointly the long-term price level. The short-run price level reflects current stocks and expectations. Any excess of the long-term price level over the short-run price level built into the system by prevailing fiscal policy causes changes in the short-run price level. The resulting price-output path, or path of output changes and price-level changes, depends on the pattern of expectational adjustments. Expectational revisions built into wage contracts and reflected by w dominate the later stages of adjustment, so effects on output are confined to the shorter run. A persistent pattern of increases in the price level maintained over longer periods of time, i.e., the emergence of an inflation problem, appears whenever one of two conditions arises: fiscal policies more or less continuously shift the def line to the right or upwards; or, open-market operations maintain the growth of money. Inflationary policies impose a persistent adjustment problem on the economy. As wage contracts become adjusted to revised expectations of financial policy, supply adjustments are made more rapidly. Persistent inflation thus attenuates output effects, enhances price effects, and speeds the adjustment to inflation.

This summary of the basic analysis conveys with rough and impressionistic strokes the role of the wage process and reinterprets the process known as "autonomous wage push." The patterns of prices, wages, output, and unemployment have suggested to many observers the operation of a "sociologically" embedded wage push. Our analysis interprets these observations in a price-theoretically coherent manner. Wage patterns exhibit an increasing dissociation from <u>current</u> market conditions whenever the underlying expectations affecting wage contracting and thus w reflect a consensus about the future trend in the budget and financial policies. Movement in w is affected very little by shorter-run retardations of output or inflation. Under the conditions of sustained inflation, a variety of incentives contribute to lower the frequency of under-estimating the longer-run policy trend.

This discussion has neglected any interaction with the outside world. Foreign influences operate via the foreign price level p^*, foreign demand for domestic output y^*, and the exchange rate e. With fixed exchange rates, foreign influences are also transmitted via the <u>b</u>alance <u>of c</u>urrent <u>a</u>ccount (boca) on B_2 and the monetary base.

Foreign influences modify both the demand and the supply schedules. An increase in p^* or e moves both schedules upwards. Imported inputs substitute for domestic materials and labor in supply, and imported output substitutes for domestic products in demand. The relative shift of the supply schedule depends on the extent to which the effects of imports used as inputs are reinforced by the effect of p^* (or e) on w. The magnitude and speed of the wage adjustment determines the division of the foreign impulse between domestic price level and output. A sensitive w raises the price effect. The other channels conveying foreign impulses--y^* on x, and B_2 (and B) on d--concentrate their full short-run effects on spending. Increases in y^* and B_2 push the expenditure curve to the right and raise domestic output and prices. With modest input price effects and w insensitive to p^* (or e), foreign impulses mainly shift d and increase domestic output. Large input price effects supplemented by a sensitive w direct the major impact of the foreign impulse to the price level. Adjustment of expectations supplements these responses. With fixed exchange rates, persistent foreign impulses generate persistent inflation with an increasing likelihood of stagflation. Figure 3 presents the analysis of foreign influences. The boca line defines all combinations of p and y that satisfy the condition of balanced current accounts, i.e., $px = imp \cdot p^* \cdot e$. The slope of the boca line is negative provided the sum of the domestic price elasticities of x and imp exceeds unity. We assume that the slope of boca is negative and lies between the slopes of the d and the def line.

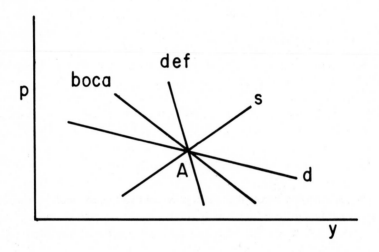

Figure 3

Point A in Figure 3 shows an equilibrium at the intersection of boca, def, d, and s. The short-run price level has converged to the long-run price level on the def line and the boca line. Full stock-flow equilibrium requires continuous adjustment of the four lines to intersect at the same point. Full equilibrium is realized only if domestic fiscal policy is adjusted to the foreign impulse, or if the exchange rate is intermittently adjusted to prevent persistent increases or decreases in B_2.[5] An independent fiscal policy is not consistent with a rigid fixed-exchange-rate system. Either the position of the def line must be adjusted to the position of the boca line, or the fixed-rate system must be abandoned.

The inherent instability of a system combining independent fiscal policies and a fixed exchange rate implies that, in the long run, exchange rates cannot remain fixed if countries pursue independent fiscal policies. In the short run, the joint operation of domestic and foreign inflation impulses appears as simultaneous movements of the def line and the boca line to the right. The impulses modify the short-run position of the spending and supply curves. But, the movements of def and boca circumscribe the enduring pattern of domestic inflation, and the size of relative shifts in def and boca determines the comparative role of domestic and foreign impulses in the inflation process.

III. A SUMMARY OF EMPIRICAL WORK

The preceding background and survey reveal two (approximately) separate issues in the inflation problem. One is the nature of underlying impulses; the other is the characteristics of the transmission mechanism. The papers in this volume address the impulse problem primarily.

The papers distinguish three sets of impulses. The monetary impulse includes the monetary effect B_1 of open-market operations and fiscal policy, and the monetary effect B_2 of the foreign impulse. The pure fiscal impulse is represented by measures of taxes, government spending, and debt. A non-monetary foreign impulse corresponds to the operation of p^* and y^* in our discussion. Examination of the impulses exploits data from the Netherlands, France, Italy, the U.S., West Germany, Australia, and the "world." The data were summarized in four magnitudes: monetary growth (or acceleration) measures the monetary impulse; a fiscal index expresses the pure net fiscal impulse including both expenditures and taxes; the foreign impulse is represented by two components, foreign price and foreign output.

---

[5]See Brunner (1976a) and Brunner and Meltzer (1976b) for a more complete analysis of fiscal policy and the balance of payments.

The data for the various countries convey in broad outline a rather similar pattern. The monetary impulse appears to operate with some regularity on changes in the price level, directly or by changing the anticipated rate of inflation. The foreign price impulse emerges as the second major force affecting the price level in the open economies investigated. The pure net fiscal impulse also exhibits some impact in most countries considered.

Among the impulses shaping the growth of output, measures expressing an unanticipated or accelerating monetary impulse figure foremost. The foreign quantity impulse also appears to affect output growth with some regularity. The foreign price impulse exhibits muted (negative) effects. A modest effect of pure net fiscal policy on output growth appears in the data for a few countries. These patterns are consistent with the implications of the underlying analysis for the comparative order of the demand curve's shift elasticity with respect to monetary and fiscal impulses. They also seem consistent with experience. Once inflation is underway, it continues even with very modest variations in foreign prices or in the pure net fiscal impulse.

Jonson and Taylor summarize the results for Australia in a statement applicable to a much broader experience. "It could be argued that considerable responsibility for increased inflation and economic instability be attributed to the failure of Australian economic policy to emphasize sufficiently monetary growth rates as crucial indicators of the stance of policy. Greater emphasis on the need for monetary stability would have involved a setting of policy instruments. . .conducive to a more stable outcome for money and economic activity."

The procedures and results presented in the papers were subjected to criticism by discussants. Their critiques, included in the volume, suggest some avenues for future research on the inflation problem.

References

Brunner, K. (1976a), "A Fisherian Framework for the Analysis of International Monetary Problems," in <u>Inflation in the World Economy</u>, eds. M. Parkin and G. Zis. Manchester: Manchester University Press.

_____(1976b), "Inflation, Money and the Role of Fiscal Arrangements: An Analytical Framework for the Inflation Problem," in <u>The New Inflation and Monetary Policy</u>, ed. M. Monti. London: MacMillan.

Brunner, K., and Meltzer, A.H. (1976a), "An Aggregative Theory for a Closed Economy," in <u>Monetarism</u>, ed. J. Stein. Amsterdam: North-Holland.

_____(1976b), "Monetary and Fiscal Policy in Open, Interdependent Economies with Fixed Exchange Rates," in <u>Recent Issues in International Monetary Economics</u>, eds. E. Claassen and P. Salin. Amsterdam: North-Holland.

_____(1976c), "Reply--Monetarism: The Principal Issues, Areas of Agreement and the Work Remaining," in <u>Monetarism</u>, ed. J. Stein. Amsterdam: North-Holland.

THE ECONOMICS OF INFLATION AND OUTPUT FLUCTUATIONS
IN THE NETHERLANDS, 1954-1975:

A Test of Some Implications
of the Dominant Impulse-cum-Rational Expectations Hypothesis

Pieter Korteweg*

Erasmus University, Rotterdam

The purpose of this paper is to give an economic explanation of the proportionate rates of change of the aggregate levels of prices and private domestic output in the Netherlands over the postwar period 1954-75.

Basic to this explanation is the contention that aggregate fluctuations in prices and output are dominated by systematic impulses operating on the economy. Four classes of such systematic impulses are distinguished: fiscal, foreign, monetary, and financial. The policies pursued by the government with respect to expenditures and tax rates impose a fiscal impulse on the economy. Changing claims of the foreign sector on domestic private output and changes in prices (and exchange rates) to be paid for domestic claims on foreign output impose foreign impulses on the economy. Finally, changes in the stocks of money and government debt brought about by monetary policy, government deficit financing, and managing the exchange rate impose monetary and financial impulses on the economy.

All these impulses have in common that they impose or release contending claims on private domestic output that have to be resolved by changes in prices and/or output. The transmission of these fiscal, foreign, monetary, and financial impulses to prices and output is governed by a relative-price stock-flow mechanism as set forth in Brunner (1976) and Brunner and Meltzer (1976a, 1976b).

Five markets are involved in this mechanism: the markets for output, money, private and government debt (credit), physical capital, and labor. Five economic agents operate in these markets: the government and the central bank, the banking system, the public and the foreign sector. The private nongovernment sector is assumed to behave rationally and to form its expectations about economic variables consistent with economic theory. In other words,

---

*In writing this paper I have benefited greatly from extensive discussions with Michele Fratianni and Eduard J. Bomhoff. The latter has also closely cooperated in devising and executing the test procedures used. I am also grateful to Wolter Klimbie and Peter Konijnenburg for high quality high-pressure research assistance. Helpful comments by the participants of the Carnegie-Rochester Conference, especially those of Anna J. Schwartz and Victor Argy, and by Ben McCallum on an earlier version of this paper, are gratefully acknowledged.

17

money illusion is absent, and expectations about economic variables are determined by the same factors which economic theory says determine the variables about which expectations are formed. However, full current information about the factors determining expectations is not available or is too costly. Informational imperfections exist. Consequently, whereas anticipated systematic impulses have only price effects and no output effects, unanticipated impulses due to imperfect information affect both the price level and the volume of output.

The paper is set up as follows.

Section I presents a highly condensed version of the model that governs the transmission of systematic economic impulses to prices and output. The model is predicated on the assumption of rational economic behavior and rational formation of expectations.

Section II constructs empirical measures of the fiscal, foreign, monetary, and financial impulses, as well as of the proportionate rates of change of the aggregate level of prices and private domestic output.

Section III develops a nonparametric test of the hypothesis according to which each of the impulse forces is both a necessary and sufficient condition for inflation and deviations of output growth from its "normal" level. (Readers in a hurry may skip this section altogether.)

Section IV discusses an analysis which regresses the proportionate rate of change of the implicit price deflator of Dutch private consumption on the anticipated and unanticipated values of the economic impulse measures, and an analysis which regresses the deviation of the proportionate rate of change of industrial production from its "normal" level on the unanticipated parts of the economic impulse measures.

In a final section, the results of the analysis of Dutch inflation and output fluctuations are summarized, and some policy implications are discussed. The main conclusions reached are that Dutch postwar inflation has been mainly a monetary phenomenon, whereas deviations of output growth from its normal level have been dominated by unanticipated foreign and financial impulses. The main policy implications are, first, that output growth cannot systematically be stimulated over and above its normal rate by traditional demand management policies, and second, that control of the growth rate of the stock of money nationally and internationally, rather than direct wage and price controls, is a necessary and sufficient condition to stem inflation.

I. A CONDENSED MODEL OF INFLATION AND OUTPUT FLUCTUATIONS

The model developed in this section is a truncated version of the one presented in Brunner and Meltzer (1976a, 1976b). Condensed to aggregate supply and demand equations for private domestic output and written in first differences of logarithms, the model for an open managed-exchange rate economy can be written as follows (see Barro and Fischer, 1976):

$$(1) \quad \hat{y} = \hat{\bar{y}} + a_1 (\hat{p} - \hat{p}^e) + u_s \text{ , aggregate supply;}$$

$$(2) \quad \hat{y} = \beta_1 (\hat{M} - \hat{p}^e) + \beta_2 (\hat{S} - \hat{p}^e) + \beta_3 (\hat{p}^* - \hat{p}) + \beta_4 FI + \beta_5 \hat{y}^*$$

$$+ \beta_3 \hat{e} + u_d \text{ , aggregate demand.}$$

Hats (^) indicate first differences of logarithms, superscript e denotes the expected value of a variable, and stars (*) refer to foreign variables. Variable y indicates the volume of private production, whereas $\bar{y}$ is the "normal" level of production, i.e., that level of production at which price expectations are realized.

Variable p is the aggregate price level of private production, M is the stock of money, S the stock of government debt outstanding, and FI some linear combination of the proportionate rates of change of discretionary real government expenditures and taxes. Variable e is the exchange rate denoting the number of domestic currency units per unit of foreign currency. Finally, u_d and u_s are random shift terms reflecting changes in tastes, productivity, etc.

For purposes of exposition, the exchange rate and the stocks of money and debt are assumed to be controlled by the government and the central bank. In reality, parts of the stocks of money and debt may be determined endogenously--via the government's budget financing restriction and via the monetary authorities' policy reaction function with respect to exchange rates, interest rates, and other economic target variables--by what happens to the aggregate level of prices and output. That is to say, money and debt may not be independent of those variables we seek to explain.

It is important to note in this respect, however, that the concern here is with the causality of money and debt with respect to fluctuations in inflation and output growth. The defining characteristic of the monetarist position, and one which is put to test in this paper, is the contention that there is a causal relationship running from money to prices and output, and that the variability of monetary impulses dominates fluctuations in the level of prices and output relative to the variability of the fiscal, foreign, and financial impulses.

On an analytical level, the issue of the endogeneity of money and government debt has no bearing on the causality of money and debt with respect to inflation and output growth. On an empirical level, however, it may result in biased estimates of the effects of monetary and financial impulses on the economy. This is, however, an empirical problem which need not concern us here and can, therefore, be reserved for a later section.

Solving for the proportionate rate of change of the aggregate price level from (1) and (2) gives:

$$(3) \quad \hat{p} = \frac{1}{A} \left[-\hat{\bar{y}} + \beta_1 \hat{M} + \beta_2 \hat{S} + \beta_3 (\hat{e} + \hat{p}^*) + \beta_4 \hat{FI} + \beta_5 \hat{y}^* \right.$$

$$\left. + (a_1 - \beta_1 - \beta_2)\hat{p}^e + u \right],$$

where $A = a_1 + \beta_3$ and $u = u_d - u_s$.

It is assumed that the expectation of inflation is formed rationally, i.e., is an unbiased predictor of actual inflation given all the information available just before the start of the period to which the expectation applies. Taking the mathematical expectation of (3) gives:

$$(4) \quad \hat{p}^e = \frac{1}{B} \left[-\hat{\bar{y}} + \beta_1 \hat{M}^e + \beta_2 \hat{S}^e + \beta_3 (\hat{e}^e + \hat{p}^{*e}) + \beta_4 \hat{FI}^e + \beta_5 \hat{y}^{*e} \right],$$

where $B = \beta_1 + \beta_2 + \beta_3$, and x^e is shorthand for $E_{t-1}(x_t)$, the mathematical expectation of some variable x_t conditioned on information available at time t-1.

Rational behavior implies that the coefficients of the actual and expected nominal variables denominated in domestic currency units $(\hat{M}, \hat{S}, \hat{e} + \hat{p}^*)$ sum to unity, implying homogeneity of degree one of actual and expected inflation in these nominal impulses. In other words, inflation and inflationary expectations are assumed to be formed rationally and free of money illusion.

Subtracting $\hat{p}^e$ from both sides of (3) and substituting (4) gives:

$$(5) \quad \hat{p} - \hat{p}^e = \frac{1}{A} \left\{ \beta_1 (\hat{M} - \hat{M}^e) + \beta_2 (\hat{S} - \hat{S}^e) + \beta_3 [(\hat{e} + \hat{p}^*) - (\hat{e}^e + \hat{p}^{*e})] \right.$$

$$\left. + \beta_4 (FI - FI^e) + \beta_5 (\hat{y}^* - \hat{y}^{*e}) + u \right\} .$$

From this equation it follows that deviations of actual from expected inflation can occur because of random events or unforeseen movements in the systematic fiscal, foreign, monetary, and financial impulse forces resulting from imperfect information. More specifically, the assumption of rational expectations implies that $\hat{p}$ and $\hat{p}^e$ differ only by a random forecast error which is uncorrelated with everything known before the beginning of the period to which the forecast applies.

Solving for the proportionate rate of change of output from (1) and (5) gives:

$$(6) \quad \hat{y} = \overset{\approx}{y} + \frac{a_1}{A} \left[\beta_1 (\hat{M} - \hat{M}^e) + \beta_2 (\hat{S} - \hat{S}^e) + \beta_3 [(\hat{e} + \hat{p}^*) - (\hat{e}^e + \hat{p}^{*e})] \right.$$

$$\left. + \beta_4 (FI - FI^e) + \beta_5 (\hat{y}^* - \hat{y}^{*e}) \right\} + \frac{a_1}{A} u_d + \frac{\beta_3}{A} u_s .$$

Note that, according to (6), deviations of output from its "normal" growth path result either from random demand and supply shifts or from unforeseen systematic fiscal, foreign, monetary, and financial impulses because of imperfect information. Systematic impulses, if foreseen, have only price effects and no output effects. By implication, there is no systematic way that the government can operate its fiscal, monetary, and financial impulses in order to stimulate output growth above its normal level. The only effect of such policies is on inflation.

21

The hypothesis embodied in (4) - (6) is that systematic impulses dominate inflation and output fluctuations and that economic behavior and expectations are formed rationally and free of money illusion. I label this hypothesis the dominant impulse-cum-rational expectations hypothesis of inflation and output fluctuations, or the DIRE hypothesis, for short.

I conclude this section with a note on the role of exchange rates and exchange rate expectations in the model. If exchange rates are fully fixed and kept constant, $\hat{e}$ and $\hat{e}^e$ are zero, and consequently, the term $\hat{e}$ and $\hat{e}^e$ disappear from (3) - (6). If, on the other hand, exchange rates are fully flexible and proximately determined by international differences between inflation rates, such that $\hat{e} = \hat{p} - \hat{p}^*$ and $\hat{e}^e = \hat{p}^e - \hat{p}^{*e}$, the terms with β_3 as a coefficient disappear from (3) - (6).

Finally, if exchange rates are neither fully fixed nor fully flexible but, instead, firmly managed as has been assumed above, exchange rate movements tend to be discrete instead of continuous and to impose impulses on the economy. The authorities intervene in the spot and future foreign exchange markets in order to stabilize exchange rates and to prevent the future exchange rate from deviating from the spot rate in excess of a certain fixed range. Exchange rate expectations may, however, be persistently different from the levels at which the monetary authorities try to set the future exchange rate. Interventions thus prevent expectations from translating into both spot and future rate. Tensions build up and accumulate until the authorities find themselves no longer able to support the exchange rates at their desired level and relent. Under such circumstances, exchange rates tend to move shockwise, and movements in $\hat{e}$ and $\hat{e}^e$ no longer reflect international differences between current actual and expected inflation rates but rather their cumulated magnitudes over time. This paper assumes a regime of firmly managed floating in which movements in the exchange rate occur in a discrete fashion and are determined not by current but rather by past international differences between actual and expected inflation rates.

In the next section, I describe and construct the empirical counterparts of the variables and impulses used to test some of the implications of the DIRE hypothesis.

II. INFLATION, OUTPUT FLUCTUATIONS, AND IMPULSE MEASURES: THE DUTCH RECORD

Changes in the price level of private domestic production will be measured by the growth rate of the implicit price deflator of private consumption $(\hat{p}_c)$. As a proxy for the growth rate of the price level of private domestic output, this measure has several weaknesses. First, only part of private domestic production consists of consumer goods and services. Moreover, only part of private domestic production of consumer goods and services is consumed domestically by the private sector. Other absorbers are the government and foreign sector. Finally, private domestic consumption involves goods and services produced not only by the private domestic sector but also by the government and foreign sector. These weaknesses do not seem to be serious. From the accompanying figures, it appears that the growth rates of the implicit price deflator of private consumption and the implicit price deflator of production of private domestic enterprises $(\hat{p}_b)$ move in unison.[1] This, as well as the fact that the growth rate of consumer prices is a central variable in public opinion and wage negotiations, motivates a preference for the growth rate of the implicit consumer price deflator as a measure of Dutch inflation.

The preferred measure of the growth rate of private domestic production will be the rate of growth of industrial production $(\hat{y})$. A disadvantage of industrial production is that it does not include private production of services, whereas a point in its favor is that it does not include agricultural production, which is partly determined by noneconomic factors like the weather. As can be seen from the accompanying figures, the growth rates of industrial production and gross production of domestic enterprises $(\hat{gdp}_b)$ move closely together.

Two salient phenomena are brought out by the figures. First, up to, say, 1969, the growth rates of consumer prices and industrial production fluctuate around a constant level of about 3 percent and 6 percent, respectively. Second, since 1969, consumer price inflation varies around an upward trend, whereas the growth rate of industrial production varies around a downward trend. This is the problem of stagflation characteristic of the late 1960s and of most of the 1970s. As can be seen from the figures also, low or stagnating growth rates of production translate into high or rising rates of excess capacity (q) and unemployment (u).

As the measure of pure fiscal impulses (FI) arising from fiscal actions of the government, annual changes in the central and local government's cash-flow

---

[1] Private domestic enterprises include, among other things, industry and agriculture.

The Dutch economic record 1954 - 1975

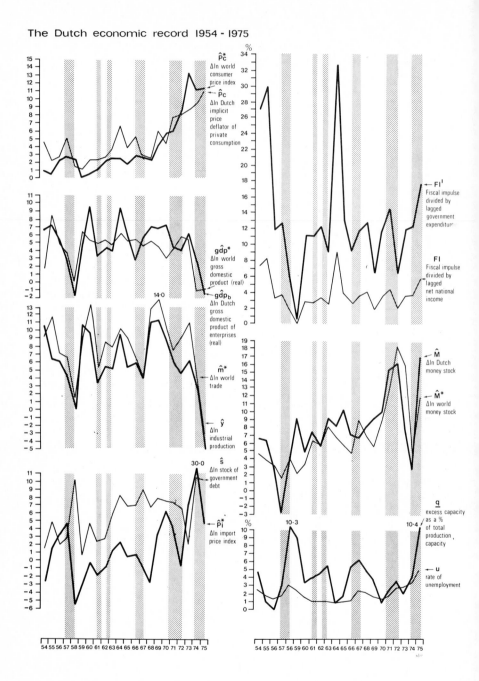

$\hat{P}_c^*$
Δln world consumer price index

← $\hat{P}_c$
Δln Dutch implicit price deflator of private consumption

$g\hat{d}p^*$
Δln world gross domestic product (real)

← $g\hat{d}p_b$
Δln Dutch gross domestic product of enterprises (real)

← $\hat{m}^*$
Δln world trade

← $\hat{y}$
Δln industrial production

← $\hat{s}$
Δln stock of government debt

← $\hat{P}_i^*$
Δln import price index

← FI^l
Fiscal impulse divided by lagged government expenditure

FI
Fiscal impulse divided by lagged net national income

← $\hat{M}$
Δln Dutch money stock

← $\hat{M}^*$
Δln world money stock

q
excess capacity as a % of total production capacity

← u
rate of unemployment

24

The Dutch economic record 1954-1975

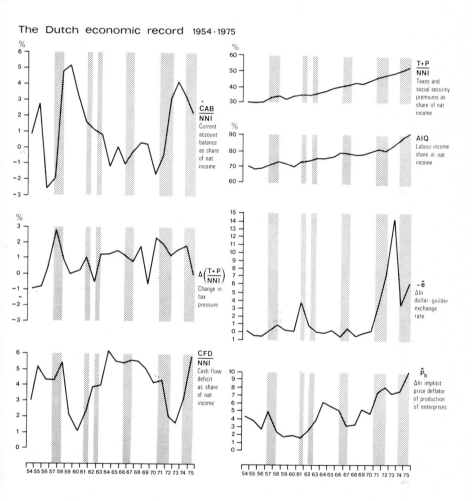

$\frac{CAB}{NNI}$
Current account balance as share of nat income

$\Delta\left(\frac{T+P}{NNI}\right)$
Change in tax pressure

$\frac{CFD}{NNI}$
Cash flow deficit as share of nat income

$\frac{T+P}{NNI}$
Taxes and social security premiums as share of nat income

AIQ
Labour income share in nat income

$-\hat{e}$
$\Delta\ln$ dollar-guilder exchange rate

$\hat{P}_b$
$\Delta\ln$ implicit price deflator of production of enterprises

54 55 56 57 58 59 60 61 62 63 64 65 66 67 68 69 70 71 72 73 74 75

25

budget deficit $(\Delta \text{ CFD})$ are used, corrected for changes in government import of foreign goods and services $(\Delta \text{ Img})$, automatic changes in the government's wage bill $(\Delta \text{ Lg})$ because of government wage-rate indexation to the overall private sector wage rate, and automatic changes in tax receipts because of changes in nominal net national income at given tax rates $(\Delta \text{ T aut})$.[2]

In addition, changes in gross nominal investment in dwellings and business buildings $(\Delta \text{ GIdb})$ are included in the fiscal impulse measure in view of the fact that they are government controlled via the operation of a building permit rationing system.[3] The fiscal impulse measure so obtained and divided by net national income (NNI) is:[4]

$$\text{FI} = \frac{\Delta \left[\text{CFD} + \text{T aut} + \text{GIdb} - \text{Lg} - \text{Img} \right]}{\text{NNI}_{-1}} \times 100 \text{ percent}.$$

The accompanying figures show that the fiscal impulse measure so calculated moves around a <u>trendless</u> average. This makes it difficult to attribute the upward trend in inflation and the downward trend in output growth discussed above to the course over time of pure fiscal impulses.

The construction of the fiscal impulse measure described above reflects in the first place a desire to separate changes in the budget deficit and in the underlying government expenditures and tax receipts into automatic and discretionary components. Secondly, it reflects that government expenditures in the Dutch case are largely set in <u>nominal</u> terms, except for government wages and salaries which are set in real terms.[5]

---

[2] For a summary of the theoretical underpinnings of the construction of fiscal impulse measures, refer to Blinder and Solow (1974). Date on ΔLg are supplied by the Dutch Ministry of Finance. The procedure to calculate $\Delta\text{T aut}$ is given in Appendix B.

[3] It should be noted in advance that both the course over time of the fiscal impulse measure and the conclusions reached later in the paper about the effects of fiscal impulses are highly independent of the absence or presence of ΔGIdb in the fiscal impulse measure constructed below.

[4] As the denominator, one could also use government expenditures lagged one period. In the accompanying figures, this impulse measure appears as FI'. It moves highly parallel to FI, be it that its average and variance are much higher. Again, none of the conclusions reached in this paper concerning the effects of fiscal impulses depend in any way on whether one uses as the impulse measure FI or FI'.

[5] For more details, see Korteweg (1975, pp. 571-77) and Dixon (1972). It should be noted in passing, first, that most of the components of our fiscal impulse measure are cash flows instead of transactions figures, and second, that the cash-flow surplus of the Dutch Social Security Funds is not included in the government's CFD used above. For some consequences of these and other properties of the fiscal impulse measure, see Korteweg (1975, pp. 575-77).

A final remark is in order regarding the measure of pure fiscal impulses. Unlike variants of the "weighted standardized surplus" proposed by Blinder and Solow (1974) and Blinder and Goldfeld (1976), the fiscal impulse measure given here implicitly assumes different kinds of government expenditures (like consumption, investment, subsidies, income transfers) and taxes (like direct and indirect taxes, income taxes, and excise taxes) to have identical effects on the level of prices and output. This may well be too strong an assumption. Different expenditures and taxes may have different effects arising from differences in multiplier-weights or from different relative-price effects. To assess the consequences of applying the same weights to discretionary changes in different government expenditures and taxes when different weights should have been applied, reference is made to two studies by the Dutch Central Planning Bureau (1963, 1971). Alternative fiscal impulse measures were constructed by applying equal weights to discretionary changes in different government expenditures and taxes in one case, and different weights obtained from the bureau's large-scale annual model in the other case. From comparison of the alternative weighted and unweighted fiscal impulse measures so obtained, it appears that they do not differ much in magnitude or time path. The hope is, therefore, that no serious distortions will take place by constructing, as has been done, fiscal impulse measures on the basis of equal weights.

Three measures will be used to indicate the operation of foreign impulses on the domestic economy. The growth rate of foreign prices $(\hat{p}^*)$ will be measured either by the growth rate of the overall index of Dutch commodity import prices $(\hat{p}_i^*)$ denominated in domestic currency units, or by the growth rate of a weighted average of consumer price indexes in the rest of the world $(\hat{p}_c^*)$. The weights applied are constant dollar real-GDP weights, the rest of the world being the twenty-four OECD-member countries excluding the country under consideration, i.e., the Netherlands.[6]

As can be seen from the accompanying figures, the growth rate of import prices has a much greater variance than the growth rate of the world price level.[7] The figures indicate, however, that the Dutch rate of consumer price inflation $(\hat{p}_c)$ moves much closer to the growth rate of the consumer price index in the rest of the world $(\hat{p}_c^*)$ than to the growth rate of Dutch import prices $(\hat{p}_i^*)$. Finally, it is interesting to note that the Dutch rate of inflation has exceeded the world rate of consumer price inflation for most of the period 1954-75.

---

[6] The calculation procedure of p_c^* is summarized in Appendix B. Note in advance that p_c^* is in dollar terms.

[7] Standard deviations over the period 1954-75 are 6.8 and 3.7, respectively.

Nonetheless, no sign of pressure has ever been shown during that period to devalue the guilder. On the contrary, revaluations took place in 1971 and 1973 for reasons which are outside the scope of this paper.[8]

Foreign absorption of domestic production depends not only on what happens to the world price level relative to the Dutch price level but also on the growth of real income abroad $(\hat{y}^*)$. Two possible measures can capture this impulse. As a fairly general indicator of the growth of foreign real income, the growth rate of the world's real gross domestic product expressed in constant dollars $(\hat{gdp}^*)$ could be used, with the world consisting of the OECD-member countries excluding the Netherlands.[9] Alternatively, as a more specific measure of the development of foreign claims on domestic production due to growth of real world income, the growth rate of world trade $(\hat{m}^*)$ could be used. The volume of world trade underlying this measure is based on the volume of Dutch exports corrected for its dependence on Dutch export prices relative to those of competitors, assuming that the distribution of all the Netherlands' trading partners' imports over countries remains unchanged from the previous period.[10]

As is shown by the accompanying figures, the growth rate of the volume of world trade $(\hat{m}^*)$ is more closely associated with the growth path of Dutch industrial production than is the growth rate of world real GDP. For that reason, the foreign impulse measures selected are the growth rates of Dutch import prices $(\hat{p}_i^*)$, of the rest-of-the-world consumer price index $(\hat{p}_c^*)$, and of world trade $(\hat{m}^*)$.

The measures used here to summarize the monetary and financial impulses on the Dutch economy are the growth rates of the Dutch stocks of money $(\hat{M})$ and government debt $(\hat{S})$. Money is defined narrowly and includes currency and demand deposits held by the private sector. The stock of government debt is defined as the stock of short-term and long-term government bonds outstanding net of government deposits with the banking system and the central bank, and excluding central bank holdings of government debt.

The stock of government debt outstanding is assumed to be policy determined since it depends on the government's cash-flow deficit (CFD), on policy decisions with respect to that part of the CFD to be financed by issuing debt, and on open market operations of the monetary authorities. The stock of money can be viewed as the product of a money multiplier and the stock of base

---

[8] As has been pointed out by Parkin (1977b), these reasons have to do with differences in productivity growth between domestic production of tradables and nontradables, with productivity growth of tradables exceeding that of nontradables.

[9] The calculation is detailed in Appendix B.

[10] The details of measuring m^* are given in Appendix B.

money. As has been found by Korteweg and Van Loo (1977), both the money multiplier and the stock of base money are determined, in the small open economy case of the Netherlands, by prices and output and interest rates which are themselves dependent on prices and output again. Other determinants include monetary policy instruments such as reserve requirements, capital flow controls, and open market policies affecting the domestic component of the monetary base and the stock of government debt. As shown by Korteweg and Van Loo, the Dutch monetary authorities could be in control of the stock of money if they wish, even in the case of a small open economy. Control of money is, however, often sacrificed for stabilizing interest rates and exchange rates. The upshot of all this is that the Dutch money stock is, in part, endogenously determined by the variables we seek to explain (inflation, output growth). This raises the issue whether the Dutch money stock and its growth rate is a suitable indicator of monetary impulses operating on the Dutch economy. A few remarks are in order in this respect.

First, the issue of the exogeneity or endogeneity of money has nothing to do with the existence or nonexistence of a causal relationship running from money to prices and output. For the development of prices and output, it is quite immaterial whether the actual monetary impulses emitted by the monetary authorities result from their discretionary behavior or from their automatic and perhaps even unconscious responses to evolving surpluses or deficits of the budget and the balance of payments. Second, as Bent Hansen has put it in his penetrating taxonomic discussion of the effects of fiscal and monetary policy, the classification of variables as endogenous and exogenous depends entirely on the question one seeks to answer: "We may ask for the effects of disturbances or discretionary measures; we may also ask for the automatic effects of built-in flexibility at disturbances in the economy; and we may ask for the total of discretionary and automatic effects in a given situation. All questions are legitimate in the sense that they can be answered, but they do lead to different classifications of variables."[11] One of the principal purposes of this paper is to distinguish the monetarist impulse hypothesis from alternative hypotheses. This can be accomplished without imposing constraints on the causal ordering of monetary and nonmonetary processes, in the sense that the monetary sector should be relatively independent of what happens in the nonmonetary sector, whereas the nonmonetary sector should depend on what happens in the monetary sector. The defining characteristic of the monetarist position is its contention that there is a causal relationship running from money to prices and

---

[11]See Hansen (1973, p. 548).

29

output, and that the pattern of variability of money dominates the fluctuations of prices and output relative to the patterns of variability of other impulses. The defining characteristic of the monetarist position is not whether or not monetary processes are highly or marginally exposed to feedbacks from the real sector! Put another way, the problem of distinguishing the monetarist impulse hypothesis from competing impulse hypotheses is one of estimating the total effect of money supply changes which lump together the effects of discretionary monetary and financial measures and the automatic effects of built-in flexibility.[12]

The upshot of the above discussion regarding the exogeneity or endogeneity of money is that the growth rate of the stock of money should not be used as a gauge for appraising the effects of monetary impulses resulting from discretionary monetary policy actions. Instead, its only relevance is in appraising the monetarist contention that anticipated changes in the stock of money are a causative and dominant force in shaping inflation, whereas unanticipated movements in money are a causative and dominant force in shaping output fluctuations. In other words, what we hope to ascertain in using money growth as an indicator of the monetary impulse is the effect of money on the economy, not of monetary policy. However, although the causality and endogeneity of money are totally different issues on an analytical level, endogenous measures of the monetary impulses may nonetheless result in asymptotically biased estimates of the effects of monetary impulses on the economy. Moreover, with money endogenous, the interpretation of a relationship between inflation and output growth, on the one hand, and money growth, on the other, as a causal relationship running from money to prices and output is liable to the charge of reverse causation. For the Netherlands, the reverse causation issue is investigated by Bomhoff (1977). Testing the Granger concept of causality by way of cross-correlation functions between appropriately prewhitened quarterly series of the growth rates of money, output, and the consumer price level leads the author to the conclusion that the hypothesis that inflation and output growth in the current period are unconnected with money growth in subsequent periods is not rejected by the facts. This means that inflation and production growth do not cause money growth in the Granger sense. In view of this, we circumvent charges of reverse causation and biased coefficient estimates either by using lagged growth rates

---

[12]The automatic effects of built-in flexibility mainly arise from the operation of a budget constraint and a balance of payments constraint on the economy. Provided that some specific monetary and fiscal arrangements exist (fixed exchange rates, progressive tax rates, etc.), such constraints imply important feedbacks from prices and output to the money supply.

of money as a measure of the monetary impulse or by introducing, as an alternative monetary impulse measure, the growth rate of world money denominated in current dollars $(\hat{M}^*)$ and defined narrowly to include currency and demand deposits, with the world consisting of the OECD-member countries excluding the Netherlands.[13]

The accompanying figures show that domestic and world money grow at rates which move closely together; both growth rates show an upward trend and increasing variance during the late 1960s and beyond. The stock of government debt grows at a somewhat higher average rate during the 1960s and 1970s than it does during the 1950s, although no definite upward trend is visible.

I conclude this description of the Dutch record of inflation and output growth and of the indicators developed to measure the thrust of the fiscal, foreign, monetary, and financial impulses operating on the Dutch economy by drawing attention briefly to the course over time of four additional economic indicators: labor income, taxes and security payments, the current account balance, and the budget deficit, all expressed as a percentage of net nominal national income. The share of labor income in national income (AIQ) has steadily increased from about 70 percent in 1954 to about 87 percent in 1975, thus leaving less and less for income from property and profits. Taxes and social security premiums paid to the government as a share of national income $(\frac{T+P}{NNI})$ have risen from about 30 percent in 1954 to more than 52 percent in 1975, thus leaving less and less income for private spending. The current account balance as a fraction of national income $(\frac{CAB}{NNI})$ has shown a surplus of some-what more than 2 percent on average over the period 1954-63, a deficit of about 1 percent on average from 1964 to 1971, and a surplus again of about 3 percent of national income on average over the period 1972-75. Finally, the cash-flow deficit of the central and local government $(\frac{CFD}{NNI})$ has moved around 3-4 percent from 1954 to 1963, around 5 percent from 1964 to 1969, taking a dip to less than 2 percent in 1972 and 1973, and rising again to more than 5 percent in 1975.

---

[13]The details of the calculation of M^* are given in Appendix B.

III. SYSTEMATIC IMPULSES
AS NECESSARY AND SUFFICIENT CONDITIONS
FOR FLUCTUATIONS IN INFLATION AND OUTPUT GROWTH

We begin by testing the DIRE hypothesis of inflation and output fluctuations by applying a comparatively weak nonparametric test to comparatively demanding data involving standardized first differences of the series used on inflation, production growth, and impulses. On the naive assumption that all anticipation variables involved in (5) and (6) can be approximated by their current values lagged one period, it follows from these equations that the DIRE hypothesis implies positive association between accelerations (decelerations) of the aggregate level of prices or production (ΔX), on the one hand, and positive (negative) first differences of each single impulse variable (ΔI), on the other.[14] Here, X and I are vectors containing $X = [\hat{p}_c, \hat{y}]$ and $I = [FI, \hat{m}^*, \hat{p}_i^*, \hat{p}_c^*, \hat{M}, \hat{M}^*, \hat{S}]$.

In testing for positive association, we make use of the newly developed nonparametric test statistic ∇p.[15] For each impulse measure, the following contingency table can be constructed of appropriately lagged impulse movements (ΔI_{-i}), on the one hand, and accelerations and decelerations of the aggregate level of consumer prices and industrial production (ΔX), on the other.

ΔX

	columns k rows j	+	-	o	Σ_j
ΔI_{-i}	+	O_{11}	O_{12}	O_{13}	O_1
	-	O_{21}	O_{22}	O_{23}	O_2
	o	O_{31}	O_{32}	O_{33}	O_3
	Σ_k	Q_1	Q_2	Q_3	N

[14] The use of first differences of X and I can be rationalized alternatively on the assumption that the variance of the anticipation variables X^e and I^e is of small order relative to the variance of X and I.

[15] See Hildebrand, Laing, and Rosenthal (1974, 1976). The ∇ p-model implies other well-known measures of association (such as Goodman's and Krushal's γ and Spearman's ρ_s) as special cases. Although the standardized ∇p - statistic is asymptotically normal, the model appears to provide reasonably accurate estimates of the relevant population parameters even in cases of modest samples (of about twenty-five observations).

The ∇p-statistic is defined as:

$$\nabla p = 1 - \frac{o_{12} + o_{13} + o_{21} + o_{23} + o_{31} + o_{32}}{e_{12} + e_{13} + e_{21} + e_{23} + e_{31} + e_{32}} ,$$

where o_{jk} is the number of actual observations in cell jk and e_{jk} the number of expected observations with $e_{jk} = O_j Q_k / N$, where N is the sample size.

The ∇p-statistic and its standardized value shall be used to test the null-hypothesis of no positive association between ΔX and ΔI_{-j}, after having normalized each of the elements involved in ΔX and ΔI_{-j} by dividing them through the standard deviation of their respective levels X and I_{-j} over the sample period 1954-75. When the standardized ∇p-statistic is positive and exceeds some critical level, the null-hypothesis of no positive systematic empirical association between ΔX and ΔI_{-j} must be rejected.[16] As the critical level of the value of the standardized ∇p-statistic, we choose a value at the 5-percent level of significance, which, in case of the appropriate one-tailed test, amounts to 1.65.[17]

The nonparametric ∇p-test set forth above is a proper test on the joint necessity and sufficiency of ΔI_{-j} for ΔX within the class of assumptions spanned by the DIRE hypothesis. Within this hypothesis, ΔI_{-j} is a necessary condition for ΔX if ΔX does not occur without ΔI_{-j}. Moreover, within this hypothesis, ΔI_{-j} is a sufficient condition for ΔX if ΔX occurs anytime ΔI_{-j} occurs.

In terms of the contingency table underlying the ∇p-statistic for each element of ΔX and ΔI_{-j}, sufficiency of ΔI_{-j} for ΔX would be tested by the frequencies in each row relative to the diagonal cell frequency in the respective rows. Necessity on the other hand would be tested by the frequencies in each column relative to the diagonal cell frequency in the respective columns. Since the ∇p-statistic simultaneously exploits all off-diagonal cell frequencies relative to those in the diagonal cells, it offers a test property bearing on the sufficiency and necessity of ΔI_{-j} for ΔX.

---

[16] Standardized $\nabla p = \nabla p / \sqrt{\text{variance } \nabla p}$,
where variance of $\nabla p = \{ n - [(1 - \nabla p)m]^2 \} / mN^2$,
with n = total proportion of sample size observed in set of error cells
m = total proportion of sample size expected in set of error cells
N = sample size.

[17] The critical value at the 1-percent significance level amounts to 2.33.

Table 1

Nonparametric Test of Joint Necessity and Sufficiency of ΔI_{-i} for ΔX, 1954-75

ΔI_{-i} \ ΔX	$\Delta \hat{p}_c$ estimated ∇p	standardized ∇p	$\Delta \hat{y}$ estimated ∇p	standardized ∇p
ΔFI	0.172	0.731	0.047	0.131
ΔFI_{-1}	- .105	- 0.658	- .299	- 1.620
$\Delta \hat{m}^*$	.069	0.258	.627	3.566[b]
$\Delta \hat{m}^*_{-1}$	.044	0.113	- .182	- 0.991
$\Delta \hat{p}_i^*$	.431	2.105[a]	.323	1.766[a]
$\Delta \hat{p}_{i-1}^*$	- .138	- 0.828	- .692	- 3.603
$\Delta \hat{p}_c^*$	.621	3.532[b]	- .015	- 0.194
$\Delta \hat{p}_{c-1}^*$	- .013	- 0.176	- .299	- 1.620
$\Delta \hat{M}$	- .304	- 1.789	- .182	- 0.991
$\Delta \hat{M}_{-1}$	.391	2.073[a]	.546	2.971[b]
$\Delta \hat{M}^*$	- .015	- 0.196	- .492	- 2.951
$\Delta \hat{M}^*_{-1}$	- .154	- 0.942	.330	1.463
$\Delta \hat{S}$	.130	0.570	.000	- 0.108
$\Delta \hat{S}_{-1}$	- 0.391	- 2.280	- 0.182	- 0.991

[a]Significant at 5-percent level.

[b]Significant at 1-percent level.

Note: Test is based on twenty-two observations over the period 1954-75. Both ΔX and ΔI are first differences normalized by dividing them through the standard deviation of the respective X and I variables. Normalized $\Delta \hat{p}_c$ for 1970 is set equal to zero in order to correct for the effects of the transition at the start of 1969 to a value-added tax system which resulted in a dramatic acceleration of p_c in 1969 and a dramatic subsequent deceleration in 1970. Note that negative signs of ∇p are a reflection of the dominance of off-diagonal cell observations, and thus of either negative or zero association.

Table 1 summarizes the estimated and standardized values of the ∇p-statistic needed to test the null-hypothesis of no positive empirical relationship between normalized accelerations of the level of consumer prices $(\Delta \hat{p}_c)$ and the volume of industrial production $(\Delta \hat{y})$, on the one hand, and normalized first differences of each of the current and one-year lagged impulse variables (ΔI), on the other.

Three conclusions follow from Table 1. First, the null-hypothesis of no significant positive empirical association between changes in the rate of consumer price inflation $(\Delta \hat{p}_c)$, on the one hand, and changes in the current growth rates of both world consumer prices $(\Delta \hat{p}_c^*)$ and import prices $(\Delta \hat{p}_i^*)$ and in the lagged growth rate of domestic money $(\Delta \hat{M}_{-1})$, on the other, has to be rejected at the 5-percent level of significance. Second, the positive association found between changes in the growth rate of industrial production $(\Delta \hat{y})$ and changes in the lagged growth rate of domestic money and in the current growth rates of world trade $(\Delta \hat{m}^*)$ and import prices cannot be attributed to pure chance either. Finally, the null-hypothesis with respect to each of the remaining impulse variables operating on the Dutch rate of inflation and output growth, specifically the fiscal and financial impulse variables $(FI, \hat{S})$, appears not to be rejected by the ∇p-test.

In general, the outcomes of this nonparametric test imply:

(1) that changes in the current growth rate of foreign prices $(\hat{p}_i^*, \hat{p}_c^*)$ and in the lagged growth rate of domestic money $(\hat{M}_{-1})$ are each of them necessary and sufficient conditions for equidirectional changes in the Dutch rate of inflation $(\hat{p}_c)$;

(2) that changes in current growth rates of world trade $(\hat{m}^*)$, import prices $(\hat{p}_i^*)$, and in the lagged growth rate of domestic money $(\hat{M}_{-1})$ are both necessary and sufficient conditions for equidirectional variations in output growth $(\hat{y})$; and,

(3) that changes in fiscal (FI) and financial $(\hat{S})$ impulses are neither necessary nor sufficient conditions for changes in inflation or output growth. The first implication mentioned above, together with the finding reported in the next section, that the variability of world consumer price inflation is dominantly determined by the variability of the growth rate of world money per unit of world output $(\hat{M}^* - \hat{gdp}^*)$ lagged between one and two years, strongly suggests that fluctuations in the Dutch rate of inflation are by and large a monetary phenomenon.

IV. TESTING SOME IMPLICATIONS OF THE DIRE HYPOTHESIS: THE RESULTS OF REGRESSION ANALYSIS

In this section, the outcomes of some tests based on a regression analysis of (4)-(6) are presented and discussed. Rewriting these equations in more general terms gives:

$$(7) \quad \hat{p}^e = f(\hat{\bar{y}}, I^e)$$

$$(8) \quad \hat{p} = \hat{p}^e + h(I - I^e) + v$$

$$(9) \quad \hat{y} = \hat{\bar{y}} + g(I - I^e) + w,$$

where I and I^e are vectors of actual and expected systematic impulse variables, $I - I^e$ is a random forecast error with respect to the impulse variables with mean zero and finite variance, and v and w random error terms with finite variance and zero mean, equal to $\frac{1}{A} (u_d - u_s)$ and $\frac{1}{A} (a_1 u_d + \beta_3 u_s)$, respectively.

The object of the regression analysis is threefold.

First, we estimate the anticipated rate of inflation $(\hat{p}^e)$. The measures of the anticipated rate of inflation will be the prediction series generated by the systematic part of a regression equation of the format of (7), in which the current rate of inflation $(\hat{p})$ is regressed on the anticipated levels of the systematic impulses (I^e) and the normal growth rate of output $(\hat{\bar{y}})$.

Second, we use the measures of the anticipated rate of inflation $(\hat{p}^e)$ to estimate regression equations of the format of (8), with the coefficient of $\hat{p}^e$ constrained to unity in one case, and estimated freely in the other. More specifically, in the one case, unanticipated inflation $\hat{p} - \hat{p}^e$ is regressed on measures of the unforeseen parts of the systematic impulses $I - I^e$, whereas in the other case $\hat{p}$ is regressed on both $\hat{p}^e$ and $I - I^e$. In case the freely estimated coefficient of anticipated inflation $(\hat{p}^e)$ is found not to be significantly different from unity, it would mean that the unanticipated impulses used to explain unexpected inflation are uncorrelated with the measures of inflationary anticipations, implying that we would have been successful in constructing correct measures of anticipated as well as unanticipated inflation.

Finally, we estimate to what extent deviations of actual from normal output growth $(\hat{y} - \hat{\bar{y}})$ can be attributed to which unanticipated systematic impulses $(I - I^e)$. To that purpose, analogous to our approach to unexpected inflation $(\hat{p} - \hat{p}^e)$, we regress measures of $\hat{y} - \hat{\bar{y}}$ in accordance with (9) on the unanticipated parts of the systematic impulses introduced above.

Before turning to the results, one final problem is left to be solved: how to measure the anticipation variables introduced in Section I. The expectation at time t-1 of some impulse variable I_t is $E_{t-1}(I_t)$, or I_t^e for short.

Two approaches will be taken in this paper to measure I_t^e. As a first and naive approach, we postulate that economic agents expect the impulses to remain unchanged from the previous period: $I_t^e = I_{t-1}$. In this case, the unanticipated impulses will be: $I_t - I_t^e = \triangle I_t$. As an alternative and more subtle approach, we obtain measures of I_t^e by fitting an ARIMA process to $\triangle I_t$ to obtain $\triangle I_t = \triangle I_t^e + \epsilon_t$, where ϵ_t is a white-noise series.[18] The I_t^e-series can then be constructed as $I_t^e = I_{t-1} + \triangle I_t^e$, which is identical to $I_t^e = I_t - \epsilon_t$. In this case, the unanticipated impulses are $I_t - I_t^e = \epsilon_t$, being serially independent forecast errors.

In order to distinguish the two approaches, we denote I_t^e and $I_t - I_t^e$, respectively, as:

I_{t-1} and $\triangle I_t$, respectively, in the naive approach,

and I_t^a and $\triangle I_t^{ua}$, respectively, in the ARIMA approach, where I is a vector of systematic impulses: $I = [FI, \hat{m}^*, \hat{p}_i^*, \hat{p}_c^*, \hat{M}, \hat{M}^*, \hat{S}]$.[19]

With respect to the normal growth rate of output $(\hat{\bar{y}})$ consistent with perfectly anticipated inflation, we assume either that $\hat{\bar{y}}$ is a constant, or, analogous to the two approaches described above, that $\hat{\bar{y}}_t = \hat{y}_{t-1}$ and $\hat{y}_t - \hat{\bar{y}}_t = \triangle \hat{y}_t$ in the naive case, and that $\hat{\bar{y}}_t = \hat{y}_t - \theta_t$ and $\triangle \hat{y}_t^{ua} = \hat{y}_t - \hat{\bar{y}}_t = \theta_t$ in the ARIMA approach.[20]

---

[18] For the ARIMA models fitted and for more details on the procedures used, see Appendix C. The ARIMA models are fitted to $\triangle I_t$, not to I_t, since we find it inappropriate to assume that economic agents know the mean of the I_t-series when predicting I_t. Nevertheless, forecasts of $\triangle I_t$ based on such ARIMA models assume that economic agents know the coefficients of these models. The proper procedure would seem to be to repeatedly fit an ARIMA model to the $\triangle I$-series prior to the period over which the forecast is made every time the forecast is made. However, data limitations preclude the application of this procedure.

[19] Note that I^e, however measured, may affect inflation with a lag (for example, information and recognition lags).

[20] Here, θ_t is again a white-noise series obtained from fitting an ARIMA process to $\triangle \hat{y}_t$. See Appendix C.

Another possibility, not pursued here because of time constraints, would have been to generate a $\hat{y}$-series from the systematic part of an equation regressing output growth on the growth rates of the labor force, the stocks of capital, money, and debt, and the absorption ratio of labor by government. This route has successfully been followed by Meltzer (1977).

37

Finally, as has been stated before, the measure of the anticipated rate of inflation will be the prediction series generated by the systematic part of a regression equation of the format of (7).

A. The Inflation Regressions

We first turn to the outcomes of our regression analysis of Dutch inflation ($\hat{p}_c$). Tables 2 and 3 summarize our findings.*

In equations 1, 6, 12, and 17, inflation is first regressed on the anticipations of all systematic impulses, with anticipations measured in the two ways indicated above, and with $\hat{\hat{y}}$ subsumed in the intercept.[21] The most appropriate lag structure proved to be half a year for each of the anticipated impulse variables.[22] The regression equations clearly suggest that the systematic impulses dominating inflation are the anticipated growth rates of domestic money ($\hat{M}^e$) and world prices, measured either by world consumer prices or import prices ($\hat{p}_c^{*e}$, $\hat{p}_i^{*e}$, respectively). Anticipations of fiscal, financial, and world trade impulses do not seem to play any role in Dutch inflation.[23]

Regression equations 2, 7, 13, and 18 show the result of rerunning the regressions with only the two dominating anticipated impulse variables included. It appears, first, that the greater part of the variance of the rate of inflation is explained by the expectations of domestic money growth and world inflation, and second, that the sum of their coefficients is never statistically different from unity at the 1-percent level of significance. These findings suggest that expectations of inflation are formed rationally and free of money illusion.

Equations 3, 8/9, 14, and 19/20 attempt to attribute unanticipated inflation to the unanticipated parts of the systematic impulse measures introduced earlier on the assumption that unanticipated inflation is properly measured by the residuals of regression equations 2, 7, 13, and 18, respectively. At first sight, it seemed that none of the unanticipated impulses worked, except for the unanticipated part of the fiscal impulse in the case of the naive approach

---

*
  Editor's note. Regression equations, displayed in Tables 2-6, are numbered consecutively from 1 to 50 without parentheses, and are so referenced in the text.

[21] Neither naive nor more subtle measures of $\hat{\hat{y}}$ as separate explanatory variables proved to be successful in terms of statistical significance and fit. According to (4) and (5), the intercept is equal to $-\frac{1}{B}\hat{\hat{y}}$. What is not taken into account in these equations, however, is the positive trend rate of growth of the velocity of money $(\hat{\hat{V}})$ because of technical progress in payments arrangements and procedures. Consequently, the constant term in regression equations 1, 6, 12, and 17 is expected to reflect not just $\hat{\hat{y}}$ but also $+\hat{\hat{V}}$.

[22] Since semiannual data are not available, we calculate $x_{t-.5}$ as $(x_t + x_{t-1})/2$.

[23] This holds independent of whether we measure the anticipated fiscal impulse in terms of FI or its alternative, $\triangle$TP; see below.

to expectations formation and with foreign inflation measured by import price changes; see regression equation 8. Further experimentation led us to introduce the unanticipated part of world trade growth jointly with an alternative indicator of unexpected fiscal impulses, namely the second-time difference of the share of taxes and social security premiums in national income, lagged half a year $(\Delta^2 TP_{-.5})$.[24] Moreover, we took account in a somewhat ad hoc fashion of a once-and-for-all institutional change when the existing excise tax system was transformed into a value-added regime on January 1, 1969. The announcement of this change in tax regime prompted enterpreneurs to postpone price increases during the last part of 1968 in order to have them concur with the transition period when all price tags would have to be changed anyway. To catch the timing effects produced by the transition, we inserted a dummy variable in the equations (shift 68/69) assuming the value of -1 in 1968, +1 in 1969, and zero otherwise.

As is shown in equations 3, 9, 14, and 20, a considerable portion of the residual variance involved in equations 2, 7, 13, and 18, respectively, can be attributed to the three variables introduced, one being a dummy variable involving the timing effects of a structural once-and-for-all change in the tax regime, and the other two being unanticipated changes of the growth rate of world trade and unforeseen changes in tax pressure.

The attribution of a sizable part of the residual variance involved in regression equations 2, 7, 13, and 18 to unanticipated fiscal impulses and world trade growth may be interpreted as constituting a partial explanation of unanticipated inflation, provided unanticipated inflation is correctly measured by the residuals of these equations. This poses the question whether we have been successful in equations 2, 7, 13, and 18 in isolating the determinants of anticipated inflation. In order to test this, we regress the actual rate of inflation $(\hat{p}_c)$ on the prediction series of inflation generated from the systematic part of equations 2, 7, 13, and 18 (i.e., $\hat{p}_c - u_i$; for i = 2, 7, 13, 18) as well as on the shift term and the unanticipated changes in world trade growth and tax pressure

---

[24]Unanticipated changes in the share of taxes and social security premiums in national income (TP) are approximated by its accelerations and decelerations lagged half a year $(\Delta^2 TP_{-.5})$ in Table 2 as well as in Table 3. Fitting an ARIMA process on the $\Delta^2 TP$-series and using its residuals lagged half a year $(\Delta^2 TP^{ua}_{-.5})$, instead of $\Delta^2 TP_{-.5}$ in equations 14 - 16 and 19 - 22 of Table 3, yields results statistically inferior to those summarized in Table 3. See Appendix D, Table D1, for equations 16 and 22 of Table 3 when $\Delta^2 TP^{ua}_{-.5}$ instead of $\Delta^2 TP_{-.5}$ is used as an indicator of unanticipated changes in tax pressure.

We take second-time differences in view of the high value of the first-order autocorrelation coefficient of the $(\Delta TP$-series, making it an ill-suited indicator of unanticipated changes in tax pressure; see accompanying figures.

Table 2

Inflation and Impulses, 1954-75

$\hat{p}_c$ regressed on $I^e = I_{-1}$, lagged half a year, and on $I - I^e = \Delta I$

Equation		VARU	$\bar{R}^2$	DW
1 (t-stat.)	$\hat{p}_c = -.58 + .23 \hat{M}_{-1.5} + .61 \hat{p}^*_{c-1.5} + .11 \hat{m}^*_{-1.5} + .13 FI_{-1.5} + .03 \hat{S}_{-1.5} + u_1$ (.43) (2.26) (5.95) (.91) (.72) (.16)	1.71	0.76	2.52
2	$\hat{p}_c = .66 + .27 \hat{M}_{-1.5} + .59 \hat{p}^*_{c-1.5} + u_2$ (1.01) (3.18) (6.29)	1.58	.78	2.30
3	$\hat{u}_2 = -.16 + 3.01 \text{ shift } 68/69 + 1.38 \Delta^2 TP_{-.5} + .12 \Delta \hat{m}^* + u_3$ (1.01) (5.11) (5.04) (2.97)	0.54	.62	2.28
4	$\hat{p}_c = -.44 + 1.06 (\hat{p}_c - u_2) + 3.07 \text{ shift } 68/69 + 1.41 \Delta^2 TP_{-.5} + .13 \Delta \hat{m}^* + u_4$ (1.18) (14.76) (5.13) (5.06) (3.06)	0.55	.92	2.38
5	$\hat{p}_c = .35 + .27 \hat{M}_{-1.5} + .65 \hat{p}^*_{c-1.5} + 3.10 \text{ shift } 68/69 + 1.41 \Delta^2 TP_{-.5} + .14 \Delta \hat{m}^* + u_5$ (.86) (5.14) (10.58) (5.03) (4.95) (3.01)	0.58	0.92	2.33
6	$\hat{p}_c = 2.08 + .52 \hat{M}_{-1.5} + .35 \hat{p}^*_{i-1.5} - .11 \hat{m}^*_{-1.5} - .05 FI_{-1.5} - .10 \hat{S}_{-1.5} + u_6$ (1.33) (4.68) (5.03) (.77) (.26) (.53)	2.13	0.70	2.23
7	$\hat{p}_c = .90 + .47 \hat{M}_{-1.5} + .33 \hat{p}^*_{i-1.5} + u_7$ (1.26) (5.44) (5.49)	1.88	.74	2.12
8	$\hat{u}_7 = -.00 + 2.22 \text{ shift } 68/69 + .24 \Delta FI + u_8$ (.01) (2.96) (2.59)	1.10	.35	2.02
9	$\hat{u}_7 = -.13 + 3.23 \text{ shift } 68/69 + 1.20 \Delta^2 TP_{-.5} + .16 \Delta \hat{m}^* + u_9$ (.61) (4.31) (3.45) (3.11)	0.88	.48	1.41
10	$\hat{p}_c = -.64 + 1.11 (\hat{p}_c - u_7) + 3.38 \text{ shift } 68/69 + 1.24 \Delta^2 TP_{-.5} + .19 \Delta \hat{m}^* + u_{10}$ (1.28) (11.49) (4.47) (3.57) (3.31)	0.87	.88	1.63
11	$\hat{p}_c = .57 + .49 \hat{M}_{-1.5} + .39 \hat{p}^*_{i-1.5} + 3.48 \text{ shift } 68/69 + 1.25 \Delta^2 TP_{-.5} + .20 \Delta \hat{m}^* + u_{11}$ (1.15) (8.21) (8.22) (4.50) (3.55) (3.38)	0.88	0.88	1.77

Table 2 -- Continued

Symbols:

$\hat{p}_c$	=	growth rate of Dutch implicit price deflator of private consumption
$\hat{p}_i^*$		growth rate of Dutch overall import price index (in guilders)
$\hat{p}_c^*$		growth rate of world consumer price index (in dollars)
$\hat{M}$		growth rate of Dutch money stock narrowly defined as currency plus demand deposits
$\hat{S}$		growth rate of Dutch stock of government debt
$\hat{m}^*$		growth rate of world trade
FI		fiscal impulse variable
TP		taxes and social security premiums as a fraction of national income
shift 68/69		dummy, - 1 in 1968, + 1 in 1969 to take account of introduction of value-added tax system, zero otherwise
VARU		error sum of squares corrected for degrees of freedom
$\bar{R}^2$		coefficient of determination adjusted for degrees of freedom
DW		Durbin-Watson statistic for autoregressive disturbances
u_i		random error terms (i = 1, . . . ,11)
$\hat{}$		first differenced logarithms (growth rates)
$\hat{p}_c - u_i$	=	anticipated rates of inflation ($\hat{p}_c^{\,e}$).

Table 3

Inflation and Impulses, 1954-75

$\hat{p}_c$ regressed on $I^e = I^a$, lagged half a year, and on $I - I^e = \Delta I^{ua}$

Equation		VARU	$\bar{R}^2$	DW
12 (t-stat.)	$\hat{p}_c = -.75 + \underset{(.25)}{.42}\, \hat{M}^a_{-.5} + \underset{(2.20)}{.62}\, \hat{p}^{*a}_{c-.5} + \underset{(3.98)}{.24}\, \hat{m}^{*a}_{-.5} - \underset{(.96)}{.07}\, FI^a_{-.5} - \underset{(.23)}{.20}\, \hat{S}^a_{-.5} + \underset{(.35)}{u_{12}}$	1.74	0.76	2.46
13	$\hat{p}_c = -.21 + \underset{(.26)}{.42}\, \hat{M}^a_{-.5} + \underset{(3.23)}{.56}\, \hat{p}^{*a}_{c-.5} + \underset{(5.47)}{u_{13}}$	1.56	.78	2.28
14	$u_{13} = -.26 + \underset{(1.48)}{2.66}\, \text{shift } 68/69 + \underset{(4.45)}{1.28}\, \Delta^2 TP_{-.5} + \underset{(4.73)}{.11}\, \Delta \hat{m}^{*ua} + \underset{(2.23)}{u_{14}}$	0.59	.59	2.11
15	$\hat{p}_c = -.39 + \underset{(.97)}{1.03}\, (\hat{p}_c - u_{13}) + \underset{(13.87)}{2.68}\, \text{shift } 68/69 + \underset{(4.36)}{1.29}\, \Delta^2 TP_{-.5} + \underset{(4.63)}{.12}\, \Delta \hat{m}^{*ua} + \underset{(2.20)}{u_{15}}$	0.62	.91	2.12
16	$\hat{p}_c = -.32 + \underset{(.62)}{.36}\, \hat{M}^a_{-.5} + \underset{(3.92)}{.63}\, \hat{p}^{*a}_{c-.5} + \underset{(8.33)}{2.83}\, \text{shift } 68/69 + \underset{(4.44)}{1.32}\, \Delta^2 TP_{-.5} + \underset{(4.70)}{.14}\, \Delta \hat{m}^{*ua} + \underset{(2.38)}{u_{16}}$	0.63	0.91	2.05

42

Table 3 -- Continued

17	$\hat{p}_c = -.26 + .64\,M^a_{-.5} + .36\,\hat{p}^{*a}_{i-.5} + .07\,\hat{m}^{*a}_{-.5} - .08\,FI^a_{-.5} + .01\,\hat{S}^a_{-.5} + u_{17}$	2.53	0.65	2.09
(t-stat.)	(.07) (2.41) (2.43) (.24) (.21) (.02)			
18	$\hat{p}_c = -.15 + .66\,\hat{M}^a_{-.5} + .36\,\hat{p}^{*a}_{i-.5} + u_{18}$	2.14	.70	2.07
	(.15) (4.83) (4.07)			
19	$u_{18} = .09 + 1.99\text{ shift }68/69 + .22\,\Delta FI^{ua} + u_{19}$	1.54	.20	2.11
	(.35) (2.24) (1.84)			
20	$u_{18} = -.27 + 2.78\text{ shift }68/69 + 1.35\,\Delta^2 TP_{-.5} + .11\,\Delta\hat{m}^{*ua} + u_{20}$	1.09	.44	1.67
	(1.14) (3.43) (3.70) (1.64)			
21	$\hat{p}_c = -.47 + 1.04\,(\hat{p}_c - u_{18}) + 2.81\text{ shift }68/69 + 1.37\,\Delta^2 TP_{-.5} + .12\,\Delta\hat{m}^{*ua} + u_{21}$	1.15	.84	1.70
	(.81) (9.85) (3.37) (3.63) (1.65)			
22	$\hat{p}_c = -.22 + .61\,M^a_{-.5} + .45\,\hat{p}^{*a}_{i-.5} + 3.09\text{ shift }68/69 + 1.45\,\Delta^2 TP_{-.5} + .17\,\Delta\hat{m}^{*ua} + u_{22}$	1.14	0.84	1.61
	(.31) (5.80) (5.56) (3.52) (3.76) (1.94)			

Note: $I^a = I_{-1} + \Delta I^a$, with ΔI^a obtained by fitting an ARIMA process on ΔI.

For explanation of other symbols, see notes to Table 2.

introduced above. Finding that the freely estimated coefficients of these measures of anticipated inflation are not significantly different from unity would suggest that the shift term and the unanticipated fiscal and world trade impulses are largely uncorrelated with the measures of anticipated inflation. This would suggest, in turn, that we would have been largely successful in correctly isolating the major determinants of inflationary expectations and in generating the correct series for expected inflation.

Regression equations 4, 10, 15, and 21 summarize the results. We find the coefficients of the anticipated inflation series generated from equations 2, 7, 13, and 18, respectively, to be not statistically different from unity at the 1-percent level of significance.[25] This suggests that in equations 2, 7, 13, and 18 we have indeed isolated the correct determinants of expected inflation, making these equations trustworthy predictors of inflation.

Finally, rerunning regression equations 2, 7, 13, and 18 with the determinants of unanticipated inflation included along with those of expected inflation gives regression equations 5, 11, 16, and 22. These equations are nothing but a compact way of summarizing the information contained in the sets of equations 2/4, 7/10, 13/15, and 18/21, respectively. In comparing equations 5, 11, 16, and 22 with 2, 7, 13, and 18, respectively, two findings stand out. First, and not surprisingly, the coefficients of anticipated money growth and world inflation remain virtually unchanged between corresponding equations with their sum not significantly different from unity. This suggests again that we have indeed successfully isolated the determinants of anticipated inflation. Second, from comparing the $\bar{R}^2$-statistics of the corresponding equations in each set it follows that the determinants of anticipated inflation, and thereby expected inflation itself, dominate actual inflation. Adding the determinants of unanticipated inflation to equations 2, 7, 13, and 18 raises the explained part of the variance of inflation by about ten percentage points only to roughly 85-90 percent. The dominant part of the variance of inflation appears to be explained by expected inflation and its determinants.[26]

---

[25]The coefficient of unity is implied by the least-squares regression model provided the unanticipated impulses are uncorrelated with the anticipated inflation series used. This means that the coefficient of unity <u>cannot</u> be interpreted as implying that economic agents raise prices at the rate they expect them to rise (absence of money illusion), nor that the expectations-augmented Phillips curve is vertical at the normal rate of output growth or the natural rate of unemployment in case inflation is fully anticipated.

[26]Introduction in the inflation regression equations of expected and unexpected exchange rate movements, measured by $\hat{e}_{-1.5}$ and $\Delta\hat{e}$, respectively, as determinants of expected and unexpected inflation produces contradictory results, as witnessed by equations $5'$, $11'$, $16''$, and $22''$ of Table D1 of Appendix D, with the coefficients of both variables being occasionally significant and occasionally not, and with the sign of $\Delta\hat{e}$ occasionally contrary to a priori expectations. Note what is noted at the bottom of Table D1 in this respect.

To summarize, our main findings are that the Dutch postwar economic experience fails to produce evidence contrary to the implications of the hypothesis that inflationary expectations are formed rationally and free of money illusion. Inflation in the Netherlands since 1954 has been dominated by inflationary expectations. Inflationary expectations in turn have been dominated by only two classes of anticipated impulses, namely, the anticipated growth rates of domestic money $(\hat{M}^e)$ and the anticipated growth rates of foreign prices (either $\hat{p}_c^{*e}$ or $\hat{p}_i^{*e}$). Unanticipated inflation can be explained partly ad hoc by invoking a dummy variable catching the timing effects on inflation of a once-and-for-all structural change in indirect tax regimes in 1969, and partly by unanticipated movements in the pressure of taxes and social security premiums on national income and unforeseen growth in world trade.

What remains to be tested is the <u>monetarist</u> impulse hypothesis that anticipated inflation is dominated directly or indirectly by anticipated monetary impulses only. To see what is involved in testing this hypothesis, we go back to the systematic parts (i.e., the inflation predictions) of regression equations 2, 7, 13, and 18. As can be seen from these equations, predicted or anticipated inflation is dominated by expected domestic money growth lagged half a year and by expected foreign inflation as measured by the growth rate of either world consumer prices or import prices, each also lagged half a year.

To test the monetarist hypothesis that inflation is a monetary phenomenon, we have to analyze the determinants of inflation in the rest of the world as measured by $\hat{p}_c^*$ or $\hat{p}_i^*$. In case anticipated world inflation proves to be dominated by anticipated growth in world money $(\hat{M}^{*e})$, the hypothesis that Dutch inflation is a monetary phenomenon would fail to be rejected by the facts.

In order to test the hypothesis that world inflation is a monetary phenomenon, we take the simplest approach possible by arguing that the world is a rational expectations quantity theory closed economy with a stable money demand function and with the supply of money policy-controllable and predetermined relative to inflation.[27]

Table 4 summarizes the results of testing this theory by way of regression analysis. The approach taken in explaining world inflation corresponds to the one summarized by (7)-(9) with respect to domestic inflation. The difference is that the only systematic impulse used on a world level of analysis is the growth rate of world money taken either at face value or per unit of world output $(\hat{M}^*$ or $\hat{M}^* - \hat{gdp}^*$, respectively).

---

[27]These assumptions are supported by the findings of Gray, Ward, and Zis (1976), and of Parkin, Richards, and Zis (1976). See also Parkin (1977a). It is recalled, moreover, that in the empirical analysis the world consists of all OECD-member countries excluding the Netherlands.

Table 4

World Inflation and World Money Growth, 1954-75

$\hat{p}^*$ regressed on $\hat{M}^{*e} = \hat{M}_{-1}^*$, lagged half a year, and on $\hat{M}^* - \hat{M}^{*e} = \Delta\hat{M}^*$

Equation (t-stat.)		VARU	$\bar{R}^2$	DW
23	$\hat{p}_c^* = 2.38 + .85 (\hat{M}_{-1.5}^* - \hat{gdp}_{-1.5}^*) + u_{23}$ (5.90) (9.29)	2.83	0.80	1.75
24	$u_{23} = -.15 + .23 (\Delta\hat{M}^* - \Delta\hat{gdp}^*) + u_{24}$ (.54) (3.46)	1.77	.34	1.81
25	$\hat{p}_c^* = -.35 + 1.05 (\hat{p}_c^* - u_{23}) + .24 (\Delta\hat{M}^* - \Delta\hat{gdp}^*) + u_{25}$ (.75) (11.92) (3.43)	1.84	.87	1.92
26	$\hat{p}_c^* = 2.14 + .90 (\hat{M}_{-1.5}^* - \hat{gdp}_{-1.5}^*) + .24 (\Delta\hat{M}^* - \Delta\hat{gdp}^*) + u_{26}$ (6.44) (11.92) (3.44)	1.84	0.87	1.92
27	$\hat{p}_i^* = -6.43 + 1.32 \hat{M}_{-1.5}^* + u_{27}$ (3.15) (4.94)	23.03	0.53	2.19
28	$u_{27} = .26 - .66 \Delta\hat{M}^* + u_{28}$ (.30) (2.81)	16.52	.25	1.87
29	$\hat{p}_i^* = .76 + .80 (\hat{p}_i^* - u_{27}) - .76 \Delta\hat{M}^* + u_{29}$ (.77) (4.39) (3.02)	16.38	.66	1.91
30	$\hat{p}_i^* = -4.40 + 1.06 \hat{M}_{-1.5}^* - .76 \Delta\hat{M}^* + u_{30}$ (2.38) (4.39) (3.02)	16.38	0.66	1.91

46

Table 4 – Continued

$\hat{p}^*$ regressed on $\hat{M}^{*e} = \hat{M}^{*a}$, lagged half a year, and on $\hat{M}^* - \hat{M}^{*e} = \Delta\hat{M}^{*ua}$

Equation		VARU	$\bar{R}^2$	DW
31 (t-stat.)	$\hat{p}^*_c = .68 + .91 (\hat{M}^{*a}_{-.5} - \hat{gdp}^{*a}_{-.5}) + u_{31}$ (1.43) (10.21)	2.42	0.83	1.41
32	$u_{31} = .28 + .25 (\Delta\hat{M}^{*ua} - \Delta\hat{gdp}^{*ua}) + u_{32}$ (1.10) (4.17)	1.29	.44	1.37
33	$\hat{p}^*_c = .18 + 1.02 (\hat{p}^*_c - u_{31}) + .26 (\Delta\hat{M}^{*ua} - \Delta\hat{gdp}^{*ua}) + u_{33}$ (.45) (13.95) (4.10)	1.35	.91	1.39
34	$\hat{p}^*_c = .87 + .93 (\hat{M}^{*a}_{-.5} - \hat{gdp}^{*a}_{-.5}) + .26 (\Delta\hat{M}^{*ua} - \Delta\hat{gdp}^{*ua}) + u_{34}$ (2.44) (13.95) (4.10)	1.35	0.91	1.39
35	$\hat{p}^*_i = -8.10 + 1.35 \hat{M}^{*a}_{-.5} + u_{35}$ (3.25) (4.62)	24.73	0.49	2.15
36	$u_{35} = .64 - .86 \Delta\hat{M}^{*ua} + u_{36}$ (.75) (3.45)	15.50	.34	1.77
37	$\hat{p}^*_i = -.28 + .82 (\hat{p}^*_i - u_{35}) - .94 \Delta\hat{M}^{*ua} + u_{37}$ (.30) (4.59) (3.60)	15.47	.68	1.82
38	$\hat{p}^*_i = -6.90 + 1.10 \hat{M}^{*a}_{-.5} - .94 \Delta\hat{M}^{*ua} + u_{38}$ (3.46) (4.59) (3.60)	15.47	0.68	1.82

Symbols: $\hat{M}^*$ = growth rate of world money narrowly defined as currency and demand deposits

$\hat{gdp}^*$ = growth rate of world real gross domestic product

Note: World is defined as the OECD-member countries excluding the Netherlands.

For other symbols, see notes to Table 2.

47

Regression equations 23, 27, 31, and 35 are used to generate world inflation prediction series $(\hat{p}_c^* - u_i;$ for $i = 23, 27, 31, 35)$ which will serve as measures of anticipated world inflation. In equations 24, 28, 32, and 36, we attempt to attribute the unanticipated part of world inflation as measured by the residuals of equations 23, 27, 31, and 35, respectively, to unanticipated world money growth (per unit of world output, if appropriate), on the assumption that these residuals are indeed correct measures of unanticipated inflation. To test this assumption, the actual rate of world inflation is regressed in equations 25, 29, 33, and 37 on the prediction series of world inflation generated by equations 23, 27, 31, and 35, respectively, as well as on unanticipated world money growth (per unit of world output). For the prediction series of inflation so generated to be correct measures of anticipated inflation, and for the prediction errors of equations 23, 27, 31, and 35 to be correct measures of unanticipated inflation, the prediction series of inflation should be independent of the series of unanticipated world money growth (per unit of world output). If that is the case, the freely estimated coefficient of the measures of anticipated inflation in equations 25, 29, 33, and 37 should be statistically equal to unity.

We first discuss the outcomes of regression equations 23 - 26 and 31 - 34 of Table 4, with world inflation measured by the growth rate of the world consumer price index $(\hat{p}_c^*)$. Several findings stand out. First, as appears from equations 23 and 31, the regression coefficients of actual world inflation $(\hat{p}_c^*)$ with respect to the anticipated growth rate of world money lagged half a year are never statistically different from unity at the 5-percent level of significance. Moreover, from the value of the $\bar{R}^2$-statistics, it follows that the dominant part (i.e., 80 percent and more) of the variance of world inflation is explained by the only determinant of world inflationary expectations, namely anticipated world money growth per unit of world output. These findings are in agreement with the implication of the rational expectations hypothesis that world inflationary expectations are formed rationally, i.e., free of money illusion.

Second, as follows from equations 24 and 32, a modest part of unanticipated world inflation as measured by the forecast errors of equations 23 and 31, respectively, can be attributed to unanticipated world money growth per unit of world output $(\Delta \hat{M}^* - \Delta \hat{gdp}^*$ or $\Delta \hat{M}^{*ua} - \Delta \hat{gdp}^{*ua})$.

Third, as follows from equations 25 and 33, the regression coefficients of actual with respect to expected or predicted world inflation--with the latter being generated from the systematic parts of quantity theory equations 23 and 31--are never statistically different from unity at the 1-percent significance level.

Fourth, as follows from comparing equations 26 and 34 with equations 23 and 31 of Table 4, respectively, inserting the determinant of unanticipated world inflation leaves the coefficient of the determinant of expected world inflation virtually unchanged and has only small effects for the better on the $\bar{R}^2$-statistics involved. These last two findings suggest that in equations 23 and 31 we have successfully isolated the dominant determinant of world inflationary expectations, that our prediction series of world inflation are correct measures of world inflationary expectations, and that expectations of world inflation are formed free of money illusion and dominate actual world inflation.

The same four conclusions elaborated above with respect to the determinants of world consumer price inflation also apply to equations 27 - 30 and 35 - 38 of Table 4, with three qualifications. First, in these equations world inflation is measured by the growth rate of the index of Dutch import prices $(\hat{p}_i^*)$ and regressed on measures of the anticipated and unanticipated parts of world money growth pure. Employing instead world money growth per unit of world output or world trade proves to worsen the regression results considerably. Exactly the opposite is true in those cases where world inflation is measured by $\hat{p}_c^*$. Second, as can be seen from comparing equations 23 - 26 with 27 - 30 and equations 31 - 34 with 35 - 38, respectively, the degree of explanation of world inflation by world money growth is sharply reduced when world inflation is measured by the growth rate of the Dutch import price index rather than by the growth rate of the OECD consumer price index. This may in part be due to the fact that import prices are expressed in domestic currency units (guilders), whereas world consumer prices are expressed in dollars. It follows that variations in the rate of import price inflation are partly due to fluctuations in the Dutch exchange rates with respect to its import partners, whereas fluctuations in the rate of world consumer price inflation are not. Fluctuations in Dutch exchange rates with respect to the rest of the world may well be determined in part by fluctuations in world money growth relative to domestic money growth. This may explain, thirdly, the negative effect of unanticipated world money growth on import price inflation, as witnessed by equations 28 - 30 and 36 - 38 of Table 4. Unanticipated accelerations of world money (relative to domestic money) depreciate the value of world money relative to that of domestic money more than anticipated. Consequently, the rate at which domestic currency exchanges for foreign currency units falls unexpectedly, thereby lowering the actual rate of import price inflation expressed in domestic currency units.[28]

Finally, we note that the quantity theory of money applied to the world as a whole implies specific constraints with respect to the constant terms of regression equation pairs 23/26, 27/30, 31/34, and 35/38. Their values should be statistically significant and close to the trend growth rate of world money velocity in the case of the $\hat{p}_c^*$-regressions, where world money per unit of world output is used as the monetary impulse measure, and close to the difference between the trend growth rates of world money velocity and world trade in the case of the $\hat{p}_i^*$-regressions, where the growth rate of world money pure is used as the monetary impulse measure. As can be seen, equations 31 and 34 of Table 4 do not meet this requirement.[29]

In the final analysis, we prefer equations 5 and 16 of Tables 1 and 2, respectively, as the equations best explaining domestic inflation, both theoretically and statistically. That is, the systematic (anticipated) part of domestic inflation is best explained by anticipated domestic money growth and anticipated world consumer price inflation, with none of the homogeneity constraints which follow from the rational behavior-rational expectations class of hypotheses violated.[30] In addition, we select equations 26 and 34 of Table 4 as the regressions best explaining world consumer price inflation without violating the constraints implied by both the quantity theory and the rational behavior-rational expectations class of hypotheses.[31]

Since domestic inflation is dominated by anticipated domestic money growth and anticipated world consumer price inflation, and since world consumer price inflation is dominated by anticipated world money growth per unit of world production, it follows that the more narrow monetarist dominant impulse hypothesis fails to be rejected by the facts. Dutch inflation has been

---

[28]This hypothesis seems to be supported by regression equations $28'$, $29'$, and $30'$ in Table D1 of Appendix D, where unanticipated world money growth is replaced by unanticipated exchange rate fluctuations as measured by $\Delta \hat{e}$.

[29]With respect to these equations, note, moreover, that the Durbin-Watson (DW) statistic for serial correlation assumes values in the inconclusive range.

[30]With respect to the preferred regression equations 5 and 16, note that the DW-test statistics for serial correlation assume values in the inconclusive range. Note further that predictions of $\hat{p}_c^*$ from equation 26 can be substituted for $\hat{p}_c^*$ in equation 5 as well as for $\hat{p}_c^{*a}$ in equation 16, since the $\hat{p}_c^*$- and $\hat{p}_c^{*a}$-series prove to be roughly equivalent (see Appendix C).

[31]Except for the constant term constraint which is violated by equation 34.

dominated by domestic and world monetary impulses and, consequently, is predominantly a monetary phenomenon. Our overall conclusion on the basis of the above analysis must, therefore, be that the rational expectations-augmented monetarist impulse hypothesis of inflation stands up remarkably well when tested against the Dutch postwar facts. As a result, we are provided with a theory of inflation that is both simple, consistent with rational economic behavior (i.e., price theory), and capable of making largely unconditional forecasts of the future rate of inflation.

B. The Output Regressions

We turn next to the outcomes of the regression analysis of the deviations of actual from normal Dutch output growth. According to the broad DIRE hypothesis embodied in (6), deviations of actual from normal output growth $(\hat{y} - \bar{y})$ are determined by unanticipated systematic economic impulses and random shifts.[32]

Ideally, as follows from substituting (5) into (1), the same unanticipated impulses found to affect the deviation of actual from anticipated inflation should also be found to affect the deviation of actual from normal output growth. This symmetry requires, however, that the underlying price level and output volume should be related conceptually such as is the case, for example, with the implicit price deflator of private consumption and the volume of private consumption. For the reasons spelled out in Section II, however, we prefer to analyze two nonmatching concepts: the growth rate of the implicit price deflator of private domestic consumption, on the one hand, and the growth rate of industrial production, on the other.[33] Consequently, a strict correspondence between the determinants of the measures of unanticipated inflation and unanticipated output growth should not be expected.

This lack of correspondence is indeed what we find in the regression analysis of the deviations of actual from normal growth of industrial production $(\hat{y} - \bar{y})$ over the period 1954-75. Table 5 summarizes the regression results. We found the most successful empirical approximation of $(\hat{y} - \bar{y})$ to be either the

---

[32] It is recalled that normal output growth is defined as that rate of output growth at which inflation is fully anticipated [see (1)] and that this rate need neither be a constant nor a trend rate.

[33] An additional empirical advantage of basing the analysis of Dutch inflation and output fluctuations on these two nonmatching concepts is the reduced dependency of possible errors in their measurement.

Table 5

Fluctuations in Output Growth and Unanticipated Impulses, 1954-75

$$\hat{y} - y = g(I - I^e) \text{ approximated by } \hat{\Delta y} = g(\Delta \hat{I}_{-i}) \text{ with } i = 0 \text{ or } 1$$

Equation		VARU	$\bar{R}^2$	DW
39 (t-stat.)	$\hat{\Delta y} = -.65 + .23\,\hat{\Delta M}_{-1} + .57\,\Delta\hat{m}^* + .20\,\hat{\Delta p}_i^* + .08\,\Delta FI + .49\,\hat{\Delta S}_{-1}$ $\quad\quad\ \ (1.44)\ \ (1.40)\quad\quad (4.21)\quad\quad (3.03)\quad\quad (.41)\quad\quad (3.44)$	4.34	0.75	1.90
40	$\hat{\Delta y} = -.64 + .71\,\hat{\Delta m}^* + .19\,\hat{\Delta p}_i^* + .48\,\hat{\Delta S}_{-1}$ $\quad\quad\ \ (1.43)\ \ (7.27)\quad\quad (2.91)\quad\quad (3.45)$	4.36	0.75	2.24
41	$\hat{\Delta y} = -.67 + .27\,\hat{\Delta M}_{-1} + .67\,\hat{\Delta m}^* + .65\,\hat{\Delta p}_{c-1}^* + .01\,\Delta FI + .27\,\hat{\Delta S}_{-1}$ $\quad\quad\ \ (1.32)\ \ (1.44)\quad\quad (4.38)\quad\quad (2.00)\quad\quad (.03)\quad\quad (2.03)$	5.47	0.69	2.46
42	$\hat{\Delta y} = -.65 + .81\,\hat{\Delta m}^* + .56\,\hat{\Delta p}_{c-1}^* + .28\,\hat{\Delta S}_{-1}$ $\quad\quad\ \ (1.28)\ \ (6.94)\quad\quad (1.75)\quad\quad (2.12)$	5.49	.69	2.73
43	$\hat{\Delta y} = -.61 + .77\,\hat{\Delta m}^* + .50\,\hat{\Delta (p_c^* + e)} + .41\,\hat{\Delta S}_{-1}$ $\quad\quad\ \ (1.29)\ \ (7.45)\quad\quad (2.39)\quad\quad (2.96)$	4.87	0.72	2.11
44	$\hat{\Delta y} = -.49 + .73\,\hat{\Delta m}^* + .25\,\hat{\Delta S}_{-1}$ $\quad\quad\ \ (.93)\ \ (6.42)\quad\quad (1.86)$	6.08	0.65	2.45

Table 5 – Continued

$$\hat{y} - \bar{y} = g(I - I^e) \text{ approximated by } \Delta\hat{y}^{ua} = g(\Delta\hat{I}^{ua}_{-i}) \text{ with } i = 0 \text{ or } 1$$

Equation		VARU	$\bar{R}^2$	DW
45 (t-stat.)	$\Delta\hat{y}^{ua} = -.71 + .11\,\Delta\hat{M}^{ua}_{-1} + .69\,\Delta\hat{m}^{*ua} + .16\,\Delta\hat{p}^{*ua}_{i} - .08\,\Delta FI^{ua} + .39\,\Delta\hat{S}^{ua}_{-1}$ $\quad\;\;(2.39)\quad(.84)\qquad\quad(6.04)\qquad\quad(3.29)\qquad\quad(.64)\qquad\quad(3.06)$	1.76	0.87	2.12
46	$\Delta\hat{y}^{ua} = -.65 + .75\,\Delta\hat{m}^{*ua} + .17\,\Delta\hat{p}^{*ua}_{i} + .42\,\Delta\hat{S}^{ua}_{-1}$ $\quad\;\;(2.31)\quad(9.92)\qquad\quad(3.49)\qquad\quad(3.56)$	1.67	0.87	2.23
47	$\Delta\hat{y}^{ua} = -.64 + .14\,\Delta\hat{M}^{ua}_{-1} + .73\,\Delta\hat{m}^{*ua} + .31\,\Delta\hat{p}^{*ua}_{c-1} - .10\,\Delta FI^{ua} + .23\,\Delta\hat{S}^{ua}_{-1}$ $\quad\;\;(1.77)\quad(.88)\qquad\quad(5.35)\qquad\quad(1.44)\qquad\qquad(.61)\qquad\quad(1.66)$	2.61	0.80	2.46
48	$\Delta\hat{y}^{ua} = -.57 + .81\,\Delta\hat{m}^{*ua} + .31\,\Delta\hat{p}^{*ua}_{c-1} + .27\,\Delta\hat{S}^{ua}_{-1}$ $\quad\;\;(1.66)\quad(8.96)\qquad\quad(1.51)\qquad\qquad(2.04)$	2.48	.81	2.68
49	$\Delta\hat{y}^{ua} = -.55 + .78\,\Delta\hat{m}^{*ua} + .34\,(\Delta\hat{p}^{*ua}_{c} + \Delta\hat{e}) + .40\,\Delta\hat{S}^{ua}_{-1}$ $\quad\;\;(1.74)\quad(9.28)\qquad\quad(2.40)\qquad\qquad\quad(2.88)$	2.12	0.84	2.41
50	$\Delta\hat{y}^{ua} = -.55 + .80\,\Delta\hat{m}^{*ua} + .23\,\Delta\hat{S}^{ua}_{-1}$ $\quad\;\;(1.56)\quad(8.57)\qquad\quad(1.71)$	2.65	0.80	2.52

Symbols: $\hat{y}$ = growth rate of industrial production

$\hat{e}$ = growth rate of guilder-dollar exchange rate.

Note: For other symbols, see notes to Table 2.

53

first time differences of $\hat{y}$ (i.e., $\Delta \hat{y}$) or the residuals of an ARIMA process fitted on $\Delta \hat{y}$ (i.e., $\Delta \hat{y}^{ua}$).[34]

In equations 39, 41, 45, and 47, these alternative measures of the deviation of actual from normal industrial production growth are regressed on alternative measures of the unanticipated parts of all systematic economic impulse forces introduced above.

Two findings stand out. First, unanticipated fiscal and monetary impulses appear not to have contributed significantly to unanticipated fluctuations in the Dutch growth rate of industrial production but are dominated, instead, by unanticipated movements in the growth rate of world trade ($\hat{m}^*$), foreign prices ($\hat{p}^*_i$ or $\hat{p}^*_c$), and domestic government debt ($\hat{S}$).

Second, from comparing equations 39 and 41 and equations 45 and 47, it appears that the unanticipated part of the rate of change of Dutch import prices ($\hat{p}^*_i$) outperforms unanticipated world consumer price inflation ($\hat{p}^*_c$) in explaining deviations of actual growth in Dutch industrial production from its normal growth level. In addition, in contrast to unanticipated $\hat{p}^*_i$, unanticipated $\hat{p}^*_c$ tends to reach statistical significance only if lagged one year. The former finding is strengthened by what happens when the nonsignificant unanticipated impulse variables are deleted from equations 39, 41, 45, and 47. The results are summarized in equations 40, 42, 46, and 48 of Table 5, respectively. Whereas the coefficient estimates of the unanticipated rate of import price inflation appear to remain practically unchanged in value and significant statistically, the coefficient estimates of the unanticipated rate of world consumer price inflation fail to reach accepted levels of significance. It is recalled, in this respect, that import prices are denominated in Dutch currency units, whereas world consumer prices are expressed in dollar units. The finding that unanticipated import price inflation outperforms unanticipated world consumer price inflation in explaining deviations of actual from normal industrial production growth thus seems to suggest that unanticipated exchange rate fluctuations are an important codeterminant of the deviation of actual from normal production growth. With the exchange rate depreciating more rapidly than anticipated, unanticipated

---

[34] See the introduction to Section IV. See Appendix C for the equation fitted. Regressing an equation like $\hat{y} = \bar{\bar{y}} + g(1 - I^e) + w$, with $\bar{\bar{y}}$ approximated by either a constant or by $\hat{y}_{-1}$ or by $\hat{y}^a$, the latter being the predictions of an ARIMA process fitted to $\Delta \hat{y}$ and then added to $\hat{y}_{-1}$ (i.e., $\hat{y}^a = \hat{y}_{-1} + \Delta \hat{y}^a = \hat{y} - \Delta \hat{y}^{ua}$), was found to give poorer outcomes, statistically, compared to those based on the measures of $\hat{y} - \bar{\bar{y}}$ mentioned in the text.

increases in the rate of foreign absorption of domestic production will occur, resulting in unanticipated output growth, and vice versa. Some support for this hypothesis may be obtained from regression equations 43 and 49 of Table 5. In these equations, unanticipated changes in the proportionate rate of change of the guilder-dollar spot rate of exchange are added to the unanticipated growth rate of world consumer prices on the assumption that the second-time difference of the logarithm of the exchange rate series ($\Delta \hat{e}$) properly measures unanticipated exchange rate movements.[35]

As appears from regression equations 43 and 49, unanticipated world consumer price inflation significantly affects the deviations of actual from normal production growth, provided unanticipated world consumer price inflation is denominated in domestic currency and used nonlagged, thereby making regression equations 43 and 49 more correspondent to equations 40 and 46 of Table 5, respectively.[36]

From Table 5, we select regression equations 40 and 46 as the preferred equations for explaining deviations of actual from normal growth of Dutch industrial production. All unanticipated impulse variables in these equations have the expected signs. Moreover, from the values of the DW-test statistic estimated for these equations, it follows that the null-hypothesis of no serial correlation cannot be rejected. The main conclusion from the output equations selected here is that the growth rate of production cannot be maintained over and above its normal level by traditional Keynesian-type systematic demand management policies. Rational expectations imply that such policies will be foreseen and ineffective. Raising fiscal, monetary, and financial impulses to maintained higher levels fails to affect production growth other than temporarily. The only maintained effects, if at all, of such policies is on the rate of inflation.

On the basis of the foregoing discussion, the preferred equations are regressions 5, 16, 26, 34, 40, and 46 of Tables 2 - 5. They are summarized for convenience in Table 6.

---

[35] Generating the residuals of an ARIMA process fitted on $\Delta\hat{e}$ for use in equation 49 seems unnecessary for the fixed rate period up to 1972 when all exchange rate fluctuations may be assumed to be unanticipated, and impossible for the managed floating period since 1972 for lack of sufficient annual observations.

[36] In addition, note the striking resemblance across these equations of the coefficient estimates of unanticipated $\hat{m}^*$ and $\hat{S}_{-1}$. Such resemblance is absent for the coefficient estimates of unanticipated world inflation denominated in domestic currency, in view of the much larger variability of the $\hat{p}_i^*$-series relative to the $(\hat{p}_c^* + \hat{e})$-series. For equations 43 and 49, including unanticipated money growth, see Appendix D, Table D1, equations 43' and 49'.

Table 6

Preferred Regression Equations

Equation		VARU	$\bar{R}^2$	DW
5	$\hat{p}_c = .35 + .27\hat{M}_{-1.5} + .65\hat{p}^*_{c-1.5} + 3.10 \text{ shift } 68/69 + 1.41 \Delta^2 TP_{-.5} + .14 \Delta\hat{m}^*$	0.58	0.92	2.33
16	$\hat{p}_c = -.32 + .36\hat{M}^a_{-.5} + .63\hat{p}^{*a}_{c-.5} + 2.83 \text{ shift } 68/69 + 1.32 \Delta^2 TP_{-.5} + .14 \Delta\hat{m}^{*ua}$	0.63	.91	2.05
26	$\hat{p}^*_c = 2.14 + .90(\hat{M}^*_{-1.5} - \hat{gdp}^*_{-1.5}) + .24(\Delta\hat{M}^* - \Delta\hat{gdp}^*)$	1.84	.87	1.92
34	$\hat{p}^*_c = .87 + .93(\hat{M}^{*a} - \hat{gdp}^{*a}) + .26(\Delta\hat{M}^{*ua} - \Delta\hat{gdp}^{*ua})$	1.35	.91	1.39
40	$\Delta\hat{y} = -.64 + .71\Delta\hat{m}^* + .19\Delta\hat{p}^*_i + .48\Delta\hat{S}_{-1}$	4.36	.75	2.24
46	$\Delta\hat{y}^{ua} = -.65 + .75\Delta\hat{m}^{*ua} + .17\Delta\hat{p}^{*ua}_i + .42\Delta\hat{S}^{ua}_{-1}$	1.67	0.87	2.23

In closing the discussion of the parametric test outcomes on the DIRE hypothesis of inflation and output fluctuations, four final notes are in order.

First, and for reasons suggested earlier, it follows from comparing the preferred equations that the determinants of the deviations of actual from normal industrial production growth do not closely match those of the deviation of actual from anticipated consumer price inflation. In fact, of all the unanticipated impulses operating on unanticipated consumer price inflation in the Netherlands, only unanticipated growth in world trade ($\Delta \hat{m}^*$, $\Delta \hat{m}^{*ua}$) is found to simultaneously affect deviations of the growth rate of Dutch industrial production from its normal level. In turn, apart from unanticipated world trade growth, none of the unanticipated impulses operating on the deviation of actual from normal industrial production growth (i.e., $\Delta \hat{p}_i^*, \Delta \hat{p}_i^{*ua}; \Delta \hat{S}, \Delta \hat{S}^{ua}$) seem to affect unanticipated consumer price inflation.[37]

Second, whereas (anticipated) consumer price inflation in the Netherlands is best explained when anticipated dollar-denominated world consumer price inflation rather than anticipated guilder-denominated import price inflation is used as a measure of anticipated world inflation, the opposite holds with respect to unanticipated growth in industrial production, which is best explained when guilder-denominated unanticipated import price inflation rather than dollar-denominated unanticipated world consumer price inflation is used as a measure of unanticipated world inflation.[38]

Third, whereas (anticipated) consumer price inflation is best explained by anticipated impulse measures lagged half a year, deviations of actual from normal industrial production growth seem best explained by unanticipated current impulses, with the exception of the unanticipated growth in the stock of government debt. Consequently, whereas predictions of inflation can conveniently be based on already known quantities, forecasts of industrial production growth must be based on quantities which need to be themselves predicted first.

Finally, as appears from the preferred output regression equations 40 and 46, the effects of unanticipated financial impulses as measured by the unanticipated growth rate of the stock of government debt ($\hat{S}$) lagged one year are not

---

[37] In addition, the indirect tax regime shift variable (shift 68/69) does not appear to have affected unanticipated industrial production growth either.

[38] The reason that world price inflation measures expressed in domestic currency reduce the statistical fit of the domestic inflation regression equations may well be that most of the period of estimation was characterized by fixed or firmly managed exchange rates. As argued in Section I, under such a regime, anticipations of exchange rate changes may well be zero approximately and, consequently, fail to show up in the inflation regression equations. See n. 25 and Table D1 of Appendix D, equations 5', 11', 16", and 22" in this respect.

only significant but also positive and strikingly strong in view of the argument made in some monetarist quarters that government expenditures financed by taxes or government debt crowd out private expenditure and production even in the short run (Carlson and Spencer, 1975). Our results imply that a one-percentage-point increase in the growth rate of the stock of government debt, if unanticipated, on average will increase the deviation of actual from normal production growth by somewhat less than one-half of a percentage point one year later.

At least two lines of reasoning can be developed to explain this finding. In the first place, it may be argued that the part of the deviation of actual from normal production attributed to unanticipated growth in the stock of government debt in fact results from unanticipated changes in government absorption of private production and taxes, which are better measured by unanticipated growth in government debt than by the measure given here of unanticipated fiscal impulses.

A second and, in our view, preferable line of reasoning is followed by Brunner and Meltzer (1976a) and Korteweg and Van Loo (1977) who argue that, although crowding out occurs in the long run, additions to the stock of government debt at first raise the market rate of interest on government debt and lower the market rate of return on (equity in) physical capital. As a result, whereas private real spending on domestic production is contracted by rising interest rates on government debt, it is stimulated by falling market rates on capital. On balance, stability of the model requires that the spending and production effects of increases in government debt are positive in the short run.[39]

V. SUMMARY, FORECASTS, AND POLICY IMPLICATIONS

This paper develops the DIRE hypothesis of inflation and fluctuations in output growth and tests some of its implications against postwar data for the Netherlands.

---

[39]The stability condition involved for $\bar{\epsilon}(y,S) > 0$ is that

$$\frac{\bar{\epsilon}(d,i)}{\bar{\epsilon}(d,i_c)} < \frac{\bar{\epsilon}(i_c,S)}{\bar{\epsilon}(i,S)} \ ,$$

where i and i_c are the market rates of return on government debt (S) and capital, respectively, y is domestic private production, d is private domestic real spending on private domestic production, and $\bar{\epsilon}$ a symbol indicating a total elasticity. See Korteweg (1976).

Four subsets of hypotheses are involved. First, it is contended that aggregate fluctuations in prices and output mainly emerge from the economy's response to systematic economic impulses, and not from the economy's exposure to random disturbances distributed over the system, nor from instability of private sector behavioral relationships, nor from any inherent dynamic instability of the system itself. Second, expectations of inflation and production growth are formed rationally and free of money illusion. Third, economic agents behave rationally and free of money illusion by changing prices in accordance with the rate of change of prices they expect. Finally, deviations of actual from anticipated inflation and of actual from normal output growth are dominated by unanticipated systematic impulses.

The main conclusion from our tests is that the major implications of the DIRE hypothesis fail to be rejected by the facts. It is found, firstly, that Dutch consumer price inflation is dominated by anticipated growth in the Dutch stock of money and the world consumer price level, with their coefficients summing to unity. Second, world consumer price inflation is dominated by anticipated growth in the world stock of money per unit of world real income, with a coefficient not significantly different from unity. Together these two findings suggest that Dutch consumer price inflation has been predominantly a monetary phenomenon. Third, we found that unanticipated growth in world trade and unforeseen changes in the pressure of taxes and social security premiums on national income significantly affect unanticipated inflation. Fourth, unanticipated growth in industrial production is found to be dominated by the unanticipated parts of three systematic impulses, namely, world trade growth, growth in the stock of government debt, and guilder-denominated world price inflation as measured either by import price inflation or world consumer price inflation in guilder terms. Finally, anticipated and unanticipated pure fiscal impulses, measuring changing claims on domestic production imposed or released by the government, are found to have had no noticeable effects on either inflation or production growth in excess of its normal rate.

The policy implications of our findings on the determinants of inflation and fluctuations in output growth give reason for optimism as well as for distress. Inflation is predominantly a monetary phenomenon and can be controlled by controlling the growth rates of domestic and world money.[40] This suggests the need for international coordination and harmonization of monetary policy as well as of the main sources of domestic money growth, i.e., government budget deficits and the way they are financed. This ties in with an additional mechanism to stem inflation, namely, slowing down the rate of increase of the share of taxes and of social security premiums in Dutch national income. However, in order for this approach to have any effect on reducing inflation, reductions of the share of taxes and of social security premiums in national income, or its rate of increase, should come as a surprise. A policy of continuous reduction in tax pressure, broadly conceived, would soon become anticipated. For such a policy to be an effective anti-inflationary device, it should be pursued unsystematically, which may well prove to be a course too difficult to devise. Finally, our analysis of inflation does not seem to provide support for the alleged effectiveness of one of mankind's oldest anti-inflationary devices: wage and price controls. Our findings suggest that domestic and foreign money growth are the dominant determinants of inflation. Continuous money growth in excess of normal production growth maintains inflation, i.e., a continuous rise in the general price level. Direct price or wage controls may have once-and-for-all effects on the level of prices and wages when installed or removed, especially if unannounced and by surprise, but there is no indication of their maintained effects on the rate of inflation. Money growth appears to be the roller coaster on which inflation rides unhampered by price and wage controls.[41]

Although our findings suggest a clear way out of inflation and are, therefore, a cause for some optimism, they are a cause for some pessimism as well. Our findings suggest that the growth rate of production cannot be made to exceed its normal level by traditional aggregate demand management policies except temporarily. Nor can such policies affect the normal rate itself. Fiscal and monetary impulses are found to fail to affect output growth at all. Financial policies, summarized by the growth rate of the stock of government debt, affect the deviation of actual from normal production growth only if unanticipated. Rational expectations imply, however, that economic agents do not make

---

[40] Can the stock of money in the small open Dutch economy be controlled by the monetary authorities? The answer is that it can be if the authorities want to control it, even under fixed exchange rates, provided foreign monetary impulses and the domestic budget deficit do not become excessive relative to the domestic source component of money and the monetary base. This is suggested by the work of Kouri and Porter (1974), whose findings imply that, with an average money multiplier of 2, a one-guilder increase in central bank domestic earning assets results in eighty-four cents of extra money, and by the work of Korteweg and Van Loo (1977), who find that a one-guilder increase in the central bank domestic earning assets will raise the money stock by more than one guilder.

[41] On this issue, we refer to the Frazer Institute (1976) and the Committee on Banking, Currency and Housing (1976).

systematic forecasting errors. Growth of production in excess of its normal rate thus requires continuous acceleration of government debt until even this policy pattern becomes anticipated.

The conclusion is that activist demand management policies cannot be counted on to <u>systematically</u> stimulate the actual growth rate of aggregate production in excess of its normal level and actual employment in excess of its natural rate. With rational expectations, any systematic policy quickly becomes foreseen and ineffective.[42] The only effect of such policies is on the rate of inflation.

Our finding that activist global demand management policies are ineffective does not imply, however, that there is no room for policies acting on the normal rate of production growth and the natural rate of employment directly. To improve these rates, however, more microeconomic policies are needed in addition to institutional reform. We can indicate such measures only briefly here, since they lie outside the scope of this paper.[43]

A higher rate of normal production growth and natural employment could be reached by measures aimed at restoring competition and removing imperfections, rigidities, and monopolies in the product and factor markets, including minimum wages, wage and price controls, and trade union monopolies. Moreover, a program for monetary stability could be enacted to restore the information content of money as a means of payment. Subsidies could be abolished or reduced for inefficient activities. The extent and duration of current unemployment benefits could be reduced and shortened or the whole system replaced by a negative income tax. The burden of taxes and tax progression could be reduced to free resources used in tax avoidance. And, trade protection and tariffs could be eliminated. This list, although not complete since it leaves many aspects of government intervention unmentioned, should serve to indicate the kinds of measures able to raise production growth and the natural rate of employment.

Finally, we want to investigate the forecasting performance of the preferred regression equations with respect to domestic and world inflation and domestic output fluctuations. To that purpose, we calculate, for each equation over the period of estimation, a so-called inequality coefficient (U_i) which is defined as:

---

[42] Poole (1976) argues that this may induce policy activists to search continuously for new policies.

[43] On this issue, see Korteweg (1977).

$$U_i = \sqrt{\frac{1}{n} \sum_t U^2_{i,t}} \quad ,$$

where $U_{i,t} = \dfrac{P_{i,t} - A_{i,t}}{\sqrt{\dfrac{1}{n} \sum_t A^2_{i,t}}}$,

and n $\quad = \quad$ number of observations

$P_{i,t}$ $\quad = \quad$ predicted value of variable i for year t,

and $A_{i,t}$ $\quad = \quad$ actual value of variable i in year t.

The lower the value of U_i, the better the forecasting performance of the equation involved. In Table 7, we compare the inequality coefficients implied by the prediction errors of the preferred equations with those implied by two naive forecasting rules, one being the "no-change" rule according to which $x = 0$, and the other being the "same-change" rule according to which $x = x_{-1}$, for $x = \begin{bmatrix} \hat{p}_c, \hat{p}^*_c, \Delta\hat{y}, \Delta\hat{y}^{ua} \end{bmatrix}$.

Table 7

Inequality Coefficients and Forecasting Performance

Regression equation and variable (i)	U_i in case of our equations	U_i in case of "no-change"	U_i in case of "same-change"
Equation 5 : $\hat{p}_c$	0.120	1.000	0.399
16 : $\hat{p}_c$	.125	1.000	0.399
26 : $\hat{p}^*_c$	.228	1.000	0.275
34 : $\hat{p}^*_c$	.196	1.000	0.275
40 : $\Delta\hat{y}$	.456	1.000	1.544
46 : $\Delta\hat{y}^{ua}$	0.331	1.000	1.383

From Table 7 it follows that the preferred regression equations, especially those with respect to inflation, easily outperform the naive "no-change" and "same-change" rules in forecasting domestic and world inflation as well as fluctuations in production growth over the sample period.

Appendix A

Variables Used

e	$=$	exchange rate (number of domestic currency units per dollar)
gdp_b		real gross domestic product of domestic enterprises
gdp^*		real world gross domestic product (in dollars)
m_f		volume of imports of foreign country f
m^*		volume of world trade weighted for structural changes in trade shares between countries
p		price level of domestic output (in general)
p^*		price level of world output (in general)
p_b		implicit price deflator of gross domestic product of enterprises
p_c		implicit price deflator of domestic private consumption
p_c^*		weighted average of consumer price indexes of OECD-member countries excluding the Netherlands (in dollar terms)
p_i^*		commodity import price index (in domestic currency)
q		100 - capacity utilization rate
x_{NL}		volume of Dutch exports of commodities
y		industrial production (daily average, seasonally adjusted), or the volume of output in general
y^*		world output
u		rate of unemployment (men and women)
CAB		current account balance
CFD		government budget deficit (central plus local government)
FI		fiscal impulse divided by net national income lagged one year
FI'		fiscal impulse divided by G lagged one year
G		net relevant government expenditures (on wages, salaries, consumption, investment, imports, net transfers, etc.)
GDP		nominal gross domestic product
GIdb		gross investment in business buildings (b) and dwellings (d)
I		vector of systematic economic impulses operating on the economy
Img		value of government imports of goods and services
$\triangle Lg$		general increases in government wages and salaries
M		domestic stock of money, narrowly defined to include currency and demand deposits (annual average)
M^*		world stock of money (narrowly defined, in dollars); world consists of OECD-member countries excluding the Netherlands
NNI		net nominal national income
S		stock of government short-term and long-term debt held by private and foreign sector
T		total amount of direct and indirect taxes (on a cash basis)
$\triangle Taut$	$=$	automatic (endogenous) change in taxes (on a transactions basis)

$\triangle$Tdisc	=	discrete (autonomous) change in taxes
TP		tax pressure, being the amount of taxes and social security premiums (T+P) as a fraction of net national income
$\hat{\ }$		first difference of the logarithm of some variable x : $\hat{x} = \triangle \ln x$
$a_{NL}, (a_f)$		share of Dutch exports in each trading partner's total volume of imports (idem, structural component)
$(1+\pi)$		macroeconomic tax progression factor $[(\triangle \text{Taut}/\text{Ta(tr)}_{-1})/\text{NNI}]$, where (tr) indicates transactions basis
∇p		nonparametric test statistic for positive or negative association between variables
DW		Durbin-Watson test statistic
$\bar{R}^2$		coefficient of determination, adjusted for degrees of freedom
VARU	=	residual variance, adjusted for degrees of freedom.

Appendix B

Calculating Procedures

1. World consumer price index relative to the Netherlands (NL):

$$
p^*_c = \left[p_{c,w} - w_{NL} \frac{e_{NL,1970} \times p_{c,NL}}{e_{NL}} \right] \Big/ (1 - w_{NL}),
$$

where $p_{c,w} = \sum_{j=1}^{24} \left(w_j \cdot \frac{e_{j,1970} \times p_{c,j}}{e_j} \right),$

and $w_j = \left[\frac{GDP_j}{e_{j,1970} \times p_{c,j}} \right] \Big/ \sum_{j=1}^{24} \left(\frac{GDP_j}{e_{j,1970} \times p_{c,j}} \right),$

with $j=1, \ldots, 24$ being the countries making up the OECD-world, including the Netherlands.

Data on p^*_c for the Netherlands are calculated and supplied to us by Michele Fratianni, EC, Brussels.

2. World gross domestic product relative to the Netherlands (NL):

$$
gdp^* = \sum_{j=1}^{24} \left(\frac{GDP_j}{e_{j,1970} \times p_{c,j}} \right) - \frac{GDP_{NL}}{e_{NL,1970} \times p_{c,NL}},
$$

where $j=1, \ldots, 24$ are the OECD-member countries.

Data source: Michele Fratianni, EC, Brussels.

3. World trade data relative to the Netherlands (m*) are supplied to us by the Dutch Central Planning Bureau. In its simplest form, the procedure involved in calculating m* can be stated as follows. Assume the following simple Dutch export function:

$$x_{NL,f} = a_{NL} \, m_f,$$

and $\quad a_{NL} = a_f \left(\dfrac{p_{c,NL}}{e_{NL} \times p_c^*} \right)^{\beta} \quad \begin{array}{l} (\beta < 0) \\ (f = 1, \ldots, F; \text{ the Netherlands' trading partners}). \end{array}$

It follows that

$$x_{NL,f} = a_f \cdot p_{c,NL}^{\beta} \cdot e_{NL}^{-\beta} \cdot p_c^{*\,-\beta} \cdot m_f.$$

Since $\quad x_{NL} = \displaystyle\sum_{f=1}^{F} x_{NL,f},$

it follows that

$$x_{NL} = p_{c,NL}^{\beta} \cdot e_{NL}^{-\beta} \cdot p_c^{*\,-\beta} \cdot \sum_f a_f \, m_f,$$

where m^* is defined as

$$m^* = \sum_f a_f \, m_f, \quad \text{with} \quad a_f = \left(\dfrac{x_{NL,f}}{m_f} \right)_{-1}.$$

4. <u>World money stock relative to the Netherlands (NL):</u>

$$M^* = \sum_{j=1}^{24} \left(\dfrac{M_j}{e_j} \right) - \dfrac{M_{NL}}{e_{NL}}.$$

Data source: Michele Fratianni, EC, Brussels.

5. <u>Automatic changes in tax receipts (ΔTaut)</u> are calculated on a transactions basis (tr) as follows:

$$\Delta \text{Taut} = (1+\pi) \cdot N\hat{N}I \cdot T(tr)_{-1},$$

where T is tax receipts, $(1+\pi)$ is the macroeconomic tax progression factor, data on which are supplied to us by the Dutch Ministry of Finance, and NNI is net nominal national income at market prices.

Discretionary changes in taxes on a cash basis can be calculated as:

$$\Delta Tdisc = \Delta T - \Delta Taut.$$

Since ΔT is defined on a cash basis, we can write:

$$\Delta T = \Delta T(tr) + \Delta[T - T (tr)].$$

It follows that discretionary taxes on a cash basis can be rewritten as:

$$\Delta Tdisc = \Delta[T(tr) - Taut] + \Delta[T - T(tr)].$$

The first term describes discretionary tax changes on a transactions basis. The second term involves changes in tax cash flows because of discrete alterations in the speed and procedures of tax collection. The sum of the two terms makes up for the discrete changes in tax receipts on a cash-flow basis.

Appendix C

Box-Jenkins Models for Inflation, Output Growth, and Impulse Variables

E. J. Bomhoff

The theoretical specification of the price and output relations requires variables for the expected and unexpected parts of the impulse measures and some other time series. This appendix describes the construction of the empirical counterparts to these concepts. The unexpected parts are the residuals ϵ_t of simple Box-Jenkins models (Box and Jenkins, 1970). Normally such models are fitted to the original series, if it is stationary, or to a differenced series if it is not. Here we always took first differences of the series to be modeled, also in those cases where the original series x_t was already stationary. This was done in order to get a series with a mean value sufficiently close to zero to be neglected. Modeling Δx_t means trying to improve upon the naive model: no change between last year and this year in x (an impulse, the growth rate of world money, or some other series). Modeling x_t, on the other hand, would have implied that we build upon the naive formula: next year x_t will be equal to its average value over the complete period. It is not attractive to assume knowledge about the mean value of the x_t when the period over which the averaging is done includes years that lie in the future. We avoid this by modeling the Δx_t-series.

There were two reasons for limiting ourselves to the simplest Box-Jenkins models, one statistical and one economic. The statistical reason is the short length of the series: at most twenty-five observations. Equally important is that the more previous values of Δx_t or ϵ_t are included in the information set used for the forecasts, the less acceptable it becomes that no other relevant series is included in the information set. If forecasts based on the adaptive expectations model or on other simple Box-Jenkins models are judged to be too coarse, then current or immediate past values of related variables seem stronger candidates for inclusion in the information set than values from the more distant past of the forecast series itself. (See McCallum, 1976, who also finds that the optimal formula lies somewhere between the simple adaptive expectations model and the type of variable that would be constructed in the first stage of a TSLS regression.)

We have not attempted to fit parameters of an order higher than 2. Of the remaining AR(1), AR(2), MA(1), MA(2), and ARMA(1,1) models, the one with the highest $\bar{R}^2$ was selected. In Table C1, summary statistics of the models are presented. The unadjusted value of R^2 is given, because it indicates the degree to which the residuals are different from the Δx_t- series itself.

In some cases models could only be fitted for a slightly different period due to outliers in the final two years (1974, 1975) of the sample. All observations more than 2.5 standard deviations away from the mean were deleted and replaced by values calculated from the model fitted to the shortened series. If the outliers had not been removed, they would have dominated the parameter values too much.

With the Box-Jenkins residuals ϵ_t as the unforeseen parts of a variable, the foreseen value of the variable is found by subtraction.

Table C1

Box-Jenkins Models

Variable	Model	R^2
$\hat{p}_c$ (t-stat.)	$\triangle\hat{p}_{c,t} = (1 - 0.64B)\ \epsilon_t$ $\qquad\qquad (0.17)$	0.27
$\hat{p}^*_i$	$(1 + 0.29B + 0.60B^2)\triangle\hat{p}^*_{i,t} = \epsilon_t$ $\quad\ (0.17)\quad (0.17)$	.24
$\hat{p}^*_c$	$\triangle\hat{p}^*_{c,t} = (1 - 0.08B^2)\ \epsilon_t$ $\qquad\qquad (0.19)$	.01
$\hat{y}$	$\triangle\hat{y}_t = (1 - 0.50B - 0.43B^2)\ \epsilon_t$ $\qquad\qquad (0.19)\ \ (0.18)$	.24
$\hat{gdp}^*$	$\triangle\hat{gdp}^*_t = (1 - 0.79B)\ \epsilon_t$ $\qquad\qquad\ (0.12)$	.32
$\hat{m}^*$	$\triangle\hat{m}^*_t = (1 - 0.33B - 0.53B^2)\ \epsilon_t$ $\qquad\qquad (0.18)\ \ (0.17)$	.24
$\hat{M}$	$\triangle\hat{M}_t = (1 - 0.22B - 0.43B^2)\ \epsilon_t$ $\qquad\qquad (0.20)\ \ (0.20)$	.15
$\hat{M}^*$	$(1 - 0.79B)\triangle\hat{M}^*_t = (1 - 0.97B)\ \epsilon_t$ $\quad\ (0.27)\qquad\quad\ (0.13)$	.08
$\hat{S}$	$\triangle\hat{S}_t = (1 - 0.89B)\ \epsilon_t$ $\qquad\qquad (0.10)$	.44
FI	$\triangle FI_t = (1 - 0.64B)\ \epsilon_t$ $\qquad\qquad (0.16)$	.16
$\triangle TP$	$\triangle^2 TP_t = (1 - 0.93B)\ \epsilon_t$ $\qquad\qquad (0.058)$	0.47

Note: B is the backshift operator, i.e., $Bx_t \equiv x_{t-1}$.

Means have been neglected (see text).

No observations were lost at the beginning of the series because an estimation procedure was used which included the so-called back-forecasting feature.

Standard deviations, in brackets below each coefficient, are based on a linearization in the vicinity of the optimum and should be regarded as approximative.

All models fitted to 1953-75, except:

$\hat{p}^*_i$ --   1953-73

$\hat{M}$ --   1953-74

$\hat{M}^*$ --   1953-73.

Appendix D

Table D1

Additional Regression Equations

	VARU	$\bar{R}^2$	DW

16' $\hat{p}_c = -1.57 + .59\,\hat{M}^a_{-.5} + .57\,\hat{p}^{*a}_{c-.5} + 2.43\text{ shift }68/69 + 1.29\,\triangle^2 TP^{ua}_{-.5} + .10\,\triangle\hat{m}^{*ua}$
    (2.02) (4.70)   (6.23)   (3.24)   (3.17)   (1.38)
                                                                                            0.92   0.87   1.80

22' $\hat{p}_c = -1.47 + .82\,\hat{M}^a_{-.5} + .37\,\hat{p}^{*a}_{i-.5} + 2.46\text{ shift }68/69 + 1.26\,\triangle^2 TP^{ua}_{-.5} + .09\,\triangle\hat{m}^{*ua}$
    (1.42) (5.60)   (3.91)   (2.46)   (2.33)   (.92)
                                                                                            1.61   .78   1.56

5' $\hat{p}_c = .30 + .25\,\hat{M}_{-1.5} + .70\,\hat{p}^*_{c-1.5} + .04\,\hat{e}_{-1.5} + 3.10\text{ shift }68/69 + 1.48\,\triangle^2 TP_{-.5}$
    (.71) (5.14)   (5.97)   (.31)   (5.46)   (5.45)
     $+ .14\,\triangle\hat{m}^* - .10\,\triangle\hat{e}$
      (3.30)   (1.61)
                                                                                    0.49   .93   2.29

11' $\hat{p}_c = .49 + .50\,\hat{M}_{-1.5} + .42\,\hat{p}^*_{i-1.5} + 3.61\text{ shift }68/69 + 1.18\,\triangle^2 TP_{-.5}$
    (1.09) (9.31)   (9.36)   (5.16)   (3.70)
     $+ .22\,\triangle\hat{m}^* + .13\,\triangle\hat{e}$
      (3.98)   (2.16)
                                                                                    0.72   .90   1.90

16" $\hat{p}_c = .25 + .32\,\hat{M}^a_{-.5} + .68\,\hat{p}^{*a}_{c-.5} + .01\,\hat{e}_{-1.5} + 2.86\text{ shift }68/69 + 1.39\,\triangle^2 TP_{-.5}$
    (.51) (3.70)   (9.44)   (6.22)   (4.88)   (5.33)
     $+ .16\,\triangle\hat{m}^{*ua} - .10\,\triangle\hat{e}$
      (2.79)   (1.93)
                                                                                   0.53   .93   1.84

22" $\hat{p}_c = -.28 + .58\,\hat{M}^a_{-.5} + .52\,\hat{p}^{*a}_{i-.5} + 3.48\text{ shift }68/69 + 1.59\,\triangle^2 TP_{-.5} + .24\,\triangle\hat{m}^{*ua}$
    (.36) (4.92)   (6.13)   (3.56)   (3.70)   (2.61)
     $+ .04\,\triangle\hat{e}$
      (.51)
                                                                                     1.47   0.82   2.26

Table D1 -- Continued

28'	$u_{27} = .28 + 1.01 \Delta\hat{e}$ $\quad\quad (.38)\quad (4.38)$	11.74	0.47	1.72
29'	$\hat{p}_i^* = .51 + .91(\hat{p}_i^* - u_{27}) + 1.03 \Delta\hat{e}$ $\quad\quad (.61)\quad (6.11)\quad\quad\quad\quad (4.37)$	12.11	.75	1.75
30'	$\hat{p}_i^* = -5.32 + 1.19 \hat{M}_{-1.5}^* + 1.03 \Delta\hat{e}$ $\quad\quad (3.54)\quad (6.11)\quad\quad\quad (4.37)$	12.11	.75	1.75
43'	$\Delta\hat{y} = -.61 + .31 \Delta\hat{M}_{-1} + .60 \Delta\hat{m}^* + .59 \Delta(\hat{p}_c^* + \hat{e}) + .42 \Delta\hat{S}_{-1}$ $\quad\quad (1.40)\quad (1.87)\quad\quad (4.53)\quad\quad (2.92)\quad\quad\quad (3.24)$	4.28	.76	2.02
49'	$\Delta\hat{y}^{ua} = -.57 + .14 \Delta\hat{M}_{-1}^{ua} + .69 \Delta\hat{m}^{*ua} + .59 (\Delta\hat{p}_c^{*ua} + \Delta\hat{e}) + .38 \Delta\hat{S}_{-1}^{ua}$ $\quad\quad (1.80)\quad (.98)\quad\quad (5.51)\quad\quad\quad (2.47)\quad\quad\quad\quad (2.78)$	2.12	0.84	2.32

Note: Generating the residuals of an ARIMA process fitted on $\Delta\hat{e}$ in order to obtain $\Delta\hat{e}^{ua}$ and $\hat{e}^a$ for use in equations 16", 22", and 49' seems unnecessary for the fixed-rate period up to 1972 when all exchange rate fluctuations may be assumed to be unanticipated, and impossible for the managed-floating period since 1972 for lack of sufficient annual observations.

73

Appendix E

Table E1

Data Series

	$\hat{p}_c$	$\hat{y}$	$\hat{p}_i^*$	$\hat{p}_c^*$	$\hat{m}^*$	FI	$-\hat{e}$	$\widehat{gdp}^*$
1952	0.0100	0.0000	-1.2376	4.0518	2.0783	1.9930	0.2101	3.4556
1953	-0.3807	9.7256	-10.5138	0.3663	3.2467	5.9905	0.1049	5.3247
1954	4.5069	10.5393	-2.6241	0.8989	9.1667	7.4392	0.1048	1.6542
1955	2.2348	6.4374	1.6267	0.6032	11.6004	8.2672	-0.5249	8.1884
1956	2.6837	6.0737	3.3918	2.4449	7.1390	3.2536	-0.5277	4.7675
1957	5.1453	4.3063	4.6311	2.7849	6.5788	3.6888	0.2114	3.6264
1958	1.5480	0.0000	-5.6253	2.5180	1.3903	1.7004	0.9459	0.2018
1959	1.2324	10.6740	-3.0975	0.2656	9.1667	0.1499	0.3133	6.5497
1960	2.4400	9.6437	-0.2904	0.6509	13.1905	2.9322	0.1042	5.3190
1961	2.3717	3.4016	-1.8673	1.2225	5.2592	2.8296	3.7817	4.9780
1962	2.5863	5.4118	-0.9344	2.4078	8.5260	3.4025	0.7992	5.4403
1963	3.6814	5.1164	1.3311	2.5785	7.8811	2.6272	0.0000	4.8190
1964	6.5788	9.5406	2.3033	2.5375	10.1654	9.1424	-0.0996	6.2843
1965	3.9028	5.3129	0.5187	2.0802	8.9841	3.8877	0.1990	5.2924
1966	5.2877	5.8590	0.7174	3.0781	6.2975	2.7628	-0.5982	5.5075
1967	2.9267	3.9746	-0.7831	2.8490	3.0529	3.6802	-0.4988	3.6987
1968	2.5278	11.0801	-2.8502	2.4293	12.8393	4.1064	-0.4988	5.2811
1969	6.0813	11.2397	3.3531	4.4026	13.9762	2.0431	-0.1001	4.6120
1970	4.4017	8.9597	6.2505	5.6758	9.8034	3.6989	0.2000	3.2409
1971	7.7516	5.8269	4.2964	6.0568	7.5107	4.5030	3.5332	4.2149
1972	8.0566	4.6091	-0.6723	8.7251	9.2579	2.1136	8.4114	5.8533
1973	8.6453	6.1154	7.1669	13.3289	10.9751	3.7409	14.3455	5.6012
1974	9.4856	2.5106	29.9882	11.2176	3.9221	3.7889	3.4720	-1.0404
1975	9.9936	-5.0858	4.0662	11.5897	-3.0459	5.7572	6.2543	-0.8859
Mean Values over the period 1954-75								
	4.7305	5.9795	2.3135	4.1067	7.8927	3.8871	1.8557	4.2366

Sources: Central Planning Bureau; The Netherlands Bank; Ministry of Finance; Central Bureau of Statistics; IMF International Financial Statistics; Michele Fratianni, EC, Brussels.

Table E1 -- Continued

	$\hat{M}$	$\hat{M}^*$	$\hat{S}$	$\hat{y}^a$	$\hat{p}_i^{*a}$	$\hat{p}_c^{*a}$	FI^a	$\hat{gdp}^{*a}$
1952	6.7045	3.5078	8.3695	0.0000	-1.2376	4.0518	1.9930	3.4556
1953	7.9253	3.2680	2.5789	4.8516	-4.0898	4.3563	3.5465	4.5617
1954	6.5981	4.7351	1.6351	9.9893	-6.2981	0.6959	4.5882	4.5302
1955	6.2938	3.8596	4.8725	7.9604	1.3437	1.5272	5.7772	3.7484
1956	2.7739	3.1789	2.0821	6.7377	-3.5762	0.9159	6.8356	4.4755
1957	-2.9464	1.6110	2.8143	6.8343	1.0931	2.8419	5.7118	4.3464
1958	4.0395	4.1065	10.1997	5.6250	3.9697	2.9970	5.1484	4.0098
1959	9.2441	2.1605	0.7594	3.6540	-2.5875	2.8496	4.0729	3.0357
1960	4.9660	3.4237	4.7522	9.3707	3.0346	0.6299	2.8262	3.5710
1961	7.5043	6.3866	2.4134	6.2846	-1.8683	1.1735	3.0276	3.7430
1962	5.5578	5.8514	2.7602	4.4958	-2.3214	1.5488	3.1205	3.8093
1963	9.2497	8.2142	6.0379	5.9694	0.4891	2.7315	3.3852	3.9540
1964	8.1977	6.7023	8.2647	4.9276	0.8643	2.8415	3.2764	3.9403
1965	10.2528	5.9165	6.8704	7.3929	1.4227	2.8772	5.5487	4.2394
1966	7.0317	4.6874	7.0491	4.1520	1.2214	2.4311	5.1158	4.2675
1967	6.7465	9.0736	9.0978	5.6796	2.4809	3.4660	4.4332	4.3347
1968	8.2346	6.8826	6.8111	3.8701	0.2968	3.1283	4.3264	4.0151
1969	9.1464	5.5709	7.8594	8.0067	-0.5889	2.8036	4.4111	4.0870
1970	9.9587	8.9923	7.5997	6.3287	3.5165	4.7828	3.7239	4.0069
1971	15.3526	12.6844	7.4770	6.0489	2.4524	5.8828	3.8780	3.6599
1972	16.2331	18.3205	6.6209	4.5911	3.8997	6.3171	4.2666	3.5853
1973	7.7911	16.1506	2.0812	4.4744	2.7139	9.0399	3.6569	3.8652
1974	2.5622	4.9095	10.5296	5.0716	8.5792	13.4756	3.8499	4.0340
1975	16.8553	11.8343	10.3775	2.8592	19.3462	11.2227	3.9922	2.7991

Mean Values over the Period 1954-75

	$\hat{M}$	$\hat{M}^*$	$\hat{S}$	$\hat{y}^a$	$\hat{p}_i^{*a}$	$\hat{p}_c^{*a}$	FI^a	$\hat{gdp}^{*a}$
	7.8020	7.0570	5.8621	5.9239	1.7947	3.9173	4.3170	3.9122

75

	$\hat{m}^{*a}$	$\hat{M}^a$	$\hat{M}^{*a}$	$\hat{S}^a$	$\triangle^2_{TP}$
1952	2.0783	6.7045	3.5078	8.3695	...
1953	5.1637	6.5733	4.1100	4.5039	- 0.20
1954	6.6527	7.2681	4.0211	4.3801	0.20
1955	9.1374	5.9758	5.3286	4.1665	0.10
1956	9.2250	6.3239	4.7189	4.3311	1.20
1957	6.2908	3.2286	4.2620	4.1723	2.40
1958	7.3733	- 0.2535	3.0705	4.1107	- 1.90
1959	2.9867	5.5611	5.2015	4.8654	- 0.90
1960	10.0965	6.4030	3.6997	4.5022	0.20
1961	8.6522	3.5113	4.8176	4.6174	0.90
1962	4.5050	7.0558	7.3344	4.4632	- 1.60
1963	8.7861	3.9827	6.9932	4.3639	1.80
1964	5.8134	8.5477	9.0243	4.6347	0.00
1965	8.9901	5.8238	7.8865	5.1194	0.20
1966	6.4425	9.2417	7.3344	5.3991	- 0.30
1967	6.1259	5.4265	6.4116	5.6668	- 0.40
1968	3.9213	7.2176	10.0856	6.1301	1.00
1969	11.3142	7.2564	8.3849	6.2924	- 2.40
1970	8.1204	8.1057	7.3923	6.5517	2.90
1971	7.6057	8.5516	10.2734	6.7540	- 0.40
1972	6.4219	12.8741	13.3905	6.9199	- 0.80
1973	8.1501	12.3851	18.1196	6.9752	- 0.40
1974	8.3081	7.1692	16.4725	6.5256	2.10
1975	3.6401	5.3633	7.3713	7.0515	- 1.30

Mean Values over the Period 1954-75

	7.2073	6.6827	7.7998	5.3634	...

References

Barro, R.J., and Fischer, S. (1976), "Recent Developments in Monetary Theory," Journal of Monetary Economics, 2: 133-67.

Blinder, A.S., and Goldfeld, S.M. (1976), "New Measures of Fiscal and Monetary Policy, 1958-73," American Economic Review, 66: 780-96.

Blinder, A.S., and Solow, R.M. (1974), "Analytical Foundations of Fiscal Policy," in The Economics of Public Finance, ed. The Brookings Institution. Washington, D.C.

Bomhoff, E.J. (1977), "Money and the Economy: Causation or Reverse Causation," working paper no. 7733, Money and Banking Workshop, Erasmus University, August 1977. Mimeographed.

Box, G.E.P., and Jenkins, G.M. (1970), Time Series Analysis. San Francisco: Holden-Day.

Brunner, K. (1976), "Inflation, Money and the Role of Fiscal Arrangements: An Analytical Framework for the Inflation Problem," in The New Inflation and Monetary Policy, ed. M. Monti. London: MacMillan.

Brunner, K., and Meltzer, A.H. (1976a), "An Aggregative Theory for a Closed Economy," in Monetarism, ed. J.L. Stein. Amsterdam: North-Holland.

_____ (1976b), "Monetary and Fiscal Policy in Open, Interdependent Economies with Fixed Exchange Rates," in Recent Issues in International Monetary Economics, eds. E. Claassen and P. Salin. Amsterdam: North-Holland.

Carlson, K.M., and Spencer, R.W. (1975), "Crowding Out and Its Critics," Review, Federal Reserve Bank of St. Louis, 57: 2-17.

Central Planning Bureau (1963), Conjunctuurpolitiek in en om de Jaren Vijftig. The Hague: Central Planning Bureau.

_____ (1971), "Conjunctuurbeleid in de Jaren Zestig," Rotterdam, May 1971. Mimeographed.

Committee on Banking, Currency and Housing (1976). Staff Report of the Subcommittee on Domestic Monetary Policy, "The Impact of the Federal Reserve System's Monetary Policies on the Nation's Economy." Washington, D.C.: U.S. Government Printing Office.

Dixon, D.A. (1972), "Techniques of Fiscal Analysis in the Netherlands," Staff Papers, 19: 615-46.

Frazer Institute (1976). The Illusion of Wage and Price Controls. Vancouver.

Gray, M., Ward, R., and Zis, G. (1976), "The World Demand for Money Function: Some Preliminary Results," in Inflation in the World Economy, eds. M. Parkin and G. Zis. Manchester: Manchester University Press.

Hansen, B. (1973), "On the Effects of Fiscal and Monetary Policy: A Taxonomic Discussion," American Economic Review, 63: 546-71.

Hildebrand, D.K., Laing, J.D., and Rosenthal, H.L. (1974), "Prediction Logic: A Method for Empirical Evaluation of Formal Theory," Journal of Mathematical Sociology, 3: 163-85.

_____(1976), "Prediction Analysis in Political Research," American Political Science Review, 2: 509-35.

Korteweg, P. (1975), "Inflation, Economic Activity and the Operation of Fiscal, Foreign and Monetary Impulses in the Netherlands: A Preliminary Analysis, 1953-1973," De Economist, 123: 559-635.

_____(1976), "The Brunner-Meltzer Model for an Open Economy: A 'Simplistic' Statement of Its Formal Properties and Underlying Assumptions," working paper no. 7513, Money and Banking Workshop, Erasmus University. Revised August 1976. Mimeographed.

_____(1977), "Stabilization Policies in the OECD Area: Their Past and Future," working paper no. 7732, Money and Banking Workshop, Erasmus University, May 1977. Mimeographed.

Korteweg, P., and Van Loo, P.D. (1977). The Market for Money and the Market for Credit: Analysis, Evidence and Implications for Dutch Monetary Policy. Leiden: Martinus Nijhoff.

Kouri, P.J.K., and Porter, M.G. (1974), "International Capital Flows and Portfolio Equilibrium," Journal of Political Economy, 82: 443-66.

McCallum, B.T. (1976), "Rational Expectations and the Natural Rate Hypothesis: Some Consistent Estimates," Econometrica, 44: 43-52.

Meltzer, A.H. (1977), "Anticipated Inflation and Unanticipated Price Change: A Test of the Price-Specie Flow Theory and the Phillips Curve," Journal of Money, Credit and Banking, 9: 182-205.

Parkin, M. (1977a), "A 'Monetarist' Analysis of the Generation and Transmission of World Inflation: 1958-71," American Economic Review, 67: 164-71.

_____(1977b), "World Inflation, International Relative Prices and Monetary Equilibrium under Fixed Exchange Rates," in The Political Economy of Monetary Reform, ed. R. Aliber. London: MacMillan.

Parkin, M., Richards, I., and Zis, G. (1976), "The Determinants and Control of the World Money Supply under Fixed Exchange Rates, 1961-71," in Inflation in Open Economies, eds. M. Parkin and G. Zis. Manchester: Manchester University Press.

Poole, W. (1976), "Rational Expectations in the Macro Model," Brookings Papers on Economic Activity, 2. Washington, D.C.: The Brookings Institution.

INFLATION AND OUTPUT GROWTH:
THE FRENCH EXPERIENCE, 1960-1975

André Fourçans[*]
École Supérieure des Sciences Économiques et Commerciales (ESSEC), Paris

I. INTRODUCTION

Much theoretical and especially empirical controversy exists as to the forces shaping the inflation phenomenon and output fluctuations. The purpose of this paper is to try to discriminate between two main theories of inflation and to test a model of French inflation and output growth. More specifically, I seek to assess to what extent four systematic stimuli can explain the inflationary experience and the rate of growth of output from the beginning of the 1960s to the end of 1975. As the French economy is considered open to foreign influences, the role of these influences on the phenomena under consideration is asserted. The respective impacts of the monetary and fiscal impulses on the behavior of the inflation rate and on the rate of growth of output are also investigated in detail.

To establish a background to the economic environment, Section II presents some basic economic facts about the French economy. The purpose of Section III is to discuss some popular views of inflation and to conduct some tests of the so-called cost-push explanation. Section IV presents the dominant impulse hypothesis of inflation, beginning with an analysis, in Section IV.A, of the institutional framework, from which evolves a discussion and a measure of the fiscal and monetary impulses. The foreign impulse, decomposed into a foreign price and a foreign quantity component, is presented in the same section. In Section IV.B, I test the dominant impulse hypothesis. Two types of tests are used: parametric and nonparametric. The first type seeks to evaluate the marginal influence of each stimulus, whereas the purpose of the second is to determine more fully if one or several impulses have a dominant influence in affecting the phenomenon under study. These two tests are also applied in Section V, where the dominant impulse hypothesis is used to analyze and explain the determinants of output growth. Finally, Section VI summarizes the main findings of the study.

[*]I wish to thank Michele Fratianni whose contribution in a previous common work (Fourçans and Fratianni, 1976) is still very much part of this paper.
This paper was written while the author was visiting at Carnegie-Mellon University.

Table 1

Basic Economic Indicators

Date	$\hat{y}$	$\hat{P}$	$\hat{CPI}$	Un
1960	6.7	3.4	3.6	0.60
1961	4.6	3.3	3.7	0.50
1962	7.9	3.7	4.2	0.50
1963	8.0	5.3	5.4	0.50
1964	4.0	3.4	2.3	0.55
1965	6.9	2.0	2.5	0.75
1966	4.7	2.8	2.8	0.75
1967	5.4	2.7	3.4	1.10
1968	8.2	6.4	5.3	1.30
1969	3.7	6.3	5.8	1.20
1970	7.2	4.6	5.5	1.55
1971	5.6	5.3	5.9	1.90
1972	5.1	5.5	6.7	2.00
1973	5.9	7.0	8.2	2.20
1974	- 2.1	14.0	14.5	3.30
1975	1.8	11.8	9.9	4.60

Sources: Tendances de la Conjoncture, INSEE; except for the CPI: Bulletin Mensuel de la Statistique, INSEE.

Note: y   =   real GDP
P   GDP price deflator
CPI   consumer price index
Un   unemployment rate, in percentage of the labor force, at year end
^   =   growth rates.

II. BASIC ECONOMIC FACTS SINCE THE BEGINNING OF THE 1960s

Until 1974 the growth of the French economy was generally substantial, even though anti-inflationary policies have, at times, been responsible for temporary slowdowns (e.g., in 1964, 1966, 1969). In spite of these policies, the trend inflation rate remained positive; at the same time, the unemployment situation deteriorated continuously. In terms of output growth, one must mention an accident such as the 1968 social disturbances that brought about a significant drop in output (from 1967-II to 1968-II, real GDP growth dropped by 2.7 percent and the index of industrial production by 8.5 percent). The output lost during this period was, however, rapidly made up during the following year (real GDP growth was 18 percent from 1968-II to 1969-II). As in the other industrialized countries, France underwent a significant depression in 1974 and 1975.

As shown in Table 1, the average rate of growth of real output was around 6 percent per annum until the 1974-75 depression (6.1 percent from 1960-I to 1973-IV, with a standard deviation of 2.6 percent). Except for these latter years, the output performance was, therefore, reasonably good. The picture is, however, not as favorable on the inflation side. Until the end of 1973, the annual rate of price increases was above 4 percent (4.5 percent for the consumer price index and 4.2 percent for the GDP deflator), with periods of accelerating and decelerating inflation. The inflation rate skyrocketed in 1974 and remained fairly high in 1975.

Roughly, four different inflationary periods can be distinguished. From 1960 to 1968, prices increased at an annual rate of about 3-4 percent, except in the 1962-63 period when the inflation rate attained 6 percent. This upsurge induced the authorities to implement a so-called stabilization plan whereby a ceiling was imposed on the rate of growth of bank credit ("encadrement du crédit," from 1963-II to 1965-II). Then, inflation decelerated and maintained a rate of about 3 percent until the beginning of 1968. From that time, the rate of price increase accelerated rapidly to attain 7-8 percent at the end of 1973, in spite of a new control imposed on the rate of growth of bank credit (from 1968-IV to 1970-II). Finally, in 1974 and 1975, in line with the rest of the world, a new boost of increasing prices characterized the French economy.

Two main periods can be distinguished in the behavior of the unemployment rate: from 1960 to the midsixties, and from the midsixties to the current period. Until about 1966, unemployment was maintained at a level always less than 1 percent even if it showed a slight tendency to increase secularly. But, it is from the middle to the end of the 1960s that the increase became more

Table 2

Monetary and Fiscal Indicators

Date	$\hat{M}$	D	G/Y (percent)	T/Y (percent)
1960	16.7	- 5.11	24.6	22.7
1961	17.2	- 4.85	24.3	22.7
1962	18.7	- 6.47	24.7	22.7
1963	14.1	-11.44	26.2	23.1
1964	9.8	- 1.29	23.4	23.1
1965	10.9	- 0.62	23.3	23.2
1966	10.6	- 3.80	23.4	22.6
1967	13.1	- 7.21	24.1	22.7
1968	11.6	-11.14	24.3	22.3
1969	6.1	5.83	23.0	23.9
1970	14.2	9.13	22.7	23.9
1971	17.6	10.37	22.2	23.5
1972	21.5	15.81	22.0	23.8
1973	14.9	22.45	21.5	23.7
1974	18.1	23.44	23.4	25.4
1975	15.9	-43.01	26.0	22.6

Sources: for $\hat{M}$, Banque de France
for D, G, and T, Statistique et Etudes Financieres, Ministere des Finances
for Y, Tendances de la Conjoncture, INSEE.

Note: $\hat{M}$ = money stock growth inclusive of bank time deposits
D   budget deficit (net government loans included) in billions of francs
G   value of government expenditures, in billions of francs
T   nominal taxes
Y = nominal GDP.

noticeable. During the five years from 1967 to 1972, the unemployment rate practically doubled, and more than doubled again in the following four years to attain almost the 5 percent mark. Two main explanations can be given for this seemingly rising trend: the arrival to maturity of the babies of the postwar boom, and the presence of a rising number of women in the labor market. Yet, the rate of growth of the total labor force has been fairly moderate, about 10 percent during the 1965-75 decade. It seems, therefore, that changes in the composition of the labor force are mainly responsible for the increasing "structural" unemployment. Finally, the rapid upsurge of unemployment in 1974 and 1975 is, at least in part, a direct consequence of the oil crisis.

The monetary and budgetary pictures are presented in Table 2. The average yearly rate of growth of the money stock is equal to 14.5 percent over the whole period. This substantial average growth is associated with large fluctuations in the monetary aggregate which oscillated from as low a value as 5 percent from the first quarter of 1969 to the first quarter of 1970, to a rate close to 23 percent from the second quarter of 1971 to the second quarter of 1972. More will be said about the forces behind this variable.

On the budgetary side, it is interesting to note that the traditional deficits that occurred until 1968 were succeeded by significant surpluses, except for the last year, 1975, when the authorities tried to stimulate the economy by increasing government expenditures and decreasing taxes, both by a significant amount. The proportion of government expenditures of total income has been fairly stable over the years, with a value around 24 percent. The same can be said about taxes which remained close to 22 percent of total income.[1] More about budgetary and fiscal arrangements follows.

It is worth mentioning that from 1960 to 1975 velocity went down at an average yearly rate of about 2.5 percent. Yet, it is interesting to note that, during the periods of relatively low monetary growth, velocity decreased much less than this average (less than 1 percent in 1963) and even increased significantly (+3 percent in 1968 and 3.9 percent in 1969). With such a long-run trend and with an average real output growth of about 6 percent a year, the money stock should have increased at an average yearly rate of about 8-9 percent in order for the long-run inflation rate to be close to zero.

Finally, Table 3 presents some data concerning the balance of payments and the exchange rate. Except for the beginning of the 1960s, the balance of trade has always been in deficit, with a very acute deficit occurring in 1974

---

[1]It must be added that these taxes do not include social security contributions, which are another form of taxation; on the average, these represent about 14-15 percent of national income. When added to the above-mentioned 22 percent, the total rate of taxation is the second highest in the Western world (after Sweden).

Table 3

The Foreign Sector

Date	Tr	Exp	Imp	Exp/Y (percent)	U	Ex
1960	2.89	33.88	30.99	12.4	10.48	4.9003
1961	2.69	35.65	32.96	11.9	15.07	4.9000
1962	- 0.79	36.33	37.12	11.1	20.06	4.9000
1963	- 3.24	39.90	43.14	10.8	24.22	4.9019
1964	- 5.30	44.39	49.69	10.8	28.02	4.9000
1965	- 1.43	49.61	51.04	11.3	31.35	4.9019
1966	- 4.83	53.79	58.62	11.2	33.18	4.9519
1967	- 4.93	56.18	61.11	10.9	34.36	4.9079
1968	- 6.17	62.58	68.75	11.1	18.64	4.9480
1969	-12.12	77.01	89.13	11.7	9.29	5.5580
1970	- 2.97	100.43	103.40	13.8	23.00	5.5199
1971	- 3.94	113.01	116.95	14.2	40.78	5.2241
1972	- 5.37	129.37	134.74	14.5	47.29	5.1250
1973	- 7.38	158.07	165.45	15.6	39.86	4.7080
1974	-32.98	217.18	250.16	18.8	37.46	4.5473
1975	- 9.90	220.75	230.65	17.4	49.65	4.4588

Sources: for Exp, Imp, Tr, Bulletin Mensuel de la Statistique, INSEE
for U, Banque de France
for Ex, Main Economic Indicators, OECD.

Note: Exp = nominal exports, in billions of francs
Imp   nominal imports, in billions of francs
Tr   Exp-Imp = trade balance
U   foreign reserves, in billions of francs
Ex = exchange rate, expressed in francs per dollar.

following the quadrupling of oil prices. It has always been a policy of the authorities to stimulate exports, and they have been reasonably successful, the percentage of national income exported exhibiting a significant upward trend. Foreign reserves grew until 1968, when the social disturbances triggered important net outflows of capital that resulted in a devaluation of the franc in August 1969. Then, the stock of reserve was brought rapidly enough (in about two years) to a "comfortable" level and remained relatively stable until the end of the period.

Under the Bretton Woods agreements, the exchange rate remained fairly constant until the 1969 devaluation of the franc. Then, it appreciated after the successive devaluations (1971 and 1973) of the dollar. Finally, in January 1974, the franc started floating against the other monies.

III. THE INFLATION PHENOMENON
AND THE COST-PUSH EXPLANATION

A. The Inflation Debate

The latest upsurge of world inflation has produced an amazing proliferation of "theories": structural, monopolist, social, ecological, anchovy, etc., explanations have been added to the more traditional cost-push versus excess-demand hypotheses. Not all of them can be presented and analyzed in an elaborate way, yet a few comments on their content are in order. Two common characteristics unite almost all of them: a generally very loose formulation, and a quasi-inability to generate empirically falsifiable statements. Unfortunately, the French literature on the subject reflects sharp preferences for this state of affairs. The search for a systematic body of testable hypotheses has produced only meager results. The following brief discussion is, thus, uncustomarily based on outputs of the popular press rather than on treatments in professional economic journals or books.[2]

A theme which recurs often in discussions is that inflation is caused by the struggle among various economic groups for a share of the national product. The intelligentsia sees in such a struggle the most visible symptoms of the contradictions inherent in a capitalist system which cannot equitably resolve claims on resources by different social groups. Although no comment will be made, in the context of this paper, on the relevance of such contradictions, it suffices to note that if such contradictions are assumed to exist they must have suddenly arisen in the 1973-74 period and as suddenly vanished in 1975 and 1976. Those who seriously entertain this hypothesis would also have to explain

---

[2]For more exhaustive surveys of inflation theories, see Bronfenbrenner and Holzman (1963), Brunner, et al. (1973), Fratianni (1974), Johnson (1967), and Laidler and Parkin (1975).

why the above-mentioned contradictions are stronger now than ever, in spite of a secularly rising government intervention in the private sector and welfare legislation. Finally, as an implication of the hypothesis, one should expect to find a positive association between accelerations of inflation and rising contradictions, and vice versa. One is at a loss to find a set of semantic rules which allows one to translate the theoretical concept of contradictions into an observable magnitude.

In the economic literature, instead, the hypothesis that competing claims on national income may be a cause of inflation can be subsumed as a particular version of Keynesian "inflationary gap" theory. The inflationary process stops when everyone adapts to his income arrangement, or when desired investment of all groups is equal to desired saving. Inflation, in other words, results from an adjustment process toward an equilibrium income distribution. A stylized version of the income-share model usually considers two groups of resource claimants: workers and capital owners. Capital owners receive profits immediately after a price increase, while wages adjust to price changes with some delay. The gap may reflect differences in information of the two groups about market processes. The occurrence of an inflationary gap raises real profit income relative to real wage income. The elimination of the inflationary gap redistributes real income against labor, provided the marginal propensity to spend of capital owners is smaller than that of the workers.

The theoretical shortcomings of this theory are that it is silent on the key question of how an inflationary gap is formed to begin with, and that it presumes that one group in society is willing to accept a lower real income to see inflation come to an end. But, more importantly, the theory does not square with the facts. In 1960, wage income in France represented 43 percent of GDP; in 1968, this proportion rose to 47 percent; and, in 1973, it had moved to 57 percent. Inflation has squeezed profit income relative to wage income.

In a recent book, Fitoussi (1973) argues that inflation can persist even in the absence of excess demand and inflationary expectations. Namely, for a given level of aggregate demand, changes in its composition cause the general price level to rise because of asymmetric price adjustments in the various sectors of the economy. The asymmetry is based on the notion that the sectors that face excess supplies of output adjust by quantity changes, whereas sectors facing excess demand adjust through price changes. It follows that as long as aggregate demand is subject to compositional shifts the general price level is doomed to rise secularly. A problem with this analysis is that each industry must have two long-run supply schedules of output: one upsloping when the demand shifts to the right, and one horizontal when the demand curve shifts to the left. In other words, the supply curve of output is not independent of the direction of shift of the demand curve. Although little knowledge is claimed here concerning quantity versus price adjustments in French industry-- nor does Fitoussi provide any--one cannot help but be puzzled by the implications of the hypothesis which suggest a) that aggregate demand shifts have become more pronounced in the 1970s than in the 1960s, and b) that they have a cyclical pattern which closely conforms to the inflation cycle. These implications appear to be disconfirmed even by the most casual observations.

A large group of social scientists attributes inflation to the power of monopolists to raise prices. The weaknesses of such an argument are well known. Briefly, it overlooks that demand is a constraint on the ability of firms to raise prices arbitrarily: profit-maximizing behavior requires that price changes can occur only if cost curves shift, shifts which must then be explained; and that the inflation of the recent past must have been accompanied by rapidly accelerating and decelerating degrees of monopolization of French industry.

All the above-mentioned (and other) explanations of inflation have in common the additional difficulty of not being directly advanced as refutable hypotheses. This feature was a further reason for discarding them from the list of potential explanations of the French inflation data set. In Sections III.B and IV, therefore, only two main classes of explanation will be tested: the so-called cost-push theory, and a competing view that builds upon an excess-demand expectations-augmented hypothesis.

B. Cost-push Explanation

One of the dominant views of inflation in the French economy is that wage increases in excess of productivity improvements result in higher prices. This argument is too well known in the literature to be examined here at any length. The important point to remember is that increases in unit labor costs are generally considered exogenous by cost-push theorists, i.e., either determined by union strength or militancy, or by some sociological rationale. Increases in unit labor costs, in turn, are automatically passed on to the consumers in the form of higher prices.

There are many variants to the basic cost-push theme (cf. Laidler and Parkin, 1975, for an exhaustive list of these variants). Some of them involve combining aggressive union behavior and highly oligopolistic product markets. The wage push that occurs in these sectors subsequently spreads quickly to other sectors via some unspecified mechanism of social awareness about "unfair" wage differentials. This view of inflation fails to take into consideration the

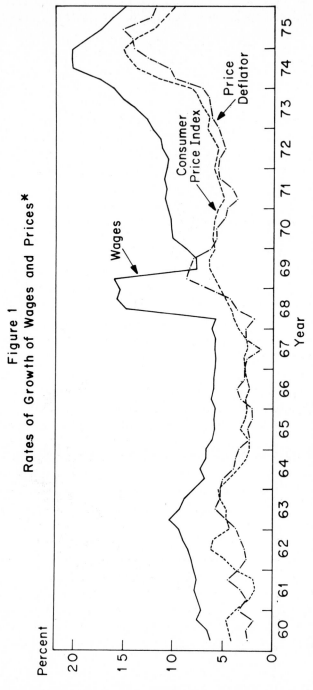

Figure 1
Rates of Growth of Wages and Prices*

*Rates of growth are calculated from quarter to quarter of corresponding years

90

excess-demand conditions that are necessary to assure persistent increases in prices (see Harry Johnson, 1967). If aggregate demand is not increased to sustain the price rise, a wage rate growth in excess of productivity improvements would create unemployment but not rising prices. The importance of this process has been well perceived by some sophisticated cost-push theorists who have argued that the behavior of the authorities is not independent of market processes but needs to be integrated into the labor market as an automatic mechanism to perpetuate inflation. More precisely, the government's commitment to maintain high employment would have created a quasi-automatic link between wages and prices. Therefore, labor unions, by correctly anticipating the response of economic policymakers, can set a wage rate which can uniquely determine the inflation rate. Inflation would then be in the hands of union leaders in a causal sense, although accommodating expansionary policy (especially through a lenient monetary policy) would be a necessary condition for inflation to persist.

This explanation is certainly worthy of attention. Yet, without a reasonably sophisticated theoretical and empirical analysis, one can hardly form a scientific opinion about its validity. One way to treat this problem would be to develop a structural model whose essential elements are wages, prices, and excess-demand or money equations. A simulation of the model should then provide useful information as to the effects of wage rises in excess of productivity with and without an accommodating behavior by the authorities. Such an endeavor will not be pursued here. Some preliminary and tentative evidence on the subject will, however, be presented. At any rate, even if the theory were "true," one very important implication for economic policy remains: inflation would not be brought under control without a concomitant control of excess demand, especially through monetary means.

Before presenting a simple formulation of the cost-push theory, a brief examination of the sample data is in order. Figure 1 shows the high comovements between wage rate increases and the inflation rate. However, such comovements are by themselves completely devoid of any information as to whether wage increases cause price increases.

The 1968 wage explosion requires some explanation. During that year, deep social unrest and a national strike ended with an agreement among labor unions, government, and firms to sharply increase wages. Such a wage increase can, of course, only be categorized as a truly exogenous shock; with cost-push proponents, it cannot be denied that the 1968 wage data had a strong impact on the price level. But, it is denied here that these wage increases had a lasting effect on the inflation rate; they merely raised the general price level, or, in a slightly different manner, one can say that they produced a transitory rate of inflation, as do oil embargoes, droughts, earthquakes, and various other accidents of nature. Once-and-for-all rather than persistent increases in the price level are produced.

From the first quarter of 1960 to the last quarter of 1975, the average yearly rate of growth of wages was 10.20 percent, whereas prices increased at an average rate of 5.30 percent. As productivity grew at an average rate of 4.50 percent per year, it is clear that over the sample period wage increases in excess of productivity growth (5.7 percent) were not significantly different from the inflation rate. This observation corroborates the hypothesis that, in the long run, real wages grow at the same rate as does productivity. But, again, this fact does not imply anything as to the direction of causation nor does it necessarily apply in the short run.

With a somewhat better knowledge of the sample data under review, the following simple but representative version of cost-push theory in an open economy can be tested:

$$\hat{P} = \beta \, (\hat{W} - \hat{Pr})_{-i} + \gamma \, \hat{PM}_{-j} + \epsilon_t \, ,$$

where P = price level
      W = wage rate
      Pr = productivity
      PM = import price level, expressed in domestic currency
      $\hat{}$ = growth rates
      i,j = "optimal" lags.

This formulation states that not only do wage increases in excess of productivity improvements generate inflation, but also increases in import prices over which a relatively small open economy like France has no control. Even if import price increases are generally considered inflationary, it must be noticed that, theoretically, they generate a variety of impulses. Besides a) affecting the aggregate supply of output, increases in PM b) provoke a substitution effect in the aggregate demand for domestic output; c) reduce the real value of financial assets, in turn inducing asset holders to lower consumption relative to saving; d) have an expansionary impact on the money stock by reducing the trade deficit or increasing the trade surplus; and e) can be understood by economic operators as signaling future price increases on the strength of the notion that inflationary expectations are based on the past behavior of both domestic and foreign inflation. With the exception of c), all other effects contribute to a higher domestic inflation rate. More important, the cost-push, item a), is only one among the various channels through which $\hat{PM}$ affects $\hat{P}$.

Notwithstanding the above arguments, I purposely strengthen the case for a cost-push view of inflation by assuming that changes in PM affect exclusively the aggregate supply of output. The tests of the proposed equation, in a closed and an open economy over two different sample periods, are presented in Table 4.[3]

Let us first examine the results over the period 1961-I to 1973-IV. Regression 1a shows that the differential between wages and productivity growth is a significant variable. Yet, the regression has no explanatory power. The introduction of the constant term in regression 1b significantly improves the fit of the equation but reduces the significance of $(\hat{W} - \hat{Pr})_{-2}$. Furthermore, the intercept explains about 75 percent of the mean value of the inflation rate. In the open economy version of the theory (regressions 2a and 2b), the rate of growth of import prices is a significant explanatory variable of $\hat{P}$. However, regression 2a, like regression 1a, explains none of the variance of $\hat{P}$. Again, the incorporation of the constant term improves the R^2 and the standard error of the estimate significantly while still explaining about 70 percent of the mean value of $\hat{P}$. Hence, over this period, the theory explains some deviations of the inflation rate from its trend value but is very inadequate to explain the total phenomenon (i.e., trend and deviation from trend).

The fits are significantly improved when the years 1974 and 1975 are added to the sample period. Yet, the R^2's are still somewhat low when the constant term is omitted. Furthermore, the latter still explains about 50 percent of the mean value of the inflation rate over the sample period when it is introduced in the regressions. Therefore, in spite of the high enough R^2 of regressions 1'b and 2'b, the theory can only explain, at the maximum, about 50 percent of the inflation rate. The fact remains that the influence of the two explanatory variables has become more important over the latter years of the period. This outcome is not surprising. First, the oil price shock definitely had a strong impact on import prices and, from there, on the rate of inflation. But, this impact is transitory and represents a once-and-for-all increase in prices. Second, in view of the acceleration of the inflation rate, the role of anticipations has probably become more important in wage negotiations. Thus, it is likely that

---

[3]Different lagged values of the independent variables were tried. Those presented gave the best fits. Tests have also been conducted by suppressing the 1968 and 1969 observations. As the results were not significantly affected, only tests over the whole sample period are presented.

Table 4

Cost-push Explanation of Inflation
(Quarterly data)

Inflation rate $(\hat{P})$	Intercept	$(\hat{W}-\hat{P}r)_{-2}$	$\hat{P}M$	R^2	S.E.	DW	Sample Period
Closed economy							
1 a (t-stat.)	: :	0.69 (10.57)	: :	*	2.66 : :	1.44 : :	1961-I-1973-IV
1 b	3.29 (10.60)	0.26 (4.63)	: :	0.30 : :	1.49 : :	0.85 : :	
1'a	: :	0.75 (17.63)	: :	.40 : :	2.57 : :	1.61 : :	1961-I-1975-IV
1'b	2.54 (7.04)	0.51 (11.02)	: :	.67 : :	1.90 : :	1.47 : :	
Open economy							
2 a (t-stat.)	: :	0.61 (9.55)	0.22 (3.45)	*	2.41 : :	1.37 : :	1961-I-1973-IV
2 b	3.06 (10.85)	0.24 (4.79)	0.14 (3.81)	.46 : :	1.32 : :	1.04 : :	
2'a	: :	0.68 (14.61)	0.07 (2.88)	.48 : :	2.42 : :	1.53 : :	1961-I-1975-IV
2'b	2.52 (7.81)	0.45 (10.05)	0.07 (3.97)	0.75 : :	1.70 : :	1.50 : :	

Table 4 -- Continued

Sources: for $\hat{P}$, Table 1
           for $(\hat{W}-\hat{P}_r)$, INSEE
           for $\hat{PM}$, International Financial Statistics, IMF.

Note: $\hat{P}$ =   rate of growth of GDP deflator
           $(\hat{W}-\hat{P}_r)$ =   wage growth in excess of productivity growth
           $\hat{PM}$ =   growth rate of import prices in domestic currency

           (The above rates of growth are calculated from quarter to quarter of corresponding years.)

           S.E.   =   standard error of the estimate
           DW   =   Durbin-Watson statistic

           * Negative values; throughout the paper, $R^2 = 1 - \dfrac{USS}{TSS - n\bar{y}^2}$ (USS = unexplained sum of squares, TSS = total sum of squares, n = number of observations, $\bar{y}$ = mean of the dependent variable) which can be negative; this definition of R^2 must be used as a measure of fit when the intercept is suppressed.

95

the adjustment of wages to price level changes has been more rapid than before 1974. One cannot also discard the idea that these anticipations have led to increases in wages which, supposedly to catch up with inflation, have, in fact, overshot the effective inflation rate and thus contributed to a transitory acceleration of the rate of growth of prices, i.e., to some "cost-push" influence.

A word of caution is in order here. None would deny that firms have a tendency to raise their prices when their unit costs, particularly their unit wage bill, increase. It is, therefore, not surprising to find a positive association between these unit costs and prices. Furthermore, to say that anticipations may, over the short run, "push" wages and, therefore, prices does not mean that the price increase could persist whatever happens to demand. If demand did not follow, prices could not keep on increasing for long; instead, unemployment would increase, anticipations of inflation would diminish, and the wage push would disappear. Hence, it is difficult to see how a "cost-push" factor may explain inflation over a long enough period of time without any reference to demand conditions. Therefore, nobody would deny, at least I would not, that increases in wages in excess of productivity growth, as well as import prices, have a role to play in the transmission of inflation over a given period and given that demand conditions validate the process. But, I would reject the cost-push view that inflation occurs because unit costs increase exogenously, i.e., independently of any market process or aggregate demand conditions. The interesting question to ask is whether wages would for long keep on increasing more quickly than productivity if demand did not follow. As noted above, this question would best be answered through a structural model whose main elements are wages, prices, and aggregate demand (or, if one wants to be more specific as to the determinants of demand, money) equations. Without going so far, I give some preliminary evidence concerning the validity of the thesis that excess demand is necessary for inflation to persist, i.e., to "validate" increases in unit cost. For that, a measure of excess demand E is introduced into the "cost-push" regressions 2a and 2'a:

Period 1961-I to 1973-IV

$$\hat{P} = 0.22 \; (\hat{W} - \hat{Pr})_{-2} \; + \; 0.06 \; \hat{PM} + 0.11 \, E$$
$$\quad\;\; (4.26) \qquad\qquad\;\; (1.43) \qquad (10.80)$$
$$R^2 = .46, \qquad S.E. = 1.33, \qquad DW = .88$$

Period 1961-I to 1975-IV

$$\hat{P} = 0.49\,(\hat{W} - \hat{Pr})_{-2} + 0.05\,\hat{PM} + 0.08\,E,$$
$$(10.96) \qquad\qquad (2.55) \qquad (6.97)$$

$$R^2 = .72, \qquad S.E. = 1.80, \qquad DW = 1.53$$

where E = one-year moving average of a quarterly capacity utilization measure.[4]

As these regressions show, the variable E is extremely significant, as are the R^2's, as the standard errors improve very significantly compared to regressions 2a and 2'a. Furthermore, the coefficients and significance of $(\hat{W} - \hat{Pr})_{-2}$ and $\hat{PM}$ decrease noticeably when E is introduced. These results strongly imply that excess demand is a variable that cannot be omitted in order to explain $\hat{P}$ in a satisfactory way. Even if it is not "foolproof," this outcome also suggests that cost-push factors need an accommodating excess demand in order for inflation to persist. Further tests of this cost-push hypothesis are conducted in Section IV.A.

At any rate, it is by comparison that an hypothesis must be judged. The next section shows more clearly how this hypothesis stands up compared to the model proposed below.

IV. THE DOMINANT IMPULSE HYPOTHESIS OF INFLATION

In the modern literature of price-setting behavior, one firm's demand function depends on its own price relative to the market average price. A negative difference between these two prices tends to increase the market share of the firm; a positive difference to lower it. Equilibrium is attained when the firm's own price equals the market price; in this situation, the market price of the firm does not change. When uncertainty is introduced, the relevant market price is replaced by the expected average price. Then, aggregation over all firms generates the testable hypothesis that the rate of price change will be an upsloping function of market excess demand as well as of the expected rate of change of the general price level. In particular, the hypothesis implies that the elasticity of the actual price level with respect to the expected price level is unitary; hence, output would grow at a rate determined by, among other things, the natural rate of unemployment (see Laidler and Parkin, 1975). This approach constitutes the microtheoretical underpinning of the expectations-augmented excess-demand hypothesis of inflation which can be represented by the equation:

---

[4]Source: Tendances de la Conjoncture, INSEE.

$$\hat{P} = e(E) + \pi \, ,$$

where E = excess demand

π = expected rate of inflation.

This presentation of the hypothesis explains inflation by its proximate determinants, i.e., by expectations and excess demand. I want to go further and examine the determinants which could explain excess demand and, ultimately, inflation.

For that, it is postulated that inflation has systematic causes rather than that it is the consequence of an infinite number of unspecified and random shocks to the macroeconomic system. These systematic causes can be essentially comprised in a) two types of real impulses: a fiscal impulse and a foreign impulse, the latter being dichotomized into a price and a quantity component; and b) a financial impulse, which will be represented by the rate of growth of the money stock. It must be noted that this latter stimulus is not totally independent of real impulses. As an example, note that an increase in the fiscal impulse, in the form of a rise in government expenditures or of a decrease in taxes, necessarily requires that base money, or government bonds, or a combination of the two, be issued to cover the deficit. If the gap between government expenditures and taxes is financed by base money creation, its impact will be reflected eventually in an increase in the money stock. If the deficit is, instead, financed entirely by government bonds, there will be a rise in the interest rate, followed by adjustments in the money market that will partly affect the money stock. It can also be mentioned that an increase in exports, which, by raising the rest-of-the-world's absorption of French output, triggers a real impulse, generates change in the financial impulse to the extent that higher exports imply a balance of payments surplus or a smaller deficit; this, in turn, raises the foreign component of the monetary base and, therefore, exerts an impact on the money stock.

It must be noted that a dominant impact of the monetary impulse on inflation relative to all other impulses would imply strict monetary conclusions.

A. Measurement of the Systematic Impulses
1. The fiscal impulse
    a) Budgetary and fiscal authorities: some institutional background

The government sector in France is very centralized. Local governments enjoy little autonomy in their economic decisions, with virtually no taxation power and, thus, total dependence on transfers from the central government (Hansen, 1969). Through the operations of the Treasury, the central authorities exert great influence on the determination and implementation of fiscal policy. Furthermore, the existence of a large nationalized sector increases such an influence in a variety of ways, from a setting of prices and tariffs to a control of sources of financing.

Traditionally, the intervention of government in economic affairs has always been fairly important. It is only since the early 1960s that the authorities have tried to attenuate the numerous constraints imposed by, and the multiple interventions of, the Treasury in the functioning of the different markets. For example, many financial advantages granted to the Treasury (preferential tax treatment for treasury bills, "floor" imposed upon banks' holdings of treasury bills, interest rate ceilings on bank deposits always lower than interest rates on government-owned savings institutions, some preferential loans granted to some industries, etc.) were partly or totally abolished in 1966 and 1967.

In spite of this "desengagement," the role played by the central government in the private sector of the economy remains large. Public expenditures are set by the prime minister and the minister of finance through their control of budget processes and expenditures outlays. Parliament has historically approved budgets which did not differ from those proposed by the executive branch of the government. The budget strictly applies over the calendar year, except for investment projects whose expenditure flows span explicitly determined numbers of years.

Each budget is supposed to be "in line" with the plan established by the planning commission ("Commissariat au Plan"). However, de facto, the budget often seems to be determined more by short-term considerations than by the long-run objectives of the plan. Public expenditures include not only expenditures on goods and services, salaries, transfer payments, and subsidies ("dépenses permanentes") but also corporate loans made by the authorities to public enterprises, local governments, and private enterprises ("dépenses temporaires"). Since the beginning of the 1960s, these government loans have been purposely reduced in accordance with the above-mentioned program of "desengagement."

b) The tax system

The French tax system is highly regressive, with the bulk of tax revenues (about 60 percent) coming from indirect taxation. The pressure of the tax system on the private sector, when social security contributions are included, is one of the highest among Western countries, just after Sweden. Direct taxes consist essentially in personal income taxes (which account for one-third of total tax revenues) and corporate income taxes (whose rate is set to 50 percent of profits), whereas the bulk of indirect tax revenues comes from the value-added tax. It must be remarked that government revenues also include income from some public enterprises as well as from other different sources.

The value-added tax which, through 1967, applied only to wholesale transactions was extended in January 1968 to the whole of the industrial and retailing sectors. Value-added tax rates have changed over the years, but four rates have always existed: a normal, a low, an intermediary, and a high rate depending on the types of goods or services to which the tax is applied. While imported goods are subject to the tax, export goods are not.

c) The measurement of the fiscal impulse

Western economies have long absorbed the basic lessons of Keynesian economics by institutionalizing in the budget an instrument to pursue economic stabilization policies. However, in the French context, the stabilizing role of fiscal policy has been officially downplayed in favor of the monetary instrument.

It is hardly surprising, therefore, that, as far as is known, both in the French literature and inside the administration, very little analysis has been done of the influence of fiscal policy on prices and output. Apparently, the budget deficit or surplus is the only measure used to evaluate the impact of expenditures and taxes on the behavior of economic agents. The measure may or may not take into consideration net loans made by the government to private and public enterprises as well as to local governments. Such a measurement is, of course, not very reliable insofar as it does not differentiate discretionary from automatic changes in budget expenditures and revenues. Particularly, it does not take into consideration the large dependence of taxes on income and prices. Because of the doubtful adequacy of the realized budgetary deficit (surplus), I have tried to construct a measure that would be relatively purged of the endogenous elements. Among these endogenous elements are items such as subsidies to agriculture and most transfer payments. Wages and salaries paid to government employees also respond partly to economic activity, to the extent that wage rates in the public sector adjust to those in the private sector.

Expenditures which have no impact on domestic markets should also be removed from the fiscal impulse. Foreign grants and government imports belong to this category. These variables are, however, of limited importance relative to the bulk of expenditures. They can, therefore, be neglected without any significant loss of content.

Finally, the impulse measure should also take into consideration the fact that different expenditures (and taxes), by acting on different markets, do not have the same effect on economic activity. Weights should, therefore, be assigned to each type of expenditure so as to represent the impact of each more adequately. Such an approach, however, requires the development of a specific model, or, in other words, the nature of the weights is only relevant to a given hypothesis (see, for example, Hansen, 1969). Unfortunately, only yearly data of the different types of government expenditures are available. Quarterly data could only be obtained for total government expenditures and net government loans. Since I wanted to build a quarterly impulse, I could not eliminate possible endogenous components and had to use total government expenditures of the central government as part of the measure of the fiscal stimulus.

Social security contributions are not included in the fiscal impulse because the system is, on the whole, a self-financing entity. When it spends more than it receives, the deficit is covered by the central government. The deficit is then included in the measure of government expenditures.

The data used are on a cash basis. A possible bias is thus introduced insofar as the effect on economic activity and prices is triggered by the placement of orders and not by the disbursement of funds. The total lag of fiscal policy should, therefore, be measured in terms of the time period elapsing from the placement of orders to the cumulative effect of placement on prices and output. There is no a priori knowledge of the magnitude of such a lag nor of the lag existing between order placements and disbursements. This issue remains, therefore, open to empirical testing.

Similarly, changes in total tax revenues can be separated into two components: a discretionary and an automatic component. The discretionary component is defined as the change in tax revenues attributable to changes in tax rates, or in tax bases; the automatic component is, by contrast, defined as the difference of total changes in tax revenues and the discretionary component.

Without any change in the tax structure, one can assume that government revenues would increase, approximately, by the same percentage as national income.[5] Hence, depending on the type of tax under consideration, it becomes possible to estimate what part of the tax changes results from changes in economic activity. The following discussion should clarify this point.[6]

The income of the preceding year constitutes the basis on which personal income taxes and corporate taxes are calculated. On a yearly basis, the automatic component of direct taxes in year t, AT_d^t, can be approximated by

[5]Of course, this statement is an oversimplification since it implicitly considers a linear tax function and does not incorporate the fact that, when the tax system is progressive, some economic agents would move from one marginal tax rate to another.

[6]The procedure is inspired by Korteweg (1975).

$$AT^t_d = T^{t-1}_d \, (1+\hat{Y}_{t-1}) \, ,$$

where $\hat{Y}_t = \dfrac{Y_t - Y_{t-1}}{Y_{t-1}}$ = annual rate of growth of nominal income

T^t_d = actual direct taxes in year t.

The discretionary component DT^t_d is expressed as

$$DT^t_d = T^t_d - AT^t_d \, .$$

This yearly component is then allocated to each quarter according to the ratio of quarterly to yearly total direct tax revenues.

Indirect tax revenues include not only the value-added tax but also all other indirect taxes and a variety of government income. One common characteristic of all these taxes is that they are ultimately determined by <u>current</u> economic activity. These taxes are generally paid quarterly, except for important firms which pay them monthly. It is thus safe to assume that the <u>quarterly</u> automatic component of indirect taxes AT^t_i is equal to

$$AT^t_i = T^{t-1}_i \, (1+\hat{Y}_t) \, ,$$

where T^t_i = total indirect taxes in quarter t.

The quarterly discretionary component is then given by

$$DT^t_i = T^t_i - AT^t_i \, .$$

Using the above-mentioned relations, the discretionary fiscal impulse is defined as

$$FI^t = \Delta \left[G^t - (DT_d^t + DT_i^t) \right] / Y_{t-1},$$

where G = total government expenditures (net government loans included)

Δ = changes from quarter to quarter of corresponding years.

2. The monetary impulse

a) Some institutional background

Money supply processes result from the interactions of the banking system and the public in response to the behavior of the authorities. The authorities consist of the Banque de France, the Treasury, and the "Caisse des Dépôts et Consignations" (CDC) which creates monetary base whenever it grants credit to the banking system. The authorities control monetary processes with essentially three instruments: rediscount and money market rates, reserve requirements, and ceilings on the volume of bank credit.

Before 1967, banks were not subject to any reserve requirements, except for a liquidity ratio ("coefficient de trésorerie") that forced them to hold a certain proportion of their liabilities in the form of liquid assets (base money, treasury bills, and commercial papers rediscountable outside the discount ceilings). Reserve requirements were introduced in January 1967, at the same time as the liquidity ratio was abolished and replaced by a "coefficient of retention," whereby banks have to hold a given proportion of their deposits of less than three-year maturity in the form of medium-term credit. Reserve requirements vary with the type of deposits. Domestic demand deposits are subject to a higher rate than domestic time deposits. The rate on foreign deposits (denominated in foreign currency or in francs by nonresidents) has been changed over the years according to balance of payments objectives. It must be added that reserve requirements have a peculiar characteristic; they are calculated as an average over a monthly period and have to be satisfied only at the end of each period. This feature was established in order to allow more flexibility to the banking system in the management of its liquid assets. However, it also diminishes the central bank's control of this liquidity and introduces uncertainty into the short-term forecasting of bank reserves.

To be complete, one must say that, at times, banks have to hold required reserves on the outstanding amount of loans.

103

Several times, the central bank has exercised direct control over the rate of bank credit expansion ("encadrement du crédit"). This measure, however, does not seem to have had a drastic influence on the volume of credit outstanding insofar as banks seem to be able to find loopholes to avoid the control.

Banks borrow heavily from the authorities. This operation encompasses the discount window and the so-called "open market operations" of the central bank and of the CDC. It may be surprising to include open market operations as part of the system's borrowing. An explanation of the institutional arrangement should clarify the issue. The difference between the rediscount desk and the open market concerns only some minor legal and administrative details. In both cases, "borrowing" operations consist in banks selling commercial papers. The authorities set the price at which they buy papers from banks (the "cost of refinancing"). When this price is set, the supply of funds is perfectly elastic, and the quantity "borrowed" is market determined. Contrary to the system in the U.S., the open market does not involve any effective quantitative control.

Another institutional characteristic of importance resides in the fact that entrance in the French money market is restricted. The market is open only to the central bank, the Treasury and its affiliates, the banking system, and since the reforms of 1967, to a few financial organizations (insurance companies, mutual funds, etc.). It is essentially the market where banks meet in order to equilibrate their daily holdings of base money.

Banks hold a very small portfolio of treasury bills (today equal to less than 2 percent of their domestic loan portfolio) which are exchanged in the interbank market. These securities cannot be traded with the public which holds another type of treasury bills. Furthermore, there is no secondary market for these bills. This institutional feature affects monetary processes dramatically insofar as the banking system cannot replenish its reserves by selling government securities to firms and households. One of the most striking consequences has been the permanent "indebtedness" of French banks to the authorities.

b) The monetary impulse measure

Several indicators could be used to measure the monetary thrust applied to the economy. Yet, many of these measures are indicators of monetary policy, whereas the object is to evaluate the impact of the monetary impulse irrespective of its origins. For this reason, the growth rate of the money stock is used as the measure of the monetary impulse. This choice does not imply, however, that money is automatically a policy variable; nor is the endogeneity or exogeneity quality of the money stock relevant to a monetary explanation of inflation.

What is relevant is the size of the impact of the total monetary impulse on prices, regardless of whether money is completely endogenous, partly endogenous, or totally exogenous. The exogeneity argument becomes important, instead, in a strategy which envisions bringing inflation under control, to the extent that money growth rates could be shown to be a major determinant of a sustained increase in the general price level. An analytical framework of how money is created and of the influence of the behavior of the monetary authorities in such creation becomes crucial in any study which, in addition to analyzing the causes of inflation, aims at proposing a cure for it.[7] The measure of the money stock is M2, i.e., currency plus postal deposits plus total bank deposits. The broad definition is used for two reasons. First, M2 is the "official" definition of money in France; second, as a result of the 1967 changes in bank regulations, it would not have been possible to calculate a narrow definition of money which would have remained homogeneous over time. In fact, in 1967, some regulations on interest rates on time deposits were relaxed with the consequence that an important shift from demand to time deposits occurred; from mid-1967 to mid-1968, the rate of growth of M2 increased, whereas that of M1 decreased. Outside this period, the two rates of growth are fairly collinear even if their magnitudes are somewhat different. M2 is also highly collinear with a broader definition of money which includes deposits in savings institutions.

c) The forces behind the monetary impulse

The equilibrium money stock is equal to

$$M = mB,$$

where B = the monetary base

m = the money multiplier.

This formulation does not rest on any assumption as to the exogeneity of the base. In fact, an important source component of B is undeniably endogenous, namely, bank borrowings from the monetary authorities A. Furthermore, in an economy largely open to international influences, and operating under a fixed exchange rates system, foreign reserves U are also endogenous. Hence, the monetary base is itself an endogenous variable equal to:

$$B = B^{na} + A + U,$$

[7]For a detailed analysis of French monetary processes, see Fourcans (1975, 1976, and forthcoming), and Melitz (1976).

105

Figure 2
Growths of Money, Base and Multiplier

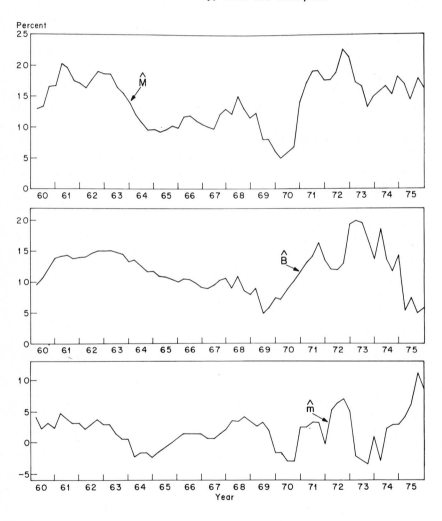

where B^{na} = net adjusted base, i.e., approximately, the government's component of the base; this variable may be considered to be under the control of the Treasury and is, therefore, exogenous.[8] From the equilibrium money stock definition, it is obvious that

$$\hat{M} = \hat{m} + \hat{B},$$

where $\hat{}$ = rates of growth.

Figure 2 shows the respective rates of growth of the money stock, the base, and the multiplier. It can be observed that the rates of growth of M and B are fairly collinear (except in 1974 and 1975), but also that $\hat{M}$ and $\hat{m}$ have a tendency to move in the same direction. If one cannot deny the important quantitative influence of the monetary base on the behavior of the money stock, then the role of the multiplier cannot be neglected either, at least in the short run. Over the long run, Table 5 demonstrates that the contribution of the base to money stock movements dominates strongly the contribution of the multiplier. It is also worth noting that the volatility (measured by the coefficient of variation) of the multiplier is significantly higher than the volatility of the base, the latter being practically identical to the money stock volatility.

Table 5

Relative Contributions of the Base and the Multiplier
to Money Stock Variations (in percentages),
Quarterly data, 1960-1973

	Mean $\overline{X}$	Standard deviation (σ)	$\sigma/\overline{X}$
m	7.98	20.89	2.62
B	92.02	93.22	1.01
M	100.00	99.10	0.99

In view of the importance of the base, a closer examination of its determinants is in order. Figure 3 exhibits some interesting features in this

---

[8] An elaborate discussion of the base can be found in Fourcans (1976, pp. 38-52).

Figure 3
Growth of the Base and Its Determinants

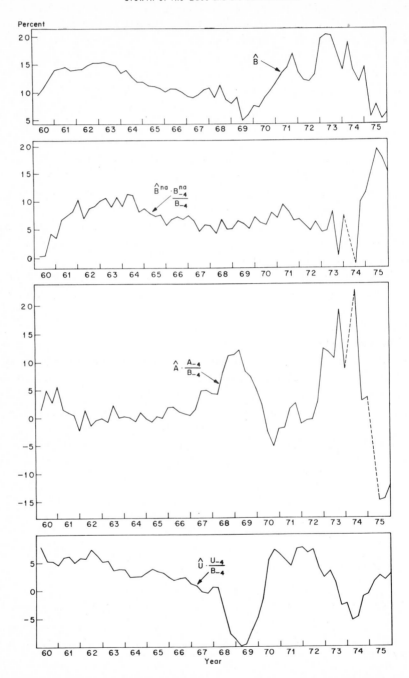

respect.[9] It shows that bank borrowings from the authorities generally vary in a direction opposite to the movements of foreign reserves. In other words, banks "compensate" any loss, or gain, of reserves due to an outflow, or inflow, of foreign exchange through their refinancing operations with the authorities.[10] This observation is interesting insofar as it shows that the banking system, through its borrowing behavior, plays a "shock absorber" role whenever funds move in or out of France. Hence, it attenuates considerably the impact of international movements of funds on the movements of the money stock.[11]

The contribution of the net adjusted base to the movements of the total base becomes more and more important from the beginning of the sample period to about the years 1964-65. After this date, a closer watch on the financing of the budget deficit by direct money creation maintained the contribution of B^{na} at a relatively more moderate and stable level, except in 1974 and 1975. Over the long run (from 1960-I to 1973-IV), the relative contribution of B^{na} to the movement of B is about 52 percent, whereas A and U accounted, respectively, for 23 percent and 25 percent. These values demonstrate that the foreign contribution is small relative to the domestic one (75 percent). Furthermore, if in the long period the policy-controlled B^{na} dominates the endogenous component A, the higher relative variability of the latter introduces a nonnegligible impediment to a monetary aggregate control over a shorter period such as the year.

3. The foreign impulse

The foreign sector of the economy may affect the rate of inflation by influencing directly either the goods market or the money stock, which in turn act upon the inflation rate. Yet, the impact of the foreign impulse on asset markets is, by definition, impounded in the monetary impulse and, as noted, the influence of the former impulse on the money stock is largely dominated

---

[9]Since $B = B^{na} + A + U$, it follows that

$$\hat{B} = \hat{B}^{na} \frac{B^{na}_{-4}}{B_{-4}} + \hat{A} \frac{A_{-4}}{B_{-4}} + \hat{U} \frac{U_{-4}}{B_{-4}},$$

where $\hat{} $ = yearly rates of growth from quarter to quarter of corresponding years, and the -4 refers to a lag of four quarters.
The dashed lines correspond to quarters for which some data were unavailable.

[10]Econometric tests (see Fourcans, 1975, 1976, and forthcoming, and Melitz, 1976) suggest that banks offset from about 70 percent to about 90 percent of their unborrowed reserves by their borrowing operations from the authorities.

[11]However, the fact that banks can obtain funds from the authorities without any significant quantitative limit may increase the sensitivity of the money stock to foreign impulses through the public's demand for credit.

by domestic components. I concentrate, therefore, on two types of external impulses which capture the total foreign stimuli.

There is an increase in aggregate demand whenever the foreign demand for domestic output increases. If the supply of output is not perfectly elastic, the excess demand so created will lead to an increase in prices and output. It is necessary, therefore, to identify a variable that would represent the impact of foreign demand on domestic aggregate demand. This variable is approximated by the growth rate of French real exports,[12] which represents the "foreign quantity" impulse.

The foreign sector was shown, in Section III.A, to have a potential influence on the domestic economy through variations in the price of imports. The rate of growth of import prices becomes, therefore, the second measure of the foreign impulse (the "foreign price" impulse).

Note that, for a relatively small economy like France, the price of imports can be safely considered to be exogenous, i.e., not influenced by domestic factors. In addition, since import prices are measured in domestic currency, the influence of foreign exchange rate changes are automatically incorporated in this measure.

B. Inflation and Dominant Impulses

In order to study the "ultimate" determinants of inflation, it is hypothesized that excess demand is a function of the unanticipated values of the set of impulses operating on the economy:[13]

$$E = f(I - I^*),$$

where I = the value of each of the four previously defined impulses

I^* = the anticipated value of each impulse.

This formulation can be transformed into an empirically falsifiable hypothesis only as long as a model about the formation of the I^*'s is established. In that respect, two very simple approaches have been tried: a) measuring the anticipated I values as a two-year moving average of each impulse; and b) assuming that the I^*'s are determined by the value of each

---

[12] Real exports growth may also be influenced by the rate of growth of prices and output. It will be shown, however, that the introduction of lagged values of this foreign quantity impulse eliminates any possible "reverse causation" from French inflation, or output, to real exports.

[13] The current and lagged values of each impulse force should have been introduced in the f function; it is only to facilitate the presentation that the formulation of the text has been adopted. The empirical analysis will shed light on the "optimum" lags involved. See especially Barro (1977), Barro and Fischer (1976), Brunner and Meltzer (1976a, 1976b), and Lucas (1973) for the literature on this subject.

stimulus one period earlier, i.e., the <u>unanticipated</u> value of each impulse is given by its first difference from one period to the next. In spite of its being very naive, the second alternative gave better and more satisfactory empirical results. In line with the view that, <u>ceteris paribus</u>, a simpler model is better than a more complicated one, it was not felt necessary to develop a more sophisticated, albeit still somewhat ad hoc, hypothesis of anticipation formation.

Hence, excess demand is empirically approximated by

$$E = g(\Delta I),$$

where ΔI = the first difference of each impulse from one period to the next.

It must be noted that since the impulses are measured as relative changes, ΔI has the dimension of an <u>acceleration</u> (or deceleration) of the money stock, of the level of the discretionary budget deficit with respect to income, and finally, of import prices and export levels.

With this hypothesis as to the determination of E, the excess-demand expectations-augmented explanation of inflation can be represented by the testable form:

$$\hat{P} = h(\Delta I) + \pi,$$

where π = the anticipated rate of inflation.

Unanticipated movements of the impulses can be expected to affect the unanticipated inflation rate positively. The dominant effect of money, of the discretionary budget deficit, and of exports should be felt through their influences on aggregate demand, whereas import prices can be expected rather to have a dominant impact on aggregate supply (see Section III.A, however, for a more elaborate discussion of this question).

Two remarks must be made with respect to this price growth equation.

First, a coefficient of π empirically close to 1 would imply the absence of a long-run trade-off between inflation and unemployment.

Second, in the long run, when the value of each impulse is totally anticipated ($I = I^*$ or $\Delta I = 0$), i.e., when each impulse does not deviate from its planned value, $\hat{P} = \pi$ (anticipations are realized).

111

Table 6

Inflation and Impulses
(Quarterly data, 1962-I-1973-IV)

Inflation rate ($\hat{P}$) (t-stat.)	$\Delta\hat{M}_{-1}$	$\Delta\hat{M}_{-2}$	$\Delta\hat{M}_{-3}$	$\Delta\hat{M}_{-4}$	$\Delta\hat{RX}_{-1}$	$\Delta\hat{RX}_{-2}$	ΔFI	ΔFI_{-1}	π	R^2	S.E.	DW
1	...	0.077 (2.79)	...	...	...	0.019 (1.69)	...	0.051 (2.33)	1.04 (37.48)	0.78	0.86	1.23
2	...	0.073 (2.61)	...	...	0.020 (1.81)	...	0.030 (1.33)	...	1.05 (36.55)	.77	.89	1.27
3	...	0.066 (2.38)	...	...	0.011 (0.96)	...	...	0.036 (1.56)	1.05 (36.82)	.77	.88	1.23
4	...	0.086 (2.96)	...	...	...	0.015 (1.32)	0.025 (1.10)	...	1.05 (35.86)	.76	.90	1.28
5	...	...	0.073 (2.70)	...	0.014 (1.20)	...	...	0.047 (2.07)	1.04 (37.00)	.78	.86	1.25
6	...	...	0.080 (2.87)	...	0.026 (2.40)	...	0.042 (1.84)	...	1.04 (36.60)	.78	.87	1.21
7	0.049 (1.72)	...	...	...	0.027 (2.26)	...	0.021 (0.91)	...	1.06 (35.14)	.75	.92	1.22
8	0.041 (1.39)	...	...	...	0.018 (1.46)	...	...	0.031 (1.24)	1.06 (35.42)	.76	.91	1.20
9	...	...	...	0.054 (1.89)	0.010 (0.83)	...	...	0.054 (2.20)	1.04 (35.38)	.76	.90	1.19
10	...	...	...	0.043 (1.49)	0.023 (1.96)	...	0.031 (1.30)	...	1.04 (34.22)	0.75	0.93	1.19

Source: for M, Banque de France
for RX, INSEE
for FI, Statistiques et Etudes Financieres
for PM, International Financial Statistics, IMF.

Note: M = money stock
RX = real exports
FI = fiscal impulse
PM = index of import prices, in francs.

In order to judge the validity of the hypothesis, I rely on two broad types of tests: a parametric test to evaluate the marginal effect of each impulse on the inflation phenomenon, and a recently developed nonparametric test statistic to evaluate the null-hypothesis of no systematic positive association between $\hat{P}$ and the impulse measures. This test allows one to isolate which impulses, if any, have a dominant influence over others in affecting the inflation rate.

1. Inflation and impulses: parametric tests

Econometric tests of the inflation rate in terms of the four impulses and anticipations are reported, over two different sample periods, in Tables 6 and 7. Table 6 reports results from the first quarter of 1962 to the last quarter of 1973, whereas Table 7 extends this period to the end of 1975. These two time periods have been chosen, essentially, to enable evaluation of the impact of the 1974-75 economic crisis on the rate of growth of prices. The symbol Δ represents yearly changes of the respective impulses from quarter to quarter of corresponding years; the lagged values are expressed in terms of quarters.[14] Only the significant lagged values are presented. The rates of growth, represented by the $\hat{}$, are also calculated from quarter to quarter of corresponding years.

The anticipated rate of inflation π is of an unobservable magnitude. One must, therefore, choose an hypothesis of expectations formation that can be translated into an empirical measure in order to conduct the regression tests. The literature proposes two approaches: the adaptive expectations and the rational expectations models. The former model is well known and does not require further theoretical explanation. The latter assumes that economic agents form their expectations by considering multiple sources of information which then constitute the input of the forecasting process. This hypothesis implies that market participants have a basic view of the way the economy operates, a view that represents the structure through which they form their expectations. Hence, agents are supposed to gather information about the exogenous variables that may enter the reduced form equation of the phenomenon to be forecast, and use them to establish their forecast. Within the dominant impulse framework, the anticipated values of the impulses are obvious candidates to represent the set of exogenous variables:

$$\pi = k \ (I^*).$$

---

[14]The data bank starts with the first quarter of 1960. The calculus of the Δ's eliminated the first year, and the lagged values of these explanatory variables to four quarters eliminated the next year. For this reason, the regression test starts in 1962-I instead of 1961-I, as was the case previously.

Table 7

Inflation and Impulses
(Quarterly data, 1962-I-1975-IV)

Inflation rate (P̂) (t-stat.)	Δ M̂_{-1}	Δ M̂_{-2}	Δ M̂_{-3}	Δ P̂M	Δ P̂M_{-1}	Δ P̂M_{-2}	Δ R̂X_{-1}	Δ R̂X_{-2}	Δ FI	Δ FI_{-1}	π	R²	S.E.	DW
1	...	0.073 (2.52)	...	0.026 (3.43)	...	...	...	0.021 (1.82)	...	0.052 (2.16)	1.08 (50.45)	0.93	0.95	1.68
2	...	0.076 (2.59)	...	0.028 (3.64)	...	...	0.017 (1.45)	...	0.059 (2.57)	...	1.08 (50.15)	.93	0.94	1.49
3	...	0.065 (2.15)	...	0.026 (3.18)	...	...	0.004 (0.31)	...	...	0.040 (1.56)	1.08 (48.35)	.92	0.98	1.64
4	...	0.087 (2.97)	...	0.028 (3.63)	...	...	...	0.017 (1.53)	0.053 (2.39)	...	1.08 (50.29)	.93	0.94	1.53
5	...	...	0.058 (1.97)	0.025 (3.11)	...	...	0.007 (0.59)	...	...	0.047 (1.82)	1.08 (48.01)	.92	0.99	1.62
6	...	...	0.076 (2.58)	0.028 (3.63)	...	...	0.023 (2.04)	...	0.068 (2.88)	...	1.07 (50.04)	.93	0.94	1.35
7	0.063 (2.14)	...	...	0.025 (3.28)	...	...	0.024 (2.02)	...	0.048 (2.09)	...	1.08 (49.10)	.92	0.96	1.43
8	0.059 (1.95)	...	...	0.023 (2.95)	...	...	0.013 (1.00)	...	...	0.032 (1.24)	1.08 (47.82)	.92	0.99	1.60
9	...	0.071 (2.48)	...	...	0.027 (3.59)	...	...	0.022 (1.91)	...	0.048 (2.05)	1.07 (50.31)	.93	0.94	1.55
10	...	0.079 (2.72)	...	...	0.026 (3.43)	...	...	0.018 (1.61)	0.036 (1.72)	...	1.07 (49.12)	.93	0.95	1.43
11	...	...	0.069 (2.33)	...	0.030 (3.53)	...	0.006 (0.52)	...	...	0.046 (1.85)	1.06 (48.02)	.92	0.96	1.55
12	...	...	0.078 (2.61)	...	0.028 (3.54)	...	0.020 (1.77)	...	0.051 (2.29)	...	1.06 (49.01)	.93	0.95	1.32

Table 7 -- Continued

13	::	0.063 (2.06)	::	::	0.020 (2.27)	::	0.020 (1.63)	::	0.026 (1.08)	1.07 (45.63)	.92	1.00	1.39
	::		::	::		::		::			::	::	::
14	::	0.069 (2.25)	::	::	0.020 (2.29)	::	0.018 (1.51)	0.022 (1.01)	::	1.06 (45.03)	.92	1.01	1.32
	::		::	::		::			::		::	::	::
15	::	::	0.058 (1.88)	::	0.023 (2.49)	0.015 (1.25)	::	::	0.017 (0.72)	1.06 (44.28)	.92	1.02	1.38
	::	::		::			::	::			::	::	::
16	::	::	0.067 (2.15)	::	0.026 (2.53)	0.023 (1.91)	::	0.036 (1.59)	::	1.06 (45.08)	0.92	1.00	1.23
	::	::		::			::		::		::	::	::

Following this procedure, π can be approximated by the estimated value of the inflation rate from a regression of $\hat{P}$ on the "long-run" (or expected, or planned) values of each impulse. To obtain such an estimate, the two empirical measures of the I^*'s discussed earlier were used. When the inflation hypothesis was tested by incorporating these measures of anticipation into the regressions, the results with respect to the influence of each unanticipated impulse and with respect to the coefficient of π were not significantly different from the outcome obtained by using an adaptive expectations scheme (presented below) to estimate the anticipated rate of inflation. Yet, the fit of the equations (in terms of R^2, S.E., and DW) was significantly worse than it would have been if the latter measure of π had been used. For this reason, only the equations incorporating the following adaptive expectations measure of π are presented in Tables 6 and 7:

$$\pi = 4 \sum_{i=0}^{5} w_i \hat{P}_{q_{t-i-1}},$$

where $w_0 = 6/21$

$w_1 = 5/21$

$\vdots$

$w_5 = 1/21$

$\sum_i w_i = 1,$

and where $\hat{P}_q$ = the rate of growth of prices from quarter to quarter.

The weights w's follow a geometrically declining lag structure over a one-and-one-half year period. It must be noted that the annualized quarterly rates of growth of prices have been used instead of the yearly rates of growth (the $\hat{P}$'s) to measure expectations. The reason for this choice is purely empirical; a measure of π using the $\hat{P}$'s leads to regressions whose fits are significantly less satisfactory than when the $\hat{P}_q$ are used to estimate π. Thus, it appears that the latter estimate of the anticipations variable is better than the former.

This result indicates that the inflation rates experienced over the last six quarters rather than over almost the last three years (since $\hat{P}_{t-7} = \dfrac{P_{t-7} - P_{t-11}}{P_{t-11}}$) influence anticipations, an intuitively sensible outcome.[15]

Finally, in order to take into consideration the possibility of an information lag, the distributed lag structure starts in period t-1 instead of period t.

It must be noticed that, as long as each ΔI affects the inflation rate significantly, this measure of π implies that the anticipated rate of inflation is a distributed lag function of the past values of the impulses. Hence, the coefficients of the ΔI's represent only the unanticipated influence of each stimulus, i.e., they measure only to what extent each stimulus contributes to the deviation of the inflation rate from its anticipated value. The total effect must also take into consideration the implicit impact of the impulses through the anticipated rate of inflation. To avoid any misunderstanding, I stress that the following discussion takes into consideration only the unanticipated impacts of the impulses.

Before discussing the results, a final remark must be made. Since the hypothesis intends to explain both the trend rate of inflation as well as deviations from the trend, the intercepts of the equations have been suppressed. At any rate, the constant term was never found to be significantly different from zero when it was introduced in the regressions. This result is, of course, favorable for the validity of the hypothesis.

Tables 6 and 7 indicate the very satisfactory fits of the regressions, with a noticeable improvement when the sample period is extended until the end of 1975. The R^2 are high by all standards, especially in Table 7. If the Durbin-Watson statistics are a little low in Table 6, the inclusion of the years 1974 and 1975 renders them more acceptable.

As the effect of the unanticipated foreign price impulse was not found to be significant over the period from 1962-I to 1973-IV, Table 6 does not report regressions including $\Delta \hat{PM}_{-i}$ (where i is a measure of lags). Yet this variable becomes extremely significant when the sample period is extended to the fourth quarter of 1975 (Table 7). Needless to say, the difference between the two periods is explained by the extraordinary oil price shock which led to a no less extraordinary increase in the import price index in 1974. Table 7 shows that changes in the rate of growth of import prices appear to have affected significantly the deviation of the inflation rate from its anticipated value during

---

[15] This measure of π also gives very satisfactory results in the estimation of demand for money functions in France (see Fourcans, 1976, and forthcoming).

the same period and two quarters ahead ($\Delta \hat{PM}_{-3}$ loses significance). As the value of $\Delta \hat{PM}$ was always around 50 for the year 1974, and as the coefficients of $\Delta \hat{PM}_{-i}$ (i = 0,1,2) are between 0.025 and 0.030, it can be inferred that the oil shock must have been responsible for about 4 percent of the inflation rate during that year (under the assumption, however, that the effect of import prices through the anticipations variable was rather minor). But, during "normal" periods, such as until the end of 1973, the unanticipated foreign price impulse seems to have played a rather minor role in explaining French inflation.

The influence of the unanticipated foreign quantity impulse does not appear to be very strong either. Indeed, if $\Delta \hat{RX}_{-1}$ and $\Delta \hat{RX}_{-2}$ are sometimes significant, their loss of significance at other times raises some doubts as to the importance of the role played by export growth on unanticipated inflation.

The marginal influence of the unanticipated fiscal impulse does not emerge very clearly either; ΔFI is not always significant, especially from 1962-I to 1973-IV. Over the longer sample periods, its significance appears more pronounced. As the value of ΔFI was always positive and relatively high in 1974 and 1975, one can infer that fiscal policy must have contributed to the acceleration of the inflation rate during the period of economic crisis.

Among the impulses, the unanticipated monetary impulse appears to be the most significant whatever the sample period under consideration. Accelerations (or decelerations) of the money stock start having a small effect on the unanticipated inflation rate after one quarter; the peak influence appears after two to three quarters, then vanishes progressively to disappear completely after about twelve to fifteen months. It is interesting to compare these lags with those of the unanticipated fiscal impulse. If it is admitted that the latter impulse exerts an impact on the deviation of the inflation rate from its anticipated value, then, apparently, it is felt more quickly (during the current period) and vanishes more rapidly (after about two quarters) than does the effect of the monetary impulse.

Finally, the coefficient of the anticipated rate of inflation is extremely significant and not significantly different from 1, a result that corroborates the "natural" rate hypothesis. It must also be noted that the t-values of the π coefficients are higher in the regressions of the extended sample period. This outcome seems to imply that the role of anticipations has become more important in the latter years of the period.

At this point, let me return to the cost-push or, more specifically, the wage-push theory of inflation. Section III.B shows that the best fits of the cost-push regressions were obtained when the differential between the rates of growth of wages and of productivity were lagged two quarters. It was also shown that the introduction of an excess-demand proxy in the representative cost-push equation improved the fit noticeably and reduced the coefficient and t-values of the $(\hat{W} - \hat{Pr})_{-2}$ variable.

It is now possible to evaluate further the role played by the wage-push factor by introducing the variable $(\hat{W} - \hat{Pr})_{-2}$ in the equations of the hypothesis. The following representative equations are given:

Period 1962-I to 1973-IV

$$\hat{P} = \underset{(2.45)}{0.063} \, \Delta\hat{M}_{-2} + \underset{(3.01)}{0.034} \, \Delta\hat{RX}_{-2} + \underset{(0.66)}{0.015} \, \Delta FI_{-1} + \underset{(16.84)}{0.90} \, \pi$$

$$+ \underset{(3.11)}{0.14} \, (\hat{W} - \hat{Pr})_{-2}$$

$$R^2 = 0.83, \qquad \sigma = 0.79, \qquad DW = 1.54$$

$$\hat{P} = \underset{(1.97)}{0.055} \, \Delta\hat{M}_{-2} + \underset{(0.25)}{0.003} \, \Delta\hat{RX}_{-1} + \underset{(0.76)}{0.019} \, \Delta FI_{-1} + \underset{(17.27)}{0.97} \, \pi$$

$$+ \underset{(1.55)}{0.07} \, (\hat{W} - \hat{Pr})_{-2};$$

$$R^2 = 0.79, \qquad \sigma = 0.87, \qquad DW = 1.34$$

Period 1962-I to 1975-IV

$$\hat{P} = \underset{(2.25)}{0.057} \, \Delta\hat{M}_{-2} + \underset{(3.25)}{0.021} \, \Delta\hat{PM} + \underset{(3.72)}{0.041} \, \Delta\hat{RX}_{-2} + \underset{(0.21)}{0.005} \, \Delta FI_{-1} + \underset{(16.33)}{0.87} \, \pi$$

$$+ \underset{(4.28)}{0.18} \, (\hat{W} - \hat{Pr})_{-2}$$

$$R^2 = 0.95, \qquad \sigma = 0.82, \qquad DW = 1.94$$

$$\hat{P} = \underset{(2.08)}{0.061} \, \Delta\hat{M}_{-2} + \underset{(3.69)}{0.027} \, \Delta\hat{PM} + \underset{(0.17)}{0.022} \, \Delta\hat{RX}_{-1} + \underset{(1.32)}{0.033} \, \Delta FI + \underset{(16.23)}{0.96} \, \pi$$

$$+ \underset{(2.15)}{0.09} \, (\hat{W} - \hat{Pr})_{-2}.$$

$$R^2 = 0.93, \qquad \sigma = 0.91, \qquad DW = 1.67$$

The coefficients of $(\hat{W} - \hat{Pr})_{-2}$ are generally significant, but their value is very small. The results imply that an increase in the differential between the rates of growth of wages and of productivity of 1 percent would, on the average, increase prices between approximately 0.05 percent and 0.20 percent. In other words, the average differential should have been between about 90 percent and 22 percent from 1962-I to 1973-IV, and between about 110 percent and 30 percent from 1962-I to 1975-IV, to explain the mean inflation rate. These values are, of course, far from the actual average differential which was around

119

5 percent for the shorter period and around 5.7 percent for the longer one. Therefore, even though one cannot reject completely the wage-push theory, its explanatory power, when excess-demand variables are taken into consideration, is indeed very minimal.

Another aspect of the results needs to be noted. The inclusion of $(\hat{W}-\hat{Pr})_{-2}$ in the equations reduces somewhat the coefficients and t-values of the π variable. This outcome suggests that the wage factor picks up some of the influence of anticipations on the inflation rate. This is not surprising in view of the persisting inflationary experience. I would not deny that anticipations of inflation may, in the short run, push wages beyond productivity and, hence, lead to an increase in prices.[16] But the wage increase would then be the consequence of market conditions and not exogenously imposed as some cost-push proponents assert. Furthermore, the increase in prices could not persist without a validating excess demand.

Let me summarize the main results of these parametric tests.

The dominant impulse expectations hypothesis gives a very robust explanation of French inflation even during the troubled latter years of the period.

There seems to be no long-run trade-off between inflation and employment. And the "long run" is rather short since the lagged structures of the result indicate that, at the most (in terms of the monetary impulse), it is about one year.

The monetary impulse appears to be the most significant in the explanation of the deviations of the inflation rate from its trend (or expected) value. The influence of the fiscal and the foreign quantity impulses cannot, however, be completely ignored even if their effect is not clearly established. The foreign price impulse was very significant as a consequence of the oil crisis, but does not seem to have any noticeable importance over "normal" periods.

Increases in wages beyond productivity gains explain only a minimal proportion of the inflationary experience when the above excess-demand variables are taken into consideration.

2. Inflation and impulses: nonparametric and dominance tests

The previous section analyzed the marginal contribution of each impulse to the inflation phenomenon given the anticipations. The purpose of this section is to evaluate the total contribution of each impulse to inflation (i.e., not contingent on the anticipated rate of price increases) and to discriminate more clearly whether one or more impulses might have a dominant influence on inflation.

---

[16]To a certain extent, this phenomenon seems to have occurred in 1974 and 1975 after the sharp rise in the price of oil.

Before embarking on a more sophisticated analysis, it is useful to look at the relationship between each impulse and the inflation rate. As Figure 4 demonstrates, only the correlation between the growth rate of money and the rate of growth of the GDP price deflator appears to be substantial. Changes in M seem to lead changes in P by about three to twelve months, with an average lead that appears to be around six months. Furthermore, it seems that prices react more quickly to an acceleration of money growth rates than to a deceleration. [17]

A closer examination of the period will shed light on this relationship. From 1960-I to 1961-I, the rate of growth of M goes from 13 percent to 20 percent, whereas inflation accelerates from about 2 percent to almost 5 percent in 1961-I. From 1961-I to 1962-I, M decreases from 20 percent to about 16 percent, and prices go down from 5 percent to 2.5 percent in 1962-I. From 1962-I to 1962-III, a new acceleration of the money growth rate (from 16 percent to 19 percent) brings about a price increase of about 3.5 percent (from 25 percent in 1962-I to 6 percent in 1963-II). Then, as money growth decelerates from 19 percent in 1962-III to 10 percent in 1965-I, the rate of inflation decelerates from 6 percent in 1963-II to about 2 percent in 1965-IV. In the following period (from 1965-I to 1967-II), the rates of growth of M and P remain fairly stable. From 1967-II to 1968-II, a new money explosion (from 10 to 15 percent) was accompanied by price rises ranging from 2 percent in 1968-I to 9 percent in 1969-I. Then, the deceleration of inflation from 9 percent in 1969-I to 4 percent in 1971-I followed the deceleration of the money growth from 15 percent in 1968-II to 5 percent in 1970-I.

The rate of growth of M accelerated sharply again from 1970-I to 1972-III, and $\hat{P}$ kept increasing, though at a fairly moderate rate, until the end of 1973; but, inflation accelerated sharply after this date until the end of 1974 in spite of the deceleration of the money stock from the end of 1972 to the third quarter of 1973. It must be noted, however, that the rate of growth of M increased noticeably in 1974 (to more than 18 percent), an occurrence that added to the oil price shock; the persistent influence of the sharp acceleration of money from 1970 to 1972 may also explain the rapidly rising price level in 1974. Finally, the growth of prices diminished somewhat during 1975, not only because the oil price increase was more or less absorbed during 1974, but also, probably, because of the deceleration of the stock of money during 1973.

---

[17] The chi-square statistic was used to test for the association between $\hat{P}$ and $\hat{M}_{t-i}$ for periods of accelerations and decelerations of inflation.
It was found that the null-hypothesis of no association between $\hat{P}$ and $\hat{M}_{t-i}$ was rejected at the 1-percent confidence level for i = 2,3,4. Furthermore, the highest confidence level at which the null-hypothesis could be rejected was obtained when i = 2, for periods of accelerating inflation, and when i = 3, for periods of decelerating inflation.

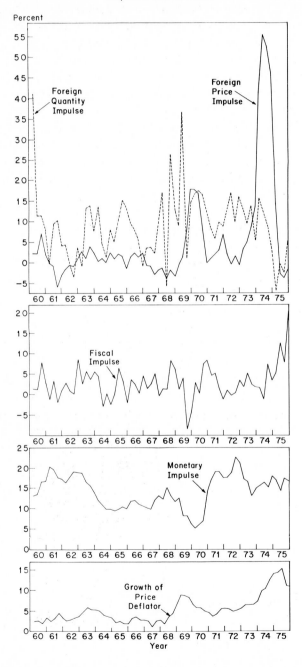

Figure 4
Impulses and Inflation

Notice that, beginning in the years 1971-72, the lag of prices behind money seems to have increased somewhat.

It is worth noting here that these observations are consistent with the view that the monetary cycle leads the inflation cycle, whereas they contradict the reverse causation argument.

I now seek with a more rigorous nonparametric test to go further than these casual observations, to test the significance of a positive association between the direction of the inflation rate and the direction of the four systematic stimuli. For that purpose, use is made of the recently developed ∇p-statistic [18] that tests for the null-hypothesis of no systematic positive association between $\hat{P}$ and each of the impulses, regardless of how the other impulses behave. The statistic is obtained from the following type of contingency table of observed movements of inflation and each impulse force.

		Inflation				
		+	-	0	Σ per row	
	+	0_{11}	0_{12}	0_{13}	M_1	+ = upward movement
Impulse	-	0_{21}	0_{22}	0_{23}	M_2	- = downward movement
	0	0_{31}	0_{32}	0_{33}	M_3	0 = no movement
Σ per column		N_1	N_2	N_3	N	N = total number of observations

If the sum of actual observations (0_{ij}) over the off-diagonal cells does not differ significantly from the sum of expected $(e_{ij} = \dfrac{N_j M_i}{N})$ off-diagonal observations, it can be inferred that the impulse under consideration and the inflation phenomenon are not positively associated. This positive association depends on the value of the ∇p -statistic:

$$\nabla p = 1 - \frac{\Sigma \text{ off-diagonal observed values}}{\Sigma \text{ off-diagonal expected values}},$$

which can be standardized (by dividing by the standard deviation of the statistic) and compared to some critical level. If this standardized value is positive and

[18] See Hildebrand, Laing, and Rosenthal (1974).

Table 8

Test of Positive Association between Impulses and Inflation
(Normalized quarterly first differences)

Impulses		Trace/N		∇p		Standardized ∇p	
Monetary	$\hat{M}_{-1}$	20/52	24/60	0.04	0.06	0.31	0.50
impulse	$\hat{M}_{-2}$	30/52	36/60	0.35	0.38	3.98	4.87
	$\hat{M}_{-3}$	24/51	27/59	0.18	0.16	1.61	1.48
	$\hat{M}_{-4}$	17/50	20/58	- 0.02	- 0.02	...	...
Foreign price	$\hat{PM}$	23/52	27/60	0.09	- 0.09	0.73	...
impulse	$\hat{PM}_{-1}$	22/51	27/59	.07	.10	0.55	0.87
	$\hat{PM}_{-2}$	23/50	29/58	.12	.17	0.98	1.59
	$\hat{PM}_{-3}$	19/49	25/57	.00	.08	0.00	0.67
	$\hat{PM}_{-4}$	17/48	24/56	- 0.05	0.05	...	0.40
Foreign quantity	$\hat{RX}_{-1}$	20/52	22/60	- 0.01	- 0.04	...	...
impulse	$\hat{RX}_{-2}$	24/51	27/59	.14	.11	1.19	0.96
	$\hat{RX}_{-3}$	15/50	19/58	- .14	- .10	...	...
	$\hat{RX}_{-4}$	20/50	23/57	0.04	0.00	0.30	0.00
Fiscal	FI	22/52	25/60	0.04	0.03	0.31	0.24
impulse	FI_{-1}	21/51	24/59	.00	.00	0.00	0.00
	FI_{-2}	20/50	20/58	.00	- .09	...	...
	FI_{-3}	23/49	26/57	.13	.10	1.06	0.85
	FI_{-4}	20/48	23/56	0.04	0.00	0.29	0.00

Note: N = number of observations.

Critical values of the standarized ∇p-statistic at
10-percent level: 1.30
5-percent level: 1.67
1-percent level: 2.39.

exceeds some given critical level, the null-hypothesis of <u>no</u> systematic positive association between inflation and the impulse must be rejected.

The 3x3 contingency tables have been constructed by taking the first difference of the inflation rate and each impulse, each of which was then normalized by their respective standard deviation. This procedure allowed for a dramatic increase in the number of sign switches vis-à-vis the original data; these switches are absolutely necessary in order to apply the test.[19] A zero change in the variables was assigned when the magnitude of the standardized variable did not exceed 0.10 in absolute value.

Table 8 presents the value of the trace (i.e., the sum of the on-diagonal observations in the contingency tables) compared to the total number of observations,[20] the ∇p-statistic, and the normalized ∇p. The values on the left-hand side of each column are obtained by testing data from 1961-I to 1973-IV, whereas the right-hand-side values are obtained by extending the sample period to 1975-IV.

The results are very clear cut; the null-hypothesis of no systematic positive association between inflation and each impulse can only be rejected at the 1-percent level for the monetary impulse ($\hat{M}$ lagged two quarters). For the other impulses, the positive association cannot be detected to be different from a pure random occurrence, at least at the 5-percent level. It must be noted that the effect of the oil crisis on the inflation phenomenon is demonstrated by the higher standardized ∇p for the foreign price impulse (especially $\hat{PM}_{-2}$) when observations for 1974 and 1975 are added to the data set. The higher standardized ∇p for $\hat{M}_{-2}$ over the extended period also suggests that the monetary impulse must have exacerbated the rate of price increases during the period of economic crisis.

It is worth emphasizing here that the parametric and nonparametric tests indicate that even if the <u>unanticipated</u> inflation rate seems to be affected by the <u>unanticipated</u> value of each impulse (see Section IV.A for details), the monetary impulse appears to dominate all the other stimuli in explaining the <u>total</u> rate of inflation, i.e., the sum of its unanticipated and anticipated components.

---

[19] Since the hypothesis can be represented by $\hat{P} = f$ $(I-I^*) + \pi$, it follows (by assuming, however, that the f function is linear) that $\Delta\hat{P} - \Delta\pi = f(\Delta I) - f(\Delta I^*)$. As the anticipated values I^* and π are much more stable than the actual values I and $\hat{P}$, it can be inferred that the variance of $\hat{P}$ dominates the variance of π, whereas the variance of I dominates the variance of I^*. From the latter equation, it follows that the variance of $\hat{P}$ should be dominated by the variance of I. That is why a positive association between the normalized values of $\Delta\hat{P}$ and ΔI is tested.

[20] The period starts in 1961-I when N=52 or 60; every time N decreases by 1 (from these values), the period starts one quarter later. The lag structures used are the cause of these small variations in the number of observations.

V. THE DOMINANT IMPULSE HYPOTHESIS OF OUTPUT GROWTH

The hypothesis was made that excess demand responded to the unanticipated values of the set of impulses operating on the economy:

$$E = f(I - I^*).$$

If excess demand is defined as the difference between the current rate of growth of output and its long-run value, then

$$\hat{y} - \hat{y}^* = f(I - I^*),$$

or

$$\hat{y} = f(I - I^*) + \hat{y}^*,$$

where $\hat{y}$ = the rate of growth of output over a given period
$\hat{y}^*$ = the long-run rate of growth of output during a given period.
This theoretical formulation can be empirically approximated by

$$\hat{y} = g(\Delta I) + \hat{y}^*,$$

where ΔI = the first difference of each impulse from one period to the next.

Remember that the ΔI's have the dimension of an acceleration (or deceleration) of the money stock, of the level of the discretionary budget deficit with respect to national income, and finally, of the level of exports and of import prices. Hence, only the accelerations (decelerations) of these four variables are supposed to affect the deviation of output growth from its long-run value. In other words, output growth may deviate from its steady state value whenever there is a change in the level of any impulse force (or when any impulse force deviates from its anticipated value). However, this deviation is only of a temporary nature, and output growth would go back to its "natural" rate $\hat{y}^*$, determined by the rate of growth of the labor force and of capital, by technological innovations, etc.

126

All of the impulses may be expected to exert a positive effect on $\hat{y}$ by influencing mainly the aggregate demand for goods and services, except for the foreign price stimulus whose impact, essentially via the aggregate supply curve, can be expected to be negative.

In this study of inflation, both parametric and nonparametric tests will be used to evaluate the hypothesis.

A. Output Growth and Impulses: Parametric Tests

The hypothesis has been tested over both the 1962-I-1973-IV and the 1962-I-1975-IV periods. Tables 9 and 10 report results obtained from the first sample period; Table 11 presents the outcome of the tests over the extended sample period.

Tables 9 and 10 measure the long-run rate of growth of output in two ways. The first, $\hat{y}_1^*$, is a two-year moving average, lagged one quarter, of the rate of growth of output $\hat{y}$. The second, $\hat{y}_2^*$, is the estimated value of output growth obtained from a regression of $\hat{y}$ against the rate of growth of capital held by firms.[21] If the traditional production function, $y = f(K,L)$, is adopted, then the long-run rate of growth depends on the rate of growth of the labor force and of capital. As the rate of growth of the labor force has been very minimal over the period, only the rate of growth of capital has been explicitly taken into consideration to estimate $\hat{y}_2^*$. The series of the stock of capital being unavailable after 1973, only $\hat{y}_1^*$ has been used to test the hypothesis over the extended sample period (Table 11).

The intercept of the equations has been suppressed whenever $\hat{y}_1^*$ or $\hat{y}_2^*$ was introduced as an explanatory variable, since the hypothesis is then supposed to explain both the trend rate of growth of output and deviations from this trend.[22] At any rate, the lack of significance of the intercept term whenever the deviation of output growth from its steady state value constitutes the dependent variable suggests that, indeed, this term has no explanatory power whatsoever.

---

[21] Over the period 1962-I-1973-IV,

$$\hat{y} = \underset{(0.49)}{4.20} + \underset{(0.21)}{0.26} \hat{K},$$
$$R^2 = .001, \qquad DW = 1.85$$

where $\hat{K}$ = rate of growth of real capital held by firms (Source: INSEE). The very bad fit of this equation implies that $\hat{y}_2^*$ is, in fact, analogous to a trend value.

[22] There is also a statistical problem involved. As the variances of $\hat{y}_1^*$ and $\hat{y}_2^*$ are very small, these variables are very close to a constant. A serious collinearity problem would, therefore, exist if both the constant term and one of these variables were introduced simultaneously as explanatory variables.

Table 9

Output Growth and Impulses
(Quarterly data, 1962-I-1973-IV)

Output growth $(\hat{y})$	Intercept	$\Delta\hat{M}_{-3}$	$\Delta\hat{M}_{-4}$	$\Delta\hat{RX}_{-3}$	ΔFI	ΔFI_{-1}	ΔFI_{-2}	$\hat{y}^*_1$	$\hat{y}^*_2$	R^2	S.E.	DW
1 a (t-stat.)	...	...	0.210 (2.70)	0.094 (2.91)	...	...	0.223 (3.54)	0.96 (15.86)	...	0.22	2.55	2.15
2 a	...	0.193 (2.36)	...	0.116 (3.48)	...	...	0.193 (3.05)	0.97 (15.70)	...	0.19	2.60	2.11
1 b	...	...	0.146 (2.00)	0.093 (3.09)	...	...	0.196 (3.34)	...	0.98 (17.20)	0.32	2.38	2.08
2 b	...	...	0.142 (1.76)	0.077 (2.41)	...	0.106 (1.60)	...	...	0.98 (15.72)	.20	2.59	2.18
3 b	...	...	0.133 (1.65)	0.069 (2.12)	0.092 (1.40)	...	...	...	0.98 (15.66)	.18	2.61	1.83
4 b	...	0.103 (1.34)	...	0.106 (3.37)	...	...	0.176 (2.96)	...	0.99 (16.89)	.29	2.44	2.04
5 b	...	0.126 (1.51)	...	0.094 (2.82)	...	0.091 (1.31)	...	...	0.98 (15.67)	.18	2.61	2.16
6 b	...	0.138 (1.63)	...	0.087 (2.62)	0.096 (1.44)	...	...	...	0.98 (15.70)	0.18	2.61	1.86
1 c	5.94 (17.19)	...	0.143 (1.97)	0.093 (3.10)	...	...	0.198 (3.37)	...	...	0.32	2.38	2.09
2 c	5.96 (16.90)	0.101 (1.31)	...	0.106 (3.10)	...	...	0.178 (3.37)	...	...	0.29	2.44	2.05

Source: for y, Tendances de la Conjoncture, INSEE.

Note: Δ = yearly first differences
y = real GDP
$\hat{y}^*_1$ = a measure of the long-run rate of growth of output, calculated as a two-year moving average of $\hat{y}$ lagged one quarter
$\hat{y}^*_2$ = a measure of the long-run rate of growth of output, calculated as the estimated value of a regression of $\hat{y}$ against the rate of growth of firms' capital stock
$\hat{ }$ = annual rate of growth from quarter to quarter of corresponding years.

Table 10
Deviation of Output Growth from Its Steady State Value and Impulses
(Quarterly data, 1962-I–1973-IV)

Deviation of output growth $(\hat{y} - \hat{y}_1^*)$	Intercept	$\Delta\hat{M}_{-3}$	$\Delta\hat{M}_{-4}$	$\Delta\hat{RX}_{-3}$	ΔFI	ΔFI_{-1}	ΔFI_{-2}	R^2	S.E.	DW
1 d (t-stat.)	-0.138 (0.37)	...	0.211 (2.69)	0.093 (2.89)	...	...	0.224 (3.53)	0.35	2.56	2.15
2 d	-0.112 (0.30)	0.195 (2.37)	...	0.116 (3.47)	...	...	0.194 (3.05)	.33	2.60	2.11
3 d	-0.166 (0.41)	...	0.211 (2.43)	0.076 (2.21)	...	0.137 (1.92)	...	.23	2.79	2.33
4 d	-0.146 (0.36)	0.224 (2.53)	...	0.104 (2.95)	...	0.118 (1.71)	...	.24	2.77	2.27
5 d	-0.149 (0.36)	...	0.197 (2.26)	0.066 (1.86)	0.112 (1.56)	...	...	.21	2.82	1.82
6 d	-0.147 (0.37)	0.239 (2.66)	...	0.095 (2.69)	0.123 (1.74)	...	...	.24	2.77	1.93
Deviation of output growth $(\hat{y} - \hat{y}_2^*)$										
1'd	-0.106 (0.31)	...	0.146 (2.00)	0.093 (3.09)	...	...	0.196 (3.34)	0.32	2.38	2.09
2'd	-0.078 (0.22)	0.103 (1.34)	...	0.106 (3.37)	...	...	0.176 (2.96)	.29	2.44	2.03
3'd	-0.126 (0.33)	...	0.142 (1.76)	0.078 (2.41)	...	0.106 (1.60)	...	.19	2.59	2.18
4'd	-0.104 (0.27)	0.126 (1.51)	...	0.094 (2.82)	...	0.091 (1.39)	...	.18	2.61	2.16
5'd	-0.115 (0.30)	...	0.133 (1.65)	0.069 (2.12)	0.092 (1.40)	...	...	.18	2.61	1.83
6'd	-0.105 (0.28)	0.139 (1.63)	...	0.087 (2.62)	0.096 (1.44)	...	...	0.18	2.61	1.86

Table 11

Output Growth and Impulses
(Quarterly data, 1962-I-1975-IV)

Output growth ($\hat{y}$)	Intercept	$\Delta\hat{M}_{4}$	$\Delta\hat{PM}_{-3}$	$\Delta\hat{PM}_{-4}$	$\Delta\hat{RX}_{-3}$	$\Delta\hat{FI}$	$\Delta\hat{FI}_{-1}$	$\Delta\hat{FI}_{-2}$	$\hat{y}^{*}_{1}$	R^2	S.E.	DW
1'a (t-stat.)	...	0.128 (1.62)	...	-0.125 (4.25)	0.093 (2.86)	...	...	0.270 (4.17)	0.94 (15.21)	0.52	2.69	2.00
2'a	...	0.101 (1.25)	-0.120 (4.28)	...	0.104 (3.18)	...	...	0.193 (3.10)	0.95 (15.32)	.52	2.68	1.84
3'a	...	0.144 (1.61)	...	-0.115 (3.35)	0.061 (1.72)	...	0.135 (1.78)	...	0.93 (13.40)	.39	3.02	1.95
4'a	...	0.096 (1.11)	-0.132 (4.30)	...	0.082 (2.42)	...	0.107 (1.56)	...	0.95 (14.36)	.45	2.86	2.02
5'a	...	0.137 (1.57)	...	-0.127 (3.69)	0.060 (1.74)	0.169 (2.40)	...	...	0.93 (13.69)	.41	2.95	1.53
6'a	...	0.094 (1.10)	-0.135 (4.46)	...	0.082 (2.46)	0.124 (1.98)	...	...	0.95 (14.53)	0.47	2.82	1.68
1'c	5.68 (15.28)	0.012 (0.15)	...	-0.184 (6.10)	0.110 (3.39)	...	...	0.245 (3.79)	...	0.52	2.68	1.79
2'c	5.51 (13.43)	0.009 (0.10)	-0.142 (4.50)	...	0.121 (3.34)	...	...	0.134 (1.93)	...	0.40	2.98	1.39

Table 11--Continued

Deviation of Output Growth from Its Steady State Value and Impulses
(Quarterly data, 1962-I-1975-IV)

Deviation of output growth $(\hat{y} - y_1^*)$	Intercept	$\Delta\hat{M}_{-4}$	$\Delta\hat{PM}_{-3}$	$\Delta\hat{PM}_{-4}$	$\Delta\hat{RX}_{-3}$	ΔFI	ΔFI_{-1}	ΔFI_{-2}	R^2	S.E.	DW
1'd	- 0.278 (0.74)	0.134 (1.67)	...	- 0.123 (4.06)	0.092 (2.82)	...	...	0.272 (4.19)	0.44	2.70	2.01
2'd	- 0.322 (0.87)	0.107 (1.31)	- 0.118 (4.17)	...	0.103 (3.15)	...	...	0.197 (3.16)	.45	2.68	1.85
3'd	- 0.309 (0.73)	0.151 (1.66)	...	- 0.113 (3.19)	0.059 (1.67)	...	0.136 (1.78)	...	.29	3.04	1.62
4'd	- 0.287 (0.73)	0.101 (1.16)	- 0.131 (4.24)	...	0.081 (2.38)	...	0.109 (1.59)	...	.37	2.86	2.03
5'd	- 0.345 (0.84)	0.144 (1.64)	...	- 0.124 (3.53)	0.058 (1.69)	0.171 (2.42)	...	...	.32	2.97	1.54
6'd	- 0.331 (0.85)	0.099 (1.16)	- 0.134 (4.39)	...	0.081 (2.42)	0.128 (2.04)	...	...	0.39	2.82	1.69

131

The fits of the equations show that the hypothesis performs better when the "troubled" years 1974 and 1975 are taken into consideration. The R^2's are somewhat lower over the 1962-I-1973-IV sample period. Over the extended period, about 50 percent of the variance of output growth (or the deviation of output growth from its steady state value) is explained. The relatively large influence of import prices on the variance of output after the "oil crisis" is, in all likelihood, responsible for the improvement of the fits.

At any rate, even if the R^2's are not very high in absolute value, they are very satisfactory in terms of the hypothesis. After all, in the short run, crops fail, strikes occur, the "economic mood" changes, etc. It is obvious that the hypothesis does not, and cannot, try to capture these short-run influences on output growth.

What is important to notice is that the coefficients of $\hat{y}_1^*$ and $\hat{y}_2^*$ are never significantly different from 1, a result that corroborates the "natural" rate of growth hypothesis. Furthermore, when the constant term replaces $\hat{y}_1^*$ or $\hat{y}_2^*$ (regressions 1c, 2c of Table 9 and 1'c, 2'c of Table 11), its coefficient takes up a value very close to the mean of the rate of growth of output (6.04 percent from 1962-I-1973-IV and 5.11 percent from 1962-I-1975-IV). This outcome suggests again that, over the long run, output grows at a rate not significantly affected by the impulse forces (from which monetary and fiscal policies could be especially isolated).

However, the significance of the other coefficients shows that output may temporarily deviate from this trend rate of growth under the influence of the impulse forces.

Changes in the foreign price impulse were not found to be significant over the 1962-I-1973-IV sample period. For this reason, the $\Delta\hat{PM}_{-i}$'s are included only in Table 11. This table demonstrates that accelerations (or decelerations) of import prices negatively affect the rate of growth of output after a period of three to four quarters. This impact was very strong in 1974 and especially so in 1975. The coefficients and the values of $\Delta\hat{PM}$ in 1974 (around 50 throughout the year) imply, approximately, that the oil shock is responsible for a drop in output growth of about 5-6 percent in 1975.

The change in the foreign quantity impulse is significant when it is lagged three quarters. The loss of exports during the economic crisis cannot, however, explain more than 1 percent of the output growth drop in the 1974-75 period.

Changes in the fiscal impulse appear to exert a significant effect upon the deviation of output from its long-run value. The impact starts being felt during the current period, but its peak influence occurs after two quarters and disappears in the third quarter (ΔFI_{-3} is never significant).

$\Delta\hat{M}_{-3}$ and $\Delta\hat{M}_{-4}$ are significant over the 1962-I-1973-IV sample period. Yet, the significance of the monetary impulse is more dubious when the last two years are taken into consideration. The results, however, appear to imply that over "normal" periods accelerations (decelerations) of the money stock influence output growth after about three quarters; the peak effect seems to occur about four quarters later. Finally, the impact disappears after about twelve to fifteen months.

In order to evaluate further the role of the impulses in explaining output fluctuations, Table 12 ascertains the influence of the quarterly changes in each impulse on the quarterly change of output growth. Now, 'the tests try to explain the acceleration of the rate of growth of the economy rather than its deviation from its steady state value. In other words, it evaluates to what extent the four stimuli influence output growth, irrespective of the initial position of the economy.[23]

As was the case previously, changes in import prices are only significant over the extended sample period, with a lag of four quarters. The influence of the foreign quantity impulse is felt after three quarters. It would appear, therefore, that it takes between nine and twelve months before any change in the foreign stimuli affects output growth changes.

The monetary and fiscal impulses act more quickly on the economy. Changes in the fiscal force exert significant positive influence on the acceleration of output during the current period. Accelerations (decelerations) of the money stock take one quarter to accelerate (decelerate) output (remember that the same variable exerts a significant impact on the inflation rate only after two to three quarters).

Let me summarize the main results of this section.

Only accelerations (decelerations) of the money stock, of the discretionary budget deficit with respect to income, of exports and of import prices seem to affect the rate of growth of the economy. However, this effect is only transitory; in the long run, output grows at its "natural" rate, determined by the rate of growth of the labor force and of capital, by technological innovations, etc.

Output seems to accelerate (decelerate) after one quarter whenever the money stock accelerates (decelerates), whereas the inflation rate is affected only

---

[23]From the hypothesis $\hat{y} = f(I - I^*) + \hat{y}^*$, it follows (if the f function is assumed to be linear) that $\partial\hat{y} = f(\partial I) - f(\partial I^*) + \partial\hat{y}^*$. As the variance of $\hat{y}^*$ and of I^* may be expected to be dominated by the variances of $\hat{y}$ and I, respectively, it follows that the variance of $\hat{y}$ should essentially depend on the variance of I. Hence, the tests are made of $\partial\hat{y}$ against ∂I, where ∂ represents the change from one quarter to the next.

Table 12

Acceleration of Output Growth and Impulses
(Quarterly data, 1962-I-1973-IV)

Acceleration of output growth ($\partial \hat{y}$)	Intercept	$\partial \hat{M}_{-1}$	$\partial \hat{RX}_{-3}$	∂FI	R^2	S.E.	DW
1 e	0.029 (0.06)	0.383 (1.70)	0.096 (2.09)	0.366 (3.22)	0.38	3.09	2.42
					...	...	...

(Quarterly data, 1962-I-1975-IV)

Acceleration of output growth ($\partial \hat{y}$)	Intercept	$\partial \hat{M}_{-1}$	$\partial \hat{PM}_{-4}$	$\partial \hat{RX}_{-3}$	∂FI	R^2	S.E.	DW
1'e	- 0.039 (0.10)	0.366 (1.84)	- 0.167 (2.26)	0.091 (2.26)	0.388 (4.34)	0.44	2.91	2.35
						...	...	...

Note: ∂ = change from one quarter to the next quarter.

134

after two to three quarters. Yet, over "normal" periods, yearly changes in the rate of growth of money appear to influence the deviations of output from its steady state value after three to four quarters and then to disappear.

Changes in the fiscal impulse exert a significant and fast (during the same period) influence on the accelerations of output. It is, however, after two quarters that yearly changes in FI appear to have their strongest impact on the deviations of output from its long-term value. Then, the influence of fiscal policy washes out.

Changes in output growth seem to be affected by changes in the two foreign stimuli after about nine to twelve months. Deviations of output growth from its steady state value depend also on the yearly changes of these impulses after about the same length of time. Though the dramatic increase in import prices had a strong influence on output and can be considered to be the main cause of the 1974-75 recession, import prices, nevertheless, do not seem to have a significant impact on the rate of growth of the economy during "normal" periods.

B. Output Growth and Impulses: Nonparametric and Dominance Tests

In order to probe the hypothesis further, a test is made of the significance of a positive association between the direction of output growth deviation from its steady state value and the direction of the four impulse forces. Again the ∇ p-statistic is used. Table 13 shows the results of this nonparametric test.

The 3x3 contingency tables necessary to build Table 13 were constructed by comparing the signs of the normalized values of $\hat{y} - \hat{y}_1^*$ with the signs of the normalized values of the yearly change of each stimulus lagged to four quarters. A zero change in the variables was assigned when the magnitude of the standardized variable did not exceed 0.10 in absolute value. In order to maintain the analysis of a positive association between impulse movements and economic activity, the foreign price impulse measure is represented by the change in import prices multiplied by -1.

Table 13 presents the trace, the ∇ p-statistic, and the normalized ∇p over two different sample periods. The values on the left-hand side for each are obtained by using the 1962-I-1973-IV period, whereas the right-hand-side values result from adding the quarterly observations for the years 1974 and 1975 to the preceding period.

The monetary impulse, with lags of three and four quarters, exhibits the highest and most significant ∇p-statistic.

The fiscal impulse, with lags of one and two quarters, is also significant, but less so than the previous stimulus. The foreign price impulse, with a two-quarter lag is significant at the 5-percent level, but only when the years 1974 and

135

Table 13

Deviation of Output Growth from Its Long-run Value $(\hat{y} - \hat{y}_1^*)$
(Normalized values)

Impulses		Trace/N		∇p		Normalized ∇p	
Monetary	$\Delta\hat{M}_{-1}$	23/48	27/56	0.10	0.15	0.79	1.35
impulse	$\Delta\hat{M}_{-2}$	23/48	26/56	0.17	0.13	1.42	1.13
	$\Delta\hat{M}_{-3}$	28/48	33/56	0.35	0.34	3.80	3.91
	$\Delta\hat{M}_{-4}$	25/48	30/56	0.23	0.25	2.11	2.53
Foreign price	$-\Delta\hat{PM}$	16/48	21/56	-0.11	-0.07	...	...
impulse	$-\Delta\hat{PM}_{-1}$	18/48	24/56	$-.04$	.00	...	0.00
	$-\Delta\hat{PM}_{-2}$	22/48	29/56	.11	.18	0.88	1.68
	$-\Delta\hat{PM}_{-3}$	20/48	28/56	.04	.15	0.29	1.35
	$-\Delta\hat{PM}_{-4}$	20/48	27/56	0.04	0.12	0.30	1.04
Foreign quantity	$\Delta\hat{RX}$	25/48	31/56	0.19	0.23	1.65	2.30
impulse	$\Delta\hat{RX}_{-1}$	21/48	26/56	.05	.07	0.37	0.58
	$\Delta\hat{RX}_{-2}$	22/48	26/56	.09	.07	0.69	0.57
	$\Delta\hat{RX}_{-3}$	23/48	27/56	.13	.10	1.05	0.84
	$\Delta\hat{RX}_{-4}$	18/48	21/56	-0.07	-0.09	...	...
Fiscal	ΔFI	23/48	26/56	0.16	0.11	1.33	0.93
impulse	ΔFI_{-1}	25/48	27/56	0.24	0.16	2.22	1.45
	ΔFI_{-2}	26/48	29/56	0.25	0.19	2.36	1.78
	ΔFI_{-3}	24/48	27/56	0.18	0.15	1.53	1.34
	ΔFI_{-4}	14/48	17/56	-0.18	-0.21	...	...

Note: N   =   number of observations

$\hat{y}_1^*$ =   two-year moving average of $\hat{y}$, lagged one period.

Critical values of the ∇p-statistic at the
      10-percent level: 1.30
      5-percent level: 1.67
      1-percent level: 2.39.

1975 are taken into consideration, an obvious consequence of the oil price shock. Even if the foreign quantity impulse exhibits high enough normalized ∇ p-values when no lags are involved, this outcome must not be taken at face value. It may be only a statistical artifact resulting from the national income identity (since no lags are involved).

Table 13 suggests that accelerations or decelerations of the money stock have been a major cause of economic fluctuations. Changes in fiscal policy also appear to have had an important and more rapid influence on these fluctuations. The role of the foreign sector is, however, more dubious, except to explain the 1974-75 recession.

Compared to the econometric analysis, this nonparametric test gives somewhat different indications as to the influence of each impulse on the deviation of output growth from its steady state value. The difference may result from the fact that the parametric tests assume a linear relationship between the dependent and independent variables, whereas the nonparametric test does not require such an assumption. Furthermore, the latter test is not plagued by the multicollinearity problem that cannot be completely eliminated from the regression analysis. Hence, it would appear that, at least for evaluating the possible dominance of one or several impulses, the nonparametric analysis is to be preferred. More work on this subject deserves to be done.

VI. CONCLUSION

The objective of this paper was to conduct empirical tests of the dominant impulse hypothesis of inflation and output growth within the French context. It evaluates the extent to which four systematic stimuli (fiscal, monetary, foreign price, and foreign quantity impulses) may shape both of these economic phenomena. Tests seeking to evaluate the so-called cost-push theory of the inflation problem were also made.

The hypothesis of inflation given here was shown to be significantly more robust than the cost-push view. Evidence was found that inflationary expectations offer a reliable explanation of the trend rate of inflation, and that excess-demand variables explain deviations of inflation from its trend rate. Furthermore, a variety of tests show that the monetary impulse dominates the other systematic stimuli in shaping the inflation phenomenon. The latter impulses appear to have a marginal effect only, except for the foreign price stimulus which explains about 4 percent of the sharp acceleration of the rate of growth of prices in 1974 and 1975. It can, therefore, be inferred that, in general, French inflation can best be explained as a monetary phenomenon.

The study also shows that, over the short run, output growth may deviate from its steady state value whenever there is an acceleration (deceleration) of the money stock, of the level of the discretionary budget deficit with respect to income, and of the levels of real exports and of import prices. But these influences are only temporary. Output goes back to its steady state growth path after a period, at the maximum, of about twelve to fifteen months. Over "normal" periods, it would appear that the fiscal and monetary impulses dominate the fluctuations of output around its "natural" value. The role of the two foreign stimuli is only significant at the margin, except for the 1974-75 recession that can readily be explained by the "oil crisis."

Note also that the fiscal impulse has a quicker, and probably more significant, effect on the economy than the monetary one. Yet, the influence of the former stimulus upon the deviation of output growth from its steady state value disappears after about two quarters, whereas the impact of the latter takes about twelve months to vanish.

Over "normal" periods, the study corroborates the "monetarist" contention that it is not the growth rate but accelerations (or decelerations) in the growth rate of the money stock that affect real economic magnitudes, particularly output and, hence, unemployment. Another monetarist hypothesis emerges from the analysis: accelerations (decelerations) of the money stock affect, first, output, then, prices. From the empirical analysis, it appears that quarterly changes in the rates of growth of the money stock induce parallel changes in the rate of growth of output, from one quarter to the next, with a lag of about one quarter, whereas they significantly affect the inflation rate only after six to nine months.

Finally, I note that empirical studies seeking to establish international comparisons on the inflation problem generally seem to have difficulties with the French economy (see, for example, Cross and Laidler, 1974, and Perry, 1975). Not only the French people but also the French economy are seen to conform to their image of the legendary individualistic Gallic spirit! Even though this study does not, of course, pretend to be the final word on inflation and output growth in France, it seems to have made significant progress in destroying this apparent idiosyncrasy.

References

Barro, R. (1977), "Unanticipated Money Growth and Unemployment in the United States," American Economic Review, 67: 101-15.

Barro, R., and Fischer, S. (1976), "Recent Developments in Monetary Theory," Journal of Monetary Economics, 2: 133-67.

Bronfenbrenner, M., and Holzman, F.D. (1963), "Survey of Inflation Theory," American Economic Review, 53: 593-661.

Brunner, K., Fratianni, M., Jordan, J.L., Meltzer, A.H., and Neumann, M.J.M. (1973), "Fiscal and Monetary Policies in Moderate Inflation: Case Studies of Three Countries," Journal of Money, Credit and Banking, 5(2): 313-53.

Brunner, K., and Meltzer, A.H. (1976a), "An Aggregative Theory for a Closed Economy," in Monetarism, ed. J. Stein. Amsterdam: North-Holland.

_____(1976b), "Monetary and Fiscal Policy in Open, Interdependent Economies with Fixed Exchange Rates," in Recent Issues in International Monetary Economics, ed. E. Claassen and P. Salin. Amsterdam: North-Holland.

Cross, R., and Laidler, D. (1974), "Inflation, Excess Demand and Expectations in Fixed Exchange Rate Open Economies: Some Preliminary Empirical Results." Paper read at the Catholic University of Louvain Conference on Bank Credit, Money and Inflation in Open Economies, September 1974.

Fitoussi, J.-P. (1973). Inflation, Equilibre et Chômage. Paris: Cujas.

Fourcans, A. (1975), "Interest Rate and Bank Credit in France: A Theoretical and Empirical Analysis," in European Finance Association, 1974 Proceedings. Amsterdam: North-Holland.

_____ (1976). La Politique de la Monnaie. Paris: Economica.

_____ (forthcoming), "The Impact of Monetary and Fiscal Policies on the French Financial System," Journal of Monetary Economics.

139

Fourcans, A., and Fratianni, M. (1976), "Cost-push versus Excess Demand Explanations of Inflation in France," in European Finance Association, 1975 Proceedings. Amsterdam: North-Holland.

Fratianni, M. (1974), "A Critical Look at Major Inflation Theories," Tijdschrift voor Economie, 3: 281-301.

Hansen, B. (1969). Fiscal Policy in Seven Countries, 1955-65: Belgium, France, Germany, Italy, Sweden, United Kingdom, United States. Paris: OECD.

Hildebrand, D.K., Laing, J.D., and Rosenthal, H.L. (1974), "Prediction Logic: A Method for Empirical Evaluation of Formal Theory," Journal of Mathematical Sociology, 3: 163-85.

Johnson, Harry G. (1967), "A Survey of Theories of Inflation," in Essays in Monetary Economics. London: George Allen and Unwin.

Korteweg, P. (1975), "Inflation and Economic Activity: The Dutch Experience, 1953-1973." Paper read at the Helsinki Conference on the Monetary Mechanism in Open Economies, August 1975.

Laidler, D., and Parkin, M. (1975), "Inflation: A Survey," Economic Journal, 85: 741-809.

Lucas, R.J., Jr. (1973), "Some International Evidence on Output-Inflation Tradeoffs," American Economic Review, 63: 326-34.

Melitz, J. (1976), "A General Model of Money Stock Determination and a Special Econometric Application to France," working paper, INSEE.

Perry, G. (1975), "Determinants of Wage Inflation around the World," Brookings Papers on Economic Activity, 2. Washington, D.C.: The Brookings Institution.

INFLATION AND UNANTICIPATED CHANGES IN OUTPUT IN ITALY

Michele Fratianni[*]

Catholic University of Louvain

and

Commission of the European Communities, Brussels

I. <u>INTRODUCTION</u>

This paper investigates the causes of inflation and of the unanticipated changes in output in Italy during the period 1952-75.

The basic research strategy will be to test three hypotheses of inflation against a common data set. The three hypotheses are the quantity theory, the monetarist theory in an open economy, and the dominant impulse hypothesis. The last of these three hypotheses purports to explain the widest range of phenomena and to generate, with suitable constraints, typically monetary explanations of inflation.

The underlying theoretical justification for each of the three hypotheses has been less than fully developed in this paper, given that the reader can easily consult existing surveys in this field (Bronfenbrenner and Holzman, 1963; Johnson, 1963; Brunner, et al., 1973; Brunner, 1973; Fratianni, 1974; Laidler and Parkin, 1975; R.J. Gordon, 1976; and Barro and Fischer, 1976), or the works cited in the text.

It must be stated at the outset that I had no interest in considering explanations of inflation which could not be reduced to a coherent and empirically testable model of demand for and supply of output. As an example, consider the frustration "theory" of inflation. How should one interpret frustration? At the level of the individual consumer, it will be safe to say that frustration results from the impossibility of moving to an indifference curve which is higher than the one that is tangent to the resource constraint. In this sense, we are all frustrated, and the statement has no empirical content. But suppose, for sake of argument, that we were to overlook the conceptual problem, how could we then measure frustration? How could we interpret the cyclical movement of inflation? By a cyclical theory of frustration, with 1973-75 being particularly frustrating years relative to the 1960s?

[*] The views expressed are my own and not necessarily those of the Commission. I want to thank Pieter Korteweg with whom I have had long discussions about both the general strategy and the methodological approach of the paper. I am also grateful to Eduard Bomhoff for his help on the Box and Jenkins computer program; Vittorio Basano for assistance with data gathering and computations; and Herbert Christie for editorial suggestions.

Figure 1 Consumption Price Deflator--Industrial Output

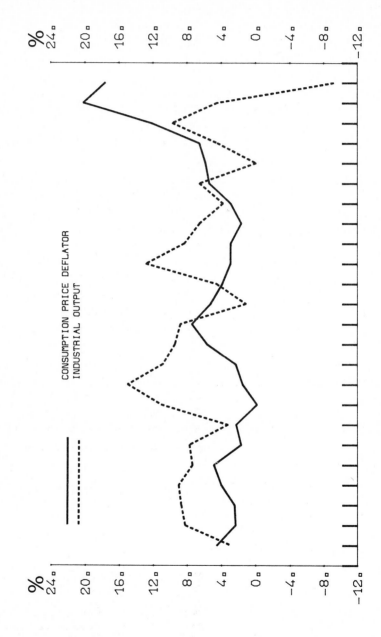

A second example of this type of reasoning, with considerably more sophistication however, is provided by the proposition that sustained increases in the general price level result from the market power of large monopolistic firms which have complete control over price determination. There are two basic arguments against such a view of the world. First, prices are determined jointly by both demand and supply schedules and not by supply forces alone. Second, the ability of a large monopolistic firm to set a price can explain at best changes in relative prices but not a continued increase in the general price level. To explain the rate of inflation of the recent past, one would have to entertain seriously the empirical proposition that accelerations of inflation are accompanied by a larger degree of monopolization in the economy and decelerations of inflation by demonopolization; cf. Brunner (1973). Given the speed with which both accelerations and decelerations of inflation have occurred, the above-mentioned thesis is self-evidently discredited by the facts.

Italian rates of inflation and output growth are illustrated in Figure 1. The former, measured by the percentage change in the personal consumption deflator, goes from 4.5 in 1952 to -0.18 in 1959, rises again to a high of 7.4 in 1963, gradually falls in the midsixties to reach a low of 1.63 in 1968. The last upswing in the time series lasts six years with the peak occurring in 1974 with a value of 20.2. In sum, the sample period encompasses two complete cycles of accelerations and decelerations in the rate of inflation. The growth rate of output, measured by the percentage change in the index of industrial production, displays a much more erratic pattern than does the rate of inflation, as evidenced by the frequent alternations of upswings and downswings, and the observation that the biggest deviation in the time series is equal to 24 percentage points.

The organization of the paper is as follows. The theory is discussed in Section II; the data and measurement procedures in Section III; the tests and findings bearing on the three hypotheses in Section IV; summary and conclusions in Section V.

II. HYPOTHESES TO BE TESTED

A. The Quantity Theory

The oldest explanation of inflation comes from quantity theory according to which a sustained increase in the general price level results from a sustained increase in the stock of money relative to output; see, for example, Schwartz (1973). Denoting with ^ above a variable relative first differences, a test of the original quantity theory is given by

(1) $\hat{P} = a + b(\hat{M} - \hat{y}) + \epsilon$,

where P = domestic price level
        M = money stock
        y = output
        ϵ = error term.

A strict application of quantity theory requires that "b" approach unity and that "a," a measure of the average percentage change in velocity, be zero. A nonzero value of "a" implies that velocity behaves independently of the expected cost of holding real cash balances. However, if the rate of return on money is zero, the expected cost of holding cash balances is the expected inflation rate; with the rate of return on money below a competitive market equilibrium, the expected cost of holding cash balances is a fraction of the expected inflation rate, the size of the fraction depending on how low relative to market equilibrium the rate of return on money has been set by a monopoly bank or by a successful cartel agreement. This is essentially the nature of the so-called South American version of the quantity theory tested by Harberger (1963) and, more recently, by Vogel (1974). The version of the quantity theory set out in (1) may be modified by introducing a variable C which captures the above-mentioned expected cost of holding cash balances:

(2) $\hat{P} = a + b(\hat{M} - \hat{y}) + d\hat{C} + \epsilon'$.

A criticism which can be directed at both (1) and (2) is that the money stock in an open economy under fixed exchange rates is not under the control of the monetary authorities. With highly interdependent national credit and money markets, any attempt by the central bank to alter the domestic component of the money stock provokes, through the ensuing fall in domestic interest rates, a net outflow of capital, with the net result that the money stock in the end does not change. This is the essence of much of the offsetting capital flows theory. Kouri and Porter (1974), who developed a three-asset-market model to test the degree to which changes in the domestic and policy-controlled domestic money stock are offset by opposite changes in the foreign component of the money stock, found "offset coefficients" significantly below unity for a variety of countries. For Italy the offset coefficient was estimated at -0.43.

144

Tullio (1977), in an application of the monetary theory to the balance of payments, finds that the average offset coefficient for Italy during the 1950-73 period was -0.50, using as a left-hand-side variable net capital flows, and -0.70, using net official reserves.[1] All of this points to the basic fact that, although Italy is an open economy with a high degree of capital market integration, monetary policy was never completely emasculated during the period of fixed exchange rates. Policymakers must take into account, however, that the open economy prevents there being a one-to-one correspondence--apart from the behavior of the money multiplier--between the domestic component of the money stock and the total money stock. So long as the leakage is predictable and different from unity, the monetary authorities can strive for a given stock of money by appropriately altering the domestic component of money.

B. Dominant Impulse and Monetarist Hypotheses

I now turn to a class of hypotheses which can be conveniently grouped under the general category of dominant impulses. This class of hypotheses was explored in a preliminary way by Brunner, et al. (1973) for Germany, Italy, and the U.S., and further developed by Korteweg (1975) for the Netherlands, by Fourcans and Fratianni (1976) for France, and by Hamburger and Reisch (1976) for Germany, the Netherlands, the U.K., and the U.S. The theoretical justification underlying the dominant impulse hypothesis can be found in many of the works by Brunner (see, for example, Brunner, 1971), by Brunner and Meltzer (for example, Brunner and Meltzer, 1976), and by Stein (1976). Here I shall briefly sketch the three principal building blocks on which I think the theory was built.

The first component of the dominant impulse hypothesis is that changes in inflation and output are proximately determined by an excess demand for output augmented by inflationary expectations.

The second element in the hypothesis explicitly recognizes that the ultimate determinants of excess demand are systematic impulses rather than random shocks. Systematic impulses, in turn, are classified as either real or financial in nature. A change in the anticipated yield on real assets (the so-called Wicksell-Keynes effect) is a real impulse; other real impulses are changes in government expenditures and taxes, changes in output absorbed by the rest of the world, and inflation abroad. Financial impulses are created (destroyed) by, among other things, government budget deficits (surpluses) and balance of payments surpluses (deficits). Changes in financial impulses are not independent

---

[1]Tullio's estimate of net reserve flows was obtained by regressing changes in reserves on domestic assets of the central bank, changes in the Italian consumer price index, permanent real income, and a long-term interest rate.

of changes in real impulses. For example, an autonomous increase in exports represents a change in a real impulse, but it also increases the monetary base and ultimately the stock of money through a higher balance of payments surplus or a smaller deficit.

Finally, and this is where the dominant impulse hypothesis generates typically monetarist implications, financial impulses dominate real impulses. This is a matter of considerable contention between Keynesians and monetarists. Keynesians analyze the private sector of the economy as if it were shocked by a sequence of unpredictable exogenous events, most of them attributable to changes in the marginal efficiency of investment. Monetarists, on the contrary, view the private sector as inherently stable, while pointing out that the source of the instability resides with the erratic behavior of the fiscal and monetary authorities. The stability of the private sector and of the demand for money has led monetarists to recommend a growth rate of the money stock which is approximately equal to the long-run output growth of the economy. Keynesians justify countercyclical policies by pointing to evidence that both velocity and the private sector are unstable. In addition, monetarists contend that there is no long-run trade-off between inflation and unemployment which, in turn, implies that current inflation has a unit elasticity with respect to expected inflation.

There are several degrees of corroboration of the dominant impulse hypothesis. There can be, for example, substantial evidence in favor of the first proposition, namely, that excess demand with inflationary expectations is the proximate determinant of inflation, and only inconclusive evidence with respect to propositions two and three. The conclusion to be drawn is that inflation responds to market forces but not to systematic impulses. Thus, an expectations-augmented excess demand view of the world should not be equated with the monetarist position: the latter implies the former but not vice versa.

A higher degree of corroboration is obtained when a set of systematic impulses is isolated from a potentially infinite number of random shocks which might cause sustained increases in the general price level. Finally, the highest degree of corroboration of the hypothesis requires that the monetary impulse dwarf all other systematic impulses.

Far from being open-ended statements, monetarist implications are very demanding of the hypothesis in the sense that they hold only if a specific set of propositions also holds. Needless to say, monetarist implications also run the risk of being easily disconfirmed. This is the inherent risk implied by a tightly constrained hypothesis.

To formalize the discussion, I begin with the monetarist model discussed by Barro and Fischer (1976), suitably extended to an open economy under fixed rates of exchange:

(3) $y^s = y_n + a_1 (P - \bar{P}) + u^s$

(4) $y^d = \beta_1 (M - \bar{P}) + \beta_2 (P^* - P) + u^d$,

where y^s = supply of output

  P = the domestic price level

  y^d = demand for output

  y_n = normal or anticipated output

  P^* = foreign price level in foreign currency

  u^s, u^d are random terms with zero mean and a constant variance

  $-$ over the variable denotes the expectation formed at time period t of the variable which will prevail next period

  $*$ refers to a rest-of-the-world variable.

All symbols denote the logarithms of the variables, and time subscripts have been ignored to keep notation to a minimum.

Equation (3) is the Lucas (1973) and Sargent (1973) aggregate supply function which states that deviation of the current supply of output from an anticipated or normal output depends on the discrepancy between current and expected prices as well as on random shifts impounded in u^s.

If term $\beta_2 (P^* - P)$ is ignored for the moment, aggregate demand (4) is nothing but (1) with the constant term (the average change in velocity) set equal to zero. The second term on the right-hand side of (4) captures the choice consumers have to buy either domestic or foreign output. The law of one price does not hold at every point in time.

The solution for the logarithm of the price level is obtained by equating (3) to (4); that is,

(5) $P = \dfrac{1}{a_1 + \beta_2} [-y_n + (a_1 - \beta_1) \bar{P} + \beta_1 M + \beta_2 P^* + u]$,

where $u \equiv u^d - u^s$.

The coefficient of the money stock can be either larger or smaller than unity depending on $\beta_1 \gtrless a_1 + \beta_2$; that of the foreign price level is between zero and one; while that of the expected price level is indeterminate. Two opposing forces are present in the effect of $\bar{P}$ on P: the cost-push term a_1, and the demand-pull term β_1. Finally, it must be noted that the sum of the money and price coefficients is equal to one.

At this point the model must be completed by specifying an hypothesis about the formation of expectations. The latter are postulated to be rational in the Muth (1961) sense; $\bar{P}$ is equal to the expected value of P in the next period. Taking the mathematical expectation on both sides of (5), the solution for $\bar{P}$ is

$$(6) \quad \bar{P} = \frac{1}{\beta_1 + \beta_2} (-y_n + \beta_1 \bar{M} + \beta_2 \bar{P}^*) ,$$

where $\bar{M}$ and $\bar{P}^*$ denote the expected values of the money stock and the foreign price level, respectively. Unlike the Barro-Fischer model of a closed economy, money here is not neutral so long as $\bar{P} \neq \bar{P}^*$. Only when the law of one price holds does money have its characteristic of neutrality.

The solution for output is obtained by replacing $P - \bar{P}$ with its determinants:

$$(7) \quad P - \bar{P} = \frac{1}{a_1 + \beta_2} [\beta_1 (M - \bar{M}) + \beta_2 (P^* - \bar{P}^*) + u] ,$$

and

$$(8) \quad y - y_n = \frac{a_1}{a_1 + \beta_2} [\beta_1 (M - \bar{M}) + \beta_2 (P^* - \bar{P}^*) + u] + u^s .$$

Deviations of output from its normal rate occur so long as the current money stock and the foreign price level deviate from their expected values (apart from the random terms u^d and u^s). To summarize briefly, the expected values of M and P^*, as well as normal output, drive the expected domestic price level which, in turn, affects the current price level with a unit coefficient. The unexpected portion of M and P^*, apart from the random terms, explains deviations of the current price level from its expected level and, thus, deviations of y from y_n.

The foreign price level can be made endogenous by treating the rest of the world as a closed economy on the assumption that the incidence of the Italian economy in the world is so small that it may be ignored. The relevant output supply and demand functions are

$$(9) \quad y^{*s} = y_n^* + a_1^* \ (P^* - \bar{P}^*) + u^{*s}$$

$$(10) \quad y^{*d} = \beta_1^* \ (M^* - \bar{P}^*) + u^{*d} .$$

The solutions for the current and expected foreign price level are

$$(11) \quad P^* = \frac{1}{a_1^*} \ [-y_n^* + \beta_1^* M^* + (a_1^* - \beta_1^*) \bar{P}^* + u^*] ,$$

and

$$(12) \quad \bar{P}^* = \bar{M}^* - \frac{y_n^*}{\beta_1^*} .$$

Replacing $\bar{P}^*$ by the right-hand side of (12) in (6), the expected domestic price level can be expressed in terms of the normal rate of output and the expected money stock at home and abroad.

According to (4), aggregate demand depends on only two exogenous impulses, namely, the domestic money stock and the foreign price level. To discriminate between a monetarist and a nonmonetarist position along the lines suggested above, it is imperative that other impulses be allowed to influence aggregate demand. I select two which, I think, are of particular importance: the fiscal impulse and real income of the rest of the world.

The study by Friedman and Meiselman (1963) for the Commission on Money and Credit and the ensuing literature bearing on the relative importance of monetary and fiscal actions as determinants of nominal economic activity make it necessary to expand the previous monetarist model to accommodate the role of fiscal policy. Foreign real income is instead taken to be, together with the relative price $P^* - P$, the basic force in determining how much of the domestic output is demanded by the rest of the world. Denoting with F the real fiscal variable, equation (4) thus becomes

$$(13) \quad y^d = \beta_1 (M - \bar{P}) + \beta_2 (P^* - P) + \beta_3 F + \beta_4 y^* + u'^d .$$

The counterparts of equations (5) - (8) are

$$(14) \quad P = \frac{1}{a_1 + \beta_2} [-y_n + (a_1 - \beta_1) \bar{P} + \beta_1 M + \beta_2 P^* + \beta_3 F + \beta_4 y^* + u'] ,$$

where $u' \equiv u'^d - u^s$;

$$(15) \quad \bar{P} = \frac{1}{\beta_1 + \beta_2} (-y_n + \beta_1 \bar{M} + \beta_2 \bar{P}^* + \beta_3 \bar{F} + \beta_4 y_n^*)$$

$$(16) \quad P - \bar{P} = \frac{1}{a_1 + \beta_2} [\beta_1 (M - \bar{M}) + \beta_2 (P^* - \bar{P}^*) + \beta_3 (F - \bar{F}) + \beta_4 (y^* - y_n^*) + u']$$

$$(17) \quad y - y_n = a_1 [\text{right-hand side of (16)}] + u^s.$$

III. THE DATA

According to the theory presented in Section II, four impulses can potentially cause an excess demand in the goods market and, thus, be ultimately responsible for inflation and unexpected changes in output. To repeat, the impulses in question are the fiscal $(\hat{F})$, monetary $(\hat{M})$, foreign quantity $(\hat{y}^*$ or $\hat{W}X)$, and foreign price $(\hat{P}^*$ or $\hat{P}M)$ impulses. I shall now develop empirical counterparts to these theoretical concepts. The variables used in the empirical work appear in Table 1.

A. The Fiscal Impulse

The fiscal impulse is defined as the theoretical equivalent of Hansen's (1969) discretionary impact of fiscal policy, namely, the total thrust of the government budget net of its induced or feedback effects. More concisely, $\tilde{F}$ is given by

150

Table 1

Data Measurement and Sources

P   =   consumption price deflator[a,b]

y   industrial production[c]

RGDP   gross domestic product at 1970 prices[a,b]

M   broad measure of the money stock = currency, bank demand and time deposits, post office demand and time deposits; quarterly averages[d]

i   yield on bonds issued by Istituti di Credito Mobiliare; monthly averages[d]

P^* $(P_W - H_I DP_I) / (1-H_I)$ = dollar-denominated price level of the rest of the world (i.e., 23 OECD countries),

      where P_W = $\sum_{i=1}^{24} H_i DP_i$ = average CPI in the 24 OECD countries

               H_i $RDG_i \sum_{i=1}^{24} RDG_i$ = weighting scheme based on real GDP converted to 1970 dollars

               H_I weight of Italy

               DP_i $(P_i/CF) CF_{1970}$ = CPI of country i expressed in dollars

               CF   currency i - dollar exchange rate

               CF_{1970} =   currency i - dollar exchange rate in 1970[e]

PM   import price deflator[a,b]

y^* rest-of-the-world output measured as the sum of the GDP at constant prices of the other 23 OECD countries; the series is converted into dollars at 1970 exchange rates.[e] See text for more details.

WX   dollar value of exports of the other 23 OECD countries deflated by P^* [e]

$\hat{F}$ fiscal impulse measured by the annual lire change of discretionary government expenditures minus discretionary tax revenues as a proportion of nominal GDP.[a,b] See text for more details.

M^* =   rest-of-the-world money stock; it is equal to the sum of the money stock M1, expressed in dollars, of the other 23 OECD countries.[e]

Sources:

[a]ISCO, Quadri della Contabilità Nazionale Italiana, Schema SEC, dati fino al 1975, Roma, 1976.

[b]Siesto, V. (1975), "I Conti Economici dell'Italia dal 1954 al 1974 secondo il nuovo schema internazionale," Economia del lavoro, 2/1975, Ceres (Centro di ricerche economiche e sociali).

[c]Istat, Bollettino Mensile di Statistica, various issues.

[d]Banca d'Italia, Bollettino, various issues.

[e]IMF, International Financial Statistics, various issues.

(18) $\hat{F} = (\Delta G_a - \Delta T_a) / GDP_{-1}$

(18a) $\Delta G_a = \Delta GC - (WLG_{-1}) \dfrac{\Delta W_{LG}}{W_{LG_{-1}}} + \Delta GIP_{-1} + \Delta GI$

(18b) $T_a = T - TDIR_{-1}$ [growth rate of nominal national income]

$\qquad - TIND_{-1}$ [growth rate of personal consumption]

$\qquad - CS_{-1}$ [growth rate of wage income],

where G   = total government expenditures
GC = government expenditures on goods and services
WLG = (LG) (W_{LG}) = expenditures on labor by government with LG denoting units and W_{LG} the wage rate
GDP = gross domestic product at current prices
GIP = government interest payment
GI   = government expenditures on capital equipment
T   = total taxes net of all transfers
TDIR = direct (income) taxes
TIND = indirect (sales) taxes
CS   = social security taxes
a   = subscript denoting discretionary effect.

Discretionary changes in government expenditures are the sum of a) changes in government labor expenditures due only to increases or decreases in labor units, on the assumption that wage rates paid by government adjust to those paid by the private sector; b) current changes in other expenditures on goods and services including capital equipment, on the assumption that the government has full control over such expenditures; and c) changes in interest payments lagged one period, where the lag is introduced to eliminate the effect of changes in interest rates on interest payments brought about by deficit financing or open market operations. Discretionary tax changes are obtained by subtracting the automatic effect of the three major components of taxes from changes in total taxes net of transfers.

It should be pointed out that this measure of discretionary fiscal policy is not equivalent to Hansen's corresponding variable. In Hansen (1969), the discretionary thrust is given by the algebraic sum of the multipliers of national income with respect to government expenditures and tax rates, using a Keynesian model of aggregate demand for output. $\hat{F}$, on the contrary, is independent of the model or models which might be adopted.

B. The Monetary Impulse

The monetary impulse is defined as the annual percentage change of a broad measure of the money stock, namely, currency, bank demand and time deposits, post-office demand and time deposits owned by the public. There is a relatively complex process underlying the formation of the money stock which is not strictly relevant here. One need only say that the growth of the money stock reflects the thrust applied by monetary policy and the joint interaction of the public and the banks in the bank credit and money markets; for more details, see Fratianni (1976). The monetary impulse absorbs the effects emanating from budget deficits, balance of payments imbalances, and changes in the composition of government debt. It follows that a monetary impulse is not totally independent of the fiscal and foreign impulses.

C. The Foreign Impulses

Two different types of foreign impulses were identified in Section II, namely, changes in foreign prices and changes in foreign demand for domestic output. For each, two alternative measures are considered. The first measure of the foreign price level is given by a weighted average of the consumer price indexes of the rest of the world which, for the purposes of this paper, consists of the other twenty-three countries of the OECD. More precisely, the consumer price index of each of the twenty-three countries was first converted to a numéraire, the dollar, by dividing its domestic-currency index by an index of (cumulative) devaluation or appreciation of that currency in relation to the dollar. The resulting indexes were then summed over all countries by weighting each index according to the incidence of the country's real GDP in the real GDP of the rest of the world. GDP figures were converted into dollars by applying the exchange rate prevailing in an arbitrary year (1970) rather than current exchange rates. Had I done the latter rather than the former, the weights would have reflected distortions arising from changes in exchange rates. For example, countries that had devalued vis-à-vis the dollar would have influenced P^* with decreasing importance even though these countries had experienced a growth rate of output not lower than countries whose currencies had not devalued in relation to the dollar.

Although the above procedure insulates the relative importance of each country in the weighting scheme from changes in the exchange rates, the measured P^* still depends, of course, on the dollar price of each currency. For example, the level and the rate of change of the German consumer price index is higher in dollar than in domestic currency, the DM having revalued on several occasions vis-à-vis the dollar during the sample period. The opposite is true for the U.K. where the dollar price of the pound has fallen.

Is it proper, then, to speak of a world inflation rate without further qualifying the term? The answer is negative. My measure of $\hat{P}^*$ is the rate of change of the dollar-denominated rest-of-the-world price level. Had I chosen the DM as the standard unit of account, the average $\hat{P}^*$ would have been lower; had I chosen the pound, it would have been higher. The choice of the dollar rather than another currency as a numéraire was not dictated by convenience but rather by the consideration that the world has been, or at least was, on a dollar standard until 1971.

The percentage annual change in the import price deflator $\hat{PM}$ was used as an alternative measure of the foreign price impulse. Unlike the measure of $\hat{P}^*$ I have just discussed, $\hat{PM}$ includes the effective devaluation or appreciation of the lira in relation to all other currencies.

The foreign output impulse has also been quantified in two alternative ways: the percentage annual change in the rest-of-the-world (the twenty-three OECD countries) real GDP converted into dollars at 1970 exchange rates $(\hat{y}^*)$, and the percentage annual change in the trade volume of the rest of the world $(\hat{WX})$. Finally, M^* is the sum of the dollar-denominated M1 monetary series of the twenty-three OECD countries.

Figures 1-5 depict the movements of the rate of inflation, output change, and the various impulses. Each impulse is paired with $\hat{P}$ so that the correlation existing between the two time series can be inspected visually. Table 2 provides basic statistics such as the sample mean, standard deviation, and simple correlation coefficients for each of the variables shown in the figures.

Table 2

Sample Mean, Standard Deviation, and Simple Correlation Coefficients

Variable	$\hat{P}$	$\hat{y}$	$\hat{RGDP}$	$\hat{M}$	$\hat{P}^*$	$\hat{PM}$	$\hat{F}$	$\hat{WX}$	$\hat{y}^*$
Mean	5.22	6.42	4.85	14.54	4.12	3.75	3.33	6.34	4.34
Standard deviation	4.89	4.92	2.48	3.34	4.01	13.31	2.40	6.51	2.36
Simple coefficient of correlation with $\hat{P}$	. . .	- 0.51	- 0.57	0.64	0.85	0.80	0.79	0.27	- 0.53

Figure 2   Consumption Price Deflator–M–Real GDP

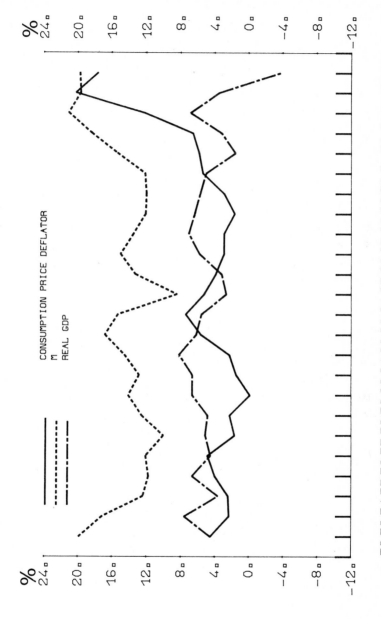

Figure 3   Consumption Price Deflator--Import Price Deflator--World CPI

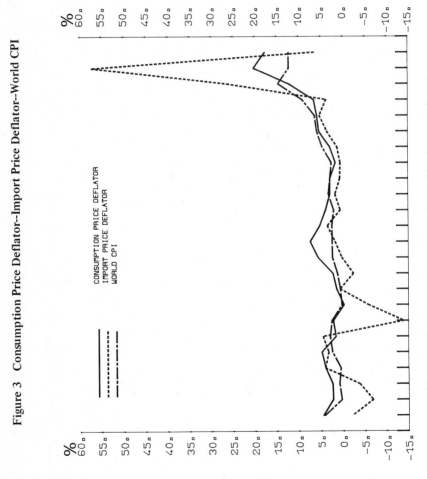

156

Figure 4 Consumption Price Deflator--Fiscal Impulse

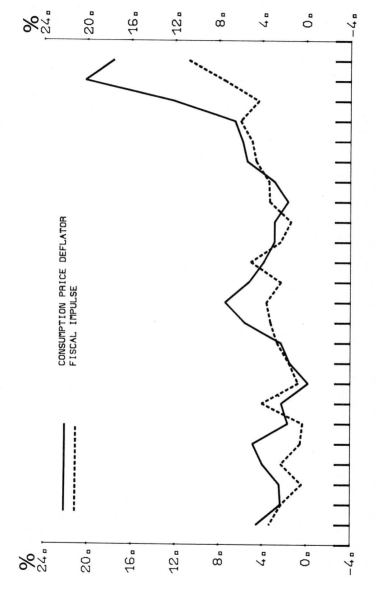

CONSUMPTION PRICE DEFLATOR

FISCAL IMPULSE

157

Figure 5 Consumption Price Deflator--World Exports--World Real GDP

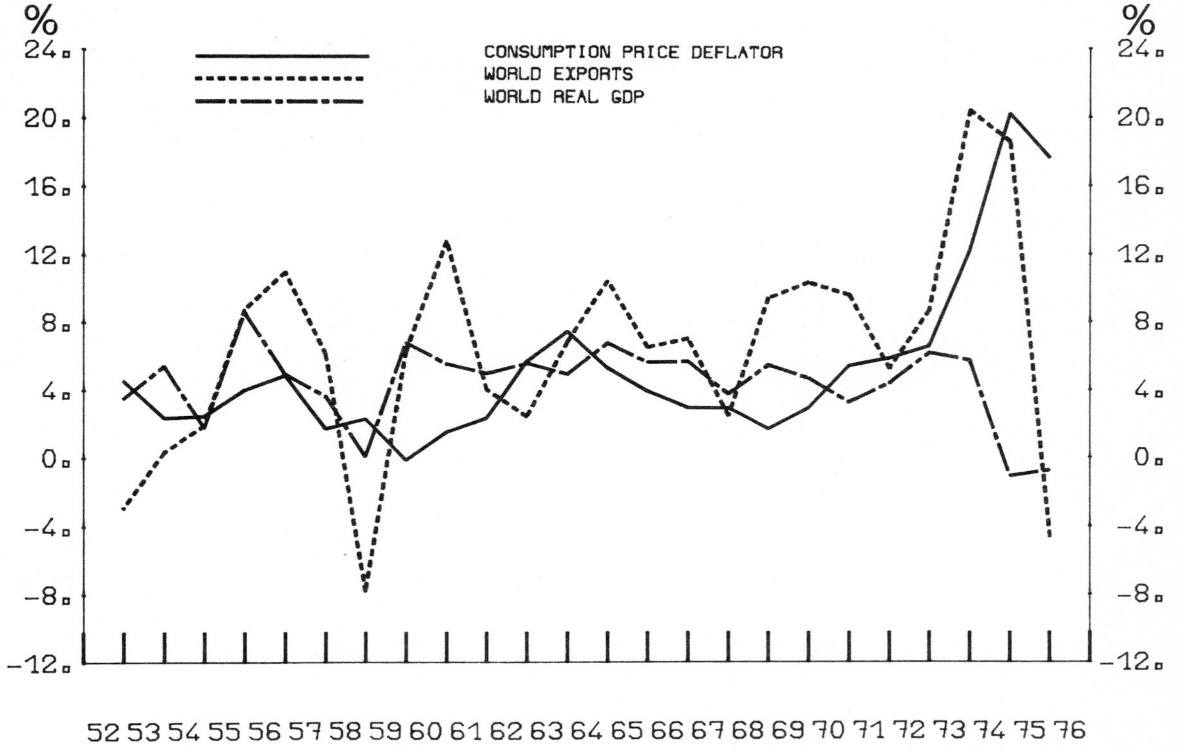

IV. TESTING THE HYPOTHESES

A. The Quantity Theory

I now develop test procedures and report findings bearing on the hypotheses developed in Section II. I begin with the quantity theory in the form of equation (1) whose determinants are shown in Figure 2. It can be seen from Table 2 that there is a negative correlation between $\hat{P}$ and $\text{RG}\hat{\text{DP}}$, and a strong positive one between $\hat{P}$ and $\hat{M}$. However, the comovement of inflation and the growth rate of money is not uniform throughout the period; it is stronger in the 1960s and 1970s than in the 1950s. In addition, there have been periods-- such as in 1959, 1960, and 1965--during which the two series moved in opposite directions.

The occurrence of isolated divergent movements in $\hat{P}$ and $\hat{M}$ should not, in principle, seriously damage the quantity theory, for it is widely recognized that this theory provides a better explanation of the long run rather than of the short run.[2] OLS regression 3.1 (Table 3) bears directly on test implication (1). Note that the estimated value of b is not unity and that the intercept cannot be considered equal to zero. Therefore, the strict version of the quantity theory does not hold. The modified version of the quantity theory is given by (2) where velocity responds to the expected cost of holding cash balances C. The percentage change in the latter was quantified in two alternative ways: by the acceleration of inflation occurring in the previous period, and by the percentage change in the nominal rate of interest i.

While the first alternative has been used before (see Vogel, 1974) and needs no further explanation, the second alternative requires a small digression. According to the well-known Fisherian relationship between the nominal rate of interest i, the real rate of interest r, and the expected inflation rate Π,

$$i = r + \Pi + (r\Pi).$$

$(r\Pi)$ can be ignored because it is presumed to be a negligible magnitude for the sample period under investigation. In accordance with classical thinking, r is determined by the stock of physical and human capital and technological

---

[2]No monetarist would deny, for example, that accidental factors such as the 1973-74 oil embargo which reduce output have an impact on the general price level. These factors produce, however, a once-and-for-all change in the price level rather than inflation. Only a continuous repetition of accidental factors could explain inflation; an acceleration of inflation would require an acceleration of accidents, and the reverse for a deceleration of inflation. It should be self-evident that the longer the sample period the more likely that accidental phenomena wash out relative to the monetary stimulus.

Table 3

Quantity Theory

Regression	Intercept	$\hat{M\text{-}RGDP}$	$\hat{\Delta P}_{-1}$	$\hat{i}$	$\hat{M\text{-}y}_n$	$\hat{\Delta P}^*_{-1}$	$\hat{y}_T$	SEE	R^2	DW
3.1 (t-stat.)	-2.95 (1.93)	0.84 (5.89)	... ...	... ...	... ...	... ...	... ...	3.11 ...	0.59 ...	1.31 ...
3.2	-0.98 (0.67)	0.61 (3.90)	0.80 (2.92)	... ...	... ...	... ...	... ...	2.48 ...	0.76 ...	2.02 ...
3.3	-1.63 (1.30)	0.67 (5.00)	0.57 (2.34)	... ...	... ...	0.76 (2.96)	... ...	2.09 ...	0.83 ...	1.72 ...
3.4	-2.92 (3.15)	0.79 (9.05)	... ...	0.22 (6.22)	... ...	... ...	... ...	1.89 ...	0.85 ...	1.25 ...
3.5	-3.76 (4.56)	... ...	... ...	0.22 (7.51)	0.93 (11.02)	... ...	0.54 (2.82)	1.51 ...	0.91 ...	1.91 ...

Note: SEE = the standard error of the estimate

R^2 = coefficient of multiple correlation adjusted for degrees of freedom

DW = Durbin-Watson statistic.

All other symbols are explained in the text.

knowledge. The small addition of the flows net investment, net income, and know-how to the existing stocks allows us to think of r as subject to minor fluctuations over a relatively short period of history; in other words, the presumption is that changes in i are dominated by changes in Π (Friedman, 1971, pp. 326-27, and Fama, 1975). Therefore, I shall quantify $\hat{C}$ by $\hat{i}$, although such a measure is not immune from criticism. Regressions 3.2 and 3.4 are a test of equation (2) with the two alternative ways of approximating the opportunity cost of holding cash balances. Regression 3.3 is based on the hypothesis that in a fixed exchange rate open economy, the inflation rate abroad directly influences expectations, and, thus, $\hat{C}$ becomes a weighted average of $\Delta\hat{P}_{-1}$ and $\Delta\hat{P}_{-1}^{*}$ (cf. Laidler, 1976). Both regressions 3.2 and 3.3 show a pronounced improvement over 3.1 in terms of explained total variance. In addition, the intercept is zero, and the value of d approaches unity. Of the two fits, 3.3 appears to be superior to 3.2. Unfortunately, no firm conclusion can be drawn from the experiment because the lagged dependent variable appears in both cases as a regressor, with the consequence that the Durbin-Watson statistic is not appropriate as a test of serial correlation. The Durbin h-statistic is also inappropriate because of the relatively small sample size (twenty-three observations). I am thus left with the specification of $\hat{i}$ as a proxy for $\hat{C}$ as shown in regression 3.4 which says that a sustained one percentage point positive deviation of the growth rate of the money stock from output growth raises the rate of inflation by 0.8 of 1 percent, whereas an increase of 1 percent in the expected cost of holding cash balances lowers the real demand for money by 0.22 percent. Ceteris paribus, this implies an increase in the general price level of 0.22 percent.

A problem with regression 3.4 is that its residuals display an appreciable degree of autocorrelation, possibly indicating a missing variable. I reformulated (2) so as to allow permanent (y_n) and transitory output (y_T) to enter the real demand for money with different weights. y_n is measured as a three-year moving average of RGDP.

The results of this experiment are shown in regression 3.5 (reported below for convenience) which is, by far, the most satisfactory explanation of the quantity theory in terms of standard statistical criteria:

$$\hat{P} = -3.76 + .93(\hat{M}-\hat{y}_n) - .54\,\hat{y}_T + .22\,\hat{i} \quad (3.5, \text{Table 3})\,.$$

Figure 6 compares the actual with the predicted time path of the inflation rate. According to 3.5, inflation can be explained in terms of the secular fall

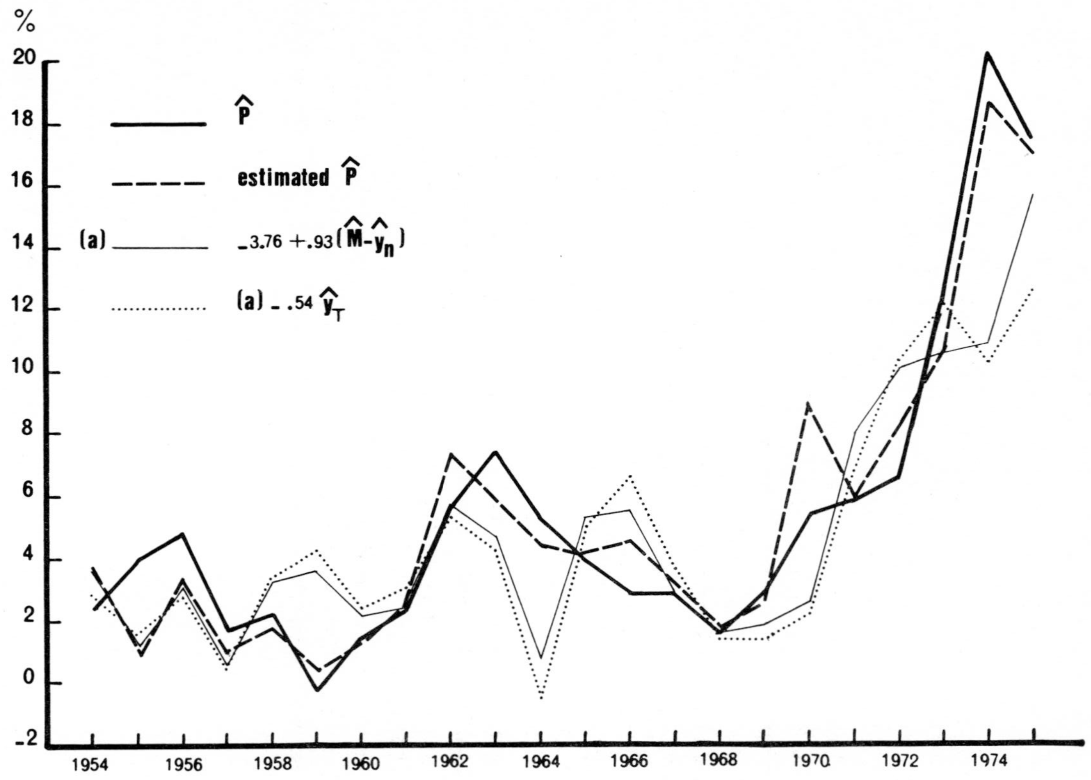

Figure 6   Regression 3.5, Quantity Theory

in velocity impounded in the intercept, the growth of the money stock in excess of long-run output, and transitory movements in velocity. Transitory velocity, in turn, responds to $\hat{y}_T$ and $\hat{i}$. In the long run, $\hat{y}_T = \hat{i} = 0$, and steady state inflation becomes $-3.76 + .93\ (\hat{M}-\hat{y}_n)$. It is to be noted that the sample mean of the average percentage change in velocity in Italy is -3.62, a value which is virtually identical to the estimate of the intercept in 3.5.

B. The Monetarist Hypothesis in an Open Economy

Consider now the simple monetarist model expressed by equations (4)-(5). The procedure is to estimate (6) and to insert the resulting estimate of the expected inflation rate $\hat{P}^s$ into (7) to arrive at an estimate of the current inflation rate. It is worth emphasizing again that the hypothesis implies that the coefficient of the expected inflation rate in (7) is equal to unity.

The expected values of the systematic fiscal, monetary, and foreign impulses will be quantified in two alternative ways. First, each expected impulse is defined to be equal to a moving average of current and past values of that impulse itself, the length and form of the moving average being ascertained on purely statistical grounds. The convention will be used here that an integer after the variable denotes the number of years over which the average is computed, e.g., $x2 = (x_t + x_{t-1})/2$.

An alternative to this procedure is to construct specific hypotheses about the way expectations are formed concerning a given impulse. Thus, it may be postulated that economic agents use all relevant information at their disposal to predict $\hat{M}$ (cf. Barro, 1977). More specifically, all information embedded in M_{-1} and a knowledge about the current value of the domestic component of the monetary base--the instrument under the control of the central bank in a regime of fixed exchange rates--are relevant to arrive at an estimate of $\hat{M}$:

(19) $\hat{M}_t = 6.81 + .30\ \hat{M}_{t-1} + .26$ [domestic component of monetary
         (3.32)   (1.81)   (2.93)
         base] $+ a_{mt}$,

$$SEE = 2.05, \qquad R^2 = .59, \qquad DW = 1.71.$$

The expected growth rate of the money stock is equal to that part which can be systematically predicted using (19), namely, $MA_t = \hat{M}_t - a_{mt}$. The unexpected component is equal to a_{mt}. The expected components of the other impulses were obtained by fitting the "best" ARIMA scheme (cf. Box and

Table 4

Monetarist Hypothesis in an Open Economy: Inflation Regressions

Regression	Intercept	$\hat{P}^*$	$\hat{P}^*2$	$\hat{M}2_{-1}$	$\hat{M}A$	$\hat{M}\text{-}\hat{M}2_{-1}$	$\hat{P}^*\text{-}\hat{P}^*2$	$\hat{M}\text{-}\hat{M}A$	$\hat{P}^s\#2$	$\hat{P}^s\#3$	SEE	R^2	DW
4.1 (t-stat.)	0.95 (1.22)	1.04 (7.60)	...	...	...	...	...	...	...	...	2.63 ...	0.71 ...	1.11 ...
4.2	- 7.34 (3.21)	...	0.91 (7.22)	0.64 (3.61)	...	...	...	...	...	...	1.83 ...	0.87 ...	1.53 ...
4.3	- 7.59 (1.97)	...	0.80 (3.80)	...	0.68 (2.15)	...	...	...	...	...	2.10 ...	0.82 ...	1.04 ...
4.4	...	...	...	...	...	0.11 (0.88)	- 0.66 (1.35)	...	1.02 (18.56)	...	1.74 ...	0.94 ...	1.36 ...
4.5	...	...	...	...	...	...	- 0.96 (1.80)	- 0.03 (0.11)	...	1.05 (16.50)	1.94 ...	0.93 ...	1.07 ...

Jenkins, 1970). The argument here is that all relevant information is restricted to that provided by the time series itself. This could be so because economic agents either have no theory about the impulses or, if they have one, they cannot obtain information which adds anything to what already exists in the time series. In any case, the adopted procedure required that a given impulse be transformed into a stationary series to which the best ARIMA scheme was then fitted. The results for $\hat{F}$ and $\hat{WX}$ are

$$(20) \quad \Delta\hat{F}_t = \underset{(3.36)}{-.671} \; \Delta\hat{F}_{t-1} - \underset{(2.88)}{.585} \; \Delta\hat{F}_{t-2} + a_{Ft}, \qquad R^2 = .25$$

$$(21) \quad \Delta\hat{WX}_t = \underset{(1.01)}{-.183} \; \Delta\hat{WX}_{t-1} - \underset{(3.23)}{.627} \; \Delta\hat{WX}_{t-2} + a_{WXt}, \qquad R^2 = .31.$$

For all other impulses, their one-year change displayed white noise properties, and, thus, the past was of no help in predicting the future. Recognizing that $\Delta\hat{F}_t - a_{FT}$ and $\Delta\hat{WX}_t - a_{WXt}$ are the one-year change in the expected impulses, it follows that

$$(20a) \quad \hat{FA}_t = \hat{F}_{t-1} + \Delta\hat{F} - a_{Ft} = \hat{F}_t - a_{Ft} = \text{expected fiscal impulse}$$

$$(20b) \quad \hat{UFA}_t = \hat{F}_t - \hat{FA}_t = a_{Ft} = \text{unexpected fiscal impulse}$$

$$(21a) \quad \hat{WXA}_t = \hat{WX}_{t-1} + \Delta\hat{WX}_t - a_{WXt} = \hat{WX}_t - a_{WXt} = \text{expected foreign impulse}$$

$$(21b) \quad \hat{UWX}_t = a_{WXt} = \text{unexpected foreign impulse.}$$

The last four equations will be employed to test the dominant impulse hypothesis. To test the monetarist theory in an open economy, which is my immediate concern, only (20) is needed. Table 4 summarizes the test I discuss beginning with regression 4.1, which bears directly on the monetary theory of the balance of payments, according to which $\hat{P} = \hat{P}^*$ under fixed exchange rates and in the long run. Although the coefficient of $\hat{P}^*$ is not statistically different from one, the low value of the Durbin-Watson statistic suggests that relevant right-hand-side variables may be missing. Regressions 4.2 and 4.3 bear

165

Table 5

Monetarist Hypothesis with Explanation of Foreign Inflation

Regression	Dependent variable	Intercept	$\hat{M}^*2\text{-}\hat{y}^*2$	$\hat{M}2_{-1}$	$\overline{\hat{P}}^{*s}\#1$	$\hat{M}\text{-}\hat{M}2_{-1}$	$\hat{P}^s\#2$	$\hat{P}^*\text{-}\hat{P}^{*s}\#1$	SEE	R^2	DW
5.1 (t-stat.)	$\hat{P}^*$	2.29 (5.88)	0.83 (10.55)	...	...	...	...	...	1.67	0.83	1.64
5.2	$\hat{P}$	-9.48 (2.74)	...	0.86 (3.16)	0.67 (3.42)	...	...	...	2.79	0.70	1.49
5.3	$\hat{P}$	...	...	...	...	0.13 (0.97)	1.00 (16.33)	1.08 (4.13)	1.95	0.95	1.87
5.3a	residuals 5.2	...	...	...	...	0.13 (0.99)	...	1.07 (4.23)	1.90	0.46	1.87

on equation (6), according to which the expected inflation rate depends negatively on $\hat{y}_n$ and positively on $\hat{\bar{M}}$ and $\hat{\bar{P}}^*$, with the coefficients of the last two variables adding to unity. The expected foreign inflation rate is here measured by a two-year moving average $(\hat{P}^*2)$; the expected money stock growth rate alternatively by $\hat{M2}_{-1}$ in regression 4.2 and by $\hat{MA}$ in 4.3.

$\hat{\bar{P}}^S\#2$ and $\hat{\bar{P}}^S\#3$ are estimates of the expected inflation rate, obtained from 4.2 and 4.3, which are then plugged into regressions 4.4 and 4.5, respectively. The regression pair 4.2-4.4 is superior to the pair 4.3-4.5 based on the criterion of serial correlation of the residuals. The sign of the coefficients conforms to theory with the domestic money stock and the foreign inflation rate providing a powerful explanation of the rate of inflation; compare the R^2 of regression 4.4. The elasticity of the current price level with respect to its expected one is unity, as theory implies. Virtually all inflation is expected in the sense that the unexpected growth rate of the money stock $(\hat{M}-\hat{M2}_{-1})$ and the foreign rate of inflation $(\hat{P}^* - \hat{P}^*2)$ add nothing to the explanatory power attributable to the expected rate of inflation.

There is, however, an important aspect of the empirical work which does not conform to theory; the coefficients of $\hat{P}^*2$ and $\hat{M2}_{-1}$ add up to 1.5 rather than unity. In addition, the estimate of the intercept which captures $-\hat{y}_n/(\beta_1 + \beta_2)$ implies a value of about 11 for $\hat{y}_n$, which is far higher than the sample mean of y; cf. Table 2.

Next, consider the monetarist model when $\hat{\bar{P}}^*$ is explained in terms of the foreign output market; cf. equations (9)-(10). Regression 5.1 (Table 5) gives an estimate of $\hat{\bar{P}}^*$. The independent variable $\hat{M}^*2 - \hat{y}^*2$ was employed because it turned out that M^*2 and y^*2, when entered separately, had coefficients of approximately equal absolute value. The simple quantity theory explains most of the variance of $\hat{P}^*$. Regressions 5.2 and 5.3 represent stages two and three, respectively, of the empirical procedure. Regression 5.1 provides an estimate of $\hat{\bar{P}}^*$, $\hat{\bar{P}}^{*S}$, which is then used as a regressor in 5.2. In turn, regression 5.2 gives an estimate of the expected domestic rate of inflation $\hat{\bar{P}}^S$ which is used as a right-hand-side variable in 5.3.

A few remarks concerning the comparison of the results of Tables 4 and 5 are in order. The explanatory power of the expected inflation rate regression is, not surprisingly, smaller when $\hat{\bar{P}}^*$ is endogenized than in the case of $\hat{\bar{P}}^*$ being equal to a two-year moving average. As in the case of regression 4.2, regression 5.2 fails to meet the homogeneity constraint. As in the case of Table 4, the coefficient of the expected rate of inflation is statistically equal to unity. However, here inflation is not completely anticipated; the unexpected growth rate of the money stock, $\hat{M} - \hat{M2}_{-1}$, and of the foreign inflation rate, $\hat{P}^* - \hat{\bar{P}}^{*S}\#1$, explain 46 percent of the variance of the residuals of regression 5.2.

Table 6

Dominant Impulse Hypothesis: Inflation Regressions

Expected impulses measured as moving averages

Regression	Intercept	$\hat{P}M2$	$\hat{W}X2$	$\hat{M}2_{-1}$	$\hat{F}2$	$\hat{P}^s$ #1	$\hat{P}M$-PM2	$\hat{W}X$-WX2	$\hat{M}$-M2$_{-1}$	$\hat{F}$-F2	SEE	R^2	DW
6.1 (t-stat.)	-2.79 (1.09)	0.27 (4.24)	0.02 (0.25)	0.34 (2.23)	0.63 (2.74)	...	...	...	...	...	1.32	0.93	1.57
6.2	...	...	...	...	...	0.99 (24.8)	0.05 (1.0)	0.0 (0.09)	0.09 (1.11)	0.10 (0.31)	1.20	0.97	1.51
6.3	-3.93 (1.70)	0.31 (6.42)	0.03 (0.41)	0.53 (2.97) [$\hat{M}A$]	0.19 (0.80)	... [$\hat{P}^s$ #3]	...	...	...	...	1.19	0.94	1.63
6.4	...	...	...	...	...	0.99 (25.91)	0.01 (0.26)	0.03 (0.29)	0.05 (0.41) [$\hat{M}$-MA]	0.17 (0.58)	1.17	0.97	1.60
6.5	-9.15 (2.85)	0.74 (3.45) [$\hat{P}*2$]	0.17 (0.61) [$\hat{y}*2$]	0.67 (3.58) [$\hat{M}2_{-1}$]	0.44 (1.09)	... [$\hat{P}^s$ #5]	... [$\hat{P}*$-$\hat{P}*2$]	... [$\hat{y}*$-$\hat{y}*2$]	... [$\hat{M}$-$\hat{M}2_{-1}$]	...	1.87	0.86	1.61
6.6	...	...	...	...	...	1.0 (17.29)	-0.68 (1.40)	-0.34 (1.42)	0.09 (0.79)	0.24 (0.59)	1.62	0.95	1.25

What conclusions can be drawn so far? First, the simplest quantity theory applied to the rest of the world goes a long way in explaining $\hat{P}^*$. Second, the expected rate of inflation responds to the movement of the exogenous or policy variables which are pertinent to the model. Expectations are thus formed rationally. Third, regardless of whether $\hat{P}^*$ is endogenized or not, the expected rate of inflation always affects $\hat{P}$ with a unit coefficient. Fourth, the unexpected portions of the impulses are a sizable determinant of $\hat{P}$ only when $\hat{P}^*$ is explained in terms of $\hat{M}^*$ and $\hat{y}^*$. Finally, although the explanatory power of the fits is very high, the results are inconsistent with degree one homogeneity in nominal magnitudes.

C. The Dominant Impulse Hypothesis

The dominant impulse hypothesis is a natural extension of the monetarist hypothesis in the sense that two real variables, the fiscal and foreign quantity impulses, are allowed to affect aggregate demand and, thus, ultimately inflation. The model is less restrictive in the sense that it is potentially open to non-monetarist solutions. The empirical work is summarized in Tables 6 and 7 for inflation and in Table 8 for unexpected changes in output. Let me begin with Table 6 in which the procedure is the same two-step one underlying Table 4. An estimate of the expected rate of inflation is obtained by regressing $\hat{P}$ on the expected values of the impulses; then, current inflation is explained in terms of its expected component and the unanticipated components of the impulses.

Regression 6.5 is the monetarist hypothesis of regression 4.2, with the addition of the expected fiscal and foreign output. Regression 6.6 is the extended counterpart of regression 4.4. It is clear that $\bar{F}$ and $\tilde{y}^*$ contribute nothing to what $\bar{M}$ and $\hat{P}^*$ already explain. Since the outcome might have been sensitive to differences in impulse measurement, $\hat{P}^*$ was changed with the growth rate in the import price $\hat{PM}$, and $\hat{y}^*$ with the growth rate of the rest-of-the-world trade volume $\hat{WX}$. The results are shown in regressions 6.1 and 6.2. Two significant changes occur: the coefficients of both the expected monetary and foreign price impulses drop by about one half, while the coefficient of the expected fiscal impulse becomes strongly positive. Again, all inflation turns out to be expected, with $\hat{\bar{P}}^S\#1$ playing the dominant role in regression 6.2.

Regression 6.1, however, is marred by the fact that the sum of the coefficients of the two nominal magnitudes is 0.60. A substantial improvement is obtained with the regression pair 6.3-6.4 in which $\hat{M}2_{-1}$ is replaced with $\hat{MA}$; the sum of the coefficients of the two nominal magnitudes is approaching

Table 7

Dominant Impulse Hypothesis
Expected impulses measured by AR schemes

Regression	Dependent variable	Inter-cept	$\hat{M}A$	$\hat{P}M2$	$\hat{W}XA$	$\hat{F}A$	$P*2$	$\hat{P}*+e$	$\hat{P}^s\#1$	$\hat{M}$-MA	$\hat{P}M$-PM2	UWX	$\hat{U}F$	SEE	R^2	DW
7.1 (t-stat.)	$\hat{P}$	-4.44 (2.10)	0.66 (4.09)	0.34 (7.73)	-0.07 (0.92)	-0.14 (0.49)	...	...	...	...	...	...	...	1.19	0.94	1.94
		...	...	...	...	...	...	...	...	...	...	...	...	...	...	...
7.2	$\hat{P}$	...	...	...	...	...	...	...	0.99 (26.64)	0.05 (0.37)	-0.002 (0.04)	0.02 (0.34)	0.23 (1.26)	1.13	0.98	1.94
		...	...	...	...	...	...	...	...	...	...	...	...	...	...	...
7.3	residuals 7.1	...	...	...	...	...	...	...	...	...	...	...	0.18 (1.32)	1.04	0.03	1.95
		...	...	...	...	...	...	...	...	...	...	...	...	...	...	...

one statistically. On the other hand, the fiscal impulse disappears as a contributor to the inflationary process.

In an effort to further improve the homogeneity properties of regression 6.3, the two-year moving average of $\hat{F}$ and $\hat{W}X$ was replaced with the auto-regressive equations (20a) and (21a), respectively. The results are shown in regression 7.1 (Table 7). While the use of $\hat{F}A$ and $\hat{W}\hat{X}A$ does not improve the case for fiscal and foreign impulses as determinants of anticipated inflation, regression 7.1 finally displays the proper homogeneity conditions. Domestic money and import prices are the two forces driving $\hat{\bar{P}}$ and give solutions which are consistent in the long run (see also Figure 7 where the actual and predicted values of the inflation rate are compared).

Recalling that foreign inflation was well explained by $\hat{\bar{M}}^*$ and $\hat{y}^*$, one can conclude that inflation is primarily a monetary phenomenon. I believe that one arrives at this conclusion without having stacked the cards in favor of the monetary interpretation of inflation. The dominant impulse hypothesis was constructed so as to leave quite open the range of determinants causing inflation: fiscalist, monetarist, or real-export solutions were accepted as possible outcomes. It was also said that a monetarist solution required that the monetary impulse dwarf all other impulses. The evidence presented so far is consistent with this view.

What role does the fiscal impulse play in the hypothesis? Having ascertained that $\hat{F}A$ has no influence on the expected rate of inflation, I checked whether the unanticipated portion of the fiscal impulse affects the unexpected rate of inflation. Regression 7.3 bears on this proposition; $\hat{U}F$ accounts for 3 percent of the variance of the residuals of regression 7.1, with the rest being pure white noise.

D. Explaining Unanticipated Changes in Output

I have concentrated on testing the models' implications concerning the rate of inflation. Consider now the determinants of output growth $\hat{y}$ which in all cases is equal to the growth of "normal" output y_n plus a transitory component which depends on the unanticipated impulses. It is about this transitory growth rate of output that the hypotheses of Section II have some-thing to say, $\hat{y}_n$ being related to the growth rate of the nation's labor force, capital stock, and technology. Output is here understood to be industrial production exclusive of housing.

Limited success was achieved in testing equation (8). The impact of the unanticipated foreign inflation rate was virtually nil and the total explanatory power of the fit low. Table 8 summarizes the tests bearing on equation (17),

Table 8

Dominant Impulse Hypothesis
Unexpected changes in output

Regression	Dependent variable	Intercept	$\widehat{WX\text{-}WX2}$	$\widehat{M\text{-}M2}_{-1}$	$\widehat{F\text{-}F2}$	$\widehat{M\text{-}MA}$	$\widehat{UWX}$	$\widehat{UF}$	$\Delta\widehat{PM}_{-1}$	SEE	R^2	DW
8.1 (t-stat.)	$\Delta\hat{y}$	...	0.73 (3.80)	0.71 (3.04)	- 1.15 (1.40)	...	...	...	...	3.32 ...	0.60 ...	2.13 ...
8.2	$\Delta\hat{y}$	...	0.75 (4.00)	...	- 1.22 (1.55)	1.25 (3.54)	...	...	...	3.22 ...	0.62 ...	2.32 ...
8.3	a_y	...	...	...	...	1.14 (3.70)	0.42 (3.72)	- 0.61 (1.37)	...	2.81 ...	0.64 ...	2.52 ...
8.4	a_y	0.14 (0.22)	...	...	...	1.02 (3.16)	0.43 (4.08)	...	- 0.13 (1.74)	2.86 ...	0.64 ...	2.46 ...

172

an implication of the dominant impulse hypothesis. In regressions 8.1 and 8.2, $\hat{y}_n$ was set equal to $\hat{y}_{-1}$, so that $\Delta\hat{y}$ represents the unanticipated growth rate of output. The unanticipated growth rate of the foreign price level, either $\hat{P}^* - \hat{P}^*2$ or PM - PM2, never showed up to be significant in the presence of the other right-hand-side variables. It was thus dropped.

Regressions 8.1 and 8.2 show that the unanticipated changes in world trade volume and domestic money have a potent and reliable impact on $\Delta\hat{y}$. The fiscal variable shows up with a negative coefficient, but the t-statistic is too low to make a claim that Italian fiscal policy has "crowded out" industrial production.[3] The evidence suggests that changes in fiscal policy have left no visible traces on transitory changes in output.

The next step was to check whether $\Delta\hat{y}$ was truly independent of its past values. It was found that a second-order autoregressive scheme could explain 18 percent of the variance of $\Delta\hat{y}$:

$$(22) \quad \Delta\hat{y}_t = \underset{(1.57)}{-.308} \; \Delta\hat{y}_{t-1} \quad \underset{(2.92)}{-.464} \; \Delta\hat{y}_{t-2} + a_{yt}, \qquad R^2 = 0.18.$$

I thus replaced $\Delta\hat{y}$ with a_y as the appropriate dependent variable in regression 8.3, whose right-hand-side variables were taken to be the residuals of (19), (20), and (21). The fit improves, although the Durbin-Watson statistic indicates negative autocorrelation in the residuals. The two relevant aspects of regression 8.3 are the dominance of the monetary impulse over the world trade impulse and the weakness of the fiscal impulse. A percentage point rise in the unanticipated money stock growth rate raises temporarily, but at least for a year, output by 1 percent. The actual and predicted values of the unanticipated changes in output are shown in Figure 8.

The last experiment, presented in regression 8.4, aimed at testing whether an unanticipated change in import prices had a net expansionary or contractive effect on a_y. The evidence, although weak, indicates a moderate deflationary impact. Such a result, in direct contrast with the theory in Section II, might leave open the door to a specification of the supply of output where import prices appear with a negative coefficient. Such a specification is more an ad hoc ex post rationalization than a carefully worked out hypothesis.

---

[3] Qualitatively similar results were obtained using a modified fiscal impulse which nets out government expenditures on capital goods.

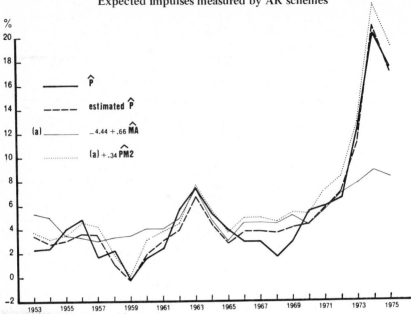

Figure 7   Regression 7.1, Dominant Impulse Hypothesis
Expected impulses measured by AR schemes

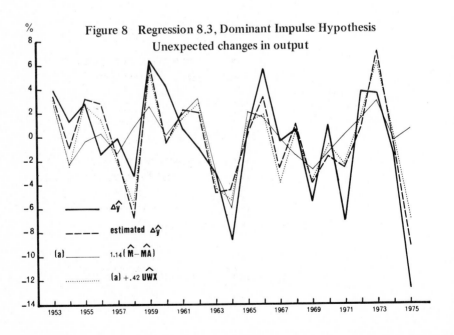

Figure 8   Regression 8.3, Dominant Impulse Hypothesis
Unexpected changes in output

174

E. Relative Forecasting Performance

I conclude with an assessment of how the three hypotheses tested fare, both relative to each other and to a naive model, in tracking the rate of inflation over the sample period 1952-75. In addition, the same models will be used to predict the rate of inflation for 1976.

The naive model was arbitrarily chosen to be $\hat{P}^S = \hat{P}_{-1}$; that is, the forecast rate of inflation this year is set equal to the value of last year's inflation rate. Table 9, column 2, reports the values of Theil's (1958) inequality coefficients applied to the best regression estimates of each hypothesis, regressions which are identified in column 1 of the table. Theil's coefficient of inequality is defined as follows:

$$(23) \quad U = \frac{\sqrt{\frac{1}{T} \Sigma (A_t - A_t^S)^2}}{\sqrt{\frac{1}{T} \Sigma A_t^2} + \sqrt{\frac{1}{T} \Sigma (A^S)^2}} \, ,$$

where A_t = values of observations

A_t^S = values predicted by the hypothesis

T = number of observations.

The lower the value of U, the more powerful is the forecasting ability of the hypothesis; at the limit, $U = 0$ when $A = A^S$ for all t.

Table 9

Relative Forecasting Performance of the Three Hypotheses

Hypothesis	U	CRP	Forecast for 1976 (actual value 17 percent)
Naive, $\hat{P}^S = \hat{P}_{-1}$	0.198	1	...
Quantity theory, regression 3.5	0.090	0.262	15.89
Monetarist theory, regression 4.4	0.112	0.367	16.5
Dominant impulse hypothesis, regression 7.2	0.070	0.141	17.32

The dominant impulse hypothesis, in the specific form of regression 7.2, has the lowest value of U, followed by the quantity theory and the monetarist theory. All three models easily outperform the naive rule $\hat{P}^S = \hat{P}_{-1}$.

To gain further insights as to how well each model performs relative to the naive rule, define the coefficient of relative performance (CRP):

$$(24) \quad CRP = \frac{\frac{1}{T}\Sigma(A_t - A_t^S)^2}{\frac{1}{T}\Sigma(A_t - A_t^N)^2} \,,$$

where A^N = values predicted by naive rule.

A value of CRP which is less than unity implies that the hypothesis under consideration outperforms the naive rule in forecasting inflation. The minimal value of CRP is zero when $A = A^S$ for all t. The computed values of CRP are shown in Table 9, column 3.

Finally, Table 9, column 4 gives the ex ante forecast of the rate of inflation for 1976. The forecasts were obtained by using only intercepts and coefficients whose t-values were above 2.07. In addition, concerning the dominant impulse hypothesis, $P\hat{M}3$ was used rather than $P\hat{M}2$ as the relevant input. This was done to smooth out the drastic variation in import prices that occurred in the 1974-76 period.

The three hypotheses perform remarkably well, with the quantity theory underpredicting the realized inflation rate of 17 percent by 110 basis points, the monetarist theory by 50 basis points, and the dominant impulse hypothesis overpredicting it by only 32 basis points.

V. SUMMARY AND CONCLUSIONS

The aim of the paper was to gather evidence, using annual data from Italy for the period from 1952 to 1975, to test three hypotheses of inflation. The strict version of the quantity theory was rejected, but a modified form proved to be a powerful explanation of the data. The modified version of the quantity theory took into consideration the secular fall in the percentage change of velocity, the growth of the money stock in excess of long-run output growth, as well as transitory movements in velocity.

The monetarist theory in an open economy posits that the domestic rate of inflation depends on the anticipated growth rate of the domestic money stock and on the foreign inflation rate. This hypothesis also turned out to be a powerful explanation of the rate of inflation. Virtually all inflation is anticipated in the sense that the unanticipated growth rates of the money stock and the foreign rate of inflation add nothing to what the expected rate of inflation already explains. Expectations, in turn, are formed rationally and, thus, depend on the behavior of the two anticipated exogenous variables. An important feature of the theory, however, was disconfirmed: the degree-one homogeneity property of $\hat{\bar{P}}$ with respect to $\hat{\bar{M}}$ and $\hat{\bar{P}}^*$.

The dominant impulse hypothesis takes a more eclectic view of which impulses are important in the inflationary process. Monetarist, fiscalist, or real-sector causes of inflation are accepted as equally possible outcomes. A monetarist solution requires that the monetary impulse dominate all other impulses. The evidence presented is consistent with this view. Out of a potentially infinite number of random shocks which might have sustained increases in the general price level, two systematic impulses emerged in the empirical work as statistically relevant, $\hat{\bar{M}}$ and $\hat{\bar{P}}M$, with their coefficients adding to unity in the $\hat{\bar{P}}$ equation. Again, virtually all inflation was anticipated, with the fiscal impulse accounting for a minimal fraction of the variance of the residuals.

Transitory changes in output respond, in accordance with the implications of the hypothesis, to the unanticipated growth of the money stock and world trade. A percentage point increase in the unanticipated money stock growth rate raises, over the period of one year, the growth rate of output by one percentage point above the growth rate of "normal" output.

The evidence that fiscal policy "crowds out" output is weak.

References

Barro, R.J. (1977), "Unanticipated Money Growth and Unemployment in the United States," American Economic Review, 67: 101-15.

Barro, R.J., and Fischer, S. (1976), "Recent Developments in Monetary Theory," Journal of Monetary Economics, 2: 133-67.

Box, G.E.P., and Jenkins, G.M. (1970). Time Series Analysis Forecasting and Control. San Francisco: Holden-Day.

Bronfenbrenner, M., and Holzman, F. (1963), "Survey of Inflation," American Economic Review, 53: 593-661.

Brunner, K. (1971), "A Survey of Selected Issues in Monetary Theory," Schweizerische Zeitschrift für Volkswirtschaft und Statistik, 1.

_____(1973), "Is Inflation Really Intractable?," University of Rochester typescript, September 1973.

Brunner, K., Fratianni, M., Jordan, J.L., Meltzer, A.H., and Neumann, M.J.M. (1973), "Fiscal and Monetary Policies in Moderate Inflation: Case Studies of Three Countries," Journal of Money, Credit and Banking, 5(1): 313-53.

Brunner, K., and Meltzer, A.H. (1976), "An Aggregative Theory for a Closed Economy," in Monetarism, ed. J. Stein. Amsterdam: North-Holland.

Fama, E.F. (1975), "Short-term Interest Rates as Predictors of Inflation," American Economic Review, 65: 269-82.

Fourcans, A., and Fratianni, M. (1976), "Cost Push Versus Excess Demand Explanations of Inflation in France, 1960-1973," in European Finance Association 1975 Proceedings, eds. R. Brealey and G. Rankine. Amsterdam: North-Holland.

Fratianni, M. (1974), "A Critical Look at Major Inflation Theories," Tijdschrift voor Economie, 3: 281-301.

178

Fratianni, M. (1976), "Domestic Bank Credit, Money and the Open Economy," in Bank Credit, Money and Inflation in Open Economies, eds. M. Fratianni and K. Tavernier, supplement to Kredit und Kapital, 3.

Friedman, M. (1971), "A Monetary Theory of Nominal Income," Journal of Political Economy, 79: 323-37.

Friedman, M., and Meiselman, D. (1963), "The Relative Stability of Money Velocity and the Investment Multiplier in the U.S., 1897-1958," in Stabilization Policies, for the Commission on Money and Credit. Englewood Cliffs, N.J.: Prentice-Hall.

Gordon, R.J. (1976), "Recent Developments in the Theory of Inflation and Unemployment," Journal of Monetary Economics, 2: 185-219.

Hamburger, M.J., and Reisch, R.D. (1976), "Inflation, Unemployment and Macroeconomic Policy in Open Economies: An Empirical Analysis," Carnegie-Rochester Conference Series, 4, eds. K. Brunner and A.H. Meltzer. Amsterdam: North-Holland.

Hansen, B. (1969). Fiscal Policy in Seven Countries, 1955-65: Belgium, France, Germany, Italy, Sweden, United Kingdom, United States. Paris: OECD.

Harberger, A.C. (1963), "The Dynamics of Inflation in Chile," in Measurement in Economics: Studies in Mathematical Economics and Econometrics in Memory of Yehuda Grunfeld. Stanford: Stanford University Press.

Johnson, Harry G. (1963), "A Survey of Theories of Inflation," Indian Economic Review, 6: 29-66.

Korteweg, P. (1975), "Inflation, Economic Activity and the Operation of Fiscal, Foreign and Monetary Impulses in the Netherlands: A Preliminary Analysis, 1953-1973," De Economist, 123: 559-635.

Kouri, P.J.K., and Porter, M.G. (1974), "International Capital Flows and Portfolio Equilibrium," Journal of Political Economy, 82: 443-67.

Laidler, D.E.W. (1976), "Inflation--Alternative Explanations and Policies: Tests on Data Drawn from Six Countries," Carnegie-Rochester Conference Series, 4, eds. K. Brunner and A.H. Meltzer. Amsterdam: North-Holland.

Laidler, D.E.W., and Parkin, M. (1975), "Inflation: A Survey," Economic Journal, 85: 741-809.

Lucas, R.E., Jr. (1973), "Some International Evidence on the Output-Inflation Tradeoffs," American Economic Review, 63: 326-34.

Muth, J.F. (1961), "Rational Expectations and the Theory of Price Movements," Econometrica, 29: 315-35.

Sargent, T.J. (1973), "Rational Expectations, the Real Rate of Interest, and the Natural Rate of Unemployment," Brookings Papers on Economic Activity, 2. Washington, D.C.: The Brookings Institution.

Schwartz, A. (1973), "Secular Price Change in Historical Perspective," Journal of Money, Credit and Banking, 5(1): 243-69.

Stein, J.L. (1976), "Inside the Monetarist Black Box," in Monetarism, ed. J.L. Stein. Amsterdam: North-Holland.

Theil, H. (1958). Economic Forecasts and Policy. Amsterdam: North-Holland.

Tullio, G. (1977), "Monetary Equilibrium and Balance of Payments Adjustment: Empirical Tests of the U.S. and the Italian Balances of Payments." Ph.D. dissertation, University of Chicago.

Vogel, R.C. (1974), "The Dynamics of Inflation in Latin America, 1950-1969," American Economic Review, 64: 102-14.

A COMMENT
ON THE KORTEWEG, FRATIANNI, AND FOURCANS PAPERS

Victor Argy

International Monetary Fund, Washington, D.C.[*]

and

Macquarie University, Australia

My comments on these three most stimulating papers will be in two parts. First, I want to evaluate the model underlying the three papers (most explicitly in Korteweg and Fratianni). Second, I want to make a number of detailed comments about some of the claims made for some of the results.

1.   The underlying structure is based on an aggregate supply equation, an aggregate demand equation, and the assumption of rational expectations.

The aggregate demand and supply equations, as they appear in Korteweg, are

$$(1) \quad \hat{y} = \hat{\bar{y}} + a_1 (\hat{p} - \hat{p}^e) + u_s$$

$$(2) \quad \hat{y} = \beta_1 (\hat{M} - \hat{p}^e) + \beta_2 (\hat{S} - \hat{p}^e) + \beta_3 (\hat{p}^* - \hat{p}) + \beta_4 \, FI + \beta_5 \, \hat{y}^* + \beta_3 \hat{e} + u_d.$$

Hats ($\hat{}$) indicate first differences of logarithms, superscript e denotes the expected value of a variable, and stars (*) refer to foreign variables. Variable y indicates the volume of private production, where $\bar{y}$ is the "normal" level of production consistent with the "natural" rate of employment and capacity utilization at which price expectations will prove to be correct. Variable p is the aggregate price level of private production, M is the stock of money, S is the stock of government debt outstanding, and FI some linear combination of the proportionate rates of change of discretionary real government expenditures and taxes. Variable e is the exchange rate denoting the number of domestic currency units per unit of foreign currency. Finally, u_d and u_s are random shift terms reflecting changes in tastes, productivity, etc.

These two equations are combined to yield a solution for the rate of inflation

---

[*]Consultant, Research Department, during 1977. The IMF is of course not responsible for the views expressed.

(3) $\hat{p} = \frac{1}{A} [-\hat{\bar{y}} + \beta_1 \hat{M} + \beta_2 \hat{S} + \beta_3 (\hat{e} + \hat{p}^*) + \beta_4 FI + \beta_5 \hat{y}^*$

$+ (a_1 - \beta_1 - \beta_2)\hat{p}^e + u]$,

where $A = a_1 + \beta_3$ and $u = u_d - u_s$.

The aggregate demand equation allows for Keynesian impulses explicitly--in the form of fiscal policies, foreign demand, and substitution effects.

I do not have any major quarrels with the aggregate demand equation. Indeed, I show in an Appendix how an equation very similar to Korteweg's can be derived as a solution from an explicit structural model.[1] I want simply to draw attention to some features of the solution, implicit in the underlying structure. The demand for money is apparently deflated by expected domestic prices, rather than by the overall price level. The expected rate of inflation does not appear in either the absorption function or the real demand for money. I take government debt to be a proxy for wealth, and it too is deflated by expected domestic prices. If government debt correctly represents wealth, and wealth appears in both expenditure and the demand for money, then its coefficient, β_2, could be either positive or negative, for reasons familiar from the work of Blinder and Solow (1973). The β_3 coefficient I take to represent the substitution effect, and it will be positive only if the Marshall-Lerner condition is met, which may not be true in the short term.

If the aggregate demand equation gives me basically little trouble, the aggregate supply equation is more worrying. First, it assumes no money illusion. Second, which follows, it assumes all variations in unemployment are voluntary, and that there are no layoffs. Third, it disregards production lags as well as lags in adjustment of wages or prices to demand or cost influences. Taking the last into account, for example, would allow a change in the expected rate of growth of money to influence the expected rate of inflation with a lag. Fourth, the aggregate supply equation should be an equation relating the difference between the unemployment rate and the natural rate of unemployment to the difference between the actual and the expected rate of inflation. Instead, it is the rate of growth of output that appears in the equation. As the equation stands, it implies

_____

[1]See Appendix below.

that when $\hat{p} > \hat{p}^e$ the actual rate of growth of output exceeds the long-run rate of growth of output, which in turn implies not that the unemployment rate is below the natural rate but that the unemployment rate is continuously falling. Strictly, therefore, one should include the level of capacity in the aggregate supply equation and the rate of growth of output in the aggregate demand equation, which complicates the mathematics a little. Fifth, the foreign rate of inflation does not appear in the aggregate supply function. With a fixed exchange rate or an adjustable peg, a trade-off or a positively sloped aggregate supply function can be generated, even with zero money illusion, because the relevant price to producers is the domestic price level, but the relevant price to suppliers of labor is the expected overall price level. In short, the aggregate supply function is too inflexible to represent the whole of the period covered by the studies.[2] Some implications of all these points for the empirical results are noted below.

Finally, rational expectations is assumed so that, with no lags in the aggregate supply function, the implication is that the rate of growth of output will be essentially a random walk.

Taking the expected values from (3) gives

$$(4) \quad \hat{p}^e = \frac{1}{B} [-\hat{\bar{y}} + \beta_1 \hat{M}^e + \beta_2 \hat{S}^e + \beta_3 (\hat{e}^e + \hat{p}^{*e}) + \beta_4 \, FI^e + \beta_5 \, \hat{y}^{*e}] \, ,$$

where $B = \beta_1 + \beta_2 + \beta_3$. Combining (1) - (4) yields

$$(5) \quad \hat{p} - \hat{p}^e = \frac{1}{A} \{ \beta_1 (\hat{M} - \hat{M}^e) + \beta_2 (\hat{S} - \hat{S}^e) + \beta_3 [(\hat{e} + \hat{p}^*) - (\hat{e}^e + \hat{p}^{*e})]$$

$$+ \beta_4 (FI - FI^e) + \beta_5 (\hat{y}^* - \hat{y}^{*e}) + u \}$$

$$(6) \quad \hat{y} = \hat{\bar{y}} + \frac{a_1}{A} \{ \beta_1 (\hat{M} - \hat{M}^e) + \beta_2 (\hat{S} - \hat{S}^e) + \beta_3 [(\hat{e} + \hat{p}^*) - (\hat{e}^e + \hat{p}^{*e})]$$

$$+ \beta_4 (FI - FI^e) + \beta_5 (\hat{y}^* - \hat{y}^{*e}) \} + \frac{a_1}{A} u_d + \frac{\beta_3}{A} u_s \, .$$

---

[2] See Appendix for a more formal demonstration of these criticisms.

Equations (4), (5), and (6) form the basis, with minor variations, of the econometric work in these three studies.

2.   The rate of inflation is regressed against the expected values of the impulses. The expected value of the impulse is identified with the best forecast of the impulse. The expected value is assumed to determine the expected rate of inflation, and in turn, the expected rate of inflation is assumed, by some mechanism which is not entirely clear, to determine fairly quickly the actual rate of inflation. If the expected values of the impulses are known, then the effect on the expected rate of inflation will be represented by the coefficient from the known structural model.

Consider one illustration, equations (1) and (2) in the Korteweg paper. With rational expectations, $p = pe$ and $\hat{y} = \bar{\hat{y}}$. Assume that $\beta_2 = 0$. Now suppose the rate of growth of money accelerates, and that this is fully anticipated. With aggregate supply effectively fixed, any excess demand must be eliminated by domestic inflation; but, domestic inflation cannot increase in the same proportion as money, because if it did, there would be a substitution effect which would produce an excess supply of goods. So, to restore equilibrium in the goods market, the coefficient of expected monetary growth must be less than 1. If, then, the expected monetary growth accelerates, the public, knowing all this, including the substitution elasticities, will quickly adjust its wages and domestic prices, but by less than the monetary growth in order to eliminate the excess demand.

If foreign prices accelerated in the same proportion as the domestic money supply, domestic inflation would also have to rise in the same proportion to eliminate the excess demand for goods. This is the rationale for a sum of 1 for the coefficients on money and foreign prices.

Now consider the estimation of the expected rate of growth of money. What is important, it seems to me, is not the anticipated rate of growth of money but the expected permanent rate of growth of money. Assuming the rate of growth of money is fully anticipated, why should it influence the expected rate of inflation when it may, in fact, represent only a transitory deviation from its long-run path? This means that fully anticipated but transitory changes in money may have real effects.[3] Consider one of Barro's (1977) estimated equations for the U.S. of the anticipated rate of growth of money, where the unemployment rate appears as an explanatory variable. If the

---

[3]The interesting theoretical question is how to rationalize this distinction within the framework of the theory of the natural rate of unemployment. The cost of adjustment is the cost of recontracting. The benefit, on the other hand, may be only marginal. When monetary growth accelerates, the real wage rate decreases, but when monetary growth decelerates, the real wage rate increases. Over the cycle, therefore, the real wage rate is unaffected.

fully anticipated acceleration in monetary growth is known to be transitory--to absorb the unemployed--the real effects may be self-fulfilling.

The question then is how to estimate the permanently expected rate of growth of money. Barro's method, which is the most efficient for forecasting the rate of growth of money, does not necessarily give the permanently expected rate of growth of money. The monetary growth in the previous period is also not very appropriate. ARIMA methods may be more appropriate, but an adaptive scheme (actually used by Carr and Smith in a recent study, 1975) may, in fact, be the most appropriate.

All of this leads to the main point which is that, given the way in which the expected impulses are measured--in terms of past values--and the way in which the expected rate of inflation is estimated--by using the actual rate of inflation--it is difficult to discriminate between a lagged adjustment model and an expectations model.[4] The apparent short lag in the adjustment of the expected rate of inflation to the expected rate of growth of money (same quarter in Fourcans, half a year in Korteweg, and variable in Fratianni) argues for the lagged adjustment model. If there had been some independent estimates of the expected rate of inflation, e.g., from surveys, it might have been possible to test the expected rate of inflation independently. I also suspect that the fact that the coefficient of the expected rate of inflation enters with a coefficient of 1 on the actual rate of inflation is simply a characteristic of the econometric estimation and says nothing about the presence or absence of money illusion.[5]

Putting aside some of my own reservations about the model and the estimated equations, are the results consistent with the model? If an expected impulse is significant in influencing the expected rate of inflation, then the unexpected component of that same impulse ought also to be significant in influencing both the actual rate of inflation[6] (with a weaker coefficient) and the deviations of the actual rate of growth of output from its long-run path. This expectation comes closest to fulfillment in Fourcans's paper, where all the expected impulses are significant for expected inflation, and in most cases, their unexpected values tend to be significant for both inflation and output. In Korteweg's and Fratianni's papers, only expected money and foreign prices are significant for expected inflation, yet their unexpected values are not significant in explaining actual inflation. In Korteweg, unanticipated money is not even significant for output. In Korteweg, therefore, it seems that

---

[4]Presumably, if a system of wage indexation is in force, only the lagged model could function.

[5]In effect, the authors are regressing the "computed" rate of inflation with the actual rate of inflation.

[6]Given, of course, the expected rate of inflation.

unexpected money does nothing. In both Korteweg and Fratianni, unanticipated foreign demand is significant in influencing output, but anticipated is not. Finally, in Korteweg, the unexpected government debt is significant in influencing unanticipated output, but its expected value does not influence expected inflation.

Fourcans concludes from his regressions on the unanticipated rate of growth of output that the theory of the natural rate of unemployment is vindicated. I suspect this is an invalid inference. Unanticipated money has transitory effects on the rate of growth of output, which means that it permanently changes the rate of unemployment. I suspect the difficulty stems from an aggregate supply function that is wrongly formulated in the first place, as suggested above.

As seen, the model apparently throws up the prediction that the sum of the coefficients on the expected rate of growth of money and the foreign rate of inflation should be 1. This is vindicated in Korteweg's work but not in either Fratianni's or Fourcans's. Korteweg's result can be rationalized in terms other than rational expectations. Take, for example, the simplest quantity theory equation:

$$\hat{p} = \hat{M} - \hat{y} + \hat{v},$$

where v represents velocity,

and

$$\hat{pc} = a_1 \hat{p} + (1 - a_1) p^*,$$

where pc is the overall price level,

then $\hat{pc} = (1 - a_1) p^* + a_1 \hat{M} - a_1 (\hat{y} - \hat{v})$. This may be simply the long-run result that Korteweg is picking up with annual data.

All the studies find foreign demand significant in influencing output. Yet, apart from Fourcans's findings, fiscal policy is not significant. Some of my own work at the IMF is consistent with these findings. The explanation may lie simply in a deficient measure of fiscal policy, or it may be more substantive. The results conform to popular thinking which, at one and the same time, tends to play down the effectiveness of fiscal policies yet assumes that a foreign induced recovery would stimulate output. Is there a theoretical rationale for this result? If we suppose that the surplus on the current account is sterilized, then the impact effects on real demand, interest rates, wealth, and asset composition are the same for increases in foreign demand and for debt-financed fiscal expansion. There are, however, two differences. First, increased foreign demand unambiguously improves the balance of payments, at least in Keynesian-type models, while fiscal expansion may or may not improve the balance of payments and almost certainly worsens the current account. Second, the fiscal expansion has continuously adverse effects on the budget deficit while, if anything, increased foreign demand will reduce the deficit. Rational or not, these may be sufficient reasons to generate an offsetting reaction from the private sector with fiscal expansion which may be absent for a foreign induced recovery.

Finally, I want to make some brief comments about the lag from the rate of change in money to the rate of inflation. These three studies agree that the rate of growth in money is significant in determining the rate of inflation. Conventional wisdom has tended to put the lag at some two years, but some studies give a longer, others a shorter lag. What does theory tell us about this lag? Consider first the expectations-augmented Phillips curve models of the type used in the three papers. According to the theory, if the acceleration in money is fully anticipated, the lag will be effectively zero. If it is unanticipated, lags could be long depending on whether or not a lag is inserted in the aggregate supply function. Now consider models with traded and nontraded goods. In these models, the acceleration in the rate of inflation will <u>lead</u> to acceleration in the rate of growth of money (implying that the expected domestic rate of growth of money should be geared to the foreign rate of inflation). In Keynesian-type models, the lags are far more complicated depending on the lags in the expenditure as well as on the money demand equations. If the source of money is large capital inflows as in the 1970-72 period, then monetary growth will lead the rate of inflation. If wage pushes or supply shocks occur and are accommodated, then again the rate of inflation will lead the rate of growth of money. Finally, under flexible exchange rates, the dynamics of adjustment are different depending on J curves, capital flow effects, etc. All of this means that the relationship between monetary growth and inflation will be a variable one depending not only on the circumstances but also on the model assumed. My guess is that the mean lag has tended to become shorter for two reasons: first, the increasing relevance of rational expectations; second, the increased integration of goods markets in foreign trade. Yet, so far as I know, there has been little work on testing for changes in the length of the lag over time.

Appendix

Aggregate Demand and Aggregate Supply:
A Framework for the Evaluation of Monetary and Fiscal Impulses [*]

Variables used:

Ar	=	real absorption
Yrd		real disposable income
Yr		real GNP
Pd		domestic prices
P		overall price level
$\overline{Pe}$		expected rate of inflation
Q		rate of growth of productivity
X		volume of exports
Wa		wage rates
M		volume of imports
Pf		foreign prices denominated in foreign currency
E		exchange rate (units of domestic currency per unit of foreign currency)
Mo		the money supply
Gr		real government expenditure
T		nominal taxes
W		wealth
Fd		real demand originating in the rest of the world
r		the interest rate
edm		elasticity of demand for imports
edx		elasticity of demand for exports
Un		natural rate of unemployment
t		rate of tax
U		unemployment rate
$\dfrac{Yr - Yf}{Yf}$		capacity utilization
Yf	=	full capacity

$\overline{}$ represents a rate of change

[*] represents the long-run growth rate.

---

[*] Work in this area is being undertaken in the IMF by V. Argy and E. Spitaeller.

An aggregate demand function

(A.1) $\quad YrPd = ArP + XPd - MPfE$

(A.2) $\quad Ar = a_1 Yrd - a_3(r - \overline{Pe}) + a_{12} \dfrac{W}{P} + Gr$

(A.3) $\quad Yrd = [\dfrac{YrPd - T}{P}]$

(A.4) $\quad T = tYrPd$

(A.5) $\quad r = a_4 Yr - a_6 \dfrac{Mo}{P} + a_{13} \dfrac{W}{P} + a_{15} \overline{Pe}$

(A.6) $\quad X = a_8 \dfrac{PfE}{Pd} + Fd$

(A.7) $\quad M = a_9 Yr + a_{10} Pd/PfE$.

If we disregard a terms of trade effect, take $a_{15} = 1$, and assume that the balance of trade is in equilibrium so $M = X$ and $Ar = Yr$, then we obtain the following reduced form solution for aggregate demand:

(A.8) $\quad \dfrac{\Delta Yr}{Yr} = (\dfrac{a_3 a_6}{k}) (\dfrac{Mo}{YrP}) [\dfrac{\Delta Mo}{Mo} - \dfrac{\Delta P}{P}] + \dfrac{1}{k} (\dfrac{Fd}{Yr}) (\dfrac{\Delta Fd}{Fd})$

$\quad\quad + (\dfrac{a_{12} - a_3 a_{13}}{k}) (\dfrac{W}{PYr}) \dfrac{\Delta(W/P)}{W/P} + \dfrac{1}{k} [\dfrac{\Delta Gr - a_1 Yr \Delta t}{Yr}]$

$\quad\quad - (\dfrac{X}{Yr}) [\dfrac{edx + edm - 1}{k}] (\dfrac{\Delta Pd}{Pd} - \dfrac{\Delta Pf}{Pf} - \dfrac{\Delta E}{E})$,

189

where $edx + edm > 1$ is the Marshall-Lerner condition, and Yk is the multiplier. Korteweg's aggregate demand equation can be obtained exactly by making the following amendments. First, deflate the demand for money by expected domestic prices instead of by the overall price level in (A.5). Second, treat government debt as a proxy for wealth, deflate it by the expected domestic price level, and allow it to influence both real absorption and the nominal interest rate. Then, the coefficient on the rate of change in expected real wealth in the solution would be ambiguous for reasons that are well known.

An aggregate supply function

$$(A.9) \quad \bar{P} = a_{14}\,\overline{Pd} + (1 - a_{14})\,(\overline{Pf} + \bar{E})$$

$$(A.10) \quad \overline{Pd} = a_{16}Q^* + a_{17}\overline{Wa} + a_{18}\left(\frac{Yr - Yf}{Yf}\right)$$

$$(A.11) \quad \overline{Wa} = a_{19}Q^* + a_{20}\overline{Pe} - a_{21}\,(U - Un)$$

$$(A.12) \quad U = Un - a_{22}\left(\frac{Yr - Yf}{Yf}\right).$$

Solving for $\overline{Pd}$ and setting $a_{16}, a_{17}, a_{19}, a_{20}$ all equal to 1 gives

$$(A.13) \quad \overline{Pd} = \overline{Pe} + (a_{21} \cdot a_{22} + a_{18})\left(\frac{Yr - Yf}{Yf}\right).$$

Solution (A.13) can be transformed into Korteweg's aggregate supply function by assuming $\overline{Pe} - \overline{Pde}$ (i.e., the expected overall rate of inflation in our model is the same as the expected domestic rate of inflation) and $\overline{Yr} - \overline{Yf} = \dfrac{Yr - Yf}{Yf}$.

References

Barro, R.J. (1977), "Unanticipated Money Growth and Unemployment in the United States," American Economic Review, 67: 101-15.

Blinder, A.S., and Solow, R.M. (1973), "Does Fiscal Policy Matter?," Journal of Public Economics, 2: 319-38.

Carr, J., and Smith, L. (1975), "A Suggestion for a New Monetary Indicator," Journal of Monetary Economics, 1: 363-68.

Fourcans, A. (1978), "Inflation and Output Growth: The French Experience, 1960-1975," Carnegie-Rochester Conference Series, 8, eds. K. Brunner and A.H. Meltzer. Amsterdam: North-Holland.

Fratianni, M. (1978), "Inflation and Unanticipated Changes in Output in Italy," Carnegie-Rochester Conference Series, 8, eds. K. Brunner and A.H. Meltzer. Amsterdam: North-Holland.

Korteweg, P. (1978), "The Economics of Inflation and Output Fluctuations in the Netherlands, 1954-1975: A Test of Some Implications of the Dominant Impulse-cum-Rational Expectations Hypothesis," Carnegie-Rochester Conference Series, 8, eds. K. Brunner and A.H. Meltzer. Amsterdam: North-Holland.

INFLATION AND OUTPUT CHANGES
IN FRANCE, ITALY, AND THE NETHERLANDS:
A COMMENT

Anna J. Schwartz

National Bureau of Economic Research, New York

These three papers are essentially similar exercises for France, Italy, and the Netherlands. The exercises are descendants of the St. Louis Andersen-Jordan (1968) one-equation model, except that the dependent variable is not nominal income change but its components, price and output change. In addition, the underlying St. Louis approach is modified in two ways: a) as supplements to the effects of money supply and fiscal changes on the dependent variables, other possible impulses from foreign sources, dichotomized into price and quantity measures--the set referred to as systematic impulses--are also examined to determine the dominant impulse; b) a distinction is introduced along the lines of "rational expectations" models between anticipated and unanticipated movements in the impulses.

Although in objectives there are obvious similarities among the papers, the one respect in which they are needlessly dissimilar is in notation.

I first summarize the papers, with some incidental comments on procedures, and at the conclusion of the summary, offer some general comments. In outline, the authors present some introductory material, derive the theoretical model, discuss the empirical measures they use in testing the model, and then present regression results, first for the inflation equations and then for transitory movements in the rate of output growth equations. Fourcans and Korteweg also give the results of nonparametric tests which I ignore.

Introductory Section

Introductory material in each paper disposes of some tangential issues. Is cost-push a satisfactory explanation of French inflation? Is a frustration theory of price behavior by monopolistic firms adequate to explain Italian inflation? Is the exogoneity or endogoneity of monetary processes relevant to the analysis of monetary effects on Dutch inflation?

Theoretical Section

The three papers offer a sketch of the dominant impulse hypothesis. In addition, Fratianni distinguishes two other hypotheses regarding inflation: the quantity theory and the monetarist theory in an open economy. I shall not comment further on these two hypotheses. To derive equations for the inflation rate and transitory movements in the rate of output growth under the dominant impulse hypothesis, Fratianni and Korteweg each begin with the Barro and Fischer (1976) formulation of aggregate supply and aggregate demand functions for an open economy (described as a managed-exchange rate economy by Korteweg, and a fixed-rate regime by Fratianni). In the theoretical model, price change, given the normal growth rate of output, is a function of the systematic impulses and expected price change. Expected price change, in turn, given the normal growth path of output, is a function of expected values of the systematic impulses. The hypothesis embodied in the expected price change equation is that expectations are formed rationally and free of money illusion. Subtracting expected inflation from actual inflation on the left-hand side, and expected from actual impulses on the right-hand side yields an equation for deviations of actual from expected inflation as the result of surprise in the systematic impulses, attributable to imperfect availability of information, and as the result of random events.

The expression for actual output growth, given the normal growth path, is then derived as a function of unexpected changes in the systematic impulses and random shifts. Expected changes in systematic impulses have only price effects and no output effects. Normal output growth is presumably determined by real factors, such as natural resource endowment, social institutions, human capacities, technology, invention, enterprise, and thrift, factors which tend to change slowly and gradually, determining the secular trend of output, not cyclical or transitory movements.

Fourcans skips the derivation of the price and output equations from the Barro-Fischer aggregate demand and supply functions and goes directly to the more general forms of the theoretical model. The equations he estimates are not derived in a manner comparable to those of the other authors. More of this below.

Measurement of the Variables

Each author presents measures of the impulses for his country.

a) The monetary impulse is measured by M1 for the Netherlands, M2 for France and Italy. Since these are open economies, in my view, the authors should have explained why it is appropriate to measure the monetary impulse in this way rather than as the rate of growth of the domestic component of the base.

b) The fiscal impulse is defined by Fratianni as "the theoretical equivalent of Hansen's (1969) discretionary impact of fiscal policy, namely, the total thrust of the government budget net of its induced or feedback effects." The empirical counterpart varies among the three countries.

c) The foreign impulse, as already noted, is measured in price and quantity dimensions. The price measure for the Netherlands and Italy is either change in import prices in domestic currency units or in a weighted average of consumer prices in the rest of the world, with constant dollar real GDP weights, and, hence, is based on dollar weights. For France, the price measure is change in French import prices. The foreign output impulse for the Netherlands and Italy is either the percentage change in the rest-of-the-world real GDP converted into dollars at 1970 exchange rates or the percentage annual change in the country's trade volume with the rest of the world. For France, the foreign output impulse is the growth rate of French real exports.

d) In addition to these impulses, Korteweg introduces a financial impulse, defined as the growth rate of Dutch government debt outstanding, both short- and long-term, net of government deposits in all banks and excluding central bank holdings of government debt.

Why the impulses should theoretically have effects on inflation and output growth rates is not explicitly treated in the papers. The possible existence of multicollinearity among the impulses is also not examined. The fiscal impulse and Korteweg's financial impulse presumably affect the domestic monetary impulse. The foreign price impulse as a proxy for the foreign money impulse presumably also affects the domestic monetary impulse. The fact that the foreign import price impulse is expressed in local currencies means that the exchange rate is implicit in the variable. The authors have indicated that the presence of different lags on the impulses means that multicollinearity is not a problem. But, if the impulses are interrelated, different lags will not answer the difficulty.

Another question may be raised with respect to the foreign inflation rate as a predictor of domestic inflation. Suppose U.S. money supply growth and U.S. inflation dominated foreign money supply growth and inflation. In that case, lagged U.S. money stock growth or inflation rather than rest-of-the-world measures should enter into nonreserve countries' expected domestic inflation rates.

The data are annual for the Netherlands and Italy, covering 1954-75 for the former, 1952-75 for the latter, but observations are lost due to lags. For France, the data are quarterly, covering 1961-I to 1975-IV. One may ask how many degrees of freedom Fratianni and Korteweg actually have when they have experimented with a number of variants of the same equation.

195

The derivation of expected values of observations in each paper is as follows.

1. For the Netherlands two approaches are used. In the first, described as naive, expectations are simply a lagged rate of change of an impulse, the lags varying with the impulse. As a second approach, an ARIMA process was fitted to changes in impulses. The normal growth rate of output was treated either as a constant in a regression, as a lagged rate of change of output, or as the anticipated value of an ARIMA process.

2. For Italy, expected values were obtained in several ways. In the first, the expected impulse was defined by Fratianni as "equal to a moving average of current and past values of that impulse itself, the length and form of the moving average being ascertained on purely statistical grounds," and the moving average in turn lagged. Alternative approaches varied with the impulses. The expected growth rate of money was obtained from predicted values of a regression of monetary change on a one-period lagged rate of monetary change and the contemporaneous domestic component of the monetary base. The use of the contemporaneous domestic component of the monetary base in such a regression seems questionable. How would knowledge of such a variable be available on a current basis? Should not the fiscal variable also be affecting the expected growth rate of money? For the fiscal impulse and the trade volume with the rest of the world, the expected growth rates were obtained by adding to the one-year lagged value of the variables the one-year change minus the surprise of an ARIMA process. Expected domestic or foreign price change was derived from predicted values of the regression of actual price change on independent variables that differ from regression to regression.

3. For France, expected values of the impulses were not used in the main regressions; instead only unanticipated values were used. Unanticipated values are the acceleration or deceleration of the systematic impulses, with various lags. The anticipated rate of inflation was first measured as the predicted value from a regression of actual price change on two-year moving averages of the systematic impulses. However, Fourcans discarded this result, and substituted anticipated rates of inflation, derived from an adaptive expectations scheme with geometrically declining weights summing to unity over a six-quarter lag structure, applied to rates of change of prices from quarter to quarter with the initial quarter lagged once. The rest of his data, except as otherwise noted, is expressed as annual percentage changes from corresponding quarters. Fourcans's unanticipated change variables, expressed as accelerations or decel-erations of growth rates, are not comparable with Fratianni's or Korteweg's measures of unanticipated change as the difference between actual and anticipated rates of change.

Let me now turn to the results the papers report, beginning with the inflation regressions.

Inflation Regressions

Because of differences in notation, in choice of variable, and in procedure, precise comparison of the results for the three countries is not possible. Table 1 summarizes the regressions Fratianni and Korteweg indicate they prefer, and one that I have selected from the array Fourcans presents since he has made no judgment. Lags of the independent variables vary within and among regressions, but are not indicated in the table. In addition, as noted, definitions of the variables and derivation of anticipated and unanticipated magnitudes vary.

For both Italy and the Netherlands, the fact that the sum of the coefficients on the anticipated money and foreign price variables approximates unity is the appeal of the inflation regressions to the authors. Fratianni achieves this result only by including the specific versions of anticipations of the fiscal and world trade variables which otherwise do not contribute to the determination of Italian inflation. Korteweg achieves his result by including unanticipated impulses for the volume of world trade and for fiscal change--an ad hoc variable he created when his original fiscal variable in its anticipated form was insignificant. In addition, he includes a dummy variable marking the shift from excise to value-added taxes. In other regressions for the Netherlands, the remaining anticipated impulses are not significant. There is no explanation for the failure of anticipations of the fiscal impulse to have an impact on the anticipated part of inflation or for the success of the impact of unanticipated fiscal change, in its ad hoc form, on the unanticipated part of inflation. Perhaps the ad hoc unanticipated fiscal variable should have been introduced in the initial regression in anticipated form.

Fratianni does not discuss the sign or the size of the coefficient of the intercept. Korteweg is bothered because the constant term fails to equal minus the normal rate of growth of real consumption--his price variable is consumer prices--but, instead, is not significantly different from zero. Although for Italy, in a regression not shown in Table 1, the unanticipated fiscal impulse explains only 3 percent of the variance of the unanticipated inflation rate, for the Netherlands, it seems to play a more important role.

Fourcans omits the first step in Korteweg's and Fratianni's procedure of regressing actual inflation on anticipated values of the impulse, from which predicted inflation rates are generated, and proceeds directly to the second step, regressing actual inflation on the inflation rate derived from an adaptive

Table 1

Comparison of Selected Regression Results for France, Italy, and the Netherlands

Inflation Regressions
Dependent variable: Rate of change in prices

Country	Intercept	Anticipated Impulses		Unanticipated Impulses		Tax shift variable	R²	DW
		Money	Import prices	Volume of world trade	Fiscal			
Italy (t-stat.)	-4.44 (2.10)	0.66 (4.09)	0.34 (7.73)	-0.007 (0.92)	-0.14 (0.49)	... ...	0.94 ...	1.94 ...
		Anticipated Impulses		Unanticipated Impulses				
the Netherlands	0.35 (0.86)	0.27 (5.14)	0.65 (10.58)	0.14 (3.01)	1.41 (4.95)	3.10 (5.03)	0.92 ...	2.33 ...
		Unanticipated Impulses				Anticipated inflation		
		Money	Import prices	Volume of French exports	Fiscal			
France	... ...	0.78 (2.61)	0.028 (3.54)	0.020 (1.77)	0.051 (2.29)	1.06 (49.01)	0.93 ...	1.32 ...

Sources: Fratianni, Table 7, regression 1; Table 8, regression 3;
Korteweg, Table 2, regression 5; Table 5, regression 40
Fourcans, Table 7, regression 12; Table 11, regression 1'd.

Table 1 -- Continued

Output Regressions

Dependent variable: Alternative measures of unanticipated output growth[a]

Country	Intercept	Unanticipated Impulses					R^2	DW
		Money	Import prices	Volume of real exports or world trade	Fiscal	Financial		
Italy (t-stat.)	: :	1.14 (3.70)	: :	0.42 (3.72)	- 0.61 (1.37)	: :	0.64	2.52
							: :	: :
the Netherlands	- 0.64 : :	: :	0.19 (2.91)	0.71 (7.27)	: :	0.48 (3.45)	0.75	2.24
							: :	: :
France	- 0.278 (0.74)	0.134 (1.67)	- 0.123 (4.06)	0.092 (2.82)	2.72 (4.19)	: :	0.44	2.01
							: :	: :

[a] Autoregressive residual of output (Italy); first difference in rate of change of output (the Netherlands); deviation of output from steady state (France).

199

expectations scheme, as noted above, plus unanticipated changes in the impulses, measured as accelerations and decelerations. Hence, this is the inflation regression shown in Table 1, reported for the full period ending 1975-IV; in the regression for a subperiod ending 1973-IV, acceleration in import prices is never a significant variable, and regressions including it are not reported. The unanticipated change in the French export impulse is not significant in either period, whereas the unanticipated monetary impulse with lags of two or three quarters is significant. The unanticipated fiscal impulse is significant only over the full period. The dominant variable, however, is the coefficient of the anticipated rate of inflation, which is not significantly different from unity. Fourcans suppresses the intercept, noting that, when introduced, it was never significantly different from zero.

The three papers conclude that domestic inflation in each country is consistent with a monetarist dominant impulse hypothesis.

Output Regressions

The dependent variables for the three countries vary, but each is expressed as a function of unanticipated impulses, variously measured. Unanticipated monetary change is significant only in Italy; unanticipated change in import prices only in the Netherlands and France. Unanticipated change in real exports or in the volume of world trade is significant in all three countries. The unanticipated fiscal impulse is significant only in France, and the unanticipated growth rate of the stock of government debt--a variable only in the Netherlands regression--has positive and significant effects on deviations of actual from normal industrial production--a rather different result from that Barro (1977) obtains for the U.S. In this case, Korteweg offers an explanation. Short-run additions to government debt, on the one hand, raise market rates of interest on government debt; on the other hand, they lower the market rate of return on equity in physical capital, hence stimulating output. Otherwise, the medley of results for the three countries is not adequately explored in the papers. For the Netherlands, unanticipated import price inflation outperforms unanticipated world consumer price inflation, suggesting that unanticipated exchange rate fluctuations are an important codeterminant of the deviation of actual from normal production growth.

General Comments

1.   The authors have estimated price and output equations. For Fratianni and Korteweg, prices are consumer prices and output, industrial production; for Fourcans, the price deflator implicit in GDP and real GDP. I assume all three

could have used symmetrical price and output series. I wonder if, as an alternative research strategy, the authors had modeled a nominal income equation and a real income equation, with the price equation determined by the identity, whether the results would have been achieved with less manipulation of the variables.

2.   I would expect some symmetry in the effects of surprises or innovations in impulses and in the effects of the anticipated parts of the impulses. Why should anticipations of monetary change affect the trend rate of inflation, but the unanticipated parts have no effect on unanticipated inflation? In general, a plethora of equations is presented with not enough explanatory material with respect to the detailed findings.

3.   From the papers it is impossible to learn the relative importance of domestic as against foreign inflationary impulses. This seems to me a lacuna in the research effort.

The papers are good examples of the state of the art in 1977, the emphasis on rational expectations reflecting the current interest in this approach. There is much we still have to learn about the transmission of inflation from one country to another--or more likely from the reserve currency country to nonreserve currency countries--and about the determinants of domestic output deviations. Still, we are indebted to the authors for putting us on the road to that goal.

References

Andersen, L.C., and Jordan, J.L. (1968), "Monetary and Fiscal Actions: A Test of Their Relative Importance in Economic Stabilization," Federal Reserve Bank of St. Louis Review, 50 (11): 11-24.

Barro, R.J. (1977), "Unanticipated Money Growth and Unemployment in the United States," American Economic Review, 67: 110-11.

Barro, R.J., and Fischer, S. (1976), "Recent Developments in Monetary Theory," Journal of Monetary Economics, 2: 133-67.

Fourcans, A. (1978), "Inflation and Output Growth: The French Experience, 1960-1975," Carnegie-Rochester Conference Series, 8, eds. K. Brunner and A.H. Meltzer. Amsterdam: North-Holland.

Fratianni, M. (1978), "Inflation and Unanticipated Changes in Output in Italy," Carnegie-Rochester Conference Series, 8, eds. K. Brunner and A.H. Meltzer. Amsterdam: North-Holland.

Korteweg, P. (1978), "The Economics of Inflation and Output Fluctuations in the Netherlands, 1954-1975: A Test of Some Implications of the Dominant Impulse-cum-Rational Expectations Hypothesis," Carnegie-Rochester Conference Series, 8, eds. K. Brunner and A.H. Meltzer. Amsterdam: North-Holland.

THE ECONOMICS OF INFLATION AND OUTPUT FLUCTUATIONS IN THE UNITED STATES, 1952-1974

Dean S Dutton*

Brigham Young University

I. INTRODUCTION

This paper presents the results of some empirical tests using annual data of the relative dominance of various impulses thought to be important in shaping the course of inflation and economic activity in the U.S. during the period 1952-74.[1] The approach is motivated by a fundamental conclusion from price theory that fluctuations in the price level and in economic activity result from the interaction of market supply and demand forces. The argument is that various impulses exert their influence on prices and output by affecting either aggregate supply or aggregate demand or both. While this approach is not inconsistent with an eclectic view that the impulses impinging on supply and demand are random and, therefore, not subject to the influence of policy decisions, the thesis advanced here is that those impulses whose effects on prices and output dominate are for the most part systematic. I argue that, while shocks which exert important effects on prices and output, occur from time to time independent of any policy decisions, persistent and sustained increases in the price level, which constitute the inflation problem as frequently perceived, and much of the variation in output growth, are due to the effect of impulses under policy control.

The effect of four different impulses on inflation and economic activity (the rate of growth of real output) are considered in this paper.

The fiscal impulse is measured by the change in the real value of some index of the federal government deficit as a percentage of real national income and affects prices and output through its effect on aggregate demand. The

---

*The work reported in this paper was begun when I was a visiting associate professor at Carnegie-Mellon University, 1974-75, and was continued at the Federal Reserve Bank of St. Louis where I was a visiting scholar during the remainder of 1975.

I am grateful to all members of the International Monetarist Consortium, particularly Allan Meltzer, Karl Brunner, and Pieter Korteweg; and to Bennett T. McCallum, Michael Hamburger, James R. Kearl, Larry T. Wimmer, Clayne Pope, James B. McDonald, and Rachel Balbach for helpful discussion; to Asa Janey, Michael Metcalf, Michael McCoy, Joan Bauer, Portia Bakker, and Ken Kruse for computational assistance; and to Carnegie-Mellon University, the Federal Reserve Bank of St. Louis, and Brigham Young University for research support.

[1]See Brunner and Meltzer (1977).

hypothesis is that inflation and increased output growth are due to increases in government demand for output not released from private-sector absorption by commensurate increases in taxes.

Two external impulses are considered–an external quantity impulse and an external price impulse. The external quantity impulse expresses the growth of the net absorption of domestic output by foreigners as a percentage of output and is measured by the change in real net exports divided by real national income. An increase in the impulse results in an increase in the contending claims on domestic output by the domestic and foreign sectors and is resolved again by either price inflation or an increase in output growth or both. Again, this impulse exerts its effect through the demand side of the economy. The external price impulse is measured by the percentage growth rate of import prices and exerts its effect through both the demand and supply sides of the economy. An increase in this impulse represents an increase in the rate of price change of imports of final and semi-final goods and services and of imports of raw materials. Substitution of domestic for foreign goods is the result of the first effect which increases aggregate demand. A reduction of supply by firms buying imported inputs is the result of the second effect which reduces aggregate supply.

The monetary impulse is measured by the percentage rate of growth of M1 and affects prices and output via the demand side.

Empirical evaluation relies on both parametric methods (i.e., regressions) and on a newly developed nonparametric test.[2] Although the discriminatory power of the nonparametric test is limited, it offers useful information complementary to the regression results. The conclusions drawn from both methods of analysis are consistent.

In an attempt to discern the effects of the extraordinary shocks that occurred in 1973 and 1974, the tests were performed on the data over the two intervals, 1952-72 and 1952-74. For the 1952-72 period, there is only weak evidence at best that anything considered except the expected rate of price change had any effect on the current rate of inflation. For the 1952-74 period, there is strong evidence that, in addition to the expected rate of price change, the external price impulse had some effect. The evidence suggests that for both periods a measure of the maintained rate of money growth was an important and probably the dominant force shaping the expected rate of price change. The monetary impulse appears consistently in both the 1952-72 and 1952-74 periods as an important and dominant determinant of fluctuations

---

[2]See Hildebrand, Laing, and Rosenthal (1974, 1976).

in output growth, whereas only for the 1952-74 period is there evidence that another impulse (viz., the external price impulse) had some effect. It was concluded, however, that the sustained rate of output growth was independent of sustained levels of the impulses.

The results obtained bear on Friedman's (1970) proposition that inflation is always a monetary phenomenon. I conclude that this is so for the 1952-72 period, but that it can be argued that at least one other impulse was important when the period is extended to include 1973 and 1974.

The term "inflation," as used here, means the current rate of price change, which includes both those changes in the price level that are persistent and sustained increases and those changes summarizing the many passing effects involving once-and-for-all increases.[3]

In the following sections I present the model relating inflation and the rate of output growth to the impulses. In the explanation of inflation, the expected rate of price change is an important ingredient, and is estimated here using a procedure similar to McGuire's (1976b) and Meltzer's (1977). The use of these estimates along with information regarding the variables generating them enables me to draw conclusions concerning Friedman's proposition.

II. THE MODEL

An expectations-augmented Phillips curve is a fundamental element in the simple model within which the data are analyzed.[4] It is assumed that the actual rate of inflation $\hat{p}$ is determined by a function of excess demand E and the anticipated rate of inflation $\hat{P}^a$:

$$(1) \quad \hat{p} = f(E) + \hat{P}^a .$$

---

[3] This definition contrasts with Meltzer's (1977) in which he defines "inflation" to be "the rate of price change maintained for a period of time" (p.183). The preference for my definition is motivated by my observation that it is the standard one, i.e., that most references to the term have this meaning behind them. Even those who prefer Meltzer's definition use the term sometimes in its conventional meaning. To have remained consistent with his definition, it seems to me that, instead of using the term "inflation," Meltzer should have said in his opening paragraph, "The Phillips curve is widely accepted as the maintained theory of [the current rate of price change]." And, "Most recent studies of [the current rate of price change] report the continuing search for variables that increase the accuracy with which the theory predicts or forecasts." To use the word "inflation," which he defines to have a different meaning, when he means the current rate of price change introduces confusion.

[4] See, for example, Friedman (1968) which laid the theoretical foundation for such an approach, and Cross and Laidler (1976), Korteweg (1975), and McGuire (1976a) for some empirical applications. See also the recent surveys of inflation by Laidler and Parkin (1976) and by Gordon (1976) which focus on the continued debate on the relevance of the Phillips curve as a useful theory of inflation.

Hats ($\hat{\ }$) denote percentage rates of change. Excess demand is proxied by the difference between the actual and the long-run "full" employment growth rate of real GNP, $\hat{y} - \hat{y}^f$, and is assumed to be determined by the deviations of the set of impulses operating on the economy from their maintained levels, defined as $DI = I - I5$, where I denotes the current value of the set of impulses and $I5$ their maintained levels (to be defined precisely later):

(2) $\quad E \;=\; \hat{y} - \hat{y}^f$

(3) $\quad \hat{y} - \hat{y}^f = E(DI)$.

The anticipated rate of inflation $\hat{p}^a$ is also assumed to be functionally determined by the impulses I. In particular, it is assumed that

(4) $\quad \hat{p}^a \;=\; g(I5)$.

From (1)-(3) it follows that:

(5) $\quad p \;=\; h(DI) + \hat{p}^a$,

so that the right-hand side of (5) summarizes the resulting effects of the impulses on inflation through market supply and demand forces.[5]

It is assumed that when $DI = 0$, then $E = 0$, which implies that $\hat{y} = \hat{y}^f$ and $\hat{p} = \hat{p}^a$. Deviations of output growth from $\hat{y}^f$ can be accomplished only by deviations of the impulses from their maintained levels, and nonzero values of impulses equal to their maintained levels will only affect inflation through their effect on the anticipated rate of inflation.

Conclusions about the effect of the impulses on inflation are drawn from regression estimates of (4) and (5). Conclusions about the effect of the

---

[5]A theory that summarizes the transmission of these fiscal, external, and monetary impulses, and their effects on aggregate supply and demand, is set forth in Brunner and Meltzer (1976). See also Korteweg (1978) for a brief summary of an aggregate supply-demand model from which an equation like (5) follows as the semi-reduced-form equation to be estimated.

impulses on fluctuations of output growth are drawn from regression estimates of (3) and from regressing $\hat{y}$ on $\hat{p}^a$.

III. THE CONSTRUCTION OF EMPIRICAL IMPULSE MEASURES

This section defines the impulse measures used in the empirical tests and outlines their construction.

A. The Fiscal Impulse Measure

I relied on two measures of the fiscal impulse—one constructed from real cash flow deficit figures (from the unified budget) and one constructed from real high employment deficit figures for the federal government. The respective nominal deficit data were deflated by the GNP deflator to generate the real deficit data. I denote the real cash flow deficit as CF and the real high employment deficit as FF. A fiscal impulse would result, however, only from changes in the deficit, i.e., from ΔCF or ΔFF. To enable comparisons of the stimulating influences of the changes in the deficit over time, the changes in the deficit for each period were divided by real national income, yr (nominal national income deflated by the GNP deflator), of the previous year. That is, the fiscal impulse measures used in this study are denoted as:[6]

$$(6) \quad FFIR = \frac{FF - FF_{-1}}{yr_{-1}}$$

$$(7) \quad CFIR = \frac{CF - CF_{-1}}{yr_{-1}} \ .$$

---

[6]In the initial stages of this study, I developed a measure of the fiscal impulse that attempted to separate that portion of the cash flow deficit resulting from the discretionary actions of the government from that portion which was automatic or endogenous.

First, engodenous changes in tax receipts were added to the cash flow deficit. If a decision is made to run a deficit of a given size which stimulates economic activity, which in turn results in an increase in tax collections, the reported cash flow deficit will be less than the planned deficit by the amount of the automatic increase in taxes.

Second, increases in the government wage bill which result from keeping government wage rates in line with private sector wage rates were subtracted from the cash flow deficit, since such increases are not the result of discretionary budget policy.

Third, government transfers abroad were subtracted from the cash flow deficit because they do not represent competing government claims on private domestic output.

I denoted this adjusted cash flow deficit deflated by the GNP deflator as F, so that the resulting fiscal impulse was defined as:

$$(8) \quad FIR = \frac{F - F_{-1}}{yr_{-1}} \ .$$

Necessary tax data for the construction of this impulse measure were unavailable to me for years after 1972. The results from the tests performed with this impulse measure over the 1952-72 period did not differ in any fundamental way from those from the tests performed with the other two impulse measures over this period. Therefore, only the results of the tests using FFIR and CFIR are reported here.

B. The External Quantity Impulse Measure

The measure summarizing this impulse is the change in real net exports NX as a percentage of real nominal income and is denoted as:

$$(9) \quad NXI = \frac{NX - NX_{-1}}{yr_{-1}} \quad .$$

C. The External Price Impulse Measure

The measure summarizing this impulse is the percentage rate of change of the import price index PI and is denoted as:

$$(10) \quad \hat{PI} = \frac{PI - PI_{-1}}{PI_{-1}} \quad .$$

D. The Monetary Impulse Measure

The percentage rate of growth of the narrowly defined money stock to include currency and demand deposits held by the private sector M is used as the measure summarizing the monetary impulse and is denoted as:

$$(11) \quad \hat{M} = \frac{M - M_{-1}}{M_{-1}} \quad .$$

Note that all impulses have the dimension of a percentage rate of change and are, therefore, pure numbers.

The hypothesis that underlies (4) is that the anticipated rate of inflation is determined by some measure of the maintained levels of the impulses, which again would have the dimension of a percentage rate of change. It is assumed that the measure of the maintained impulse is the five-year moving average of the percentage rate of change of the respective index or other entity for which each impulse is the one-year percentage rate of change and is denoted as I5, where I is the respective impulse. For example, the maintained monetary impulse for the current year $\hat{M5}_t$ is defined to be the average annual compound rate of change that is required for the money stock to grow from its level five years ago to its current level and is denoted as:

$$\hat{M5}_t = (\frac{M_t}{M_{t-5}})^{\frac{1}{5}} - 1 \; ,$$

where the subscript t denotes the current year.

The maintained external price impulse $\hat{PI5}_t$ is an analogous concept and is computed in like manner, i.e.,

$$\hat{PI5}_t = \left(\frac{PI_t}{PI_{t-5}}\right)^{\frac{1}{5}} - 1 \, .$$

The construction of the maintained external quantity impulse and the maintained fiscal impulse requires an additional step, however. The monetary impulse $\hat{M}$ and the external price impulse $\hat{PI}$ are the one-year percentage rates of change of observable empirical entities. Such is not the case for the external quantity impulse NXI and the fiscal impulse $FFIR(CFIR)$, however. While the dimension of NXI is a percentage rate of change, for example, there is no observable empirical entity of which NXI is the percentage rate of change; likewise for $FFIR(CFIR)$. I define an artificial index $FFC(CFC)$ of which $FFIR(CFIR)$ is the percentage rate of change. Likewise I define the artificial index NXC of which NXI is the percentage rate of change, i.e.,

$$NXC_t = NXC_{t-1}(1 + NXI_t)$$

$$FFC_t = FFC_{t-1}(1 + FFIR_t)$$

$$CFC_t = CFC_{t-1}(1 + CFIR_t).$$

The maintained external quantity impulse for the current year $NXI5_t$ and the maintained fiscal impulse for the current year $FFIR5_t(CFIR5_t)$ are therefore denoted as:

$$NXI5_t = \left(\frac{NXC_t}{NXC_{t-5}}\right)^{\frac{1}{5}} - 1$$

Table 1

Estimate of $\hat{p}$ [a]

Regression	Constant	$FFIR5_{-1}$	$CFIR5_{-1}$	$NXI5_{-1}$	$\hat{PI5}$	$\hat{M5}_{-2}$	R^2/DW	Period*
1 (t-stat.)	-0.0049 (-1.07)	0.21 (0.72)		1.25 (1.55)	-0.20 (-1.66)	1.16 (6.96)	0.86/1.49	1952-72(C-O)
2	-0.0010 (-0.14)	0.24 (0.62)		2.71 (2.57)	0.24 (3.11)	0.92 (3.79)	.90/1.47	1952-74(C-O)
3	-0.0048 (-0.89)		0.13 (0.38)	1.08 (1.61)	-0.18 (-1.49)	1.14 (6.12)	.86/1.50	1952-72(C-O)
4	0.00081 (0.12)		-0.19 (-0.42)	2.30 (2.83)	0.24 (3.11)	0.86 (3.73)	.89/1.54	1952-74(C-O)
5	0.0013 (0.19)					0.83 (4.18)	.80/1.35	1952-72(C-O)
6	-0.0082 (-1.59)					1.22 (8.28)	0.77/1.23	1952-74(C-O)

*The expression (C-O) following the period indicates that the Cochrane-Orcutt iterative technique was applied to the regression.

$$FFIR5_t = (\frac{FFC_t}{FFC_{t-5}})^{\frac{1}{5}} - 1$$

$$CFIR5_t = (\frac{CFC_t}{CFC_{t-5}})^{\frac{1}{5}} - 1.$$

IV. EMPIRICAL TESTS: THE RESULTS FROM REGRESSION ANALYSIS

A. The Inflation Regressions

The first step was to estimate the anticipated rate of inflation. The price variable used throughout was the GNP deflator. The measure of the anticipated rate of inflation used here is the prediction series generated by the systematic part of a regression equation of the format of (4), in which the current rate of inflation $\hat{p}$ is regressed on the maintained levels of the impulses FFIR5(CFIR5), NXI5, $\hat{PI}5$, and $\hat{M}5$. The regression results are presented in Table 1.[7]

Using estimates of $\hat{p}^a$ from the regressions in Table 1, a regression equation of the form of (5) was estimated. The results of that estimation are presented in Table 2.

The results of regressing the unanticipated rate of inflation on the changes in the impulses are reported in Table 3.

The results of regressing $\hat{p}^a$ on $\hat{p}^{am}$ are reported in Table 4.

Examination of regressions 1-6 of Table 1[*] yields some useful information about the formation of expectations under the hypothesis. It appears that neither measure of the fiscal impulse had a statistically significant effect on anticipated inflation. From regressions 1 and 3, I conclude that over the 1952-72 period the maintained rate of monetary expansion was the sole determinant of anticipated inflation, since only the coefficient on the monetary impulse is statistically significant. In 1973 and 1974 the picture changes. When the period is extended, both the sustained external quantity and price impulses enter regressions 2 and 4 with statistically significant coefficients. A rationalization of these results might easily be that, although economic agents consider all four of the impulses, no importance was attached to the external price and quantity

---

[7] In all the regressions in this section, an attempt was made to choose that lag structure of the variables that most favored the hypothesis of a positive effect of the respective impulse on inflation.

[*] Editor's note. Regression equations, displayed in Tables 1-5, are numbered consecutively from 1 to 36 without parentheses, and are so referenced in the text.

Table 2

Estimated Coefficients of $\hat{p}$

Regression	Constant	DFFIR	DCFIR	$DNXI_{-1}$	$\hat{DPI}$	$\hat{DM}_{-1}$	$\hat{p}^a$	$\hat{p}^{am}$	R^2/DW	Period*
7 (t-stat.)	-0.00098 (-0.28)	-0.11 (-0.99)		-0.17 (-0.56)	0.0036 (0.062)	-0.052 (-0.55)	1.04 (8.36)		0.88/1.59	1952-72
8	0.0087 (1.24)	0.027 (0.20)		0.014 (0.048)	0.12 (3.07)	0.060 (0.67)	0.61 (3.07)		.94/1.42	1952-74(C-O)
9	-0.00044 (-0.12)		0.017 (0.16)	-0.26 (-0.76)	-0.00034 (-0.0058)	-0.021 (-0.20)	1.02 (7.91)		.87/1.54	1952-72
10	0.0081 (1.11)		0.021 (0.21)	-0.028 (-0.084)	0.12 (3.02)	0.069 (0.67)	0.62 (2.99)		.93/1.46	1952-74(C-O)
11	0.026 (8.36)	0.028 (0.11)		0.33 (0.47)	0.18 (1.86)	0.071 (0.35)			.20/0.38	1952-72
12	0.026 (8.90)	0.00019 (0.00084)		0.46 (0.88)	0.22 (6.29)	0.11 (0.62)			.70/0.44	1952-74
13	0.026 (8.40)		0.095 (0.39)	0.23 (0.31)	0.18 (1.87)	0.10 (0.47)			.21/0.42	1952-72
14	0.026 (8.95)		0.088 (0.39)	0.37 (0.67)	0.22 (6.39)	0.14 (0.73)			.70/0.46	1952-74
15	0.0051 (0.90)	-0.062 (-0.47)		0.037 (0.11)	0.10 (1.42)	-0.0061 (-0.066)		0.80 (4.25)	.85/1.62	1952-72(C-O)
16	0.011 (1.84)	-0.019 (-0.14)		0.21 (0.74)	0.16 (5.35)	0.025 (0.28)		0.55 (3.38)	.94/1.61	1952-74(C-O)
17	0.0060 (0.95)		-0.058 (-0.55)	0.12 (0.33)	0.12 (1.66)	-0.029 (-0.28)		0.76 (3.75)	.85/1.61	1952-72(C-O)

*The expression (C-O) following the period indicates that the Cochrane-Orcutt iterative technique was applied to the regression.

Note: In each equation where DFFIR or DCFIR appears, the sustained level of the respective impulse was used in the estimate of $\hat{p}^a$ in that equation.

The estimates of $\hat{p}^a$ in regressions 19 and 20 come from regressions 1 and 2. The variable $\hat{p}^{am}$ is the estimate of the anticipated rate of inflation from regressions 5 and 6.

Table 2 -- Continued

18	0.010 (1.76)		-0.050 (-0.48)	0.28 (0.89)	0.16 (5.24)	0.0041 (0.043)		0.56 (3.40)	0.94/1.59	1952-74(C-O)
19	0.0011 (0.30)						0.96 (8.09)		.86/1.61	1952-72(C-O)
20	-0.0011 (-0.29)						1.03 (10.96)		.90/1.60	1952-74(C-O)
21	0.0022 (0.59)							0.94 (7.37)	.83/1.72	1952-72(C-O)
22	-0.00022 (-0.040)							1.05 (7.02)	0.79/1.37	1952-74(C-O)

impulses until the relatively dramatic shocks of 1973 and 1974, at which time their effects were taken into account in the formation of expectations.

Another measure of the anticipated rate of inflation $\hat{p}^{am}$ was devised by regressing the current rate of price change $\hat{p}$ on the maintained monetary impulse alone. The anticipated rate of inflation series $\hat{p}^{am}$ is again the prediction series from this regression. A simple quantity theory of money in which the growth rate of money is policy determined would yield this result.[8] This measure of the anticipated rate of inflation will be used to test Friedman's (1970) proposition that inflation is a monetary phenomenon.[9]

Another interesting feature of regressions 1-6 is apparent. The estimated coefficients of the monetary impulse are larger in regressions 1 and 3 for the 1952-72 period than in regressions 2 and 4 for the longer 1952-74 period, again supporting the notion that in the longer period when other impulses that affect anticipations of inflation came into play, the importance of the monetary impulse is reduced. The relative sizes of the coefficient estimates in regressions 5 and 6 are just reversed. This suggests, at least, that the relatively large coefficient estimate in regression 6 for the longer period relative to the coefficient estimates in regressions 2 and 4 is biased upward, i.e., that the estimated coefficient on the monetary impulse includes the effects of the omitted variables in the 1952-74 period.

Table 2 summarizes most of the information from the tests of the relative dominance of the impulses on inflation. The general flavor of the conclusions can be sensed from regressions 7-10. Neither measure of the deviation of the fiscal impulse from its sustained level is ever statistically significant. And further, in no other case is the deviation of an impulse measure from its main-tained level significant at the 5-percent level for the 1952-72 period, implying that the anticipated rate of inflation fully explains the current rate of inflation during that period. This conclusion is further supported by the results of regressions 15 and 17 where the anticipated rate of inflation is measured by $\hat{p}^{am}$. The results of regressions 15 and 17 do not differ in any fundamental way from the results of regressions 7 and 9, in the sense that in both cases the coefficients of $\hat{p}^{a}$ and $\hat{p}^{am}$ are not statistically different from 1, implying that during the 1952-72 period not only is the expected rate of price change wholly determined by the sustained rate of money growth but that the current rate of inflation is so determined as well.

---

[8]Sims (1972) concludes that for the U.S. there is no evidence to contradict the assumption that money can be treated as exogenous in a quantity theory relationship.

[9]See Dutton (1977) and Berman (1977) for other evidence regarding this phenomenon.

Table 3

Estimated Coefficients of $(\hat{p} - \hat{p}^a)$

Regression	Constant	DFFIR	DCFIR	$DNXI_{-1}$	$\hat{DPI}$	$\hat{DM}_{-1}$	R^2/DW	Period*
23 (t-stat.)	0.00010 (0.080)	-0.10 (-1.00)		-0.16 (-0.54)	0.014 (0.29)	-0.051 (-0.56)	0.10/1.51	1952-72
24	-0.0023 (-0.69)	-0.019 (-0.14)		-0.091 (-0.29)	0.056 (2.09)	0.082 (0.84)	.26/1.58	1952-74(C-O)
25	0.00016 (0.12)		0.019 (0.18)	-0.26 (-0.77)	0.0054 (0.11)	-0.020 (-0.20)	.05/1.49	1952-72
26	-0.0028 (-0.80)		0.0051 (0.045)	-0.15 (-0.41)	0.062 (2.26)	0.095 (0.87)	0.24/1.58	1952-74(C-O)

*The expression (C-O) following the period indicates that the Cochrane-Orcutt iterative technique was applied to the regression.

Table 4

Estimated Coefficients of $\hat{p}^a$ on $\hat{p}^{am}$

Regression	Constant	$\hat{p}^{am}$	R^2/DW	Period[*]
27 (t-stat.)	0.0027 (0.97)	0.92 (10.00)	0.89/2.10	1952-72(C-O)
28	-0.00043 (-0.14)	1.01 (11.50)	.87/1.42	1952-74
29	0.0022 (0.99)	0.94 (12.46)	.92/2.21	1952-72(C-O)
30	0.0010 (0.29)	1.01 (10.84)	0.89/1.21	1952-74(C-O)

[*]The expression (C-O) following the period indicates that the Cochrane-Orcutt iterative technique was applied to the regression.

Note: The estimates of $\hat{p}^a$ in regressions 27 and 28 come from regressions 1 and 2, respectively. The estimates of $\hat{p}^a$ in regressions 29 and 30 come from regressions 3 and 4, respectively.

The variable $\hat{p}^{am}$ is the estimate of the anticipated rate of inflation from regressions 5 and 6.

It is interesting to note the small magnitude and the lack of statistical significance of the estimated parameter of the deviation of the one-year rate of money growth from its maintained level in all the regressions. The effect of money on inflation is expressed wholly through the expected rate of price change.

For the 1952-74 period, the implications of regressions 8 and 10, where $\hat{p}^a$ is used as the measure of anticipated inflation, do not differ from those of regressions 16 and 18 where $\hat{p}^{am}$ is used as the measure of anticipated inflation. In addition to the anticipated rate of inflation, the deviation of the rate of change of import prices from the sustained level exerts a significant effect on the current rate of inflation. One notes that the estimated coefficients on DPI in regressions 16 and 18 are somewhat larger than the corresponding estimated coefficients in regressions 8 and 10. This is probably due to the fact that in regressions 8 and 10 part of the effect of the external price impulse on current inflation is exerted through the anticipated rate of inflation $\hat{p}^a$. Since in regressions 16 and 18 the anticipated rate of inflation $\hat{p}^{am}$ excludes the effect of any impulses except money, the total effect of the external price impulse on inflation must come through the estimated coefficient of DPI, hence, the larger estimated coefficient.

Regressions 11-14 and 19-20 and 21-22 imply that the deviations of the impulses from their maintained levels, on the one hand, and the measures of anticipated inflation, on the other, are sufficiently independent that regressions of $\hat{p}$ on them separately do not alter the results in any fundamental way. Indeed, the explanatory power of regressions 19-22 is almost as good as that of regressions 7-10 and 15-18.

Table 3 summarizes the results of the regressions where the coefficient of $\hat{p}^a$ is constrained to be equal to 1. Again the results from these regressions are in fundamental agreement with those presented earlier.

The implication of the regressions of $\hat{p}^a$ on $\hat{p}^{am}$, presented as 27-30 in Table 4, imply that the $\hat{p}^{am}$-series essentially summarizes the information contained in the $\hat{p}^a$-series. This is consistent with the regression results 7-22, viz., that the results obtained by using the $\hat{p}^a$-series as the measure of anticipated inflation do not differ in any fundamental way from the results obtained using the $\hat{p}^{am}$-series as the measure of anticipated inflation.

If the conclusion is correct that, during periods free of extraordinary shocks, inflation can be explained exclusively by the rate of money growth, then one would expect to be able to forecast the inflation rate for 1976 with reasonable accuracy using regressions 5 and 21. Probably by 1976 the effects of the extraordinary shocks of 1973 and 1974 had mostly worn off. Using the

Table 5

Estimated Coefficients of $\hat{y}$

Regression	Constant	DFFIR	DCFIR	DNXI	$\widehat{DPI}_{-1}$	$\widehat{DM}_{-1}$	$\hat{p}^a$	R^2/DW	Period[*]
31 (t-stat.)	0.033 (5.67)	0.046 (0.085)		-1.20 (-0.96)	-0.030 (-0.20)	1.18 (3.14)		0.48/1.95	1952-72(C-O)
32	0.031 (6.18)	0.52 (1.10)		-0.43 (-0.41)	-0.23 (-2.11)	1.24 (3.79)		.48/1.81	1952-74
33	0.033 (5.42)		0.083 (0.23)	-1.22 (-1.85)	-0.033 (-0.25)	1.23 (2.96)		.48/1.93	1952-72(C-O)
34	0.030 (5.87)		0.13 (0.34)	-0.84 (-0.82)	-0.18 (-1.76)	1.21 (3.26)		.45/1.63	1952-74
35							-0.28 (-0.62)	.02/2.28	1952-72
36							-0.44 (-1.59)	0.11/2.14	1952-74

[*]The expression (C-O) following the period indicates that the Cochrane-Orcutt iterative technique was applied to the regression.

estimated parameter values of regression 5 and the maintained rate of money growth for 1974, the anticipated rate of inflation $\hat{p}^{am}$ for 1976 was obtained and plugged into regression 21, which yielded a forecasted rate of increase of 5.3 percent in the GNP deflator for 1976. The actual inflation rate for 1976 was 5.1 percent. This result provides a useful test strengthening the conclusions presented here.

B. The Output Regressions

Equation (3) states that $\hat{y} - \hat{y}^f = E(DI)$. I make the simplifying assumption that the long-run "full" employment growth rate of real GNP, $\hat{y}^f$, is constant, and estimate the following equation:

$$\hat{y} = \hat{y}^f + E(DI) .$$

Regressions 31-34 of Table 5 summarize the results.[10] In each regression, the constant is the estimate of the growth rate of long-run "full" employment real GNP, $\hat{y}^f$. In each case it is highly statistically significant and is between .030 and .033.

In the two time intervals considered, neither the net export impulse DNXI or either measure of the fiscal impulse, DFFIR or DCFIR, ever has a statistically significant effect, but the monetary impulse $\hat{DM}_{-1}$ always has a rather large and highly statistically significant effect. Import prices $\hat{DPI}_{-1}$ do not have a statistically significant effect in the 1952-72 period, but the regressions provide some evidence that they did affect output growth negatively in 1973-74.

The evidence summarized here plus the results from the inflation regressions are contrary to the Phillips curve argument in which some measure of the full employment gap (such as the $\hat{y} - \hat{y}^f$ used here) is related to the rate of price change, so that monetary policy has very little influence on inflation once unemployment reaches a critical level.[11] The regressions 31-34 strongly imply that deviations of the rate of money growth from its maintained level affect output growth and, thus, the full employment gap, $\hat{y} - \hat{y}^f$. The very

---

[10]Here, again, the lag structure of the deviations of the impulses from their maintained levels, DI = DFFIR(DCFIR), DNXI, DPI$_{-1}$, DM$_{-1}$, was chosen which most favored the hypothesized effect of this impulse on output growth, viz., DFFIR(DCFIR), positive; DNXI, positive; $\hat{DPI}_{-1}$, negative; $\hat{DM}_{-1}$, positive.

[11]See Gordon (1976), Modigliani and Papademos (1975), and Tobin (1975).

small and statistically insignificant estimate of the coefficient of $\hat{DM}_{-1}$ in the inflation regressions implies that changes in the gap, $\hat{y} - \hat{y}^f$, caused by changes in the one-year acceleration of money have no effect on inflation. Indeed, the inflation rate is dominated by the maintained rate of money growth independent of the one-year deviations from that maintained level.

Regressions 35 and 36 imply that the rate of growth of output and the anticipated rate of inflation are independent. This finding in conjunction with other results implies that the rate of output growth is independent of the maintained rate of money expansion. One concludes that output cannot systematically be stimulated over and above its normal rate of growth by traditional demand management policies.

V. AN ADDITIONAL EMPIRICAL TEST OF THE DOMINANCE OF THE ONE-YEAR IMPULSES

Taking first differences of (5) yields

$$\Delta \hat{p} = h(\Delta DI) + \Delta \hat{p}^a .$$

It is assumed that the variability of $\hat{p}^a$ is small relative to the variability of $\hat{p}$ so that

$$\Delta \hat{p} - \Delta \hat{p}^a \approx \Delta \hat{p} .$$

From this assumption it follows that

$$(12) \quad \Delta \hat{p} = h(\Delta DI)$$

is a good approximation of the relationship between the rate of inflation and the one-year impulses.

From (3) and the assumption that $\hat{y}^f$ is constant, it follows that

(13) $\Delta \hat{y} = E(\Delta \, DI)$

is a good approximation of the relationship between output growth and the one-year impulses.

Within the context of (12) for inflation and (13) for output growth, I make use of the newly developed nonparametric test statistic ∇p[12] to test the hypothesis of positive association of $\hat{p}$ and $\hat{y}$, on the one hand, and DI with the appropriate lags, on the other.[13] That is, the positive association for inflation is tested by comparing series of $\Delta \hat{p}$ and $\Delta \, DI$, and is tested for output growth by comparing series of $\Delta \hat{y}$ and $\Delta \, DI$. The appropriate lags for the one-year impulses are those specified in the respective regression equations.

The ∇p-statistic and its standardized value are used to test the null-hypothesis of no positive association between the phenomenon $\hat{p}$ or $\hat{y}$ and the impulse DI. This involves comparing $\Delta \hat{p}$ or $\Delta \hat{y}$ with $\Delta \, DI$ after having normalized each of the elements involved in $\Delta \hat{p}$, $\Delta \hat{y}$, and $\Delta \, DI$ by dividing them by one-third the standard deviation of the respective series, $\hat{p}$, $\hat{y}$, and $\Delta \, I$, over the respective sample periods, 1952-72 and 1952-74. When the standardized ∇p-statistic is positive and exceeds some critical level, the null-hypothesis of no positive systematic empirical association between $\hat{p}$ and DI or between $\hat{y}$ and DI must be rejected. I chose the 5-percent level of significance to reject the null-hypothesis. The appropriate one-tailed test is satisfied when the value of the standardized ∇p-statistic amounts to 1.65.

Table 6 summarizes the estimated and standardized values of the ∇p-statistic needed to test the null-hypothesis of no positive empirical association between the rate of inflation and output growth, on the one hand, and the deviations of the impulses from their maintained levels, on the other. The results are in complete agreement with and strengthen the conclusions drawn from the regression analysis.

The null-hypothesis of no positive association between $\hat{p}$ and the set of impulses DI can be rejected only for the external price impulse $\hat{DPI}$ for the

---

[12]See Hildebrand, Laing, and Rosenthal (1974, 1976) for the development of the test, and Korteweg (1978) for a detailed description of its application to a problem of this type.

[13]The hypothesis as conceived assumes a negative relationship between $\hat{y}$ and $\hat{DPI}_{-1}$. In order to maintain the general rule of positive association between impulse movements and output growth, the $\hat{DPI}_{-1}$ series was multiplied by -1 for this test.

Table 6

**Nonparametric Test of Positive Association
of the Relevant Phenomenon and the Impulse Measures,
1952-72 and 1952-74**

Impulse	Phenomenon $\hat{\triangle p}$		Phenomenon $\hat{\triangle y}$		Period
	estimated ∇p	standardized ∇p	estimated ∇p	standardized ∇p	
$\triangle$DFFIR	0.1538	0.761			1952-72
	.0363	0.145			1952-74
$\triangle$DCFIR	- .2174	- 1.702			1952-72
	- .0544	- 0.504			1952-74
$\triangle$DNXI$_{-1}$	- .0074	- 0.168			1952-72
	.0336	0.125			1952-74
$\triangle$D$\hat{P}$I	.2135	1.075			1952-72
	.3372	2.013*			1952-74
$\triangle$D$\hat{M}_{-1}$	- .0405	- 0.379			1952-72
	- 0.0308	- 0.338			1952-74
$\triangle$DFFIR			0.0156	- 0.024	1952-72
			- .0126	- 0.173	1952-74
$\triangle$DCFIR			- .1538	- 1.142	1952-72
			- .1358	- 1.045	1952-74
$\triangle$DNXI			- .2353	- 1.241	1952-72
			- .1871	- 1.108	1952-74
- $\triangle$DPI$_{-1}$			.1765	0.893	1952-72
			.2853	1.888*	1952-74
$\triangle$D$\hat{M}_{-1}$			.5078	2.835*	1952-72
			0.4840	2.902*	1952-74

Note: Starred (*) values of the standardized ∇ p-statistic are significant at at least the 5-percent level.

1952-74 period, implying, as did regressions 7-22, that no evidence of an effect of the deviation of any impulse from its maintained level was found except for the rate of change of import prices for the 1952-74 period.

The null-hypothesis of no positive association between $\hat{y}$ and $\hat{DPI}_{-1}$ for the 1952-74 period or between $\hat{y}$ and $\hat{DM}_{-1}$ for both periods is rejected, again supporting the conclusions drawn from regressions 31-36. This result implies that, while strong exogenous shocks can affect output growth, the most important source of variations in output growth among the impulses considered over the 1952-74 period was the deviations of the rate of money growth from its maintained level.

VI. CONCLUSIONS

For the period 1952-72, the results reported here imply that the rate of inflation was determined exclusively by the maintained rate of money growth. While other factors were shown to have had important effects on the rate of inflation in 1973 and 1974, money was, nevertheless, found to be dominant. The main conclusion from this study of the 1952-74 period is that inflation is predominantly a monetary phenomenon, and in periods free of extraordinary exogenous shocks, exclusively so. A useful test of this conclusion was made by comparing the forecasted rate of inflation for 1976 from the model estimated over the 1952-72 period, in which money exclusively is the driving force, with the actual rate. The forecasted rate for 1976 was 5.3 percent and the actual rate was 5.1 percent.

It was concluded also that, at least over the 1952-72 period, the rate of inflation was independent of the "unemployment gap" as measured by the deviation of output growth from full employment output growth, $\hat{y} - \hat{y}^f$, i.e., the Phillips curve played no role in either exacerbating or mitigating the inflationary forces emanating from the maintained rate of money expansion.

It was found that during the entire period deviations of money growth from its maintained level were the most important causes of the fluctuations in the growth rate of output. There was some evidence also that the sharp acceleration of import prices in 1973 and 1974 affected output growth negatively.

The principal policy implications are, first, that output growth cannot systematically be stimulated over and above its normal rate by traditional demand management policies, and second, that control of the domestic money stock is a necessary and sufficient condition to control inflation. And further, since those impulses found to be dominant in shaping the course of inflation and those impulses found to be dominant in causing fluctuations in output growth were--it can be argued--to a substantial degree at least under the control of the government policymaker, then the government policymaker must take a major part of the credit for the inflation and recessions experienced in the U.S. during the 1952-74 period.

Appendix

Relevant Data Series

	P	y	FFC	CFC	NXC	PI	M
1947	74.64	309.90	63.02	74.81	102.16	74.10	113.10
1948	79.57	323.70	64.80	74.14	99.33	81.90	111.58
1949	79.12	324.10	66.95	77.21	99.21	78.00	111.20
1950	80.16	355.30	65.87	76.58	97.23	84.70	116.20
1951	85.64	383.40	66.97	76.38	97.91	106.20	122.70
1952	87.45	395.10	68.76	76.87	97.38	100.60	127.40
1953	88.33	412.80	69.45	78.59	96.76	96.50	128.80
1954	89.63	407.00	67.73	77.02	97.21	98.50	132.30
1955	90.86	438.00	66.57	76.91	97.26	98.30	135.20
1956	93.99	446.10	66.19	75.49	97.81	99.30	136.90
1957	97.49	452.50	66.27	76.47	98.24	101.20	135.90
1958	100.00	447.30	66.90	78.16	97.27	96.20	141.10
1959	101.66	475.90	66.06	74.96	96.73	94.50	143.40
1960	103.29	487.70	65.09	75.80	97.63	96.00	144.20
1961	104.62	497.20	65.53	77.68	97.96	94.60	148.70
1962	105.78	529.80	65.90	77.47	97.83	92.40	150.90
1963	107.17	551.00	65.48	77.27	98.00	93.20	156.50
1964	108.85	581.10	66.40	77.36	98.50	95.50	163.70
1965	110.86	617.80	66.88	77.24	98.21	96.50	171.30
1966	113.94	658.10	67.36	77.38	97.79	99.20	175.40
1967	117.59	675.20	68.39	77.72	97.74	100.00	186.90
1968	122.30	706.60	67.66	78.44	97.33	101.00	201.70
1969	128.20	725.60	65.92	76.18	97.23	104.20	208.70
1970	135.24	722.50	66.30	77.79	97.41	111.60	221.40
1971	141.35	746.30	67.03	77.43	97.04	117.40	235.30
1972	146.12	792.50	67.51	78.20	96.40	126.10	255.80
1973	154.31	839.20	66.73	77.41	97.43	149.60	271.50
1974	170.18	821.20	66.18	77.55	97.30	222.10	284.40

	$\hat{P}$	$\hat{y}$	FFIR5	CFIR5	NXI5	$\hat{PI5}$	$\hat{M5}$
1952	0.0211	0.0305	0.0176	0.00544	-0.00954	0.0631	0.0241
1953	.0101	.0448	.0139	.0117	- .00522	.0334	.0293
1954	.0147	- .0141	.00232	- .000516	- .00408	.0478	.0354
1955	.0137	.0762	.00212	.000870	.0000654	.0302	.0308
1956	.0344	.0185	- .00234	- .00234	- .000207	- .0133	.0221
1957	.0372	.0144	- .00734	- .00105	.00176	.00119	.0130
1958	.0257	- .0115	- .00745	- .00109	.00104	- .000623	.0184
1959	.0166	.0639	- .00500	- .00539	- .000992	- .00826	.0162
1960	.0160	.0248	- .00447	- .00292	.000749	- .00472	.0130
1961	.0129	.0195	- .00199	.00574	.000315	- .00965	.0167
1962	.0111	.0656	- .00112	.00261	- .000821	- .0180	.0212
1963	.0131	.0400	- .00428	- .00228	.00150	- .00632	.0209
1964	.0157	.0546	.00103	.00631	.00364	.00211	.0268
1965	.0185	.0632	.00543	.00378	.00120	.00104	.0350
1966	.0278	.0652	.00551	- .000768	- .000342	.00954	.0336
1967	.0320	.0260	.00744	.000655	- .000199	.0159	.0437
1968	.0401	.0465	.00659	.00299	- .00138	.0162	.0521
1969	.0482	.0269	- .00145	- .00306	- .00260	.0176	.0498
1970	.0549	- .00427	- .00174	.00143	- .00163	.0295	.0527
1971	.0452	.0329	- .000983	.000116	- .00155	.0343	.0605
1972	.0337	.0691	- .00260	.00124	- .00276	.0475	.0648
1973	.0560	.0589	- .00276	- .00263	.000207	.0817	.0612
1974	0.103	-0.0215	0.000777	0.00358	0.000135	0.163	0.0639

	FFIR	CFIR	NXI	$\hat{PI}$	$\hat{M}$
1952	0.0267	0.00643	- 0.00543	- 0.0527	0.0383
1953	.0100	.0224	- .00628	- .0408	.0110
1954	- .0247	- .0201	.00459	.0207	.0272
1955	- .0172	- .00135	.000544	- .00203	.0219
1956	- .00566	- .0185	.00560	.0102	.0126
1957	.00124	.0129	.00440	.0191	- .00730
1958	.00946	.0222	- .00984	- .0494	.0383
1959	- .0126	- .0410	- .00558	- .0177	.0163
1960	- .0146	.0111	.00930	.0159	.00558
1961	.00678	.0249	.00342	- .0146	.0312
1962	.00565	- .00272	- .00129	- .0233	.0148
1963	- .00645	- .00253	.00170	.00866	.0371
1964	.0141	.00108	.00512	.0247	.0460
1965	.00722	- .00151	- .00296	.0105	.0464
1966	.00720	.00185	- .00426	.0279	.0239
1967	.0153	.00440	- .000573	.00806	.0656
1968	- .0107	.00918	- .00421	.0100	.0792
1969	- .0258	- .0288	- .000981	.0317	.0347
1970	.00574	.0212	.00187	.0710	.0609
1971	.0110	- .00468	- .00387	.0520	.0628
1972	.00712	.0101	- .00658	.0741	.0871
1973	- .0115	- .0102	.0107	.186	.0614
1974	- 0.00836	0.00182	- 0.00135	0.484	0.0475

	DFFIR	DCFIR	DNXI	$\hat{DPI}$	$\hat{DM}$
1952	0.00913	0.000990	0.00411	- 0.0116	0.0142
1953	- .00394	.0107	- .00106	- .0741	- .0183
1954	- .0270	- .0196	.00867	- .0271	- .00819
1955	- .0193	- .00222	.000469	- .0323	- .00883
1956	- .00332	- .0161	.00581	.0235	- .00957
1957	.00858	.0140	.00264	.0179	- .0203
1958	.0169	.0233	- .0109	- .0488	.0199
1959	- .00760	- .0356	- .00459	- .00941	.0000600
1960	- .0101	.0141	.00855	.0206	- .00739
1961	.00877	.0191	.00311	- .00493	.0145
1962	.00677	- .00533	- .000469	- .00523	- .00637
1963	- .00217	- .000250	.000200	.0150	.0162
1964	.0130	- .00523	.00148	.0226	.0192
1965	.00179	- .00529	- .00416	.00943	.0114
1966	.00169	.00262	- .00392	.0184	- .00965
1967	.00789	.00375	- .000374	- .00787	.0218
1968	- .0173	.00619	- .00283	- .00620	.0271
1969	- .0243	- .0257	.00162	.0141	- .0151
1970	.00748	.0197	.00350	.0415	.00820
1971	.0120	- .00480	- .00232	.0177	.00226
1972	.00972	.00882	- .00382	.0266	.0223
1973	- .00869	- .00753	.0105	.105	.000140
1974	- 0.00914	- 0.00176	- 0.00149	0.321	- 0.0163

228

	$\hat{p}^a_{53\text{-}72}$	$\hat{p}^a_{53\text{-}74}$	$\hat{p}^{am}_{53\text{-}72}$	$\hat{p}^{am}_{53\text{-}74}$
1952	...	...	...	...
1953	0.0133	0.00857	0.0220	0.0224
1954	.0103	.0225	.0145	.0169
1955	.0195	.0196	.0219	.0257
1956	.0383	.0251	.0240	.0310
1957	.0288	.0287	.0290	.0294
1958	.0231	.0268	.0256	.0211
1959	.0124	.0115	.0155	.00907
1960	.0162	.0136	.0191	.0172
1961	.0161	.0147	.0145	.0117
1962	.0131	.00708	.0110	.00726
1963	.0139	.0120	.0146	.0130
1964	.0200	.0231	.0178	.0179
1965	.0231	.0259	.0169	.0165
1966	.0259	.0261	.0235	.0253
1967	.0336	.0342	.0378	.0366
1968	.0320	.0335	.0301	.0324
1969	.0438	.0433	.0437	.0492
1970	.0475	.0494	.0505	.0583
1971	.0456	.0516	.0485	.0539
1972	0.0451	.0530	0.0465	.0553
1973	...	.0573	...	.0604
1974	...	0.0932	...	0.0701

Note: The prediction series $\hat{p}^a_{53\text{-}72}$ and $\hat{p}^a_{53\text{-}74}$ are taken from regressions 1 and 2, and the prediction series $\hat{p}^{am}_{53\text{-}72}$ and $\hat{p}^{am}_{53\text{-}74}$ are taken from regressions 5 and 6. Each series begins in 1953 because of the application of the Cochrane-Orcutt iterative technique to the regressions.

References

Berman, P.I. (1977), "The Short-run Relationship between Money and Inflation," The Conference Board, New York. Multilithed.

Brunner, K., and Meltzer, A.H. (1976), "An Aggregative Theory for a Closed Economy," in Monetarism, ed. J. Stein. Amsterdam: North-Holland.

_____(1977), "The Explanation of Inflation: Some International Evidence," American Economic Review, 67: 148-54.

Cross, R., and Laidler, D. (1976), "Inflation, Excess Demand, and Expectations in Fixed Exchange Rate Open Economies," in Inflation in the World Economy, ed. M. Parkin and G. Zis. Manchester: Manchester University Press.

Dutton, D.S (1977), "A Model of Self-perpetuating Inflation: The Confederacy, 1861-65; Germany, 1922-23." Brigham Young University. Multilithed.

Friedman, M. (1968), "The Role of Monetary Policy," American Economic Review, 58: 1-17.

_____(1970). The Counter-revolution in Monetary Theory. London: International Economic Association for the Wincott Foundation, occasional paper no. 33.

Gordon, R.J. (1976), "Recent Developments in the Theory of Inflation and Unemployment," Journal of Monetary Economics, 2: 185-220.

Hildebrand, D.K., Laing, J.D., and Rosenthal, H. (1974), "Prediction Logic: A Method for Empirical Evaluation of Formal Theory," Journal of Mathematical Sociology, 3: 163-85.

_____(1976), "Prediction Analysis in Political Research," American Political Science Review, 70: 509-35.

Korteweg, P. (1975), "Inflation, Economic Activity and the Operation of Fiscal, Foreign and Monetary Impulses in the Netherlands: A Preliminary Analysis, 1953-1973," De Economist, 123: 4.

Korteweg, P. (1978), "The Economics of Inflation and Output Fluctuations in the Netherlands, 1954-1974: A Test of the Dominant Impulse-cum-Rational Expectations Hypothesis," Carnegie-Rochester Conference Series, 8, eds. K. Brunner and A.H. Meltzer. Amsterdam: North-Holland.

Laidler, D., and Parkin, M. (1976), "Inflation: A Survey," Economic Journal, 85: 741-809.

McGuire, T. (1976a), "Price Change Expectations and the Phillips Curve," Carnegie-Rochester Conference Series, 2, eds. K. Brunner and A.H. Meltzer. Amsterdam: North-Holland.

_____ (1976b), "On Estimating the Effects of Controls," Carnegie-Rochester Conference Series, 2, eds. K. Brunner and A.H. Meltzer. Amsterdam: North-Holland.

Meltzer, A.H. (1977), "Anticipated Inflation and Unanticipated Price Change: A Test of the Price-Specie Flow Theory and the Phillips Curve," Journal of Money, Credit and Banking, 9: 182-205.

Modigliani, F., and Papademos, L. (1975), "Targets for Monetary Policy in the Coming Year," Brookings Papers on Economic Activity, 3. Washington, D.C.: The Brookings Institution.

Sims, C.A. (1972), "Money, Income, and Causality," American Economic Review, 62: 540-52.

Tobin, J. (1975), "Monetary Policy, Inflation, and Unemployment." Yale University. Multilithed.

THE IMPULSE-THEORETIC EXPLANATION
OF CHANGING INFLATION AND OUTPUT GROWTH:
EVIDENCE FROM GERMANY

Manfred J.M. Neumann[*]
Freie Universität Berlin

I. INTRODUCTION

A. The Aim of the Paper

An explanation of the accelerations and decelerations of the German price level as well as of output of the private sector observed over the past twenty years is attempted. The basic approach is to concentrate on explanations that are reconcilable with price theory and to neglect the "ad-hocery" of institutionalist approaches.

Price theory seeks to explain economic fluctuations as resulting from sequences of real and financial shocks that are transmitted to output and the price level through changes in the structure of relative prices of financial and nonfinancial assets, where the channels and the relative speed of transmission are conditioned by the distribution of relative costs of information and adjustment; see Brunner (1970a). Price theory per se does not discriminate among the various kinds of shocks operating on the private sector. Additional hypotheses are required for differentiation. Acknowledgement is made that a large variety of once-and-for-all events occurring at random influences the observed rates of change of the price level and of output, but the contention here is that the more persistent changes of the price level result from a small set of systematically changing impulse forces.

The relevant impulse forces are the following: the Keynes-Wicksell impulse of autonomous changes of the anticipated net yield on real capital; the domestic fiscal impulse force emitting pure fiscal and financial effects; foreign monetary and fiscal impulse forces emitting financial and real effects; and finally, the monetary impulse. I dismiss a priori the Keynes-Wicksell impulse as an impulse force operating on both inflation and real growth, since for Germany there is no evidence that real rates of return move positively with the rate of inflation. Fiscal actions create pure fiscal and financial effects. The pure fiscal effects will be taken care of by an appropriately defined impulse measure, and the financial effects enter the analysis through the monetary

[*] I am grateful to Karl Brunner and the participants at the Carnegie-Rochester Conference for valuable comments and suggestions, and to Herbert Buscher for research assistance.

Table 1

Selected Economic Indicators

Cycles	Δy	Δx	U	Δg	Δp	Δp^g	Δp^I	ΔM	Contribution of foreign reserve flows to ΔM
1955-58	6.9	13.2	4.0	4.4	2.3	4.0	- 0.7	10.2	20.0
1959-63	5.7	8.1	1.2	7.6	2.3	3.9	- 0.9	9.3	4.2
1964-67	3.8	8.2	1.1	2.3	2.7	5.4	1.0	6.1	0.5
1968-71	6.1	10.5	1.0	4.3	3.0	8.1	0.3	8.2	13.1
1972-75	1.5	7.3	2.4	4.1	6.4	9.6	8.8	9.4	12.5
1955-75	4.8	9.4	1.9	4.7	3.3	6.1	1.6	8.7	9.8

Note: Annual averages are given as percentages.

Δz = annual percentage rate of change of variable z.

Variables:

y = total output
x = real exports
U = unemployment ratio
g = real government consumption
p = cost-of-living index
p^g = deflator of government consumption
p^I = import price index
M = narrowly defined money stock.

234

impulse by changing the monetary base from the sources side as well as by changing the money multiplier (through relative price effects). Similarly, the financial effects of foreign impulse forces become part of the monetary impulse, while their real effects have to be measured separately.

The paper has two main aims. The first is to develop a consistent explanation of the observed accelerations and decelerations of the German price level and of domestic output by tracing them back to the interaction of rationally anticipated and unanticipated changes of the impulse forces mentioned above. Particularly, I wish to test the accelerationist hypothesis (Friedman, 1968; Phelps, 1967) that changes in the observed rate of inflation are exclusively determined by changes in the anticipated rate of inflation. The tests are based on a weak form of rational expectations (Muth, 1961; Lucas, 1972; Sargent and Wallace, 1976) and assume that changes in the anticipated rate of inflation are determined by agents' expectations of changes in the impulse forces. Due to the lack of perfect foresight, agents will experience "surprises." The approach implies that the "surprises" induce transitory accelerations or decelerations of output.

The second aim is to gain insight into the relative order of magnitude of the impact elasticities of the various impulses. Specifically, we are interested to find evidence that allows evaluation of the monetarist hypothesis that changes of monetary impulses dominate changes of fiscal impulses in shaping the broad contours of fluctuations in the rates of inflation and of output; see Brunner (1970b) and Friedman (1970).

The organization of the paper is as follows. This section terminates with a brief discussion of the main economic developments in Germany since the midfifties. Section II explains the basic model, the hypotheses on the formation of expectations, and the test procedures. The empirical approximations of the price level, of output, and of the impulse variables are described in Section III. Section IV presents the tests, and Section V summarizes the results.

B. Economic Developments since the Midfifties

The overall performance of the German economy in the last twenty years has not been too bad, as can be read from the economic indicators presented in Table 1. On the average, the real rate of growth has been close to 5 percent per annum, the unemployment ratio not more than 2 percent, and the rate of change of the cost-of-living index about 3.5 percent per annum. Evaluated, however, on the basis of individual cycles, the performance has been much less satisfactory. The percentage rates of change of total output as well as of the consumer price level experienced a considerable amount of variation, indicating that the German authorities have not contributed to holding the economy on an even track.

On the balance-of-payments side, the picture that emerges is typical of an open economy that, for most of the period, was running on the basis of a permanently undervalued currency. On the average, the rate of change of real exports was twice as high as the real rate of growth of the economy, pushing the share of real exports in total output continuously upward, from about one-fifth in the late fifties to more than one-third in the early seventies. The openness of the economy also contributed to impede monetary management. Most noteworthy is the tremendous cycle-to-cycle variation in the contribution of international reserve flows to the growth of the narrowly defined money supply; see the last column of Table 1. Nevertheless, even a casual inspection of the data indicates that, on the average, the German authorities managed quite well to dampen the impact of those fluctuations.

With respect to the German fiscal scene, it is noteworthy that, on the average, real government consumption stayed in line with the growth of total domestic output. The average rate of change of the government's consumption expenditure deflator, on the other hand, increased almost twice as fast as the corresponding rate of the cost-of-living index. Even if one excludes the expenditure for the civil service, one finds that the remaining index exhibits higher rates of change than does the cost-of-living index.

II. THE MODEL

The model used in this study builds on an expectations-augmented Phillips curve, but goes beyond the simple excess demand notion by explaining excess demand as a function of unanticipated changes in selected impulses. Table 2 provides a complete description of the model.

A. The Basic Structure

The core of the model consists of three equations. The familiar price equation (1) explains the observed rate of inflation Δp as a positive function of excess demand E and of the anticipated rate of inflation Δp^*. Equation (2) relates excess demand to the difference between the observed and the "normal" rate of growth of output, $\Delta y - \Delta y^p$. Equation (3) links excess demand with unanticipated impulse variables, $I - I^*$. The vector I summarizes monetary, fiscal, and real foreign impulses; their empirical counterparts are described in Section III. Stars denote expected values of the variables.

236

Table 2

The Model

(1) $\quad \Delta p = f(E) + \Delta p^*,\quad$ with $f > 0$

(2) $\quad E = e(\Delta y - \Delta y^p),\quad$ with $e > 0$

(3) $\quad z = g(I - I^*),\quad$ with $g > 0$.

I is a vector referring to the impulse variables: ΔM, ΔF, Δx, and Δp^I.

Solutions:

(4) $\quad \Delta p = f(I - I^*) + \Delta p^*$

(5) $\quad \Delta y = g(I - I^*) + \Delta y^p,$

or, equivalently,

(6) $\quad \Delta^2 p = f(\Delta I - \Delta I^*) + \Delta^2 p^*$

(7) $\quad \Delta^2 y = g(\Delta I - \Delta I^*) + \Delta^2 y^p,\quad$ with $\Delta^2 y^p = 0$.

A. Dominance Variance Hypothesis

(8a) $\quad \dfrac{v(\Delta^2 p^*)}{v(\Delta^2 p)}\quad$ is of small order;

(8b) $\quad \dfrac{v(\Delta I^*)}{v(\Delta I)}\quad$ is of small order.

Given (8a) and (8b), solutions (6) and (7) may be simplified to

(9a) $\quad \Delta^2 p = f(\Delta I)$

(10a) $\quad \Delta^2 y = g(\Delta I)$.

Estimates of (9a) and (10a) are presented in Tables 4 and 5.

B. Rational Expectations Hypothesis

$$(11) \qquad \Delta^2 p^* = f^* (\Delta I^*), \qquad \text{with } f^* > 0.$$

Estimates of (11) are presented in Tables 7 and 9, applying the following alternative hypotheses on the formation of expectations on the impulse variables.

Expectations Hypothesis 1

$$\Delta^2 M^* = \Delta^2 M_{-2}$$

$$\Delta^2 F^* = \Delta^2 F_{-1}$$

$$\Delta^2 x^* = \Delta^2 x_{-2}.$$

Expectations Hypothesis 2

$$\Delta I_t^* = (1/m) \sum_{i=1}^{m} \Delta I_{t-i} .$$

The estimates of (11) are used to test the validity of restrictions (12a) and (12b) in (9b).

$$(12a) \qquad f = 0$$

$$(12b) \qquad a^* = 1$$

$$(9b) \qquad \Delta^2 p = f(\Delta I - \Delta I^*) + a^* (\Delta^2 p^*).$$

Estimates of (9b) are presented in Tables 7 and 9.

$$(10b) \qquad \Delta^2 y = g(\Delta I - \Delta I^*).$$

Estimates of (10b) based on the alternative expectations hypotheses are presented in Tables 8 and 10.

C. A Modification: Asymmetrical Weights

(13a) $\quad f_t = au_t,$ $\qquad$ with $a > 0$

(13b) $\quad g_t = \beta s_t,$ $\qquad$ with $\beta > 0$

(14a) $\quad u_t = w_t,$ $\qquad$ for $\Delta I_t > 0$

$\qquad u_t = v_t,$ $\qquad$ for $\Delta I_t < 0$

(14b) $\quad s_t = v_t,$ $\qquad$ for $\Delta I_t > 0$

$\qquad s_t = w_t,$ $\qquad$ for $\Delta I_t < 0,$

with $\quad w_t = CAP_{t-1} / \dfrac{1}{n} \sum_{i=1}^{n} (CAP_{t-1})_i$

$\qquad v_t = (1\text{-}CAP_{t-1}) / \dfrac{1}{n} \sum_{i=1}^{n} (1\text{-}CAP_{t-1})_i .$

Substituting (13a) through (14b) into the alternative price and output equations derived under A and B yields:

(9a') $\quad \Delta^2 p_t = a(u_t \Delta I_t)$

(10a') $\quad \Delta^2 y_t = \beta(s_t \Delta I_t)$

(11') $\quad \Delta^2 p^* = a^*(u_t \Delta I_t^*)$

(9b') $\quad \Delta^2 p_t = a(u_t \Delta I_t - u_t \Delta I_t^*) + a^* (\Delta^2 p^*)$

(10b') $\quad \Delta^2 y_t = \beta(s_t \Delta I_t - s_t \Delta I_t^*) .$

Solving the model for relative rates of change of the price level and of output gives equations (4) and (5) of Table 2:

(4) $\quad \Delta p = f(I - I^*) + \Delta p^*$

(5) $\quad \Delta y = g(I - I^*) + \Delta y^p,$

where Δy^p is the rate of growth of "normal" output consistent with the natural rate of unemployment. The model states that the observed rate of output growth will be equal to its normal rate, $\Delta y = \Delta y^p$, and that the observed rate of inflation will equal the anticipated rate, $\Delta p = \Delta p^*$, when the impulses I are fully anticipated, $I = I^*$.

The actual rate of output growth will (transitorily) deviate from its normal rate only if economic agents experience "surprises" with respect to the movements of the impulses, $I \neq I^*$.

B. Additional Hypotheses

To put the model to test requires an additional hypothesis that allows the replacement of unobservable expectations variables by observables. We introduce three alternative hypotheses.

The first hypothesis says that anticipated variables bypass most of the noise in the system and consequently exhibit a much smaller variance than do the corresponding actual variables; see Table 2, section A. Given this dominance variance hypothesis, anticipated variables may be eliminated as explicit regressors from the price and the output equation without seriously affecting the estimates.

As the dominance variance hypothesis circumvents the expectations issue, it is of limited interest. Alternatively, an explicit expectations hypothesis based on the general concept of rational expectations may be used. Rational expectations imply that the relevant economic theory is used for predicting the future rate of inflation. Given our model, the anticipated change of the rate of inflation is determined by the "anticipated" changes of the impulse variables.

We experiment with two alternative expectations hypotheses. Both of them simplify matters by assuming the following scenario. In period t-1, economic agents use current or past observations of the impulses for predicting the future rate of inflation in period t. When period t is reached, agents behave in their market decisions as if they had correctly anticipated the actual rate of inflation. If by rare chance the actual changes of the impulses in period t are equal to the values of past changes that were used by agents for predicting the

Table 3

The Numerical Order of the Weights

State of capacity utilization	Explanation of $\Delta^2 p$	$\Delta^2 y$
$CAP_{t-1} = 1$		
$\quad I_t > 0$	> 1	0
$\quad I_t < 0$	0	< 1
$CAP_{t-1} > Av(CAP_{t-1})$		
$\quad I_t > 0$	> 1	< 1
$\quad I_t < 0$	< 1	> 1
$CAP_{t-1} = Av(CAP_{t-1})$		
$\quad I_t > 0$	1	1
$\quad I_t < 0$	1	1
$CAP_{t-1} < Av(CAP_{t-1})$		
$\quad I_t > 0$	< 1	> 1
$\quad I_t < 0$	> 1	< 1

Note: $Av(CAP_{t-1})$ = average rate of capacity utilization over the period 1955-74.

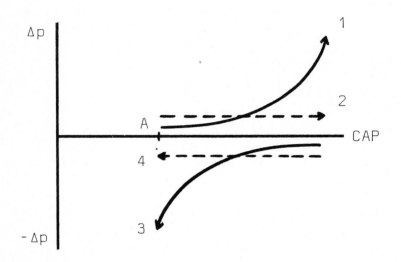

Figure 1

rate of inflation of period t, no output effect will occur. Alternatively, if the actual changes of the impulses of period t differ from their past values, output effects will arise, but the rate of inflation will equal the rate predicted, except for modifying random disturbances.

The two expectations hypotheses differ with respect to their assumptions concerning which current or past observations of the impulses are used by agents for predicting the future rate of inflation. Expectations hypothesis 1 assumes that agents know the estimates of the price equation derived under the dominance variance hypothesis and use one of them for predicting the future change of the rate of inflation. Expectations hypothesis 2 assumes that agents consider "maintained" changes of the impulses to be the more relevant predictors of future changes of the rate of inflation; see Meltzer (1977). "Maintained" changes are approximated by moving averages; see Table 2, section B.

C. Weighted Impact Elasticities

In Section IV, first estimates of the alternative price and output equations are provided based on the usual assumption of constant impact elasticities: ϵ (p, I) = f = constant, and ϵ (y, I) = g = constant. Thereafter, the estimates are repeated under the assumption that the impact elasticities vary with the state of the economy and with the direction of the change of the impulse variables. The estimates were accomplished by using asymmetrically weighted data on the changes of the impulses. The weights applied are defined in Table 2, section C; the numerical order of the weights is given in Table 3.

The application of asymmetrically distributed weights serves as a test of the following hypothesis about the pricing policies of suppliers of goods: suppliers respond the more to given changes in demand by adjusting prices the more they become convinced that an observed change in demand will not remain a temporary event but be followed by further changes of demand in the same direction.

Suppose a supplier finds himself in a state of low capacity utilization (point A in Figure 1) and observes a given increase in demand. Also assume that further increases in demand of equal strength will occur during the next periods, but that this is not known to the supplier. Under the circumstances, the supplier will initially suspect that the observed demand increase is a temporary one and, therefore, will respond with only a minor increase of his product price, if any. During the following periods, however, the continuouly increasing demand will more and more convince him that a lasting upward trend of demand has taken place. Consequently, he will turn to larger and larger upward revisions of his

243

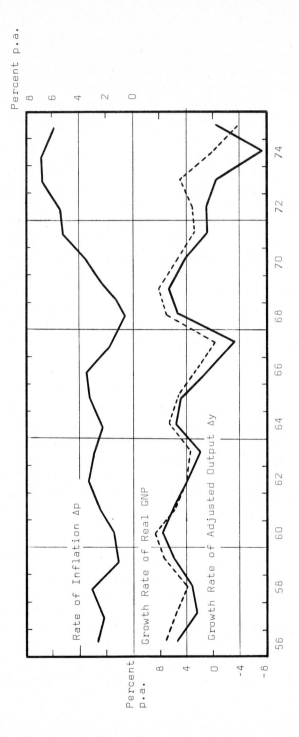

Figure 2

244

product price. It needs no elaboration that the same reasoning can be applied to the case of deflationary movements of demand.

If the hypothesis stated is valid, one should observe that a constant positive (negative) growth rate of total demand is associated with a progressively rising rate of price increase (decrease) as described by arrow 1(3) in Figure 1 instead of with the constant rate of price increase (decrease) that is pictured by arrow 2(4).

III. MEASUREMENT OF INFLATION, OUTPUT, AND IMPULSE FORCES

A. Measurement of Inflation and Output

The rate of inflation is approximated by the relative rate of change of the official cost-of-living index as published by the Federal Statistical Office. One minor adjustment has been made to take into account a once-and-for-all change in the price index that resulted from a fundamental revision of the turn-over tax system in 1968. Beginning that year, the former cascading turnover tax (tax rate 4 percent) was replaced by a value-added tax with an initial tax rate of 10 percent that, in mid-1968, was raised to 11 percent. As a result of this change in the tax structure, the cost-of-living index increased in 1968 by approximately 1 percent.

Output of the private sector differs from the conventionally defined real gross national product mainly in that it excludes the services produced by government employees. Therefore, we have subtracted from real GNP the real expenditure for the civil service, $l^g w/p^g$. The resulting variable has been further adjusted for real exports x. Real exports are excluded from the output variable in order to avoid spurious correlation in the empirical explanation of accelerations of output when real exports enter as an explanatory variable. Thus, the output measure y is defined as

$$y = GNP/p - l^g w/p^g - x.$$

Figure 2 pictures the time paths of the annual rate of inflation and of the annual rates of growth of the output measure as well as of real GNP adjusted for real expenditure on the civil service. From 1956 to 1969, the rate of inflation moved around a trend rate of about 2.5 percent. Thereafter, it started rising almost continuously, reaching a maximum rate of almost 7 percent in 1974. The time paths of the relative rates of change of both output variables

245

are very similar, except for 1975. While the export-adjusted output variable exhibits a turnaround from deceleration to acceleration, the unadjusted output variable does not, due to the exceptionally large deceleration of real exports in 1975 (-22 percent).

B. The Fiscal Impulse Measure

The construction of a summary measure of the pure fiscal impulses emitted by fiscal authorities is based on the initial stimulus concept as originally developed by Oakland (1969) and Corrigan (1970). The initial stimulus combines in one measure the initial effects of all discretionary fiscal policy actions. Such discretionary actions are the setting of government expenditure (in nominal or real terms) and the setting of tax rates, tax bases, and terms of tax payment. The application of this straightforward concept within the German institutional framework poses some statistical problems, mainly with regard to the estimation of the initial effects of tax policy. We discuss these problems separately for expenditure and tax receipts.

1. Government expenditure

Budgetary policies are investigated in a narrower sense. We concentrate on fiscal authorities only, i.e., on those public authorities that intend to integrate their budgetary policies into a joint frame of fiscal policy. Thus, we have included the expenditures of federal government (Bund) and state governments (Länder), but we have excluded the expenditure of local communities, of the Social Security System, of the Equalization of Burdens Fund, and of public enterprises as far as their expenditures are not financed by transfers from the Bund and/or the Länder.

The expenditure figures used here are cash figures. They deviate from official accounting figures mainly because they are not recorded at the time they are entered into budgetary accounts but at the time of the actual payment. Making use of cash figures raises the problem of the timing relationships. Cash expenditures lag behind the orders placed by the government for the acquisition of domestic product. The effect on economic activity and inflation, on the other hand, can be expected to be initiated with the placement of the orders or the actual acquisition, depending on the kinds of goods or services demanded. Our interpretation of cash expenditure data is thus affected by the relative length of two distinct lag structures, i.e., the lag of cash flows behind orders or acquisition, and the lag of economic activity and inflation behind the initial fiscal impulse applied. We surmise that the second lag is not shorter than the first. It appears very improbable that the mean value of the second lag is less than one quarter. The mean value of the cash flow lag, on the other hand, is not more than one quarter. For a majority of government expenditure, we know that this lag is much less. Moreover, since we concentrate on the annual time unit, it follows that the expenditure effect cannot be expected to lead our cash expenditure observations.

The expenditure component of the fiscal impulse measure has been derived by a) summing cash expenditures of Bund and Länder, b) subtracting net transfer payments passed from the Bund to the Länder, c) subtracting the expenditures on the civil service, and d) subtracting expenditures directed to recipients outside the country.

The exclusion of civil service expenditure takes care of the endogeneity bias resulting from the necessity of keeping wage increases in the government sector more or less in line with concurrent wage increases in the private sector. However, as a matter of fact, the rates of change of the fiscal stimulus measure are not much affected by this adjustment; see Figure 3.

The elimination of cash expenditures directed to recipients outside the country may not be exhaustive, but it includes the vast majority of such government transactions: payments and prepayments for direct government imports, payments for foreign services (e.g., the use of foreign military installation), indemnification payments, net payments to the European Economic Community and to other international organizations.

2. Tax receipts

Following the initial stimulus concept, we wish to approximate the initial effects of discretionary changes in tax policies by isolating from total changes in tax revenues those which result from changes in tax rates, tax bases, and tax payment terms. This leads to various problems.

The main problem, of course, is the availability of suitable data. While, for most of the period under investigation, detailed surveys of changes in tax legislation are available and, for the period since the beginning of 1965, even official estimates of the initial revenue effects are published, we lack complete and comparable statistics for the period prior to 1958. It is for this reason that we have constructed two different tax policy measures.

The first measure, to be used for the years prior to 1959, rests on a very simple concept. Discretionary tax revenue effects are approximated by the change in the effective average tax rate multiplied by the relevant tax base lagged one period:

$$\Delta T_t^{Discr.} = (t_t - t_{t-1})\, TB_{t-1}\,.$$

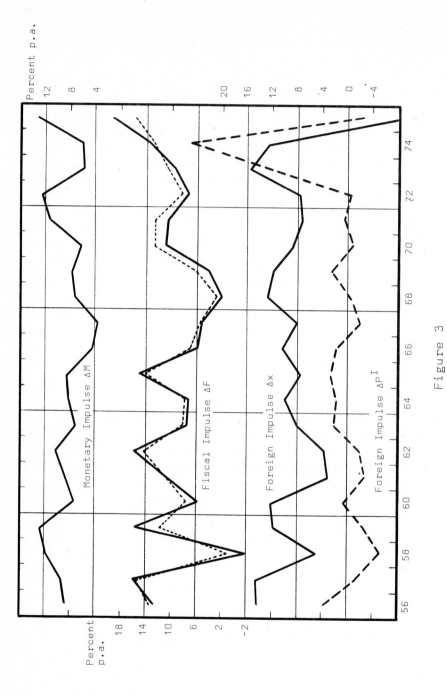

Figure 3

Only three kinds of taxes were differentiated: a) the wage tax with total wages as tax base, b) the assessed income tax with total profits as tax base, and c) the indirect taxes with nominal GNP as tax base. Finally, the discretionary changes in tax revenues were cumulated starting in 1952.

The main defect of this tax policy measure is probably the implied inclusion of the progression factor. With growing income, a progressive income tax system raises the average tax rate over time. Our tax policy measure erroneously treats the resulting tax revenue effects as discretionary rather than automatic. The relative importance of this bias, however, can be expected to be small for the fifties. In any case, the combined measure of government expenditure and discretionary tax revenue effects will not be seriously affected, due to the small contribution of the latter.

The second tax policy measure, used for the period since 1959, is defined as the sum of the initial revenue effects of discretionary tax changes, cumulated since the end of 1957.

For the period since the end of 1964, we have fallen back on official estimates of the initial revenue effects.[1] Those estimates are available separately for the various kinds of taxes changed. They are calculated in such a way that they present the total initial effects over the first four quarters after a change in tax legislation has been put into effect.

For the period 1958-64, we had to estimate the initial effects on our own. This was done in the following way. On the basis of surveys of changes in tax legislation, the effective dates of tax changes were first located. The initial revenue effects for each individual tax change were then separately identified by inspection of the quarterly growth of revenues and of the respective tax base. Not unexpectedly, the effects of many minor changes in tax legislation were not reliably identifiable. More seriously, in the case of income taxes, the estimation of discretionary revenue effects was impeded by the fact that the lag between the official and the effective date of tax changes varies with the business cycle and depends on the direction of a tax rate change as well.[2]

The construction of the tax policy measure is again given by

$$\Delta T_t^{Discr.} = \sum_{m=1}^{n} TB_m \, \Delta r_m \, ,$$

where TB denotes the tax bases and r the tax rates.

---

[1] See Bundesministerium der Finanzen, Jährliche Finanzberichte, section: Überblick über die Steuerrechtsänderungen.

[2] The lag is shortest if tax rates are lowered during a recession; it is longest if tax rates are increased during a boom.

3. Fiscal stimulus

Our measures of government expenditure and of tax policy have been combined into one fiscal stimulus measure by assuming equal impact multipliers:

$$F_t = G_t - \sum_{\tau=1952}^{\tau=t} \Delta T_t^{Discr.} \; .$$

We approximate the fiscal impulse by the relative rate of change of the fiscal stimulus, denoted by ΔF.

C. Foreign Impulse Measures

Foreign impulses transmitted to the domestic economy result mainly from the working of financial and fiscal forces in the rest of the world. There are two main channels of transmission: a monetary-sector channel and a real-sector channel. The first enables foreign forces to work via the balance of payments on domestic financial asset markets, creating monetary effects that are transmitted to the domestic output market in the same way as are domestic monetary impulses. The foreign monetary effects are integral parts of the total monetary impulse force, given fixed exchange rates. Therefore, the foreign monetary effects do not have to be measured separately.

With respect to the real-sector channel, we have selected two complementary impulse measures. One is the growth rate of real exports Δx intended to approximate the direct effects of changing foreign real income on domestic inflation and output growth via total demand for domestic product. The second measure is the relative rate of change of an index of German import prices ΔP^I, denominated in German currency. Changes in the index of import prices reflect the direct operation of foreign forces on both the demand for and the supply of domestic product.

The rationale underlying the second impulse measure is the following. An acceleration of import prices, denominated in German currency, induces in the short run a substitution of domestic demand for foreign product by domestic demand for domestic product, thus shifting the demand schedule for domestic output upward. At the same time, the supply schedule will also shift upward as domestic suppliers will be induced to raise their supply prices in response to increasing import prices. Thus, market forces will push up the domestic rate of inflation. The induced behavior of the growth rate of domestic output, on the other hand, depends on the relative order of magnitude of the shift elasticities. We lack any a priori information about the numerical magnitudes of these elasticities but expect an unanticipated increase in the import price index to suppress temporarily the rate of output growth.

D. The Monetary Impulse Measure

The total monetary impulse is approximated by the relative rate of change of the exclusive money stock ΔM. This variable serves as a composite measure of the monetary impulses emitted by foreign forces, domestic fiscal policy, domestic monetary policy, and autonomous changes in the behavior patterns of domestic banks and of the public. Whatever the causes of monetary impulses, they are uniformly transmitted from financial asset markets to the output market via the operation of relative prices, and they have uniform effects.

Two interrelated objections to using ΔM as an approximation of the total monetary impulse force may be taken up briefly. One is the controllability of the money supply; the other is the reverse causation issue.

The standard controllability objection goes like this. Fixed exchange rates hinder the authorities of a small open economy in implementing an effective monetary policy even in the shorter run. Any attempt at controlling the money supply will be rendered fruitless by interest-rate-induced capital flows that completely offset the money supply effects of policy actions. Therefore, the domestic money supply variable is endogenous rather than exogenous and cannot be used in reduced form regressions as an explanatory variable.

Although it can be shown that offsetting capital flows posed much less of an obstacle to German monetary policy during the sixties than previous research seemed to indicate,[3] the controllability objection can easily be dismissed on the simple grounds that it is irrelevant with respect to the validity of the monetary explanation of inflation. Even if domestic authorities had a zero influence on the German money supply, changes in that aggregate would have systematic and predictable effects on the domestic price level and output, provided the monetarist hypothesis is valid.

The reverse causation objection, in contrast, cannot be dismissed a priori but has to be investigated. The portfolio behavior of banks and of the public contributes to shaping the time path of the money multiplier and, thus, the growth rate of the money supply. Therefore, it is conceivable that current changes in real income and inflation dominate the current and future development of the money supply. For Germany, the reverse causation issue has been investigated by Gebauer (1975). Applying Granger's (1964, 1969) approach to a money demand function estimated with quarterly data, Gebauer found no

---

[3] Kouri and Porter (1974) and Kouri (1975) have reported offset coefficients ranging from -0.6 to -1.0 for Germany over the period of fixed exchange rates. A reexamination of the German evidence by Neumann (1978) resulted in lower offset coefficients of -0.4 to -0.5.

Table 4

Dominance Variance Hypothesis

Test equation: $\Delta^2_p = g(\Delta I)$

Regression	Period	$\Delta^2 M_{-2}$	$\Delta^2 F_{-1}$	$\Delta^2 x_{-2}$	$\Delta^2_p I$	Constant	$\bar{R}^2$	DW
4.1 (t-stat.)	1956-75	0.12 (1.83)	0.07 (3.26)	0.10 (2.53)	0.04 (1.42)	0.16 (0.97)	0.42	1.40
4.2	1956-73	0.12 (1.77)	0.08 (3.42)	0.11 (2.81)	0.05 (1.16)	0.23 (1.31)	0.45	1.29
Asymmetrical Weights								
4.3	1956-75	0.12 (2.41)	0.07 (4.13)	0.09 (2.98)	0.04 (1.82)	0.21 (1.50)	0.59	1.54
4.4	1956-73	0.12 (2.54)	0.07 (4.55)	0.10 (3.53)	0.07 (1.91)	0.26 (1.68)	0.66	1.42

evidence supporting the hypothesis of dominant reverse causation from prices to the narrowly defined money stock, while the evidence with regard to a potential existence of dominant reverse causation from output to the money stock was inconclusive. I return to this issue when estimates of the output equation are presented.

IV. TESTS

This section presents regression estimates of the model's price and output equations using the alternative auxiliary hypotheses discussed in Section II. The estimates are based on annual data and cover the sample periods 1956-73 and 1956-75. All variables are measured as second differences of the logarithms of the levels.

A. Dominance Variance Hypothesis

Under the dominance variance hypothesis the price and the output equation simplify to

$$(9a) \quad \Delta^2 p = f(\Delta I)$$

$$(10a) \quad \Delta^2 y = g(\Delta I).$$

Table 4 gives the best estimates of the price equation obtained from trying different lags. All estimates suggest that accelerations of the price level can be explained by lagged accelerations of the money stock M, the fiscal stimulus measure F, and real exports x. The monetary impulse variable receives a larger regression coefficient than the fiscal impulse variable (0.12 compared to 0.07); the coefficients, however, are not significantly different from each other. The parameter estimated for the import price variable carries the expected positive sign but becomes significant at the 0.05-significance level only if the impulse variables are weighted; see regressions 4.3 and 4.4. The application of asymmetrically distributed weights resulted in a reduction of the estimated standard errors and thus improved the estimates. These, nevertheless, are not too satisfactory because they do not provide homogeneity of degree one.

Estimates of the output equation are presented in Table 5. Regressions 5.1 and 5.5 cover the sample period 1956-74 and show that accelerations of output can be explained by current accelerations of the money stock, of real

Table 5

Dominance Variance Hypothesis
Test equation: $\Delta^2 y = g(\Delta I)$

Regression	Period	Δ^2_M	Δ^2_{F+1}	Δ^2_F	Δ^2_x	$\Delta^2_p I$	Constant	$\bar{R}^2$	DW
5.1 (t-stat.)	1956-74	0.53 (2.36)	0.28 (3.03)		0.70 (3.93)	-0.35 (-2.22)	-0.37 (-0.57)	0.46	1.82
5.2	1956-73	0.60 (2.62)	0.25 (2.69)		0.56 (2.64)	-0.13 (-0.54)	-0.38 (-0.60)	0.40	1.75
5.3	1956-75	0.47 (1.51)		-0.06 (-0.53)	0.35 (1.80)	-0.33 (-1.96)	-0.21 (-0.26)	0.20	1.70
5.4	1956-73	0.64 (2.21)		-0.10 (-0.95)	0.30 (1.35)	0.15 (0.57)	-0.57 (-0.74)	0.13	1.59
Asymmetrical Weights									
5.5	1956-74	0.40 (2.18)	0.19 (2.63)		0.51 (4.01)	-0.26 (-1.84)	-0.66 (-1.12)	0.55	1.63
5.6	1956-73	0.55 (3.02)	0.17 (2.55)		0.36 (2.59)	0.04 (0.22)	-0.66 (-1.23)	0.58	1.62
5.7	1956-75	0.51 (2.17)		-0.04 (-0.40)	0.32 (2.27)	-0.29 (-2.11)	-0.36 (-0.52)	0.40	1.77
5.8	1956-73	0.69 (3.18)		-0.08 (-1.02)	0.24 (1.58)	0.22 (0.97)	-0.74 (-1.18)	0.42	1.49

exports, and of the import price index, and by future accelerations of the fiscal stimulus measure. If future values of the fiscal impulse variable are replaced by its current values (regressions 5.3 and 5.6), the variable receives an insignificant coefficient, and the total explanation fails drastically.

These observations suggest that dominant reverse causation may be present. To test for it, we have applied the test for unidirectional causality developed by Sims (1972). Table 6 gives the results. Note that the data were not prefiltered; for second differences the assumption of serially uncorrelated residuals seems to be quite safe. As the computer program could not accommodate more than nine explanatory variables at a time, the test was conducted in two steps.

The results confirm that we cannot reject the hypothesis of dominant reverse causation for the fiscal impulse. Deleting $\Delta^2 F_{t+1}$ from the first test equation led to an F-value of 5.09 which is significant at the 0.05-significance level. This result is interesting but not completely unexpected because Elliott (1975) has come up with a similar result for the U.S. from reestimates of the St. Louis equation. Government's behavior apparently is less Keynesian than we are used to believe. It is most noteworthy, on the other hand, that the test did not detect the existence of dominant reverse causation for the remaining impulse forces and, in particular, not for the monetary impulse. However, we acknowledge that the test does not preclude current changes of the money supply and of exports to be determined by concurrent changes of output.

The Sims test suggests that the specification of regressions 5.3, 5.4, 5.7, and 5.8 is more appropriate. They uniformly attribute a zero influence on accelerations of output to the fiscal impulse. Regressions 5.3 and 5.7 cover the total sample period. The largest impact elasticity found is the one for the monetary impulse (about 0.5). The parameter estimate attached to the import price variable is negative (-0.3), as expected. Note, however, that it switches sign and becomes insignificant if the years 1974 and 1975 are deleted from the sample period; see regressions 5.4 and 5.8. Apparently the significant negative coefficient for the import price variable in the regressions covering the total sample period is dominantly caused by the exceptionally large swing of $\Delta^2 p^I$ from +13 percent in 1974 to -27 percent in 1975.

B. Expectations Hypothesis 1

An explicit incorporation of expectations requires estimating the price equation

$$(9b) \quad \Delta^2 p = f(\Delta I - \Delta I^*) + a^* (\Delta^2 p^*),$$

255

Table 6

Test for Reverse Causation
(1966-74 period)

Test equation: $\Delta^2 y_t = g (\Delta I_{t+1}, \Delta I_t)$

ΔI	Regression coefficient	t-ratio	F-value, if deleted
$\Delta^2 M_{t+1}$	- 0.25	- 0.89	0.80
$\Delta^2 F_{t+1}$	0.31	2.25	5.09[a]
$\Delta^2 x_{t+1}$	- 0.26	- 1.24	1.55
$\Delta^2 P^I_{t+1}$	0.18	1.05	1.12
$\Delta^2 M_t$	0.52	1.97	3.90
$\Delta^2 F_t$	0.04	0.31	0.09
$\Delta^2 x_t$	0.51	2.12	4.52
$\Delta^2 P^I_t$	- 0.37	- 1.61	2.62

Constant = - 0.59 (- 0.82), $\bar{R}^2 = 0.40$,   DW = 1.91.

Test equation: $\Delta^2 y_t = g (\Delta I_t, \Delta I_{t-1})$

ΔI	Regression coefficient	t-ratio	F-value, if deleted
$\Delta^2 M_t$	0.56	1.93	3.73
$\Delta^2 F_t$	- 0.03	- 0.17	0.03
$\Delta^2 x_t$	0.46	2.16	4.68
$\Delta^2 P^I_t$	- 0.15	- 0.77	0.60
$\Delta^2 M_{t-1}$	0.28	0.94	0.89
$\Delta^2 F_{t-1}$	- 0.07	- 0.55	0.31
$\Delta^2 x_{t-1}$	0.51	2.04	4.19
$\Delta^2 P^I_{t-1}$	- 0.39	- 1.30	1.69

Constant = - 0.10 (- 0.12), $\bar{R}^2 = 0.31$,   DW = 2.07.

[a]Significant at the 0.05-significance level.

Note: Data are not prefiltered.

with

(11) $\Delta^2 p^* = f^*(\Delta I^*)$.

The first expectations hypothesis is straightforward. We hypothesize that rational agents know the estimates of the price equation derived under the dominance variance hypothesis and consider them the best tools at hand for forecasting future accelerations of the price level. The hypothesis is equivalent to assuming that

$$\Delta^2 M^* = \Delta^2 M_{-2}; \qquad \Delta^2 F^* = \Delta^2 F_{-1}; \qquad \Delta^2 x^* = \Delta^2 x_{-2}.$$

The import price variable is excluded from the estimation in equation (11) since no significant influence of lagged accelerations of the import price index was detectable in the estimates of the price equation, given the dominance variance hypothesis. We hypothesize that agents ignore this variable in view of the potentially high costs involved in forecasting a variable that seems to contribute only marginally to the forecast of future accelerations of the price level.

Before turning to the estimates, a brief clarification of the nature of the anticipation variables defined above may be useful. They must not be interpreted to be "anticipated" in the sense that rational agents are naive enough to believe that the lagged changes of the impulses, used for predicting the future change of the rate of inflation, will again prevail in the next period. Rather, these changes of the impulses are "anticipated" in the sense that they are considered to be the relevant determinants of the anticipated acceleration of the price level.

Regressions 7.1 to 7.4 (Table 7) provide alternative estimates of equation (11), and regressions 7.5 to 7.8 are the corresponding estimates of price equation (9b). The first four regressions generate estimates of the anticipated changes of the rate of inflation. All the estimated impact elasticities are significant at the 0.05-significance level, and the largest is the one received for the anticipated changes of monetary impulses. Note, however, that we again do not find homogeneity of degree one; the sum of the coefficients for $\Delta^2 M^*$ and $\Delta^2 F^*$ does not exceed 0.24.

The alternative inflation predictions obtained from regressions 7.1 to 7.4 are used as inputs in the following estimates of the price equation (9b). The latter estimates test the validity of the restriction:

Table 7

Expectations Hypothesis 1

Test equation: $\Delta^2_p{}^* = f^*(\Delta I^*)$

Regression (t-stat.)	Period	$\Delta^2_M{}^*$	$\Delta^2_F{}^*$	$\Delta^2_x{}^*$		Constant	$\bar{R}^2$	DW
7.1	1956-75	0.17 (2.70)	0.07 (3.16)	0.09 (2.24)		0.17 (0.98)	0.38	1.43
7.2	1956-73	0.13 (1.98)	0.08 (3.50)	0.11 (2.69)		0.26 (1.48)	0.44	1.24
Asymmetrical Weights								
7.3	1956-75	0.16 (3.34)	0.07 (3.84)	0.08 (2.50)		0.22 (1.50)	0.53	1.52
7.4	1956-73	0.13 (2.70)	0.07 (4.36)	0.10 (3.11)		0.31 (2.13)	0.60	1.37

Test equation: $\Delta^2_p = f(\Delta I - \Delta I^*) + a^*(\Delta^2_p{}^*)$

Regression (t-stat.)	Period	$\Delta^2_p{}^*$	$\Delta^2_M{}^u$	$\Delta^2_F{}^u$	$\Delta^2_x{}^u$	$\Delta^2_p{}^I$	Constant	$\bar{R}^2$	DW
7.5	1956-75	1.12 (2.24)	0.04 (0.73)	0.00 (0.23)	-0.00 (-0.07)	0.04 (1.33)	-0.03 (-0.19)	0.40	1.52
7.6	1956-73	0.90 (2.04)	0.02 (0.35)	0.00 (0.02)	-0.03 (-0.74)	0.08 (1.59)	-0.01 (-0.07)	0.48	1.16
Asymmetrical Weights									
7.7	1956-75	1.38 (3.57)	0.08 (1.64)	0.01 (0.82)	0.03 (0.80)	0.03 (1.14)	-0.08 (-0.52)	0.62	2.02
7.8	1956-73	1.11 (3.28)	0.04 (1.07)	0.01 (0.50)	-0.00 (-1.10)	0.09 (2.02)	-0.08 (-0.54)	0.70	1.48

(12a) $f = 0.$

The necessary time series of unanticipated changes of the impulses are generated by a consistent decomposition of the observed changes. The anticipated changes of the impulses defined above were subtracted from the actual changes, $\Delta I^u = \Delta I - \Delta I^*$:

$$\Delta^2 M^u = \Delta^2 M - \Delta M^2_{-2},$$

$$\Delta^2 F^u = \Delta^2 F - \Delta^2 F_{-1},$$

$$\Delta^2 x^u = \Delta^2 x - \Delta^2 x_{-2}.$$

Regressions 7.5 to 7.8 uniformly confirm the validity of restriction (12a). None of the unanticipated changes of impulses ($\Delta^2 M^u$, $\Delta^2 F^u$, $\Delta^2 x^u$) affects significantly the observed changes of the rate of inflation. It is also in accordance with our hypothesis that the alternative parameter estimates for the anticipated inflation variable $\Delta^2 p^*$ are not significantly different from unity. The latter result, however, must not be stressed as it can be rationalized on purely statistical grounds.

Table 8 presents the corresponding estimates of the output equation:

(10b) $\Delta^2 y = g (\Delta I - \Delta I^*).$

A comparison of regressions 8.1 to 8.4 with regressions 8.5 to 8.8 shows that the application of asymmetrically distributed weights raises the explanatory power by generally reducing the standard errors of the parameters. Hence, we discuss regressions 8.5 to 8.8 only. The first two indicate that unanticipated accelerations of the fiscal stimulus measure have a zero effect on accelerations of output and, therefore, may be neglected. Unanticipated accelerations of the money stock and of real exports, in contrast, significantly contribute to the explanation of accelerating output. As in the estimates based on the dominance variance hypothesis, the largest impact elasticity is the one found for the monetary impulse variable. We also find again a significant negative impact

Table 8

Expectations Hypothesis 1

Test equation: $\Delta^2 y = g\,(\Delta I - \Delta I^*)$

Regression	Period	$\Delta^2_M{}^u$	$\Delta^2_F{}^u$	$\Delta^2_x{}^u$	$\Delta^2_p I$	Constant	$\bar{R}^2$	DW
8.1 (t-stat.)	1956-75	0.32 (1.77)	0.03 (0.48)	0.19 (1.64)	-0.23 (-1.56)	-0.47 (-0.59)	0.22	2.08
8.2	1956-73	0.34 (2.04)	0.03 (0.46)	0.15 (1.26)	0.14 (0.64)	-0.68 (-0.87)	0.08	1.95
8.3	1956-75	0.32 (1.88)		0.19 (1.64)	-0.23 (-1.55)	-0.49 (-0.62)	0.25	1.97
8.4	1956-73	0.35 (2.17)		0.15 (1.25)	0.16 (0.71)	-0.69 (-0.91)	0.14	1.84
Asymmetrical Weights								
8.5	1956-75	0.35 (2.78)	0.03 (0.60)	0.20 (2.16)	-0.22 (-1.81)	-0.59 (-0.85)	0.43	2.14
8.6	1956-73	0.38 (3.29)	0.02 (0.56)	0.16 (1.74)	0.15 (0.80)	-0.83 (-1.27)	0.37	1.96
8.7	1956-75	0.36 (2.95)		0.20 (2.20)	-0.22 (-1.81)	-0.58 (-0.87)	0.45	2.01
8.8	1956-73	0.39 (3.48)		0.15 (1.78)	0.16 (0.86)	-0.83 (-1.30)	0.40	1.81

elasticity for the import price variable if the years 1974 and 1975 are included in the sample period.

C. Expectations Hypothesis 2

This alternative expectations hypothesis assumes that agents consider "maintained" changes of the impulses as efficient predictors of future changes in the rate of inflation. The anticipated changes of the impulses are measured by one-period lagged moving averages:

$$\Delta^2 M^* = (1/3) \sum_{i=1}^{3} \Delta^2 M_{t-i} \, ,$$

$$\Delta^2 F^* = (1/2) \sum_{i=1}^{2} \Delta^2 F_{t-i} \, ,$$

$$\Delta^2 x^* = (1/3) \sum_{i=1}^{3} \Delta^2 x_{t-i} \, .$$

The import price variable is again omitted since none of the various moving averages tried resulted in a significant positive contribution when equation (11) was estimated. For the remaining impulse variables, moving averages of different lengths were also tried but gave inferior performance in the estimates. As before, the unanticipated changes of the impulses were computed by subtracting the anticipated changes from the actual changes, $\Delta I^u = \Delta I - \Delta I^*$.

Regressions 9.1 to 9.4 (Table 9) are estimates of equation (11) and directly comparable to regressions 7.1 to 7.4. A comparison reveals that expectations hypothesis 2 allows us to estimate a much larger impact elasticity for the anticipated monetary impulse variable; the parameter estimates range between 0.45 and 0.62. Hence, expectations hypothesis 2 produces estimates that are much closer to fulfilling the homogeneity condition than do the previous estimates. Still the condition is not met. The sum of the regression coefficients of $\Delta^2 M^*$ and $\Delta^2 F^*$ reaches 0.70 in the best case, regression 9.1, while the sum of their standard deviations is 0.22. But, note that the coefficient of the anticipated fiscal impulse variable $\Delta^2 F^*$ is significant at the 0.1-significance level only in regressions 9.1 and 9.2, and even worse if asymmetrically distributed weights are applied.

Regressions 9.5 to 9.8 provide the corresponding estimates of price equation (9b). They test and confirm the validity of restriction (12a). As

Table 9

Expectations Hypothesis 2

Test equation: $\triangle^2_p{}^* = f^*(\triangle I^*)$

Regression (t-stat.)	Period	$\triangle^2_M{}^*$	$\triangle^2_F{}^*$	$\triangle^2_x{}^*$		Constant	$\bar{R}^2$	DW
9.1	1956-75	0.62 (3.37)	0.08 (1.59)	0.18 (1.95)		0.24 (1.39)	0.39	1.91
9.2	1956-73	0.56 (2.83)	0.08 (1.63)	0.20 (2.07)		0.30 (1.62)	0.38	1.90
			Asymmetrical Weights					
9.3	1956-75	0.50 (3.31)	0.04 (0.85)	0.15 (1.78)		0.28 (1.70)	0.42	2.20
9.4	1956-73	0.45 (2.76)	0.04 (0.96)	0.17 (2.00)		0.36 (1.99)	0.43	2.24

Test equation: $\triangle^2_p = f(\triangle I - \triangle I^*) + a^*(\triangle^2_p{}^*)$

Regression (t-stat.)	Period	$\triangle^2_p{}^*$	$\triangle^2_M{}^u$	$\triangle^2_F{}^u$	$\triangle^2_x{}^u$	$\triangle^2_p{}^I$	Constant	$\bar{R}^2$	DW
9.5	1956-75	0.95 (2.63)	0.02 (0.31)	-0.00 (-0.00)	-0.02 (-0.41)	0.04 (1.16)	-0.01 (-0.07)	0.37	1.94
9.6	1956-73	0.93 (2.62)	0.05 (0.72)	0.00 (0.14)	-0.05 (-1.17)	0.11 (1.92)	-0.03 (-0.17)	0.46	1.82
				Asymmetrical Weights					
9.7	1956-75	1.10 (3.19)	0.07 (1.06)	-0.01 (-0.68)	0.01 (0.31)	0.04 (1.10)	-0.03 (-0.17)	0.45	2.30
9.8	1956-73	1.10 (3.40)	0.10 (1.67)	-0.01 (-0.70)	-0.02 (-0.36)	0.13 (2.50)	-0.10 (-0.61)	0.60	2.02

before, under expectations hypothesis 1, we find that unanticipated changes of the impulses do not significantly contribute to observed changes of the rate of inflation. Since the import price variable was not used in the estimation of anticipated inflation, it appears as an explanatory variable in the price equation, and it is interesting to find that the variable receives a regression coefficient significant at the 0.05-significance level if the years 1974 and 1975 are excluded from the sample period; see regressions 9.6 and 9.8.

Table 10 gives estimates of output equation (10b). These are broadly in line with those generated by expectations hypothesis 1 and suggest that unanticipated accelerations of the fiscal stimulus variable have no role in the determination of the time path of output. Unanticipated accelerations of the money stock and of real exports, on the other hand, appear as significant determinants of accelerations of output. The impact elasticity assigned to the latter impulse variable is larger under the second than under the first expectations hypothesis (0.3 to be compared to 0.2) and not significantly smaller than the impact elasticity assigned to the unanticipated monetary impulse variable.

The estimates also point to an important impact on output of the exceptionally large variation of import prices during the years 1974 and 1975. A comparison of the estimates in Tables 9 and 10 indicates that, during the essentially fixed-exchange-rate period from 1956 to 1973, accelerations of the import price level exerted a significant impact on accelerations of the domestic price level but not on those of output. Thereafter, the responsiveness of the domestic price level to changes in import prices, expressed in domestic currency, seems to have fallen, while real economic activity appears to have become more sensitive.

V. SUMMARY AND CONCLUSIONS

The general frame developed here integrates the hypothesis of rational expectations with an impulse-theoretic explanation of accelerations of the general price level as well as of domestic output. The theory goes beyond the simple excess demand explanation to discriminate among members of a small set of anticipated and unanticipated impulse forces that shape the broad contours of economic fluctuations. Testing three variations of the general approach with annual data from Germany for the 1956-75 period, it was found that a weak rational expectations formulation which differentiates anticipated from unanticipated impulses permits a consistent explanation of observed accelerations of the price level as well as of output that is in accordance with the accelerationist hypothesis.

Table 10

Expectations Hypothesis 2

Test equation: $\Delta^2 y = g\,(\Delta I - \Delta I^*)$

Regression	Period	$\Delta^2 M^u$	$\Delta^2 F^u$	$\Delta^2 X^u$	$\Delta^2 P^I$	Constant	$\bar{R}^2$	DW
10.1 (t-stat.)	1956-75	0.32 (1.19)	0.03 (0.41)	0.30 (2.04)	-0.32 (-2.13)	-0.33 (-0.42)	0.25	2.02
10.2	1956-73	0.46 (1.78)	0.00 (0.01)	0.28 (1.64)	0.11 (0.42)	-0.67 (-0.88)	0.14	1.90
10.3	1956-75	0.35 (1.41)		0.30 (2.18)	-0.31 (-2.15)	-0.34 (-0.42)	0.29	1.90
10.4	1956-73	0.46 (1.93)		0.28 (1.73)	0.11 (0.44)	-0.67 (-0.91)	0.20	1.90
Asymmetrical Weights								
10.5	1956-75	0.34 (1.84)	0.02 (0.37)	0.27 (2.49)	-0.29 (-2.34)	-0.51 (-0.75)	0.44	2.06
10.6	1956-73	0.46 (2.50)	-0.00 (-0.07)	0.23 (1.90)	0.12 (0.57)	-0.86 (-1.34)	0.40	1.91
10.7	1956-75	0.36 (2.05)		0.28 (2.71)	-0.29 (-2.40)	-0.50 (-0.76)	0.47	1.93
10.8	1956-73	0.45 (2.64)		0.23 (2.01)	0.12 (0.59)	-0.86 (-1.39)	0.44	1.93

The main results may be summarized as follows.

First, observed accelerations of the domestic price level are dominated by rationally formed anticipations of inflation. The anticipated changes of impulse forces determine the observed accelerations of the price level via the anticipated accelerations.

Second, the unanticipated changes of the impulses have a zero-effect on inflation, but determine the observed accelerations of output.

Third, the evidence corroborates the monetarist hypothesis that monetary impulses dominate fiscal impulses in shaping economic fluctuations. The impact of anticipated changes of the monetary impulse on accelerations of the price level appears to be a multiple of the impact of anticipated changes of the fiscal impulse. Moreover, unanticipated changes of the fiscal impulse have a zero-effect on output. Unanticipated changes of the monetary impulse, in contrast, emerge as the dominant driving force of short-run fluctuations of adjusted output. We also note the apparent presence of dominant reverse causation from output to fiscal impulses, while no reverse causation is detectable for monetary impulses.

Fourth, anticipated accelerations of real exports contribute to accelerations of the price level. Their impact elasticity, however, appears to be much smaller than the respective impact elasticity of monetary impulses. A smaller impact elasticity with respect to output is also found for unanticipated accelerations of real exports than for unanticipated accelerations of the money stock M1. In evaluating this unexpectedly weak performance of real exports, one has to consider, however, that the output measure used was adjusted for real exports in order to avoid spurious correlation. Reestimates of the output equation using unadjusted output point to a larger impact elasticity that exceeds the one assigned to unanticipated monetary impulses.

Fifth, during the period of fixed exchange rates, accelerations of the import price level, denominated in domestic currency, appear to have influenced moderately the domestic rate of inflation but not the growth rate of output. After 1973, the situation seems to have changed completely: the estimates suggest relatively large contractionary effects of accelerating import prices on the growth rate of output and no measurable impact on the rate of inflation. A definite conclusion, however, should not be drawn as a sufficient number of observations is lacking.

Sixth, the application of asymmetrically distributed weights proved to be successful in estimation. It almost uniformly raised the explanatory power of the price and output regressions. This suggests that a fruitful hypothesis may be to assume that anticipated as well as unanticipated changes of the impulses have asymmetrical effects on the rates of change of the price level and of output,

265

depending on the direction of the impulse changes and on the inherited state of capacity utilization.

In sum, it is found that rationally formed anticipations of the future rate of inflation dominantly determine the division of the total effects of changes in impulses into effects on the rate of inflation and effects on the rate of growth of output.

Appendix

Variables Used

CAP	=	rate of capacity utilization
E		excess demand
F		fiscal stimulus measure
I		impulse
M		narrowly defined money stock
U		unemployment ratio
p		cost-of-living index
p^I		index of import prices (converted into domestic currency)
x		real exports of goods and services
y	=	domestic output adjusted for real exports and real civil service expenditure.

Note: All variables are measured as logarithms. Anticipated variables are denoted by a star. Unanticipated variables carry a superscript u.

References

Brunner, K. (1970a), "Eine Neuformulierung der Quantitätstheorie des Geldes: Die Theorie der relativen Preise, des Geldes, des Outputs und der Beschäftigung," Kredit und Kapital, 3: 1-30.

_____(1970b), "The 'Monetarist' Revolution in Monetary Theory," Weltwirtschaftliches Archiv, 105: 1-29.

Corrigan, E.G. (1970), "The Measurement and Importance of Fiscal Policy Changes," Monthly Review, Federal Reserve Bank of New York, 52.

Elliott, J.W. (1975), "The Influence of Monetary and Fiscal Actions on Total Spending," Journal of Money, Credit and Banking, 7: 181-92.

Friedman, M. (1968), "The Role of Monetary Policy," American Economic Review, 58: 1-17.

_____(1970). The Counter-revolution in Monetary Theory. Occasional Paper. London: Institute of Economic Affairs.

Gebauer, W. (1975), "Die Kausalitätsbeziehungen zwischen Geldmenge, Preisen und Produktion," Zeitschrift für die gesamte Staatswissenschaft, 131: 603-26.

Granger, C.W.J. (1964). Spectral Analysis of Economic Time Series. Princeton: Princeton University Press.

_____(1969), "Investigating Causal Relations by Econometric Models and Cross-spectral Methods," Econometrica, 37: 424-38.

Kouri, P.J.K. (1975), "The Hypothesis of Offsetting Capital Flows: A Case Study of Germany," Journal of Monetary Economics, 1: 21-39.

Kouri, P.J.K., and Porter, M. (1974), "International Capital Flows and Portfolio Equilibrium," Journal of Political Economy, 82: 443-67.

Lucas, R.E., Jr. (1972), "Expectations and the Neutrality of Money," Journal of Economic Theory, 4: 103-24.

Meltzer, A.H. (1977), "Anticipated Inflation and Unanticipated Price Change: A Test of the Price-Specie Flow Theory and the Phillips Curve," Journal of Money, Credit and Banking, 9: 182-205.

Muth, J.F. (1961), "Rational Expectations and the Theory of Price Movements," Econometrica, 29: 315-35.

Neumann, M.J.M. (1978), "Offsetting Capital Flows: A Reexamination of the German Case," Journal of Monetary Economics, (forthcoming).

Oakland, W.H. (1969), "Budgetary Measures of Fiscal Performance," Southern Economic Journal, 35: 347-58.

Phelps, E.S. (1967), "Phillips Curve, Expectations of Inflation and Optimal Unemployment over Time," Economica, n.s. 34: 254-81.

Sargent, T.J., and Wallace, N. (1976), "Rational Expectations and the Theory of Economic Policy," Journal of Monetary Economics, 2: 169-84.

Sims, C.A. (1972), "Money, Income, and Causality," American Economic Review, 62: 540-52.

INFLATION AND OUTPUT FLUCTUATIONS
IN THE UNITED STATES AND GERMANY:
A COMMENT ON THE DUTTON AND NEUMANN PAPERS

Michael J. Hamburger[*]
Federal Reserve Bank of New York

The Dutton and Neumann analyses have many features in common with the other Western European studies in this volume. Using parametric and non-parametric empirical tests, the authors seek to advance our understanding of inflation and aggregate output movements, with particular reference to the experiences of the U.S. (Dutton) and Germany (Neumann) from the early 1950s through the midseventies. As in the other studies, attention is focused on explanations that are consistent with price theory, i.e., the interaction of market supply and demand forces. Little or no attention is given to institutionalist approaches.

The principal objectives of both authors are: a) to evaluate the relative importance of various impulse forces in shaping the course of a nation's inflation and economic activity, b) to determine the role of rationally formed expectations in influencing these developments, and c) to assess the usefulness of the Phillips curve in analyzing and understanding inflation. The impulse forces are intended to summarize the pressures on the productive resources of an economy emanating from fiscal policy actions, monetary actions, and the external sector. As such, they are viewed as the systematic determinants of fluctuations in output and the price level.

The studies are generally of high quality. Nevertheless, they are not uniformly successful in meeting the authors' objectives. The most interesting results are those associated with the relative importance of the impulse forces. The least persuasive are those which relate to the role of the Phillips curve in the analysis of inflation. This discussion of the papers is organized around the objectives listed above.

1. The Systematic Determinants of Macroeconomic Fluctuations

In their separate analyses, Dutton and Neumann draw heavily on the theory of rational expectations. Although Dutton is not very explicit about this, his reliance on the theory is clear. Assuming that expectations are formed rationally has two important implications. It means that allowing for

[*] The views expressed are the author's and do not necessarily reflect those of the Federal Reserve Bank of New York.

expectations does not require that any additional variables be included in the analysis, i.e., that expectations about price and output movements are determined by the same impulse forces that ultimately cause these movements. Second, it implies that the effects of changes in the impulse forces depend on whether or not the changes are anticipated. Anticipated changes are expected to have their principal effect on the rate of inflation, while unanticipated movements are likely to produce transitory accelerations or decelerations in the growth of output. In the remainder of this section, Dutton's and Neumann's findings regarding the basic determinants of macroeconomic fluctuations are considered. The formation of expectations is taken up subsequently.

Using multiple regression analysis fitted to annual observations of the variables, Dutton obtains results that are similar to those of other recent studies[1] and that support the monetarist approach to macroeconomic analysis. Over the period 1952-72, deviations of monetary growth from its trend are found to be the principal cause of fluctuations in output, while the trend in monetary growth determines the inflation rate. In both cases, the estimated elasticities are not significantly different from 1, but the speeds of adjustment are different from each other. According to Dutton's estimates, the response of output to deviations in monetary growth occurs initially with a mean lag of about a year. The effect on inflation takes longer and appears to take hold only after there has been a change in the trend in monetary growth--after approximately two years.

Other impulse forces included in the analysis, but found to have little or no impact on aggregate output and inflation in the U.S. during the 1952-72 period, are: a) the fiscal impulse--measured as the change in the federal government deficit (in constant prices) divided by real GNP; b) the external quantity impulse--measured as the change in real net exports as a percentage of real GNP; c) the external price impulse--measured as the percentage rate of change in import prices. Questions may be raised regarding many of these measures. For example, it is not clear why the external price impulse is restricted solely to import prices. One would expect that an increase in the (world) price of a country's exports would also put upward pressure on domestic prices. Moreover, Dutton gives no indication of whether his import price index is denominated in local or foreign currencies. It is clearly the local currency that is appropriate, to allow for changes in exchange rates as well as explicit movements in foreign prices.

Despite these potential problems, Dutton's findings for the period through 1972 correspond reasonably well to those obtained by others. His conclusions suggest that variations in monetary growth account for most of the short-run

---

[1] See, for example, Meltzer (1977), Committee on Banking, Currency and Housing (1976), and Andersen and Karnosky (1972).

(annual) movements in nominal GNP. The initial impact of these variations is on output, but, if they persist, the main effect will be on the rate of inflation.

When Dutton's sample period is extended through 1974, the external price and quantity impulse elasticities become statistically significant. With this exception, the results are the same: the estimated effects of the monetary impulse are essentially unchanged, while the fiscal policy impulse continues to be of no practical importance. This implies that although money may be the principal determinant of economic activity, large movements in other factors, such as those that occurred in the external impulse forces in 1973 and 1974, may have some effects. In this connection, it is interesting to note that the estimated elasticities of the external price impulse with respect to aggregate output and the inflation rate are almost exactly offsetting. Hence, the net effect of this impulse force on nominal income in the U.S. appears to be very close to zero, even during the 1973-74 period.

Using analogous techniques, Neumann obtains results for Germany that are quite similar to Dutton's for the U.S. The main differences are those that examination of a more open economy might be expected to reveal. Variations in monetary growth once again appear to be the most consistent and the most important determinant of price and output movements. However, real exports also seem to be a significant force in shaping the future course of inflation and real economic activity for Germany. The results with respect to the fiscal and external price impulse forces are more ambiguous. These are less important than the monetary and external quantity impulses, but appear to have larger impacts than they do in the U.S. In particular, Neumann's estimates suggest that the fiscal stimulus has some influence on inflation but little or no effect on fluctuations in output growth. On the other hand, import prices (denominated in domestic currency) are found to have a modest, positive effect on domestic inflation throughout the sample period (1956-75), but to affect output growth (negatively) only after the shift away from fixed exchange rates (i.e., after 1973). All of Neumann's other results are independent of whether the sample period is terminated in 1973 or extended through 1976.

This analysis, like Dutton's, is subject to some methodological questions. For example, the dependent variables in almost all of Neumann's regression equations are expressed as second time differences (i.e., the acceleration in the inflation rate). This approach differs from that used in the other papers on Western Europe in the volume and in most other studies of this type. Generally the dependent variables are expressed as first time differences (e.g., the rate of inflation). While there may be a clear economic or statistical reason for proceeding in this way, Neumann does not indicate what it is. However, the general consistency of his results with macroeconomic theory and with those obtained by others suggests that this may not be a very important consideration. Of great concern is the treatment of the expectations-augmented Phillips curve in the two papers, to which I now turn.

2. Expectations and the Phillips Curve

As indicated by Dutton and Neumann, the expectations-augmented Phillips curve is a fundamental element of their models. Accordingly, the actual rate of inflation $\dot{p}$ is viewed as a positive function of excess demand E and the anticipated rate of inflation $a(\dot{p})$:

(1) $\dot{p} = F(E) + a(\dot{p}).$

The Dutton and Neumann analyses of expectations are examined first, and then their specifications of the Phillips curve are considered.

Both authors interpret their empirical results as providing strong support for the hypothesis that the anticipated rate of inflation plays a major role in determining the actual rate. Indeed, Dutton argues that over the 1952-72 period, "the anticipated rate of inflation fully explains the [actual] rate." The basis for this conclusion is the authors' common two-step empirical procedure. First, the observed inflation rate is regressed on a number of hypothesized determinants, i.e., impulse forces. Defining the calculated values from these equations as "anticipated inflation," the second step involves regressing the actual inflation rate on its "anticipated" value and a number of other variables. For the most part, anticipations provide the bulk of the explanatory power in the second-stage regressions. The authors' conclusions regarding the role of expectations in determining inflation follow from these results.

The problem with this approach is that there is no independent measure of anticipations. Without such a measure, it would seem difficult to draw any firm conclusions regarding the formation of expectations or their role in explaining macroeconomic fluctuations. Put another way, the procedure employed by Dutton and Neumann provides no systematic means of differentiating between an incomplete set of inflation determinants in the first step and inaccurate or irrational expectations.

A similar type of problem besets the authors' discussions of the Phillips curve, a construct that is customarily viewed as indicating the relationship between the level of excess demand (i.e., the unemployment rate) and the rate of inflation. But, this is not the sense in which Dutton and Neumann use this concept. For them, the Phillips curve relates the change in the "unemployment gap" to the inflation rate. Thus, in (1), E is defined as "the difference between the actual and the long-run 'full' employment growth rate of real GNP," by Dutton, and as "the difference between the observed and the 'normal' rate of growth of output," by Neumann, rather than in the more standard way as the difference between the levels of current and "full employment" output. Leaving aside the question of whether it is the level or the change in the "gap" (or perhaps both) that should be used to explain inflation, it is clear that the present studies are not very helpful in evaluating the relevance of the Phillips curve as it is customarily defined.

3. Conclusion

In summary, the Dutton and Neumann investigations increase our understanding of the systematic determinants of price and output fluctuations in the U.S. and Germany. As do numerous other studies, the papers suggest that movements in the money stock are the most important cause of such fluctuations. Under certain circumstances, other factors (e.g., fiscal and external impulses) may play a role, but their effects appear to be not nearly so robust as those of the money stock. Moreover, the results for both countries imply that an acceleration in monetary growth above its maintained level may stimulate output growth for a time, but that this effect will be only temporary. Ultimately (beginning in about two years), the full impact will show up as a higher rate of inflation. Thus, the studies cast doubt on the ability of traditional debt-management policies to stimulate systematically the growth rates of output over and above their longer-term rates in the U.S. and Germany.

The sections of the Dutton and Neumann papers dealing with the Phillips curve and expectations are less helpful. The authors' specifications of the Phillips curve are different from the standard one, and, hence, it is not clear what bearing their evidence has on the latter. Their analyses of the role of expectations in macroeconomic fluctuations are also seriously flawed. Here the problem relates to the authors' empirical measures of anticipated inflation. In the absence of an independent means of judging the quality of these measures, it is difficult to attribute much significance to the evidence presented. These deficiencies do not appear, however, to be of much consequence for the remainder of the Dutton and Neumann analyses.

References

Andersen, L.C., and Karnosky, D.S. (1972), "The Appropriate Time Frame for Controlling Monetary Aggregates: The St. Louis Evidence," in Controlling Monetary Aggregates, II: The Implementation. Federal Reserve Bank of Boston.

Committee on Banking, Currency and Housing (1976). The Impact of the Federal Reserve's Money Policies on the Economy. Hearings before the Subcommittee on Domestic Monetary Policy, House of Representatives. Washington, D.C.: U.S. Government Printing Office.

Dutton, D.S (1978), "The Economics of Inflation and Output Fluctuations in the United States, 1952-1974," in Carnegie-Rochester Conference Series, 8, eds. K. Brunner and A.H. Meltzer. Amsterdam: North-Holland.

Meltzer, A.H. (1977), "Anticipated Inflation and Unanticipated Price Change: A Test of the Price-Specie Flow Theory and the Phillips Curve," Journal of Money, Credit and Banking, 9: 182-205.

Neumann, M.J.M. (1978), "The Impulse-Theoretic Explanation of Changing Inflation and Output Growth: Evidence from Germany," Carnegie-Rochester Conference Series, 8, eds. K. Brunner and A.H. Meltzer. Amsterdam: North-Holland.

INFLATION AND OUTPUT FLUCTUATIONS:
A COMMENT ON THE DUTTON AND NEUMANN PAPERS

Bennett T. McCallum[*]

University of Virginia

The studies by Dutton and Neumann attempt to discover which, of several hypothesized impulses, are the more important determinants of annual output growth and inflation rates in the U.S. and Germany, respectively. As in the Fourcans (1978), Fratianni (1978), and Korteweg (1978) papers, monetary, fiscal, and (two) foreign impulse variables are considered, with each decomposed into anticipated and unanticipated components. The empirical findings are somewhat different for the two countries, but they agree in broad outline.

Properties of the Consortium Model

In discussing details of the Dutton and Neumann papers, it will be helpful to have in mind some aspects of the general picture that emerge from the afore-mentioned studies--which I shall refer to as the "Consortium" studies--taken together. My first impression was that, as a group, these five papers provided wide-ranging empirical support for a monetarist viewpoint of the rational expectations variety, that is, for a view of the economy such as that expressed in the macroeconometric model of Sargent (1976). This impression was created not only by the papers' numerous references to expectational rationality[1] but also by their tendency to agree in finding: no long-run trade-off between inflation and output growth; inflation attributable primarily to anticipated monetary expansion; and output growth attributable mainly to unanticipated impulse components, with the monetary impulse especially important.

A more careful reading reveals, however, that the empirical findings in some of these papers differ in one very important way from those of Sargent, and also from those of other related studies, including Lucas (1973) and Barro (1977). This is the finding that unanticipated monetary impulses have no effect on the inflation rate, or in other words, that there exists no short-run Phillips-type trade-off--not even one of the nonexploitable variety. This finding is of considerable interest in its own right, especially as it denies the existence of the perceived empirical regularity that led Lucas to carry out his fundamental reformulation of aggregate supply theory. In addition, the finding would appear

---

[*] In preparing this comment, I have drawn upon research supported by the National Science Foundation.

[1] Such references are not present in the paper by Dutton.

to have some possible implications relevant to stabilization policy. Specifically, the finding seems to imply that (in a closed economy) the price level is a supply-determined variable, entirely unresponsive to contemporaneous shocks in aggregate demand. This, in turn, might be thought to suggest that aggregate demand must impinge on output, possibly providing the monetary authorities with the means for systematically affecting output--a situation contrasting with that depicted by Lucas, Sargent, and Barro.

In order to investigate this possibility, and also the statistical procedures used in several of the studies, it will be useful to refer to an explicit model. To keep matters as simple as possible, I adopt one that recognizes only one impulse and is more streamlined than, but consistent with, my view of the modal Consortium specification. It is

(1) $\quad p_t = a_1(y_t - \bar{y}_t) + a_2 p_t^a + u_t$, aggregate supply;

(2) $\quad y_t = \beta_0 + \beta_1 (m_t - p_t) + v_t$, aggregate demand;

(3) $\quad m_t = \mu_0 + \mu_1 m_{t-1} + \mu_2 y_{t-1} + e_t$, monetary policy;

(4) $\quad p_t^a = E_{t-1} p_t$, rational expectations.

Here p_t, y_t, $\bar{y}_t$, and m_t are price, output, capacity, and money stock variables that are subject to two alternative interpretations. The first, used by Dutton and in some other Consortium studies, is that these are rate-of-growth variables: p_t = inflation rate, y_t = output growth rate, etc. The second is that the variables represent detrended logarithmic measures.[2] Either way, the random disturbances u_t, v_t, and e_t are taken to be generated by temporally independent white noise processes. Also, u_t and v_t are independent of $e_{t-\tau}$ for $\tau = 0, \pm 1, \pm 2, \ldots$. In (4), $E_{t-1} p_t$ denotes the conditional expectation of p_t, given values of all variables from all periods prior to t. Capacity is exogenous and predictable: $E_{t-1} \bar{y}_t = \bar{y}_t$. Equations (1)-(4) would constitute a fairly orthodox, if miniscule, macroeconomic model if it were not for the omission from (2) of a term such as

---

[2]Michael Parkin and David Laidler have argued--convincingly, in my opinion--that the latter formulation is more appropriate. But the reader may take his choice.

$p^a_{t+1} - p^a_t$, where the superscript a means "expected as of period t-1." It is my impression that the absence of such a term is of no consequence for the issues at hand.

It is clear that, if $a_1 > 0$ and $a_2 = 1$, then (1) becomes equivalent to a supply function of the type used by Lucas (1972) and by Sargent and Wallace (1975). In this case, as is well known, monetary policy will (under rational expectations) be powerless to affect output, in the sense that a solution equation for y_t will not involve any of the parameters μ_0, μ_1, or μ_2. In several of the Consortium studies, $a_2 = 1$, but $a_1 = 0$--the finding mentioned above. Under that condition, the aggregate supply function (1) determines p_t, and then, with p_t and m_t given, the aggregate demand curve (2) determines y_t. It is this pairing that might lead to a conjecture that monetary policy would affect output in this model.

Such a conjecture would, however, be incorrect. With $a_1 = 0$ and $a_2 = 1$, the following expressions constitute a solution to the model (1) - (4):[3]

$$(5) \quad p_t = \mu_0 + (\beta_0/\beta_1) - (\bar{y}_t/\beta_1) + \mu_1 m_{t-1} + \mu_2 y_{t-1} + u_t$$

$$(6) \quad y_t = \bar{y}_t - \beta_1 u_t + v_t + \beta_1 e_t.$$

Here none of the policy parameters appears in (6), so output behavior is independent of monetary policy, even though p_t is unresponsive to the demand shocks v_t and e_t.

The properties of the model with $a_1 = 0$ are, however, somewhat unsatisfactory. The solutions (5) and (6), unlike those to the models of Sargent (1976) or Lucas (1973), imply that $y_t - \bar{y}_t$ is serially uncorrelated. Thus, the model does not account for persistently high or low values of output. A more basic problem, however, is that (5) and (6) would remain solutions if another variable (or constant) were inserted in place of $\bar{y}_t$.[4] In other words, the model does not explain why output fluctuates around capacity, rather than around some other path. The presence of $\bar{y}_t$ in (5) and (6) is entirely ad hoc.

---

[3] This can be verified by substitution of (5) and (6)–and p^a_t obtained from (5) via (4)–into (1) - (3).

[4] This point is more basic in the sense that, if $\rho_1 \bar{y}_t + \rho_2 y_{t-1}$ were inserted, the previous point would no longer apply.

Alternative Statistical Procedures

Consequently, the statistical procedures used to obtain the finding that $a_1 = 0.0$--and also that $a_2 = 1.0$--deserve scrutiny. One strategy for statistical analysis of the issues of interest would be to specify a complete model (including impulse-generating equations), estimate parameter values, and analytically deduce measures describing the impact of the various impulse components (anticipated or unanticipated) on the endogenous variables. In terms of my one-impulse model, one would estimate the parameters of (1) - (3)--including disturbance variances--and then draw conclusions about impulse effects from the analytically obtained solution equations (5) and (6).

This is not, however, the strategy employed by Dutton (whose analysis I emphasize not only because his paper is skillfully executed and clearly exposited, but also because his approach is fairly representative of the Consortium as a group). I focus on the results in his Table 2, as these are the ones which are used to indicate that, "the anticipated rate of inflation fully explains the current rate of inflation," i.e., that $a_2 = 1.0$ and $a_1 = 0.0$, in my notation. Dutton's procedure is, first, to obtain a measure of p_t^a by OLS regression of p_t on maintained impulse values (Table 1) and, then, to regress p_t on this measure of p_t^a and first differences of raw (not maintained) impulse values (Table 2).[5] The fact that the resulting regression coefficients are insignificantly different from 1.0 and 0.0, respectively, is used as evidence for the propositions at hand. To interpret this procedure in terms of my one-impulse framework, let us suppose that the maintained impulse values coincide with rationally expected impulse values. Then, from (4), the maintained impulse is $\mu_0 + \mu_1 m_{t-1}$, if it is assumed (as it will be henceforth) that $\mu_2 = 0$. So, Dutton's first step is to regress p_t on m_{t-1} and to retrieve the fitted values, say $\tilde{p}_t$, for use as measures of p_t^a. The second step is to regress p_t on $\Delta m_t = m_t - m_{t-1}$ and $\tilde{p}_t$, obtaining regression coefficients denoted $\tilde{a}_1$ and $\tilde{a}_2$ as follows:[6]

---

[5] In the revised version of his paper, included in this volume, Dutton uses the discrepancy between raw and maintained impulse values rather than the first difference of the raw values. Thus, the details of the following discussion apply to the preliminary version of Dutton's paper.

[6] Actually, Dutton uses an average of $m_{t-1}, \ldots, m_{t-5}$ instead of m_{t-1}. Analysis similar to that which follows could be conducted given this condition--and would yield the same basic result--but would be more tedious. In the expressions that follow, I ignore constant terms.

$$
(7) \quad
\begin{bmatrix} \tilde{a}_1 \\ \\ \tilde{a}_2 \end{bmatrix}
\equiv
\begin{bmatrix} \Sigma \Delta m_t^2 & \Sigma \Delta m_t \tilde{p}_t \\ \\ \Sigma \tilde{p}_t \Delta m_t & \Sigma \tilde{p}_t^2 \end{bmatrix}^{-1}
\begin{bmatrix} \Sigma \Delta m_t p_t \\ \\ \Sigma \tilde{p}_t p_t \end{bmatrix} .
$$

As stated above, the fact that the values obtained for $\tilde{a}_1$ and $\tilde{a}_2$ are close to zero and unity, respectively, is used as evidence that a_1 and a_2 have those values. To see whether this conclusion is warranted, I derive probability limits for the estimators $\tilde{a}_1$ and $\tilde{a}_2$ as follows:

$$
(8a) \quad \text{plim} \, \tilde{a}_1 = \frac{a_1 \beta_1}{1 + a_1 \beta_1}
$$

$$
(8b) \quad \text{plim} \, \tilde{a}_2 = \frac{a_2 (\mu_1 - 1)}{\mu_1 (1 + a_1 \beta_1)} + \frac{1}{\mu_1} .
$$

Thus, the statistics are not consistent estimators for the crucial parameters a_1 and a_2, and so are not reliable guides for the conclusions drawn by Dutton.[7]

The reason for the difficulty is very simple; there is no rigorous analytical basis for the specification of the equation estimated in Dutton's Table 2. In particular, the use of the first differences of the impulse variables (Δm_t in my setup) is, though appealing intuitively, not otherwise justified.[8] The equation is not a structural, reduced form, or final equation for the model at hand.

There are, of course, difficulties involved in estimating equations with unobservable expectational variables. It is, nevertheless, possible to obtain consistent estimates of a_1 and a_2. One way would be to estimate the structural equation (1) by the instrumental variable technique, using $\tilde{p}_t$ in place of p_t^a and $\tilde{y}_t$ as an instrument for y_t (with $\tilde{y}_t$ retained from a regression of y_t on m_t and m_{t-1}).[9] The estimators in this case would be

---

[7] It will be noted that, for $a_1 > 0$, $\tilde{a}_1$ is asymptotically biased toward zero. This bias should not be large, however.

[8] Note that this point is in no way dependent on my identification of maintained and rationally expected impulse values. Nor is it affected by the fact that, on rather ad hoc grounds, Dutton uses the lagged change for the monetary impulse.

[9] Note that this procedure is not the one described in McCallum (1976), which is inapplicable to (1).

$$(9) \quad \begin{bmatrix} \tilde{a}_1 \\ \\ \tilde{a}_2 \end{bmatrix} = \begin{bmatrix} \Sigma \tilde{y}_t y_t & \Sigma \tilde{y}_t \tilde{p}_t \\ \\ \Sigma \tilde{p}_t y_t & \Sigma \tilde{p}_t \tilde{p}_t \end{bmatrix}^{-1} \begin{bmatrix} \Sigma \tilde{y}_t p_t \\ \\ \Sigma \tilde{p}_t p_t \end{bmatrix} .$$

It can straightforwardly be shown that these estimators are consistent:

$$(10) \quad \text{plim} \begin{bmatrix} \tilde{a}_1 \\ \\ \tilde{a}_2 \end{bmatrix} = \text{plim} \begin{bmatrix} \Sigma \tilde{y}_t y_t & \Sigma \tilde{y}_t \tilde{p}_t \\ \\ \Sigma \tilde{p}_t y_t & \Sigma \tilde{p}_t \tilde{p}_t \end{bmatrix}^{-1} \begin{bmatrix} \Sigma \tilde{y}_t (a_1 y_t + a_2 p_t^a + u_t) \\ \\ \Sigma \tilde{p}_t (a_1 y_t + a_2 p_t^a + u_t) \end{bmatrix}$$

$$= \begin{bmatrix} a_1 \\ \\ a_2 \end{bmatrix} + \text{plim} \begin{bmatrix} \Sigma \tilde{y}_t y_t & \Sigma \tilde{y}_t \tilde{p}_t \\ \\ \Sigma \tilde{p}_t y_t & \Sigma \tilde{p}_t \tilde{p}_t \end{bmatrix}^{-1} \begin{bmatrix} \Sigma \tilde{y}_t u_t \\ \\ \Sigma \tilde{p}_t u_t \end{bmatrix} = \begin{bmatrix} a_1 \\ \\ a_2 \end{bmatrix} .$$

Here, the second equality is justified by the results $\text{plim } T^{-1} \Sigma \tilde{p}_t (\tilde{p}_t - p_t^a) = 0$ and $\text{plim } T^{-1} \Sigma \tilde{y}_t (\tilde{p}_t - p_t^a) = 0$, while the third comes from $\text{plim } T^{-1} \Sigma \tilde{y}_t u_t = \text{plim } T^{-1} \Sigma \tilde{p}_t u_t = 0$. It would seem to be more appropriate that tests of the issues at hand be based on these estimators, or others that are statistically consistent.

To avoid possible misunderstanding, it should perhaps be mentioned explicitly that the foregoing argument is not a claim that estimation of structural equations is necessarily more productive than estimation of reduced form or final equations. It is, rather, a claim that the parameters estimated, whatever the type of equation in which they occur, should be related to the model under study in some rigorous fashion. Otherwise it will not be possible to draw logical conclusions about the model from the estimates. In terms of its observance of this simple but important principle, Myhrman's (1977) study of impulse effects in Sweden scores much higher than the studies in this volume.

The statistical procedure used by Dutton is, nevertheless, distinctly preferable to one in which p_t is regressed on $\tilde{p}_t$ and measures of the unanticipated components of the impulses, with the coefficient of $\tilde{p}_t$ used as an estimate of a_2. In the case of system (1) - (4), the "estimators" thus defined would be

$$
(11) \quad
\begin{bmatrix} \tilde{c}_1 \\ \\ \tilde{c}_2 \end{bmatrix}
=
\begin{bmatrix} \Sigma e_t^2 & \Sigma e_t \tilde{p}_t \\ \\ \Sigma \tilde{p}_t e_t & \Sigma \tilde{p}_t^2 \end{bmatrix}^{-1}
\begin{bmatrix} \Sigma e_t p_t \\ \\ \Sigma \tilde{p}_t p_t \end{bmatrix}
,
$$

if e_t were measured accurately.[10] Now, since $\tilde{p}_t$ is a linear function of m_{t-1}, it is orthogonal to e_t, the unanticipated impulse component. Therefore, the off-diagonal elements in the matrix in (11) are zeros, and the "estimator" $\tilde{c}_2$ reduces to

$$
(12) \quad \tilde{c}_2 = \Sigma \tilde{p}_t p_t / \Sigma \tilde{p}_t^2 .
$$

But, since $\tilde{p}_t = \tilde{\pi} m_{t-1}$, with $\tilde{\pi} = \Sigma p_t m_{t-1} / \Sigma m_{t-1}^2$, we derive

$$
(13) \quad \tilde{c}_2 = \frac{\Sigma p_t \tilde{\pi} m_{t-1}}{\Sigma \tilde{\pi}^2 m_{t-1}^2} = \frac{\Sigma p_t m_{t-1}}{\tilde{\pi} \Sigma m_{t-1}^2} = \frac{\tilde{\pi}}{\tilde{\pi}} .
$$

Thus, $\tilde{c}_2$ takes on the value 1.0 no matter what the values of the system's parameters are! It is entirely uninformative regarding a_2.

The estimates reported in equations (7.5) - (7.8), Neumann's Table 7, are essentially of the type just described; the inflation rate[11] is regressed on the anticipated inflation rate (measured as fitted values from a prior regression on

---

[10] If e_t were measured imperfectly but consistently, the equalities in (13) would hold in the limit, i.e.,

plim $\tilde{c}_2 = 1.0$.

[11] Neumann's use of second differences does not affect the point.

impulse values) and unanticipated components of the impulses.[12] The coefficient on the anticipated inflation variable is not exactly 1.0 in these cases because the unanticipated components of the impulses were not obtained by a method that makes them orthogonal to the anticipated components.[13] But, this is hardly a virtue, for one requirement of expectational rationality is precisely this orthogonality condition. More generally, any correlation between unanticipated and anticipated components implies that the forecaster is passing up virtually costless opportunities to improve his forecasting. Indeed, this nonorthogonality exemplifies the second main weakness of the Neumann and Dutton papers, namely, inadequate attention to the task of separating impulses into anticipated and unanticipated components. An instructive contrast is provided by an important recent paper by Barro (1977).

There is one other set of statistical results that I feel compelled to mention, namely, those based on the "newly developed nonparametric test statistic" used by Dutton (Table 6) and others. I state my concern in the form of a question, as follows. What is there about this test statistic that enables it to overcome the main weakness of an ordinary simple Pearsonian correlation coefficient, i.e., the failure to net out effects of other relevant variables (eliminate "specification bias")? Is not the nonparametric statistic simply a less informative measure of the same sort of gross bivariate association as the ordinary Pearsonian coefficient?

Conclusions

Despite my reservations concerning the procedures used by Dutton and Neumann, I consider their studies to be quite interesting and worthwhile. It is entirely possible--perhaps even likely--that most of their conclusions would continue to hold if more appropriate statistical procedures were utilized. And the emphasis which their papers, and the others in the volume, place on the study of aggregate supply relations is highly desirable. While there may be certain differences of opinion regarding some dynamic aspects of aggregate demand, it is clear that "monetarists" and "Keynesians" disagree far more over the nature of aggregate supply relationships.[14] And, these conflicting views

---

[12]This sort of procedure is also used by Fratianni (1978) in his Tables 4 and 6. Korteweg (1978) obtains estimates similar to $\tilde{c}_2$, but correctly recognizes that they cannot be used to test hypotheses concerning a_2.

[13]In fact, the decomposition is not based on the time-series properties of the impulse variables at all, but on the extent to which single annual values help to explain p_t in the regression used to generate $\tilde{p}_t$.

[14]On this particular point, monetarists should be in agreement with the contention of Modigliani (1977).

regarding supply are crucially relevant for stabilization policy. After all, if the Lucas-Sargent theory of supply is valid, then neither fiscal nor monetary policy will be effective for activist stabilization of output and employment.

References

Barro, R.J. (1977), "Unanticipated Money Growth and Unemployment in the United States," American Economic Review, 67: 101-15.

Dutton, D.S (1978), "Economics of Inflation and Output Fluctuations in the United States, 1952-1974," Carnegie-Rochester Conference Series, 8, eds. K. Brunner and A.H. Meltzer. Amsterdam: North-Holland.

Fourcans, A. (1978), "Inflation and Output Growth: The French Experience, 1960-1975," Carnegie-Rochester Conference Series, 8, eds. K. Brunner and A.H. Meltzer. Amsterdam: North-Holland.

Fratianni, M. (1978), "Inflation and Unanticipated Changes in Output in Italy," Carnegie-Rochester Conference Series, 8, eds. K. Brunner and A.H. Meltzer. Amsterdam: North-Holland.

Korteweg, P. (1978), "The Economics of Inflation and Output Fluctuations in the Netherlands, 1954-1975: A Test of Some Implications of the Dominant Impulse-cum-Rational Expectations Hypothesis," Carnegie-Rochester Conference Series, 8, eds. K. Brunner and A.H. Meltzer. Amsterdam: North-Holland.

Lucas, R.E., Jr. (1972), "Econometric Testing of the Natural Rate Hypothesis," in The Econometrics of Price Determination Conference, ed. O. Eckstein. Washington: Board of Governors of the Federal Reserve System.

_____(1973), "Some International Evidence on Output-Inflation Tradeoffs," American Economic Review, 63: 326-34.

McCallum, B.T. (1976), "Rational Expectations and the Natural Rate Hypothesis: Some Consistent Estimates," Econometrica, 44: 43-52.

Modigliani, F. (1977), "The Monetarist Controversy or, Should We Forsake Stabilization Policies?" American Economic Review, 67: 1-19.

Myhrman, J. (1977), "Inflation and Economic Activity: The Swedish Experience, 1953-1973." University of Stockholm. Mimeographed.

Neumann, M.J.M. (1978), "The Impulse-Theoretic Explanation of Changing Inflation and Output Growth: Evidence from Germany," Carnegie-Rochester Conference Series, 8, eds. K. Brunner and A.H. Meltzer. Amsterdam: North-Holland.

Sargent, T.J. (1976), "A Classical Macroeconometric Model for the United States," Journal of Political Economy, 84: 207-37.

Sargent, T.J., and Wallace, N. (1975), "'Rational' Expectations, the Optimal Monetary Instrument, and the Optimal Money Supply Rule," Journal of Political Economy, 83: 241-54.

INFLATION AND ECONOMIC STABILITY IN A SMALL OPEN ECONOMY: A SYSTEMS APPROACH

Peter D. Jonson and John C. Taylor[*]
Reserve Bank of Australia

I. INTRODUCTION

In the past six years, Australia has experienced its third major inflation of the twentieth century. It has shared this inflationary episode with the rest of the world, but in several ways its experience has differed from that in earlier times and in other countries. Indeed, the recent Australian experience offers evidence of the effects of several impulses: worldwide inflation impinging on an economy that initially maintained a relatively fixed exchange rate and then first revalued and later devalued its currency; strong expansion of the government sector, with government outlays, tax receipts, and the budget deficit increasing rapidly; a wage explosion generated to a considerable extent by large increases in centrally determined wages; and rapid increases in credit that, with the monetary effects of the other impulses, raised monetary growth from an average annual rate of 8 percent in the 1960s to a maximum of 26 percent in 1972/73, and to around 15 percent for about the last four years. The net effect of these impulses has been an entrenched inflation, a marked cycle in real product, and an unemployment rate that is approximately three times the average for the 1960s.

It is difficult to disentangle the effects of the various interrelated impulses. Nevertheless, analysis of a structural model of the Australian economy , yields some tentative judgments about the proximate role of the various factors listed above. This analysis is put into perspective in Section II with an overview of recent economic experience. In Section III, simulation analysis of this experience is presented, using an aggregate macroeconometric model, with the usual stock and flow adjustment mechanisms, some innovative monetary feedbacks, and allowance for the centralized wage-fixing institutions in Australia. Section IV discusses the interdependencies among the impulses examined in Section III, and Section V draws some conclusions.

[*] We are grateful to several people for comment and assistance, including André Cohen, Jan Eberhardt, Jim Henderson, Chris Higgins, Neil Johnston, Lyle Procter, and Don Stammer, although neither they nor our employer is necessarily in agreement with the arguments or conclusions.

Table 1

Some Aggregate Economic Indicators

	Real growth[a] (product)	Inflation[a] (product prices)	Inflation[a] (average weekly earnings)	Unemployment rate (percent)	Share of labor[b]	Volume of money[a] (M3)	International reserves[a]
1958/59-1968/69 (average)	5.1	2.9	5.8	1.4	0.51	7.7	5.4
1969/70	5.8	4.5	9.1	1.4	.52	6.1	2.9
1970/71	4.4	5.3	13.1	1.4	.54	6.8	45.1
1971/72	4.2	7.1	7.6	1.9	.55	10.5	67.9
1972/73	4.6	8.9	11.5	2.1	.54	25.8	29.5
1973/74	5.8	14.5	19.2	1.6	.55	14.5	- 8.1
1974/75	- 0.1	17.6	21.6	3.4	.59	15.4	- 10.6
1975/76	1.5	15.3	14.7	4.3	0.58	13.8	- 25.2

[a] Annual percentage change.

[b] Measured as the ratio of total wages, salaries, and supplements to nominal GDP.

290

II. RECENT AUSTRALIAN EXPERIENCE: AN OVERVIEW

In the first half of the 1970s, a variety of impulses came together to generate the third major acceleration of prices of the century; from 1969/70 to 1975/76, price rises averaged around 11 percent,[1] which compares with about 3 percent during the decade of the 1960s. As indicated in Table 1, inflation, as measured by the GDP deflator, accelerated to a peak of around 17.5 percent per annum in 1974/75 and then declined somewhat.[2] Wage rises on average exceeded price rises by more than can be explained by rises in productivity, resulting in an increase in the share of wages in GDP from an average of .51 in the 1960s to .59 in 1974/75. A major determinant of this higher share was a series of strong increases in arbitrated award wages, which in 1970/71 rose by 11.5 percent, in a year in which prices increased by 5.3 percent, and in both 1973/74 and 1974/75 by around 24 percent, also substantially in excess of price rises.[3]

The prices of traded goods, as represented by the export and import price deflators, were on average almost stable through the 1960s, and rose relatively little until 1972/73, in the case of export prices, and 1973/74, in the case of import prices, then increased strongly in line with the worldwide explosion in the price of traded goods, particularly primary commodities. Australia's exchange rate with the U.S. dollar remained fixed throughout the 1960s, then revalued substantially from 1971 to 1973, and subsequently devalued.[4] The relatively slow growth of Australian prices, and particularly of export prices, combined with the effects of major mineral discoveries to produce high export growth. These relative price effects contributed to strong growth of output and an intense domestic boom in 1973/74.

The large trade surplus was reinforced by large capital inflows to produce increases in international reserves that reached a peak year-on-year rise of 68 percent in 1971/72. Despite this increase, monetary growth (represented by growth in M3) remained below its average for the 1960s of slightly less than

---

[1]In the last two major inflationary episodes, average rises in the GDP deflator were around 8 percent (1913/14 to 1919/20) and 11 percent (1945/46 to 1952/53).

[2]In the calendar year to the end of 1976, preliminary national accounts indicate a decline in inflation and a substantial recovery in real product.

[3]During the 1960s, the annual rise in average weekly earnings averaged 5.8 percent, compared with average annual price increases of 2.9 percent.

[4]There were net revaluations relative to the U.S. dollar of 6 percent in 1971/72, 16 percent in 1972/73, 5 percent in 1973/74, and devaluations of 12 percent in 1974/75 and 7 percent in 1975/76. Late in 1976 the exchange rate was devalued by 17.5 percent; then a series of small revaluations pegged the devaluation back to approximately 12.5 percent by the end of the year.

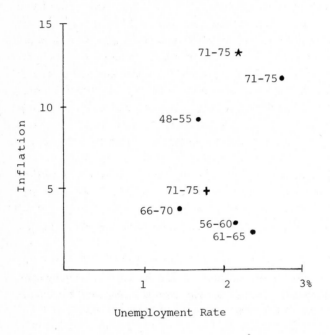

* Control Solution.   + Combined Tight Policies Solution.

Figure 1:   Inflation/Unemployment Combinations 1948-1975

8 percent per annum, until 1971/72 when it reached 10.5 percent. The low rates of domestic credit expansion of the early 1970s resulted from relatively low rates of growth of government spending on goods and services, fiscal drag, and quite large nonbank take-up of government securities in 1971/72, reflecting the effects of traditional stabilization policy responses to the rising inflation. In 1972, however, budgetary policy was relaxed somewhat, and combined with an explosion of bank lending in 1973 to generate an enormous expansion of domestic credit. The strong growth in domestic credit was reinforced by a 30 percent increase in international reserves[5] to raise the money stock by 26 percent in 1972/73. In subsequent years rapid domestic credit expansion continued, fueled by fast growth in government outlays,[6] although falling international reserves helped restrain average growth in money supply to rates around 15 percent.[7]

An indication of the degree to which inflation has become entrenched is provided by an index of price expectations constructed from a survey of manufacturers;[8] this measure suggests that, while in the June quarter of 1972 manufacturers expected price increases at an annual rate of approximately 8 percent, their expectations of price increases had risen to 14 percent by June 1973, 18 percent by June 1974, 16 percent by June 1975, and 16 percent by June 1976.

As in other countries, the greatly increased inflation has been accompanied by low growth of real product and increased unemployment. As Table 1 indicates, by 1975/76 the unemployment rate was about three times its average value for the 1960s; and growth in real product was negative in 1974/75 and relatively small in 1975/76.[9]

The recent performance of the Australian economy is put into a slightly broader perspective in Figure 1 which presents average rates of inflation and unemployment since 1948. After the first seven years, which were strongly influenced by the economic instability of the Korean War years, the apparent

---

[5] All the increase in international reserves occurred before the revaluation of December 1972. Revaluation, accompanied by quite stringent capital controls and high domestic demand, rapidly turned the balance of payments from surplus to deficit.

[6] Public sector outlays were around 27 percent of GDP in 1958/59, 32 percent in the late 1960s, and around 38 percent in the last three financial years.

[7] Although a short-lived monetary squeeze temporarily reduced the year-on-year growth rate to only 6.6 percent by September 1974, with the (seasonally adjusted) money stock actually falling in July and August of that year.

[8] See Danes (1975).

[9] Although, as noted, growth in real product seems to have recovered somewhat in calendar 1976.

"trade-off" between inflation and unemployment was very stable for Australia. For the years from 1971 to 1975, however, both inflation and unemployment are considerably higher, as in many other countries in the same period.[10]

III. A SIMULATION ANALYSIS OF AUSTRALIAN INFLATION

The analysis in this paper is based on simulation of a structural model of the Australian economy. The model is intended to reflect the major mechanisms and institutional features of the Australian economy; it is discussed briefly in Section III.A, and the complete model is set out in Appendix A.[11] Section III.B discusses the degree to which the model explains the recent takeoff in inflation and fluctuations in other important variables, and Section III.C presents some counterfactual simulation analysis. This analysis proceeds by eliminating in turn the various proximate causes of the inflationary takeoff, to give an idea of the contribution of each of the impulses listed in the introduction. Section IV draws together the threads of the simulation analysis and discusses some ways in which the impulses were interdependent.

A. The Model: Crucial Features

A basic feature of the model is its representation of economic processes as reflecting partial adjustment toward a moving equilibrium determined by a set of long-run behavioral schedules. Thus, for example, desired consumption is determined by disposable income and interest rates, business fixed investment by adjustment to equate the marginal product of capital with the cost of capital, desired imports and domestic output by sales and price of imports relative to those of domestic output. Actual consumption, investment, imports, output, etc., are in general assumed to adjust toward the desired level with a first-order adjustment process, although adjustment is also importantly influenced by the gap between actual and desired levels of buffer stocks. The buffer stocks, consisting of money in the case of households and of inventories of goods in the case of firms, allow smoothing of the relevant path in the face of unexpected disturbances, and play an important role in the dynamics of the model.

---

[10]Figure 1 contains two further points for the period 1971-75; one, denoted by the asterisk, represents the control solution trade-off for the RBA76 model used in the current analysis, and the other, denoted by the cross, represents the trade-off when all policy variables grow smoothly in the model. The alternative solutions are discussed below.

[11]The model is in the tradition of those developed at the International Monetary Research Program at the London School of Economics. It is discussed more fully in Jonson, Moses, and Wymer (1976).

The actual quantity of each buffer stock is determined residually in the short run, reflecting its role as a shock absorber. Thus, for example, the stock of money is determined as the net outcome of all other private and government decisions, as indicated by equation (18) in the model (see Appendix A). An important feature of the money supply process[12] in Australia since the Second World War has been a persistent tendency for bank lending to the private sector to increase more rapidly than bank deposits; that is, there has been a rising money multiplier for much of the sample period.[13] This is reflected in the equation (14) determining bank lending by a term representing the minimum asset ratio of the banks and by another representing the effect of excess demand for funds; one of the simulation experiments involves setting the parameter on excess demand at zero and holding the asset ratio constant.

The wage-price sector of the model, equations (6) and (9), is built around a wage-price interaction that is intended to capture implicitly the effects of past and future price movements. Money wages adjust with a lag to bring real wages into line with the marginal product of labor, while prices adjust to a mark-up over unit labor costs. This specification insures that the effects of past price changes are built into wages and that wage rises feed in turn into prices (in each case with allowance for movements in productivity). Within the framework of the model, however, information about future price movements is provided by the level of real money balances relative to desired real money balances; our results to date suggest that there are statistically significant and numerically important direct effects of excess money balances on price and wage dynamics.[14] In addition, labor market disequilibrium is included in the wage equation to represent the short-run Phillips effect of demand pressure in the labor market.

A further direct effect on wages, which is important in the Australian case, is that of the centralized wage-fixing authorities. In Australia, commonwealth and state arbitration commissions set a range of minimum award wages. The important effect of award wages in wage determination, found in almost all empirical work in this area for Australia,[15] can be rationalized in two ways

---

[12] It should be noted that the model uses a relatively broad (M3) measure of "money"; "credit" is correspondingly defined as bank credit. Future work will investigate alternative treatments which allow for a nonbank credit market in the model.

[13] Until recently, the statutory minimum cash ratio tended to be reduced more or less as the banks ran up against their lending limits as part of a policy to strengthen the competitive position of the banks.

[14] A comparison of the values of the relevant parameters in equations (6) and (9) when they are estimated with data for different sample periods suggests that they are rising in recent times.

[15] A survey of earlier results is provided by Jonson, Mahar, and Thompson (1974); in the current work, the effect of award wages comes through strongly, as indicated by equation (9). The weight of .4 on awards relative to trend is consistent with earlier results suggesting that increases in awards are not fully passed into earnings.

which have not yet been empirically distinguished. One theoretical rationalization would be provided by a two-sector model in which one sector has its wages determined by a markup on awards and the other with wages market determined. The second explanation relies on expectational effects; thus, Parkin (1973) suggests that decisions about award wages are an important part of the wage-expectations generating mechanism in Australia and, for this reason, includes a distributed lag on award wages in an equation for average weekly earnings. In the current model, this approach is modified somewhat and combined with work on the determinants of award wages. This work suggests that awards are usually adjusted for price changes and for trend productivity growth.[16] In the current model, it is assumed that it is only award wages that are higher or lower than those which would be expected on the basis of price changes and the regular productivity changes that influence market wages. If, for example, real award wages are above the level regarded as normal, then this serves as a signal that market rates should be increased, and vice versa if awards are below normal levels.[17]

The other general feature of the model is the way in which it endogenizes movements in the bond rate and the exchange rate by the inclusion of policy reaction functions for the relevant variables. Equations (20) and (21) explain an interest rate on government securities and the U.S.-dollar exchange rate, respectively; the corresponding financial quantities (the net value of government securities held by the nonbank sector and the level of international reserves) are determined by the relevant demand functions [equation (12) for government securities, equations (3), (4), (8), (13), and (21) for the components entering the balance of payments identity given in equation (17)]. The policy reaction functions include terms representing the usual stabilization policy objectives and also dummy variables representing the timing of the several major changes, particularly in the exchange rate, that have occurred in recent times. As is likely to be inevitable with a jumping-peg exchange rate regime, these changes were anticipated to a degree. Hence, a further dummy, representing the extent to which exchange rate expectations built up prior to each of the discrete exchange rate changes,[18] is influential in the trade equations and in the asset demand functions of the model. There is also an endogenous

---

[16]See Jonson, Mahar, and Thompson (1974) for the most recent work and a discussion of earlier results.

[17]As noted above, award wages have recently risen well in excess of historical norms. One of the simulation experiments involves hypothetically removing this deviation from historical trends.

[18]These exogenous exchange rate expectation effects are set at zero in some simulations in which a more flexible exchange rate regime is assumed.

aspect to exchange rate expectations, represented simply in the model by the exchange rate relative to an "equilibrium" exchange rate calculated from considerations of purchasing power parity.

In contrast to interest rate and exchange rate policy, budgetary policy, as represented by tax rates and real government outlays, is assumed to be exogenous. The deviation of real award wages from trend is also assumed to be exogenous in the model. The distinction between the degree of endogeneity of the different policy instruments is not clear-cut, however: on the one hand, the interest rate and especially the exchange rate equations contain exogenous explanatory variables; on the other hand, the instruments of budgetary policy, and the decisions of the arbitration commissions, react to some extent to economic conditions. The choice of which policy instruments to endogenize in a macroeconometric model is obviously somewhat arbitrary, and reflects a judgment about the extent to which the exogenous influences dominate over the sample period. If this were the only criterion, the exchange rate would probably be exogenous in the current model, but a further important point is that the exchange rate cannot remain fixed in the face of substantial changes in budgetary or monetary policy.[19] Therefore, it is necessary to allow the exchange rate to fluctuate if sensible counterfactual simulations are to be constructed; this is the main reason for endogenizing the exchange rate in the model. On the other hand, in a complete analysis, it is necessary to consider that even the policy instruments regarded as exogenous in estimating and simulating the model are endogenous to a degree; in Section IV, an attempt is made, therefore, to allow for the extent to which the variables regarded as exogenous in the simulations in Section III are endogenous and interdependent.

B. Control Simulation against Actual Changes

The panels in Figure 2 provide actual and simulated values since 1970 of proportional changes in real output, prices, international reserves, and the money stock; the unemployment rate; and a measure of monetary disequilibrium. The control solution values are obtained from a dynamic simulation of the model from a starting point in 1966. Dynamic simulations which allow errors to cumulate provide a rigorous test of a model's tracking ability, and a subjective assessment of the model's performance is "moderate."[20]

---

[19]Unless draconian direct controls are imposed, and even these are likely to be unsuccessful if macroeconomic policy is highly destabilizing.

[20]It is extremely difficult to devise objective tests of the performance of alternative macroeconometric models as indicated, for example, by the discussion in Dhrymes, et al. (1972). The approximate root mean square percentage errors for key variables in the dynamic control solution of the current version of the model from 1966 to 1975 are as follows: price of output, 3.9; earnings, 4.4; employment, 1.0; real product, 2.6; international reserves, 13.5; money, 3.5.

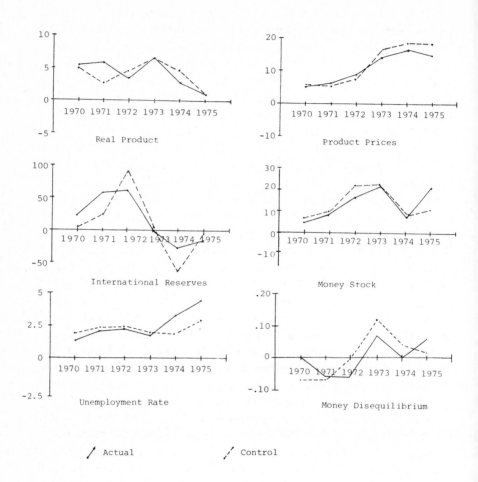

Figure 2:

Actual and Control Simulation Values for Growth Rates of
Key Variables, Unemployment Rate and a Measure of Money
Disequilibrium

The model's ability to explain levels of each variable is quite high, and the main weakness is the failure to accurately explain short-term fluctuations in output and employment. Typically, the model underpredicts output and employment in booms and overpredicts during slumps, although in the disturbed period from 1970 to 1972 the timing of output fluctuations is also somewhat astray.[21] In contrast, fluctuations in international reserves are greater in the control solution than in the economy for recent years. The takeoff in inflation and the major recent cycle in the balance of payments and the monetary growth rate are explained reasonably well, although the model tends to overpredict inflation in recent years somewhat, and the growth in money in 1975 is seriously understated.

The model also captures the major movements in monetary disequilibrium (real money supply less real money demand) reasonably well, although the underestimate of the monetary growth rate in 1975 translates into an error in the direction of movement in money disequilibrium. In the control simulation, the supply of money is exceeded by demand in 1970 due mainly to the underprediction of interest rates. This underprediction of interest rates also occurs in 1971, but its effect on money demand is offset by the underprediction of real income. The strong growth in unemployment in 1974 and 1975 is not captured by the model, partly due to its aggregated labor market. The wage equation is based on adult male units, whereas the equations modeling labor demand and labor supply refer to males plus females, and as a result, the model tracks movements in the unemployment rate of adult males better than it does the average for the whole economy,[22] although still not capturing fully the sharp rise at the end of the period.

The point denoted by an asterisk in Figure 1 illustrates the control solution trade-off between inflation and unemployment in the model for the period 1971-75. As noted, the model somewhat overpredicts inflation and underpredicts unemployment, especially in 1974 and 1975. The underprediction of unemployment is related mainly to the failure to allow for the wage relativity effects given in footnote 22; these effects are virtually impossible to capture in a highly aggregated model.

Despite the model's imperfect fit, it performs well enough to justify its being used for a series of simulation experiments designed to indicate the proximate causes of the inflationary takeoff in Australia.

---

[21]The two problem areas are exports and inventories, where short-run movements are not captured particularly well.

[22]Wages and unemployment rates for females and juniors have risen by considerably more than the average for the work force as a whole in recent years.

C. Some Counterfactual Simulation Experiments

The results of simulating the model with somewhat different assumptions about the policy regimes and by hypothetically removing some of the impulses that impinged in the past six years are presented. First, a managed float from early in 1971 is assumed;[23] next, a managed float with monetary tightness, achieved by raising interest rates in 1972 and 1973, by fixing bank liquidity ratios, and by assuming that bank advances did not, therefore, respond to demand pressures;[24] then, a managed float with monetary and fiscal tightness (the previous simulation is repeated, with government outlays growing steadily at a slower rate in recent years); and finally, a managed float with monetary and fiscal tightness and with real award wages assumed to grow at a slower rate, corresponding to an assumption that arbitrated wage increases occurred at a rate that did not raise wage expectations in the labor market. Appendix B specifies precisely the nature of these experiments.

The hypothetical nature of these simulation experiments cannot be stressed too strongly, and for two reasons, the results should be treated with considerable caution. The first is that the various impulses were not independent, or totally exogenous, as might be thought to be implied by the simulation strategy. Some ways in which the variables assumed to be exogenous were, in fact, endogenous, and interdependent, are discussed in Section IV, and the results of the simulation analysis cannot be considered apart from this discussion.[25]

The second reason for caution is even more fundamental. Since private sector reactions will not be invariant to the policy regime, as argued by Lucas (1976), one cannot be sure that the outcome would be the same as that predicted by the model if different policies had been followed. The

---

[23] In the discussion of the exchange rate reaction function above, it was noted that equation (21) contains both endogenous determinants, such as the level of and changes in the money stock and international reserves, and the level of prices relative to world prices, and exogenous dummy variables, to allow for the timing of the several major changes in parity that occurred. In simulating a managed float, the dummies representing the major changes in parity are set at zero, and the endogenous influences determine the rate. Further discussion is presented below, but it should be noted that a variety of market or policy reaction functions could in principle be substituted to provide alternative ways to simulate a flexible exchange rate.

[24] This is a somewhat clumsy way to represent a tight money policy within the traditional institutional framework. In practice, it might be more convincing to simulate such a policy by substituting a market reaction function for the policy reaction for interest rates, and by including a market-determined bank lending rate, but there are problems of the sort discussed by Lucas (1976) in imposing such a major change of structure on the model.

[25] In principle, this point would be covered by including reaction functions for all the instruments of policy and award wages, and by including some more structural detail in the financial sector of the model. The impulses would be removed by setting at zero those dummy variables which represented the economically exogenous determinants of policy reactions. In practice, knowledge of policy reaction is far too imprecise at present to implement this first-best approach. The discussion at the end of Section III.A is relevant here.

methodology of this paper is designed to weaken the force of this objection in two respects. First, the analysis uses a structural model that is designed to enable consequent adjustments to the structure of private sector reactions to be made when the policy regime is altered.[26] Second, the alternative policy regimes are in some respects within the range observed in the sample period: the exchange rate changes under the managed float are less than those that occurred with the variable peg;[27] changing official interest rates and bank cash ratios is a common policy reaction; and, the rate at which government outlays and award wages grow in the alternate simulations are similar to those achieved in the latter part of the 1960s.[28] Nevertheless, the issue raised by Lucas is a further reason for caution in interpreting the results.

1. A managed float

In this simulation, the exchange rate reaction function operates without the major revaluations of 1972 and 1973, or the devaluation of 1974. The exchange rate revalues slowly but steadily from 1971 under the influence of the relative price, balance of payments, and monetary target variables in the exchange rate reaction function. By the end of the simulation period, the rate has revalued slightly more than in the control simulation, but this is achieved without the major revaluations followed by devaluation that occur in the control simulation.[29] The major fluctuations in the trade account and capital accounts of the balance of payments that occur in the control simulation are, therefore, absent.

Figure 3 compares the control solution with that obtained under the managed float. As indicated, the managed-float simulation removes the major cycle in the balance of payments and the resulting rapid acceleration in the monetary growth rate in 1972 and 1973. Money growth increases from 1973 under the managed-float regime, however, because the high domestic credit expansion is not offset by loss of international reserves as in the control solution, and in 1974 and 1975 the monetary growth rate is higher under the managed float.

---

[26]In particular, when a managed float is substituted for the movable-peg exchange rate regime, the dummy variable representing expectations of the once-and-for-all changes in the exchange rate (denoted QE) is set equal to zero.

[27]Although it should be noted that there is no example of a managed float during the sample period.

[28]Indeed, the control solution tracks, although imperfectly, with policy and other variables well outside the range in much of the sample period. Jonson, Moses, and Wymer (1976) give estimates for the periods to 1971-IV and 1974-IV; it is possible to check the extent to which omitting the highly disturbed observations in 1972, 1973, and 1974 changes the key structural parameters.

[29]In 1975, the rate of revaluation slows although there is no devaluation, despite the strong expansion of the budget deficit in the last two years. If exchange rate expectations were closely geared to the budget or monetary position, this conclusion might be altered, in which case there would be devaluation and increased inflation toward the end of the sample period with the managed float.

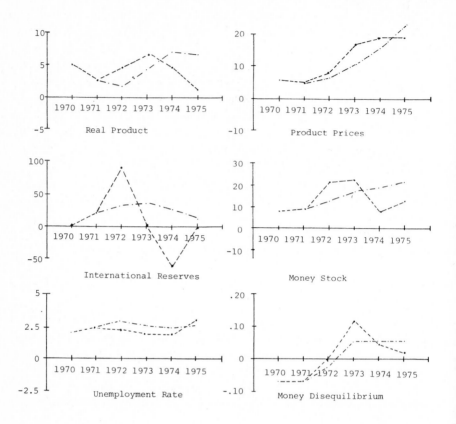

Figure 3:

Control Solution and Managed Float: Growth Rates of
Key Variables, Unemployment Rate and a Measure of
Money Disequilibrium.

Inflation is less than that in the control simulation by approximately seven percentage points in 1973, slightly lower in 1974, four percentage points higher than in the control simulation in 1975, and accelerating sharply. Output growth falls in 1972 as the stimulus provided by expectation of a major revaluation[30] is removed under the assumption of a managed float, but, thereafter, it accelerates steadily to reach an inflationary peak of almost 7 percent per annum in 1974. The levels of real product and employment are considerably lower in 1973 than in the control solution.

The unemployment rate in this simulation rises above the control solution value in 1972 and remains high until 1974. In 1975 the increased real growth produces a small reduction in the unemployment rate. The influence of the initially reduced growth in international reserves and money is seen in the behavior of monetary disequilibrium. The lower growth of money until 1973 means that the inflationary consequences of monetary disequilibrium are lessened considerably. After 1973, however, monetary disequilibrium is greater than in the control solution, largely due to the faster growth in the money supply.

2. Managed float with tighter money

In this simulation,[31] money is tightened by raising interest rates in 1972 and 1973, fixing the bank asset ratio at its initial value, and assuming that bank lending did not respond to demand.[32] The effect is to reduce the money multiplier, substantially eliminating its rise during the sample period, and to increase sales of government securities. As in the previous simulation, a managed float of the exchange rate is also assumed, so that lower domestic credit expansion is not offset by a buildup of international reserves as would tend to occur with a fixed exchange rate.

The panel depicting monetary growth in Figure 4 shows that, with a managed float and tighter money, the money growth rate is about one percentage point less from the beginning of the 1970s, with the major gain occurring toward the end of the simulation period, when monetary growth is reduced by over 4 percent. International reserves are growing at a slightly greater rate throughout, partly because of the effect of higher interest rates on capital flows, and the stronger current account. These factors combine to cause money supply to fall by more than money demand, although money

---

[30]Which operates to encourage exports and postpone imports and, therefore, to encourage domestic production in the control simulation.

[31]In this and subsequent simulations, the control solution is plotted in addition to the two simulation paths that are being compared directly.

[32]N. 24 gives reasons for using this approach.

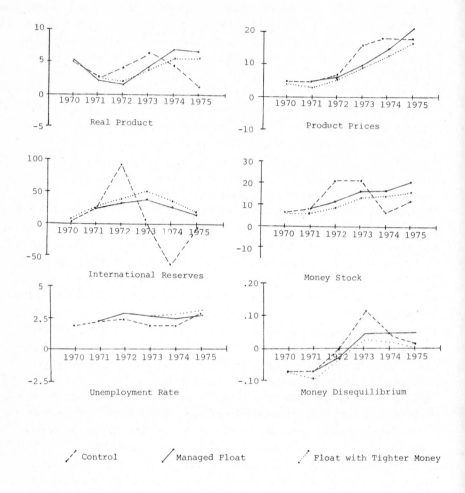

Figure 4:

Managed Float and Tighter Money: Growth Rates of
Key Variables, Unemployment Rate and a Measure
of Money Disequilibrium

demand decreases due to lower real income and higher interest rates. Decreased monetary disequilibrium has strong anti-inflationary consequences, particularly in 1974 and 1975, although at a relatively slight cost in terms of a higher unemployment rate. The rate of inflation is reduced by about a quarter throughout the simulation period, which more than offsets the effect of revaluation on exports and imports. Higher exports and lower imports both contribute to the slightly increased output growth in 1971 and 1972, as is evident in the first panel of Figure 4.

Despite tighter monetary policy and a revaluing exchange rate, prices are still rising (although at a slower rate than in the previous simulation) at the end of the sample period. This is due both to demand pressures in the goods market and to the effects of strong wage increases.

3. Managed float, tighter money, and tighter budgetary policy

As noted above, budgetary policy was relatively tight in the early 1970s, then became highly expansionary. Although there were important influences on the revenue side of the budget, these are largely endogenous in the model. On the outlays side, the growth of government spending on goods and services declined somewhat in the early 1970s, and transfers were growing relatively slowly; then, transfers expanded strongly from 1971/72 as did spending on goods and services from 1973/74. The current simulation, which is compared with the previous one in Figure 5, consists of maintaining growth of both spending and transfers, at the rates achieved in the late 1960s, into the 1970s. Thus, spending on goods and services is actually higher for a time, then markedly lower.

In the simulation, the effect is to produce higher growth in real product until 1973; after that time, product growth is slightly lower and unemployment slightly higher. The net effect of a smoother path for real government outlays is smoother growth of real product. Inflation is slightly lower at first, as the effect of higher productivity on unit labor costs offsets the higher degree of demand pressure in the commodity markets. The cumulative effect of lower prices on the trade account is sufficient to almost offset the output effect of smaller government outlays late in the simulation period. The monetary growth rate is over one percentage point lower at the end of the period, mainly reflecting the lower budget deficits, and the inflation rate is over two percentage points lower than in the previous simulation, again largely due to reduced monetary disequilibrium.

4. Managed float, tighter money, tighter budgetary policy, and steady growth of award wages

The final simulation experiment is to remove the large increases in award wages, especially in 1970/71, 1973/74, and 1974/75. The policy changes in the

305

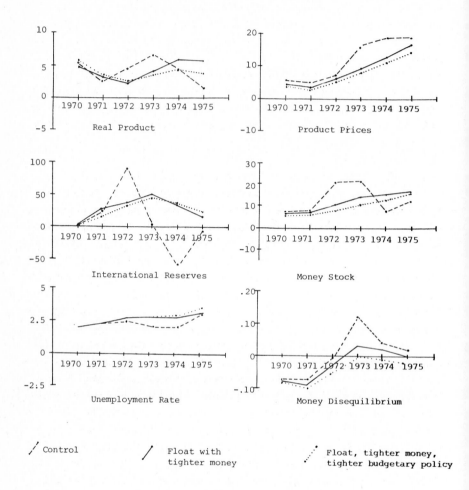

Figure 5 :

Managed Float, tighter money and tighter budgetary policy:
Growth Rates of Key Variables, Unemployment Rate and a
Measure of Money Disequilibrium

306

previous simulation are retained, so the comparison of the simulation paths illustrated in Figure 6 indicates the effect of the large award wage increases.

The results of this simulation are similar to those of the previous one, except that the inflation rate is lower throughout, and dramatically so in 1974 and 1975. Monetary growth is also substantially lower, reflecting largely the effect of lower wages on government outlays, which is partly but not entirely offset by lower tax collections. An important effect of lower awards is that unemployment is substantially lower, as lower real wages[33] combine with higher real output. As might be expected, the tighter monetary and budgetary policies in the previous simulations both reduce employment relative to the control solution values (although the growth of employment is smoother). When the real wage impulse is also removed, in the final simulation, employment is considerably higher throughout, relative to both the previous simulation and to the control solution (except in 1973).

5. Control solution compared with all variables growing steadily

Comparing the control simulation results with those of the final simulation path, it is evident that removal of the various monetary, budgetary, and wages impulses, combined with a managed float, have largely eliminated the dramatic acceleration of inflation that occurs in the control simulation. The slight acceleration of money and inflation in 1973, 1974, and 1975 in the final simulation occurs because the sizable revaluation resulting from the managed float is not enough to entirely offset the effects of the massive commodity price rises of recent years. A relatively steady set of policies has produced a smoother output path and a more favorable combination of inflation and employment in the model. This is seen most clearly in the average inflation-unemployment combination for the 1971-75 period in the final simulation, denoted by the cross in Figure 1; it is interesting that the average trade-off achieved in this simulation is similar to those in the late 1950s and 1960s. The improved trade-off is also indicated by a comparison of the simulation paths in the first and second panels of Figure 6, where the growth rate of output is smoother, and higher at the end, and that of prices substantially lower than in the control simulation. Since real wages are lower in the final simulation, there are favorable employment effects in excess of those indicated by the higher output.

There is still a recession, indicated by the relatively low growth of real product, in 1971 and 1972, partly as a result of the world recession[34] and the

---

[33] In the short run, lower award wages have a larger effect on earnings than on prices.

[34] World activity is represented in the model by a measure of world trade, which influences the demand for Australian exports.

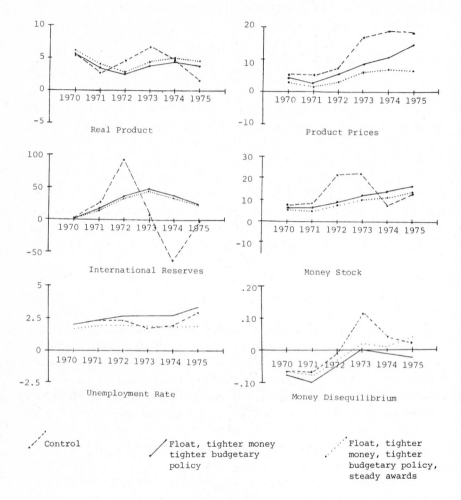

Figure 6:

All policy Variables growing steadily: Growth
Rates of Key Variables, Unemployment Rate and
a Measure of Money Disequilibrium

revaluation of the Australian dollar;[35] the growth of real product also turns down in 1975, again mainly because of the effects of the world recession on exports. It is evident that the managed float of the exchange rate assumed in the current analysis cannot insulate the economy fully from either sharp fluctuations in world prices, particularly when there are changes in the terms of trade, or from major fluctuations in world activity.[36]

IV. INTERDEPENDENCIES AMONG THE IMPULSES: TOWARD A GENERAL EVALUATION

There are two general reasons for interdependencies among the impulses: technical factors, such as the government budget constraint, the bank lending function, and other endogenous responses which transmit and may amplify the effect of each impulse throughout the system; and the broader factors relating to the stabilization policy rules followed and the policy objectives chosen by successive governments. It is necessary to consider these factors in any general evaluation of the reasons for the inflationary takeoff in Australia, even though the second set involves consideration of relationships which are to some extent outside the formal framework of the model.

A. Technical Factors

The basic technical factor is that the government budget constraint combined with the traditional policy of setting important prices, such as the exchange rate and the yields on government securities, rather than financial quantities, so that each of the impulses acted to raise the monetary growth rate. Thus, the buildup of international reserves, the increase in government outlays, and the rise in award wages all contributed at various times to the excessive increase in money. The reductions in bank cash ratios, and the banks' traditional tendency to expand lending in response to demand,[37] multiplied the monetary effects and contributed to excessive demand in the commodity market (via the effects on consumption), and to price and wage rises (through expectational effects).

The dependence of wages on prices and of prices on wages triggered a wage-price spiral, which was underpinned by a largely accommodating monetary

---

[35] Other factors include the depressing effect of a trough in the Australian investment cycle.

[36] It is worth noting that a perfectly flexible exchange rate could not insulate an economy from such fluctuations either.

[37] With demand for credit reinforced by lending rates below market rates.

policy in the early phases of the wage-price takeoff, and then by the adoption of wage indexation. There were, of course, some negative or dampening feedbacks, such as the rise in tax receipts due to the interaction of highly progressive income tax schedules and the rise in nominal incomes, the rise in interest rates, and the increase in inflation. These dampening feedbacks operated partly by reducing real product; it is worth noting that the specification of the price expectations effect in the model as a disequilibrium real balance effect has an important implication for the "trade-off" debate. If increased inflation and economic instability reduce real output and raise interest rates, the likely result is a reduction in the demand for money,[38] which, given supply, increases the excess supply of money. This excess supply of money will, in turn, produce a higher price level for any given money stock, and during the adjustment to a higher price level, the inflation rate will be greater, in parallel with lower activity and employment.

B. Policy Rules and Policy Objectives

A complete analysis of the influence of policy rules and policy objectives in Australia's recent experience would require a major study; this section can do no more than point to some of the important factors in this area which need to be considered in understanding the inflationary takeoff.

As already noted, economic policy was conducted in the 1960s under fixed exchange rates and by pegging a range of nominal interest rates and bank liquidity ratios. These policy instruments, and the rate of growth of government outlays and statutory tax rates, tended to respond systematically to the conventional targets of stabilization policy. Reinforced by progressive personal income tax schedules, the policy responses were probably stabilizing in the face of domestically generated inflation. They were far less appropriate instruments for maintaining economic stability with the increase in world inflation, however. Indeed, as suggested by Porter's (1974) analysis of capital movements, the tightening of budgetary policy in the early 1970s helped to generate the enormous buildup of international reserves and the self-fulfilling expectations of exchange rate revaluation.[39] The larger-than-usual increase in award wages in 1970/71 can be related in part to the exceptionally strong balance of payments at the time, and contributed to a rise in the unemployment rate

---

[38] Although increased uncertainty associated with increased instability may partly or in some conditions wholly offset this negative effect on the demand for money. See Brunner and Meltzer (1971) for a discussion of this issue.

[39] The failure to revalue in 1971 stemmed partly from distributional factors. The country party members of the government coalition were reported to have threatened to leave the government if the rate were revalued.

above that which had in the past triggered expansionary policy responses. In 1972 tax rates were cut and social service payments increased more quickly than usual, although, in common with many other countries, the unemployment rate remained somewhat higher than usual.

One of the first economic policy changes of the Labor Government elected late in 1972 was a revaluation of the exchange rate and a tightening of capital controls. Revaluation was repeated twice in 1973, with an across-the-board tariff cut in the middle of the year providing a further external policy initiative. Budgetary policy eventually became extremely inflationary, and an adviser to the Labor Government, in an article entitled "What Went Wrong?" (Gruen, 1976), gives considerable weight both to the use of the labor market as the major indicator of domestic demand pressure and to the unusually high levels of unemployment, especially after the onset of recession in the middle of 1974.[40] While labor governments might in any case be expected to increase government outlays more rapidly than more conservative parties, it can be argued that in recent Australian experience a further inflationary factor was that the high level of international reserves inherited from previous years meant that a traditional constraint on expansionary social policies was missing. The strongly rising tax revenues also provided a permissive background for the Labor Government's policymaking. From a situation combining a tight budgetary policy with an undervalued exchange rate, the economy moved to a higher and more flexible exchange rate, but with much more rapid domestic credit expansion.

The general air of permissiveness extended to the wage-fixing authorities, who were in fact encouraged to grant large wage increases by the government's submissions to the 1973 and 1974 national wage cases.[41] A further impetus to wage rises was provided by the phasing in of equal pay for females over the three years following the 1972 national wage case, and by other innovations such as a 17.5 percent loading for holiday pay; then, the adoption of wage indexation tended to put a floor under before-tax real wages. After a sharp monetary contraction in the middle of 1974, the thrust of macroeconomic policy was quickly reversed and the exchange rate devalued in an attempt to boost demand; the rapid turnaround in policy is likely to have had effects on consumer and business confidence which, while difficult to quantify, may be quite important. As noted elsewhere, the relationship between increased policy

---

[40]Gruen also discusses the effects of errors in forecasting, a certain degree of mutual suspicion between the government and the Treasury, and the inflationary situation inherited by the Labor Administration.

[41]The Labor Government's concern to raise the share of wages provides another example of the weight of distributional objectives being raised for some time relative to that of stabilization objectives.

variance and a worsening trade-off between inflation and unemployment is an area in which further analysis is indicated.[42]

V. CONCLUDING COMMENTS

The simulation analysis presented in this paper illustrates how several related impulses contributed to a rise in the monetary growth rate and to a buildup of inflation, with its associated economic instability, in Australia. The results emerge from a highly aggregated structural model which contains the usual channels for the influence of policy and foreign variables. The discussion of the various simulation experiments indicates how these standard channels operated in Australia in recent years. Two somewhat unusual channels also contribute significantly to the results: the first is the effect of monetary disequilibrium on consumption expenditure and on the adjustment of wages and prices; the second is the important role of the arbitration commissions which, the model implies, have provided substantial exogenous wage push in recent Australian experience. The wage push was underwritten and reinforced by budgetary and monetary expansion.

Section IV discusses interdependencies among the various impulses, and shows how the rise in world inflation and the resulting balance of payments surpluses contributed to high wage increases and somewhat contradictory monetary and budgetary policy responses. When the propensity of a new labor government to expand the government sector was reinforced by the rising unemployment rate, high international reserves, and rapidly increasing tax receipts, further instability was added to the system. While there was an autonomous element to each of the impulses whose effects are examined above, it is also necessary to recognize the complex interdependencies among the various impulses during the inflationary takeoff. It can reasonably be argued that the buildup of inflation, while not inevitable, was highly likely in view of world instability, the distributional and other objectives of successive governments, and the attitudes and institutions inherited from the earlier period of relatively low inflation, fixed exchange rates, and an entrenched belief in the efficacy of discretionary macroeconomic policymaking.

At the most general level, it could be argued that considerable responsibility for increased inflation and economic instability be attributed to the failure of Australian economic policy to emphasize sufficiently monetary

---

[42]See Lucas (1973) for a theoretical analysis and an across-country comparison, and Jonson (1977) for a discussion of recent British experience. The comments in Section IV.A and in Jonson (1976) are also relevant.

growth rates as crucial indicators of the stance of policy. Greater emphasis on the need for monetary stability would have involved a setting of policy instruments–including wages policy–conducive to a more stable outcome for money and economic activity. A conclusion suggesting a link between monetary and economic stability for Australia would be based in part on the correlation between lower inflation, steadier growth of real product, and more stable money in the simulations presented above; but, as in the analysis by Friedman and Schwartz (1963), this conclusion would have to be supported by a judgment that the monetary instability was triggered by factors exogenous to the normal working of the economy. As Section IV attempts to indicate, such a case could be put for the recent Australian experience; but, it is not proven in any formal sense, and further work on the determinants of economic policy reactions is required.

Appendix A

The Model

The specification of the model is as follows:

(1) Household expenditure, demand for money

$$\text{Dlog } d = .55 (\log \hat{d} - \log d) - .26 (\log \hat{m} - \log {}^M/_P)$$

$$\log \hat{d} = d_0 + \log (y - {}^{T_1}/_p + c) - .06 \log r$$

$$\log \hat{m} = m_0 + \log y - .18 \log r - .14 \log r_w - .01QE + .10 \log {}^{EP_w}/_P$$

(2) Net business fixed investment

$$Dk = .99 [.10 (.3 {}^{y-g}/_K - r + \text{Dlog } P) + \lambda_1 - .30 \text{ Dlog } P - k]$$

$$\lambda_1 = .012$$

(3) Exports of goods and services

$$\text{Dlog } x = 3.9 (\log \hat{x}^d - \log x) + 2.0 (\log \hat{x}^s - \log x) - .49QE$$

$$\log \hat{x}^d = x_0 + \log x_w - .51 \log ({}^{P_x}/_{EP_w})$$

$$\log \hat{x}^s = x_0' + \log y + .50 \log ({}^{P_x}/_p)$$

(4) Imports of goods and services

$$\text{Dlog } i = .54 (\log \hat{i} - \log i) + 1.2 (\log \hat{v} - \log v * e^{\lambda_1 t})$$

$$\lambda_1 = .012$$

(5) Output, desired inventories

$$\text{Dlog } y = .50 (\log \hat{y} - \log y) + .07 (\log \hat{v} - \log v)$$

$$\hat{i} = [i_0 (\frac{EP_i(1+t_3)}{P})^{-.41} e^{.28QE}] S$$

$$\hat{y} = [1 - i_0 (\frac{EP_i (1+t_3)}{P})^{-.41} e^{.28QE}] S$$

$$\hat{v} = v_0 S$$

$$S = d + DK + DK_g + x + g$$

Note: A subscript of zero indicates a constant.

(6) Price of output

$$\text{Dlog } P = .42 (\log \hat{P} - \log P) - .23 (\log \hat{m} - \log {}^M\!/_P)$$

$$\hat{P} = P_0 \frac{WL}{y_0 e^{\lambda_3 t} L^{.7} K^{.3}}$$

$$\lambda_3 = .0029$$

(7) Price of government current goods and services

$$\text{Dlog } P_g = 1.4 (\log \hat{P}_g - \log P_g)$$

$$\log \hat{P}_g = .81 \log W + .19 \log P$$

(8) Price of exports

$$\text{Dlog } P_x = .44 (\log \ EP_i - \log P_x) + .31 \log ({}^P\!/_{EP_w}) + .01 QE$$

(9) Average weekly earnings

$$\text{Dlog } W = .20 [\log (.7^y\!/_L) - \log {}^W\!/_{P'}] + 1.7 \log {}^L\!/_{\theta_0 N}$$

$$+ .40 \log ({}^{W}A\!/_{w_0} \ e^{\lambda_3 t}) - .21 (\log \hat{m} - \log {}^M\!/_P)$$

$$\log P' = P'_0 + .20 \log EP_w + .80 \log P$$

$$\lambda_3 = .0029$$

(10) Labor supply

$$\text{Dlog } N = .16 (\log \hat{N} - \log N)$$

$$\log \hat{N} = N_0 - .18 \log [\frac{(1-t_1)WL}{Py}] + \log L$$

(11) Labor demand

$$\text{Dlog } L = .09 [\log (.7^y\!/_L) - \log {}^W\!/_P] + .008 \log ({}^g\!/_{g_0} e^{\lambda_1 t})$$

$$\lambda_1 = .012$$

(12) Nonbank demand for government securities

$$\text{Dlog } B = .06\, (\log \hat{b} - \log {}^B/_p)$$

$$\log \hat{b} = b_0 + \log y + .89 \log r - .89 \log r_w - .20QE + 2.2 \log {}^{EP}w/_p$$

(13) Net capital inflow

$$\text{Dlog } F = .06\, (\log \hat{f} - \log {}^F/_p)$$

$$\log \hat{f} = f_0 + \log y + .79 \log r - .79 \log r_w - .59QE$$

$$+ 2.5 \log {}^{EP}w/_p - .02QF$$

(14) Bank advances

$$\text{Dlog } A = .26\, (\log \hat{A} - \log A) + .15 \log \left[{}^{Py}/_{(Py)_0} e^{\lambda_2 t} \right]$$

$$\log \hat{A} = A_0 + \log (1-Z)\, M - .22 \log r + .17 \log r_w - .009QA + .02QF$$

$$\lambda_2 = .015$$

(15) Direct taxes

$$\text{Dlog } T_1 = 2.8\, (\log \hat{T}_1 - \log T_1)$$

$$\log \hat{T}_1 = T_{01} + \log t_1 Py$$

(16) Indirect taxes

$$\text{Dlog } T_2 = .11\, (\log \hat{T}_{21} - T_2) + .74\, (\log \hat{T}_{22} - \log T_2)$$

$$\log \hat{T}_{21} = T_{02} + \log t_2 Pd$$

$$\log \hat{T}_{22} = T_{03} + \log T_{04}\, WL$$

(17) Balance of payments

$$DR = P_x x - EP_i i + DF$$

(18) Supply of money

$$DM = DR + P_g g + P\,(DK_g) + Pc - T_1 - T_2 - DB + DA + f\,(rB)$$

(19) Change in inventories

$$Dv = y + i - d - DK - x - g - DK_g$$

(20) Bond rate

$$\text{Dlog } r = .05 \log {}^{r}0/_{r} - .03 \log {}^{R}/_{\phi_0 M} + 1.2 \log {}^{L}/_{\theta_0 N}$$

$$+ .14 \log ({}^{M}/_{M_0} e^{\lambda_2 t}) + .09 QS + .79 (\text{Dlog } M - \lambda_2)$$

$$- .22 (\text{Dlog } R - \lambda_2)$$

$$\lambda_2 = .015$$

(21) Exchange rate

$$\text{Dlog } E = .05 \log {}^{P/P_w}/_{E} - .02 \log {}^{R}/_{\phi_0 M} - .22 \log {}^{L}/_{\theta_0 N}$$

$$- .07 \log ({}^{M}/_{M_0} e^{\lambda_2 t}) + .11 QUS + .06 QER + .50 (\text{Dlog } M - \lambda_2)$$

$$- .12 (\text{Dlog } R - \lambda_2)$$

$$\lambda_2 = .015$$

(22) Business fixed capital stock

$$\frac{DK}{K} = k.$$

Variables Used in the Model[a]

A	=	all bank advances to private sector
B		bonds held by private (nonbank) sector
c^*		real cash benefits to persons
d		real household expenditure
E		exchange rate ($A/$US)
F		net Australian capital owned by overseas residents
g^*		real Australian government current spending
i		real imports of goods and services
k		net real business fixed investment
K		stock of business fixed capital
K_g^*		real Australian government capital stock
L		labor demand
M		nominal stock of money (M3)
N		labor supply
P		price of output
P_g		price of government goods and services
P_i^*		Australian import prices ($US)
P_x		price of exports
P_w^*		world prices ($US)
QA*		dummy variable for requests to limit advances, 1961
QE*		dummy variable for exchange rate expectations, 1972-75
QER*		dummy variable for timing of exchange rate changes, 1972, 1973, 1974
QF*		dummy variable for capital controls, 1973-74
QS*		dummy variable for credit squeeze, 1961, 1973
QUS*		dummy variable for devaluation of $US, 1973
R		foreign exchange reserves
r		bond rate
r_w^*		world interest rate
t^*		time
t_1^*		income tax rate
t_2^*		expenditure tax rate
t_3^*	=	tariff rate

---

[a]The precise definitions and sources for all variables are given in Appendix B of Jonson, Moses, and Wymer (1976). Lower case variables b, f, and m correspond to real values of B, F, and M, respectively.

*The items marked with an asterisk are exogenous for estimation purposes. As discussed in Section IV, however, some of these items are at least in part endogenous in the real world.

T_1	=	direct tax receipts
T_2		indirect tax receipts
v		stock of inventories
W		average weekly earnings
w_A^*		real award wages
x		real exports of goods and services
x_w^*		real world exports
y		real output (net of depreciation)
z^*		required asset ratio for all banks
λ_1		target rate of growth of inventories
λ_2		target rate of monetary growth
λ_3	=	regular growth of real award wages.

Appendix B

Simulation Procedures

Section III of the paper discusses five simulations of the model of the Australian economy set out in Appendix A. The period for the simulations, which are all dynamic nonstochastic simulations, is 1966-III to 1975-IV.

1. The control solution

This simulation has all exogenous variables taking on their historical values; all lagged endogenous variables are the solution values from the previous period. Any errors are thus allowed to cumulate, in contrast to their treatment in a nondynamic simulation.

2. Managed float

In this simulation, the dummy variables in the exchange rate equation (21) which represent the timing of the major changes in parity that occurred in the sample period (QER, QUS) are set equal to zero, and the authorities are assumed to react continuously, rather than at discrete times, to the level and changes in the money stock, in international reserves, and to the level of prices relative to world prices.

It is assumed that, if such a managed float had been adopted, the capital controls imposed in 1972 would not have been necessary, and hence, the dummy variable (QF) representing these is also set at zero. It is also assumed that the behavior of exchange rate expectations would have been different, and in consequence, the dummy variable indicating the degree to which expectations built up prior to each of the major changes in the exchange rate (QE) is also set equal to zero.

3. Managed float with tighter money

The changes included in simulation 2 are made, and in addition higher interest rates on government securities are imposed in 1972 and 1973, and the aggregate bank liquidity ratio is not reduced from its value at the start of the simulation period. It is assumed that a policy with higher official and bank interest rates early in the inflationary period would have prevented bank lending from responding to demand, and accordingly, the parameter on $Py/(Py)_0 e^{\lambda_2 t}$ in equation (14) is set equal to zero. This package represents a somewhat clumsy way to simulate a tight money policy within the traditional institutional framework, and it might eventually be more convincing to simulate such a policy by introducing explicitly an interest rate on bank lending, which would be market determined. There are, of course, some difficult issues to be resolved before such a major change of structure could be imposed on the model.

4. Managed float, tighter money, and tighter budgetary policy

The changes described in simulations 2 and 3 are made, and in addition government outlays are assumed to increase steadily from their 1966-III values as follows:

$$\log g = 6.48 + .010t$$
$$\log c = 5.75 + .008t$$
$$\log K_g = 10.48 + .012t.$$

The growth rates in these aggregates are approximately those achieved in the second half of the 1960s.

5. Managed float, tighter money, tighter budgetary policy, and steady growth of award wages

All of the changes in simulations 2-4 are again made, and real award wages are assumed to grow at the rate of growth of productivity indicated by the estimate of λ_3:

$$\log w_A = -.0052 + .0029t.$$

References

Brunner, K., and Meltzer, A.H. (1971), "The Uses of Money: Money in the Theory of the Exchange Economy," American Economic Review, 61: 784-805.

Danes, M.K. (1975), "The Measurement and Explanation of Inflationary Expectations in Australia," Australian Economic Papers, 14: 75-87.

Dhrymes, P.J., et al. (1972), "Criteria for Evaluation of Econometric Models," Annals of Economic and Social Measurement, 1: 291-324.

Friedman, M., and Schwartz, A.J. (1963). A Monetary History of the United States, 1867-1960. Princeton: Princeton University Press.

Gruen, F.H.G. (1976), "What Went Wrong? Some Personal Reflections on Economic Policies under Labor," Australian Quarterly, 48: 15-32.

Jonson, P.D. (1976), "Money, Prices and Output: An Integrative Essay," Kredit und Kapital, 4: 499-518.

_____(1977), "Inflation and Growth in the United Kingdom: A Longer-run Perspective," Journal of Monetary Economics, 3: 1-24.

Jonson, P.D., Mahar, K.L., and Thompson, G.J. (1974), "Earnings and Award Wages in Australia," Australian Economic Papers, 13: 80-98.

Jonson, P.D., Moses, E.R., and Wymer, C.R. (1976), "A Minimal Model of the Australian Economy," Reserve Bank of Australia discussion paper 7601, Sydney.

Lucas, R.E., Jr. (1973), "Some International Evidence on Output-Inflation Tradeoffs," American Economic Review, 68: 326-34.

_____(1976), "Econometric Policy Evaluation: A Critique," Carnegie-Rochester Conference Series, 1, eds. K. Brunner and A.H. Meltzer. Amsterdam: North-Holland.

Parkin, J.M. (1973), "The Short-run and Long-run Trade-offs between Inflation and Unemployment in Australia," Australian Economic Papers, 12: 127-44.

Porter, M.G. (1974), "The Interdependence of Monetary Policy and Capital Flows in Australia," Economic Record, 50: 1-20.

Further Reading

Additional material on aspects of the economic policy debate in Australia is contained in the following books.

Arndt, H.W., and Stammer, D.W. (1972). The Australian Trading Banks. Melbourne: Cheshire.

Corden, W.M. (1968). Australian Economic Policy Discussion: A Survey. Melbourne: Melbourne University Press.

Nevile, J.W. (1975). Fiscal Policy in Australia: Theory and Practice. Melbourne: Cheshire.

Niland, J.R., and Isaac, J.E., eds. (1975). Australian Labour Economics: Readings. Melbourne: Sun Books.

Perkins, J.O.N. (1975). Macro-economic Policy in Australia. Melbourne: Melbourne University Press.

INFLATION AND PRICE CHANGES:
SOME PRELIMINARY ESTIMATES
AND TESTS OF ALTERNATIVE THEORIES

Pieter Korteweg

Erasmus University, Rotterdam

and

Allan H. Meltzer*

Carnegie-Mellon University

In countries experiencing real and nominal shocks, output, relative prices, and the price level do not adjust instantly from one set of long-run equilibrium values to the next. Economists have speculated on the reasons for slow or gradual adjustment without reaching firm conclusions. Currently, the most widely accepted hypothesis to describe the phenomenon is some type of Phillips curve relating the current rate of change of prices to some measure of unemployed resources and to the anticipated rate of price change.

Although there are many versions of the Phillips curve, there is a common theme; see Laidler and Parkin (1975) and Gordon (1976). The rate of price change deviates from the anticipated or equilibrium rate of change in direct relation to the size of aggregate excess demand. The Phillips curve is a price adjustment equation, and is generally treated as an aggregate supply relation, so there is a positive association between the level of output and the rate of price change. In the usual statement of the Phillips curve,

$$(1) \quad \hat{p} = h(y - y_0) + \hat{p}^a,$$

where $\hat{p}$ and $\hat{p}^a$ are the actual and anticipated rates of price change, and $y-y_0$ is the difference between actual (y) and full employment (y_0) output or real income. In some versions, y and y_0 are logarithms of actual and full employment output. At times, the unemployment rate replaces $y-y_0$ as the measure of excess demand.

The Phillips curve is a disequilibrium relation that developed in the attempt to extend Keynesian theory to a world of rising prices and money

*We are indebted to Karl Brunner for many discussions, to Dean Dutton, Martin Feldstein, David Laidler, and Johan Myhrman for their helpful suggestions, and to Dipankar Chakravarti for his assistance.

wages. Conventional Phillips curves make the deviation from full employment output relevant for pricing decisions even if there is no reason to anticipate that full employment will be restored within the period for which price and output decisions are made. A unit of full employment "gap" has the same effect in deep depressions as in mild recessions. A known, or anticipated, gap changes $\hat{p}$ relative to $\hat{p}^a$ instead of changing $\hat{p}^a$ and anticipated output.

An alternative theory of supply starts with a micro supply curve relating price and output. Linear aggregation of the micro supply curves yields a relation between the price level and aggregate output that differs from the Phillips curve. The rate of price change depends on the rate of change of output or income, not on the level of income. Large changes in the rate of change of real income have larger effects than do small changes. If the aggregate supply curve is significantly nonlinear, the level of output, or the gap between actual and anticipated or actual and full employment output, may also affect the rate of price change, though these effects would not be the principal or dominant influences.

The difference between the two theories of supply becomes clearer if (1) is rewritten as:

$$(2) \qquad \hat{p}_t = h \left[(\hat{y} - \hat{y}_0)_t + (\ell n \; y - \ell n \; y_0)_{t-1} \right] + \hat{p}_t^a ,$$

where the $\hat{}$ indicates a relative rate of change and ℓn is a natural logarithm. The terms between the brackets are a rearrangement of $\ell n \; y - \ell n \; y_0$ in (1).

In the conventional Phillips curve, y_0 is best thought of as full employment output. Both terms between brackets are treated as equal with respect to their influence on $\hat{p}$. The difference between actual and anticipated rates of price change depends on the full employment gap, as before.

In the alternative theory, y_0 is best taken as representing anticipated output. The first term of (2) dominates the second. The difference, $\hat{p} - \hat{p}^a$, depends mainly on the difference between actual and anticipated rates of growth of output. The gap between the anticipated and past levels of output has its principal effect on $\hat{p}^a$. Once $\hat{p}^a$ is determined, this gap has a minor and much less significant role.

It is useful to regard the alternative theory as an equilibrium theory and the conventional Phillips curve as a disequilibrium theory of the output market. In an equilibrium theory, price and output are determined at the intersection of the aggregate demand and aggregate supply curves. All available information about the position of the output market affects the anticipated rate of change of output and the anticipated rate of price change. There is no unused information about the rate of price change in the "gap" between current output and full employment output. In contrast, the conventional Phillips curve assigns significance to the current or lagged value of the full employment gap. The gap is a measure of disequilibrium, and the rate of price change depends on the size of the disequilibrium.

The equilibrium theory need not be treated as the limiting case of a standard Phillips curve. An equilibrium relation between the rate of price change and the rate of change of output can be obtained starting from the first-order condition derived from a standard production function. As in Brunner and Meltzer (1976), we rearrange the first-order condition to obtain

$$p = p\,(y, K, w), \qquad\qquad p_1, p_3 > 0 \qquad p_2 < 0$$

where p, y, K, and w are, respectively, the price level, real output, real capital, and the money wage. Let capacity output y_0 be

$$y_0 = y(K),$$

and let the money wage depend, inter alia, on the anticipated price level p^a, so that

$$w = w(p^a, \dots) .$$

Then,

$$p = p(y, y_0, p^a)$$

is a supply curve relating price and output that holds as an equilibrium relation whenever the first-order condition holds.

Suppose that the first-order condition always holds. Measured unemployment is now a consequence of misperception, unforeseen shocks, or incorrect anticipations, as in Lucas's (1975) equilibrium model of the business cycle.

Further, assume that the supply curve is linear in the logarithms of the variables. Differentiating, we obtain

$$(3) \quad \hat{p} = a_0\hat{y} - a_1\hat{y}_0 + a_2\hat{p}^a,$$

which can be further constrained by setting $a_0 = a_1$ and $a_2=1$ to test well-known propositions in economic theory.

Meltzer (1977) compared the equilibrium theory to the standard Phillips curve and concluded that, for the U.S. during this century, the data give more support to the equilibrium theory. In this paper, we test the alternative theories on several sets of data.

Most studies of the Phillips curve treat excess demand as a given to concentrate on the determinants and speed of adjustment of supply. Monetary and fiscal policies, real shocks, and other disturbances are assumed to shift aggregate demand and to set off a process that changes wages, prices, output, and balances of payments or exchange rates. The relative importance of monetary, fiscal, and other impulses on aggregate spending, a major issue in contemporary economics, is left unresolved by these studies.

The monetary theory of the balance of payments takes a different approach; see Mundell (1968) and Johnson (1972). By assumption--the "law of one price"--prices of (tradable) goods and interest rates are equal everywhere, so the principal, and perhaps the only, effect of monetary and fiscal policies and real shocks is on the balance of payments, on the exchange rate, or on the relative price of nontradable to tradable goods. These propositions appear to hold in an approximate way given a long enough period, but, if these propositions were always true, there would be little opportunity to observe differences in rates of inflation across countries. Evidence for annual or shorter periods gives either very weak support, or no support at all, to the law of one price; see Genberg (1976), Pattison (1976), and Cross and Laidler (1976).

In contrast, the recent work of Brunner (1976) and Brunner and Meltzer (1976) analyzes economies with fixed exchange rates in which prices and incomes, interest rates and asset prices may differ from country to country in the short term, but are connected by the reallocation of expenditure, borrowing and lending, and balances of payments. The long-run equilibrium price level and rate of price change for each country reflect the influence of domestic and foreign stimuli, as in the monetary approach. Countries' policies affect the short-term path of economic activity and cause rates of inflation to diverge.

This paper compares the alternative approaches and obtains estimates of the effects of monetary, fiscal, and other influences on the rate of change of prices for several countries and groups of countries called blocs. In the sections that follow, we first introduce a model of anticipations, assume equilibrium in the output market, and solve for the current rate of price change as a function of the anticipated rate of price change. We test the model using a sample drawn from twenty-four countries, differing in size, stages of development, and degrees of openness to foreign trade, but restricted to annual observations for a brief period, the years of the "dollar standard," 1957 to 1972. These data have some limitations. We discuss the data, present some evidence, and draw the implications of our estimates for theory and policy. Then we estimate some alternative models, similar to those proposed in recent literature on the Phillips curve, and compare the equilibrium and disequilibrium theories of supply. Finally, we summarize the results and the conclusions they appear to support.

I. A MODEL OF ANTICIPATED AND MEASURED RATES OF PRICE CHANGE

Economic theory distinguishes between real and nominal shocks and between inflation and one-time adjustments of the price level. Technical change, crop failures, abundant harvests, and changes in the degree of monopoly are among the factors that raise or lower the price level. Such changes are distinct from the maintained rates of price change resulting from sustained growth in the world gold stock or from government policies that maintain the growth of money above the rate of growth of real output.

The model we test against alternatives is adapted from a recent study of rates of price change in the U.S. by Meltzer (1977) and earlier work by McGuire (1976) that separate maintained inflation and once-and-for-all price changes. Some adjustments are made to reflect the influence of foreign monetary and fiscal policies. Others adjust the model to the available data.

Along a steady growth path, the fully anticipated rate of price change remains constant. Economic theory implies that in equilibrium the fully anticipated rate of price change $\hat{p}^a$ is the difference between the maintained rate of monetary expansion μ and the maintained rate of growth of output g. Equation (4) expresses this relation:

$$(4) \quad \hat{p}^a = \mu - g .$$

Departures from long-run equilibrium give rise to an excess demand for, or supply of, money and goods. The anticipated rates of change of prices and output depart from steady state values. The size of the departures varies over time and between countries, and depends on factors such as the source of the disturbance and the speed with which information becomes available. As Lucas (1975, 1977) emphasizes, separation of absolute and relative price changes poses a particularly difficult problem for the decision makers in a market economy who observe rates of change of prices, income, money, and other variables.

Similar problems arise for the economy as a whole. Relative prices change permanently as a result of such real shocks as sustained changes in technology, population, real resources, taxes, and tariffs. Monetary shocks and temporary real shocks have short-term effects on relative prices that must be separated from the effects of permanent real shocks. The true value of μ must be inferred from current monetary and fiscal policies. With fixed exchange rates, foreign as well as domestic policies influence μ. Separating once-and-for-all price changes from maintained rates of price change provides additional opportunity for error.[1]

Shocks and errors cause current rates of change of prices and income to fluctuate around the long-term path and to induce changes in velocity. The quantity equation, with all terms written as relative rates of change, relates the current rates of change of aggregate expenditure, $\hat{M} + \hat{V}$, to the nominal value of current income, $\hat{p} + \hat{y}$:

$$(5) \quad \hat{M} + \hat{V} = \hat{p} + \hat{y} .$$

Equations (4) and (5) constrain the system to positions of long- and short-run equilibrium. Rational agents know that (4) does not hold always and everywhere. But, (4) contains information about the evolution of the economy that affects the anticipated rate of inflation and, therefore, affects the current demand for money. Departures from long-run equilibrium are fully reflected in the demand for money and, therefore, in monetary velocity.

The demand for nominal money balances depends on the market rate of interest i, on stocks of base money B, and of debt S, on nominal income yp, and on actual and anticipated prices:

---

[1] Changes in a fixed weight price index will reflect some changes in relative prices, as well as real shocks, changes in the degree of monopoly, and maintained inflation.

$$M = L(i, p, p^a, B, S, yp).$$

$$L_1, L_3 < 0, \qquad L_2, L_4, L_5, L_6 > 0$$

We assume the demand function is homogeneous of first degree in prices and the value of financial assets. Velocity, the ratio of current income to the demand for money, is then

$$V = v(i, \frac{p^a}{p}, \frac{B}{p}, \frac{S}{p}, y),$$

$$v_1, v_2 > 0, \qquad v_3, v_4 < 0, \qquad v_5 \geq 0$$

where $i = r + \hat{p}^a$, with r being the market rate of return on physical capital. We postulate that

$$r = \frac{p}{c_0 p^a} \, n(y - y_0, \frac{B}{p}, \frac{S}{p}, y_0),$$

$$n_1, n_3 > 0, \qquad n_2, n_4 < 0$$

where y_0 is capacity output. By assumption, the replacement cost of existing capital is proportional to the anticipated price level. The ratio $p/c_0 p^a$ expresses the effect on measured real rates of return of changes in the price of current production relative to the replacement cost of existing capital.

Taking logarithms of the V and r equations and differentiating both equations, we obtain relative rates of change of V and r, written as $\hat{V}$ and $\hat{r}$. The parameters v_i and n_i are now treated as elasticities. Let $\hat{i} = \hat{r} + \dfrac{d\hat{p}^a}{\hat{p}^a}$, where the latter term is the expected rate of price acceleration. Substitute for $\hat{r}$ in the $\hat{V}$ equation and combine terms to obtain (6):[2]

---

[2] The coefficients of (6) are elasticities that are formed from linear combinations of the coefficients of the V and r equations. The combinations are

$$
\begin{aligned}
w_1 &= (1 - n_2 - n_3) v_1 - (v_2 + v_3 + v_4) < 1 \\
w_2 &= (v_2 - v_1) > 0, \text{ if } v_2 > v_1 \\
w_3 &= v_3 + v_1 n_2 < 0 \\
w_4 &= v_4 + v_1 n_3 \\
w_5 &= v_5 + v_1 n_1 > 0 \\
w_6 &= v_1 (n_4 - n_1) < 0.
\end{aligned}
$$

(6) $\quad \hat{V} = w_1\hat{p} + w_2\hat{p}^a + w_3\hat{B} + w_4\hat{S} + w_5\hat{y} + w_6g.$

A small term, the anticipated rate of price acceleration, is omitted; g is the rate of growth of capacity output, $\dfrac{dy_0}{y_0}$.

The system is assumed to be in short-run equilibrium whenever we observe values of $\hat{p}$, so we substitute (6) into (5) and solve for $\hat{p}$. Current rates of monetary change are given by $\hat{B}$, used as our measure of $\hat{M}$ in (5) and elsewhere. We obtain

(7) $\quad \hat{p} = \dfrac{w_2}{1-w_1}p^a + \dfrac{1+w_3}{1-w_1}\hat{B} + \dfrac{w_4}{1-w_1}\hat{S} + \dfrac{w_5-1}{1-w_1}\hat{y} + \dfrac{w_6}{1-w_1}g.$

To reduce problems of estimation, let the anticipated acceleration of output $\Delta\hat{y}$ be equal to the difference between current $\hat{y}$ and long-run normal growth g. This assumption avoids the problem of finding measures of capital stock and other variables affecting supply. Clearly, our assumption is not applicable or appropriate for all periods, but we believe it is a useful approximation for many countries during the period used for our estimates. Since w_5 and w_6 are assumed to be approximately equal in magnitude, but have opposite signs, we can now rewrite (7) as[3]

(8) $\quad \hat{p} = \dfrac{w_2}{1-w_1}\hat{p}^a + \dfrac{1+w_3}{1-w_1}\hat{B} + \dfrac{w_4}{1-w_1}\hat{S} + \dfrac{w_7}{1-w_1}\Delta\hat{y} - \dfrac{1}{1-w_1}g.$

Below, we introduce additive error terms, define μ, and estimate (4) and (8) for the period 1957-72. Then, we test our hypothesis by comparing estimates obtained using a standard Phillips curve.

---

[3]The coefficient of $\Delta\hat{y} = \hat{y}$-g is $\dfrac{w_7}{1-w_1}$. The numerator is $(w_5 -1)$ or $-(w_6+1)$. The two terms are equal in magnitude if v_5 and v_1n_4 are both small or are of similar order and opposite sign. (See note 2 above.) The term $\dfrac{-1}{1-w_1}$ g is included in the intercept below, along with any other variables that affect $\hat{p}$ without affecting the right-hand side of (7).

II. THE DATA

Our data set consists of twenty-four countries that reported most of the variables required for our tests to the International Monetary Fund (IMF) from 1956 to 1972. The countries are listed in note 4.[4] Seventeen countries were grouped into four major blocs. Five of the original members of the EEC (Luxembourg is included with Belgium) are treated as a bloc; four Nordic countries are a second bloc; three European members of the former Free Trade Area are a third bloc. A more heterogeneous grouping--Australia, Canada, Japan, New Zealand, and the U.S.--are grouped in a "Pacific" bloc.

Each country is treated as an independent entity, and relative rates of change of base money, debt, prices, etc., are computed for the world, for the country, and for the rest of the world as seen from that country. The "rest of the world" consists of the remaining twenty-three countries. Rest-of-the-world variables have a superscript r.

Several conventions were adopted. These affect all of the variables in our analysis and the interpretation of our results.

First, real income and all nominal stocks and flows were converted to U.S. dollars at annual IMF conversion factors before rates of growth were computed. This procedure adjusts country gross real domestic product, our measure of real income, for gains or losses in country purchasing power relative to the world when the world was on a dollar standard. GDP growth after adjustment is closer to a measure of income growth than to a measure of the growth of physical output. Similarly, base money, debt, and our measure of government spending--the cash flow surplus or deficit--are converted to U.S. dollars at current conversion rates before computing growth rates.

Second, the world and rest-of-the-world price levels are weighted averages with weights h_{zt}:

$$h_{zt} = \frac{DG_{zt}}{\sum\limits_z DG_{zt}} \; .$$

The numerator of h_{zt} is real gross domestic product of country z in year t converted to U.S. dollars at the annual conversion ratio. The denominator

[4]The data are taken from International Financial Statistics. Descriptions and detailed statement of sources are available on request. The seventeen countries with complete data have been grouped into blocs. Countries are listed by blocs, followed by the seven countries for which some fiscal measures or debt are not available for all or most of the period. ECC bloc: Belgium, France, Germany, Holland, Italy; Nordic bloc: Denmark, Finland, Norway, Sweden; other Europe bloc: Ireland, Switzerland, U.K.; Pacific bloc: Australia, Canada, Japan, New Zealand, U.S.; ungrouped countries: Austria, Greece, Iceland, Portugal, Spain, Turkey, Yugoslavia.

Table 1

Simple Correlations

Range	$\hat{B},\hat{B}^r$	$\hat{p},\hat{p}^r$	$\hat{S},\hat{S}^r$	$\hat{y},\hat{y}^r$	γ,γ^r	$\triangle\hat{B},\triangle\hat{B}^r$	$\triangle\hat{p},\triangle\hat{p}^r$
Negative	1	0	2	1	5	4	4
0 to .20	0	0	3	3	3	5	3
.21 - .40	2	4	5	1	7	5	8
.41 - .60	7	6	5	6	2	1	2
.61 - .80	6	7	1	6	0	2	0
.80 and above	1	0	1	0	0	0	0
Median of 17 countries	0.55	0.53	0.38	0.52	0.30	0.20	0.25
U.S.	0.25	0.68	0.40	0.17	0.51	- 0.59	0.42
Denmark	- 0.14	0.53	0.29	0.53	0.40	- 0.06	0.40
Holland	0.59	0.49	0.51	0.69	0.30	0.26	- 0.39

Note: B = monetary base
 p   price index (CPI)
 S   government debt outstanding
 y   gross domestic product (real)
 γ $\triangle$ cash flow deficit/gross domestic product (nominal) of the previous year
 ^ = relative rates of change.

is the sum of the real dollar value of GDP in the twenty-four countries. The world price level is, then,[5]

$$p^w_t = \sum_z p_{zt} h_{zt} .$$

The domestic consumer price index is used as the measure of the price level.

Third, relative rates of change are obtained in the usual way. The relative rate of change for the rest-of-the-world price level for country z in year t is denoted $\hat{p}^r_{zt}$, such that

$$\hat{p}^r_{zt} = \frac{(p^w_t - h_{zt}p_{zt}) - (p^w_{t-1} - h_{zt-1}p_{zt-1})}{p^w_{t-1} - h_{zt-1} p_{zt-1}} .$$

Similar procedures are used to compute all rest-of-the-world rates of change. The rate of change of domestic prices is $\hat{p}_{zt}$. The rate of acceleration for any variable is obtained by taking the first difference of the relative rate of change.

To obtain some preliminary information about the degree to which the seventeen countries contain information that is not entirely common, we computed simple correlations between the relative rates of change of some principal variables for each of the seventeen countries and for the twenty-three countries comprising the rest of the world as seen from that country. As a standard of comparison, we chose a large country, the U.S., and two small open economies, Holland and Denmark. Table 1 shows frequency distributions of the correlation coefficients for relative rates of change and for accelerations of base money and prices in seventeen countries, and compares the median correlation for the seventeen countries to the measured correlation for the large and the two small open economies.

Contrary to versions of the monetary approach to the balance of payments that do not distinguish short- and long-term adjustment, the data show substantial variability in the relation between domestic and rest-of-the-world rates of growth of monetary and fiscal variables. The median correlation is highest for growth rates of base money and lowest for cash flow deficits. Although the median correlation between domestic and world growth rates

---

[5] The weights were not constrained to sum to unity. This introduces an error in price levels, but the error has very small effect on the relative rates of price change, the variable we seek to explain.

of base money is relatively high, the greater part of the variance of the growth of the domestic base is not explained by synchronous changes in "world money." Further, there is considerable dispersion in the correlations and very little evidence of systematic association between accelerations and decelerations of the domestic and rest-of-the-world base money.[6]

Comparison of the median correlations with the correlations for the U.S., Denmark, and Holland does not permit any simple conclusions to be drawn. Domestic and rest-of-the-world rates of price change and rates of price acceleration are more highly correlated for the U.S. than for the median country or for the two small open economies. Correlations for rates of change of debt and the cash flow deficit for the U.S. are as high or higher than in the median country. The growth rates of the U.S. and Danish base appear to be relatively independent of the short-term rate of growth of base money in the rest of the world; the growth rate of the base in Holland is more closely related to the rate of change of base money in the rest of the world.

A final comparison suggests that monetary expansion in the rest of the world affects domestic rates of price change through several different variables. Frequently, $\hat{p}$ is most closely related to $\hat{B}^r$. The median correlation of $\hat{B}^r$ and $\hat{p}$ is 0.57 for the seventeen countries, and in thirteen countries, the correlation is 0.50 or above. For the European countries, with one exception, $\hat{p}$ is more closely correlated with $\hat{B}^r$ than with $\hat{B}$, and usually $\hat{B}^r$ is more closely correlated with $\hat{p}$ than with $\hat{B}$. In the countries of the Pacific bloc, relationships differ. $\hat{B}^r$ is often more highly correlated with $\hat{B}$ than with $\hat{p}$. These differences suggest that there is not a simple, uniform mechanism linking foreign money to domestic money and then to prices through the trade account or the base. The short-run effects of foreign variables appear to operate through a number of channels.

III. ESTIMATES AND IMPLICATIONS

To compute the anticipated rate of inflation $\hat{p}^a$, we define μ and g in (4) and use the values predicted by the equation as estimates of $\hat{p}^a$. The actual rate of price change can differ from the anticipated rate of inflation when there are real shocks affecting $\hat{\Delta y}$ or unanticipated changes in government fiscal and monetary policies. The estimated $\hat{p}^a$ is only one of the variables determining the observed rate of price change $\hat{p}$. In this section, we use the

---

[6]Using the z-transformation with seventeen observations, the 0.95 confidence interval for the correlation coefficients is approximately 0.50. This test implies that r $<$0.50 is not significantly different from zero.

estimate of $\hat{p}^a$ from (4) with other variables in (8) to separate the effects of sustained and current impulses and to test an equilibrium theory of inflation.

The effect on the price level of financing fiscal policy by issuing debt is one of the principal issues in recent comparisons of monetarist and Keynesian theories. Christ (1968) finds that the effect of debt finance on prices is ambiguous; Stein (1976) concludes that the effect is small in the U.S. and can be neglected. Brunner and Meltzer (1976) show that, in an open economy, differences in fiscal stimuli are sufficient for devaluation of exchange rates. To compare the long-term effect of sustained changes in debt and base money, we define μ as a weighted sum:

$$\mu = a_1 \hat{\bar{B}}_{-1} + a_2 \hat{\bar{B}}^r_{-1} + a_3 \hat{\bar{S}}_{-1} + a_4 \hat{\bar{S}}^r_{-1} \, ,$$

where $\hat{\bar{B}}_{-1}, \hat{\bar{B}}^r_{-1}, \hat{\bar{S}}_{-1}, \hat{\bar{S}}^r_{-1}$ are three-year moving averages of measured rates of growth of the monetary base and the stock of outstanding government debt in each country and in the rest of the world as seen from the country. Each of the components of μ is lagged one year to impose a two-year average lag in the effect of monetary and fiscal impulses on the anticipated rate of inflation. The same procedure is used for $\hat{\bar{y}}$; a three-year moving average of the rate of change of real income, lagged one year, is taken as the maintained rate of growth, g. A two-year average lag has been found in several studies of recent inflation; see Hamburger and Reisch (1976), Weintraub (1976), and Meltzer (1977). The two-year lag is not a constant of nature, but its use seems preferable to the alternative--using some of our few degrees of freedom to gain the appearance of a better estimate. Substituting for μ and g in (4) and assuming that the true $\hat{p}^a$ is observed with an additive error, we estimate $\hat{p}^a$ for seventeen countries, five blocs, and the twenty-four-country world. Table 2 summarizes the findings.[7]

Five conclusions seem warranted. First, the combined response to B^r and $\hat{B}$ generally falls in the neighborhood of 0.4. Second, the response to $\hat{B}^r$ is the most reliable of the five responses, as measured by the t-statistics. Third, the effect of debt finance is small and insignificant for each of the blocs and for many of the countries. An important exception is the response to $\hat{\bar{S}}^r$ in the bloc called Other Europe. Fourth, the coefficient on $\hat{\bar{y}}$ is substantially below unity and occasionally positive. Consequently, this variable gives little support

---

[7]Individual country regressions can be obtained from the authors.

Table 2

Estimates of $\hat{p}^a$

Group	Intercept	$\hat{\bar{B}}_{-1}$	$\hat{\bar{B}}^r_{-1}$	$\hat{\bar{S}}_{-1}$	$\hat{\bar{S}}^r_{-1}$	$\hat{\bar{y}}_{-1}$	$\bar{R}^2$/DW
EEC (80)	1.24	- 0.01	0.38	- 0.04	1.01	0.09	0.11/
(t-stat.)	(1.51)	(0.09)	(3.21)	(0.80)	(0.41)	(0.73)	
Other Europe (48)	0.11	- 0.12	0.65	0.05	0.55	- 0.05	.51/
	(0.14)	(1.14)	(5.62)	(1.19)	(2.37)	(0.34)	
Nordic (64)	1.61	0.01	0.42	- 0.01	- 0.07	0.24	.24/
	(1.82)	(0.15)	(3.05)	(0.22)	(0.24)	(2.24)	
Pacific (80)	2.17	0.15	0.26	0.01	- 0.16	- 0.14	.15/
	(2.68)	(2.42)	(2.56)	(0.86)	(0.79)	(1.13)	
World (16)	1.70	0.46	. . .	- 0.28	. . .	- 0.06	.39/1.90
	(1.47)	(2.84)	. . .	(1.01)	. . .	(0.21)	
Median of 17 countries	- 0.46	0.07	0.31	- 0.07	0.10	0.25	0.53/1.90

Note: Sample size for countries and blocs is shown after the group name. DW-statistics for blocs are meaningless and are not shown.

to our hypothesis about anticipations. Fifth, no more than half the variance in $\hat{p}$ is explained by the regressions in Table 2. Most of the variation in the rate of price change cannot be explained as a result of past policies or lagged average rates of output change. One reason, consistent with our hypothesis, is that much of the price change may be accounted for by once-and-for-all changes in the price level that do not affect the anticipated rate of inflation.

The estimate of $\hat{p}^a$ obtained from the regressions for each group and country in each year is used to test the hypothesis in (8).[8] The current rate of price change depends on anticipated inflation, on current domestic policy, and on the current rate of acceleration of output. The effect of the maintained growth rate and all other independent influences on $\hat{p}$ are combined in an intercept. Table 3 shows the responses of $\hat{p}$ to the arguments of (8).

The anticipated rate of price change dominates all other variables. The response of $\hat{p}$ to $\hat{p}^a$ is approximately unity for the median country and for many of the individual countries and the blocs. There is, also, a small negative effect of $\Delta\hat{y}$ on $\hat{p}$. Both $\hat{B}$ and $\hat{S}$ are statistically significant at $t \geqslant 2.0$ in only a few cases, but both have a positive effect in each of these cases. The small intercept for the world, the median country, and several blocs suggests that there is no unexplained "trend" rate of price change.

The last column of Table 3, labeled Σ, shows the sum of the coefficients of all nominal values to check on the homogeneity of the $\hat{p}$ equation. Most of the countries lie within 10 percent of unity, and for the median country the sum is 0.97. The results support the homogeneity assumption. By far, the largest contribution to the sum comes from the anticipated rate of inflation.

The near unit coefficients for $\hat{p}^a$ and near zero coefficients for $\hat{B}$ and $\hat{S}$ place some strong restrictions on the coefficients of (8) and permit a check of the consistency of the estimates. The coefficient of $\hat{S}$ is close to zero if and only if w_4 is approximately zero. From note 2 above, we see that, for $w_4 = 0$,

$$v_4 = -v_1 n_3 .$$

The response of velocity to the government debt depends on the wealth effect (v_4) and the effect of debt on interest rates (n_3) and of interest rates on velocity

---

[8] Our procedure treats $\hat{p}^a$ as an instrument variable. The procedure would be equivalent to two-stage least squares if the regressions for $\hat{p}^a$ are taken as the first stage and the regressions in Tables 3 and 5 are treated as the second stage.

Table 3

The Current Rate of Price Change

Group or Country	Intercept	$\hat{p}^a$	$\hat{B}$	$\hat{S}$	$\hat{\Delta y}$	$\bar{R}^2$/DW	Σ
EEC	0.56	0.82*	0.02	- 0.01	- 0.14*	0.19	0.83
Other Europe	0.19	0.95*	- .02	.08*	- .05	.58	1.00
Nordic	0.69	0.91*	- .04	- .00	- .08*	.35	0.87
Pacific	0.54	0.74*	.05*	.00	- .07*	.25	0.79
World	0.19	0.77	.06	.06	- .15	.54/1.66	0.90
Median of 17 countries	0.02	0.94	0.01	0.01	- 0.06	0.72/1.81	0.97
Germany	0.20	0.75*	0.05*	- 0.01	- 0.05	0.89/1.56	0.79
France	0.35	0.87	.05	.04	- .23	.17/1.81	0.97
Holland	0.02	1.17*	- .10	- .00	.01	.42/2.14	1.06
Belgium	- 0.05	1.03*	- .02	.01	.01	.74/2.77	1.02
Italy	- 1.45	0.79*	.19*	- .01	- .06	.80/2.36	0.97
U.K.	- 0.32	1.10*	- .01	.01	- .12	.74/1.61	1.09
Switzerland	1.56*	0.68*	- .02	.14*	- .28*	.93/2.79	0.80
Ireland	- 0.01	1.08*	- .04	.14	- .06	.68/1.63	1.18
Sweden	- 0.06	0.73*	.18	.01	- .16	.41/1.63	0.92
Norway	- 1.32	0.80	.14	.08	- .30	.32/1.45	1.01
Denmark	0.35	1.00*	- .05	- .02	- .01	.91/2.70	0.93
Finland	0.77	0.89*	- .01	- .02	- .04	.39/1.76	0.85
U.S.	0.08	0.98*	.01	- .02	- .08	.63/0.97	0.96
Canada	- 0.23	0.99*	.01	.02	- .04	.88/2.07	1.02
New Zealand	0.34	1.06*	.04*	- .17	- .02	.80/2.44	0.92
Australia	0.21	0.93*	.14*	- .18	- .10*	.72/1.53	0.89
Japan	- 0.32	0.94*	0.02	0.01	- 0.08	0.60/2.10	0.97

Note: DW = Durbin-Watson statistic.

Detail may not add to sum due to rounding.

*Indicates t ⩾ 2.0.

(v_1). The two effects of debt are offsetting in most countries. From (8), we find that zero coefficients for $\hat{B}$ and $\hat{S}$ occur together only if

$$w_3 = -1,$$

and

$$w_4 = 0.$$

This implies (see note 2) that

$$v_1 = -\frac{1+v_3}{n_2} = -\frac{v_4}{n_3},$$

or, in terms of the elasticities of velocity and the anticipated return, n:[9]

$$\epsilon(V,i) = -\frac{\epsilon(V,S)}{\epsilon(n,S)} = -\frac{1+\epsilon(V,B)}{\epsilon(n,B)}.$$

The finding of near zero coefficients for $\hat{B}$ and $\hat{S}$ does not imply that monetary and fiscal changes have no effect. On the contrary, both $\hat{B}$ and $\hat{S}$ change interest rates and wealth and induce changes in the balance of payments position and, thus, in $\hat{B}^r$. If the wealth and interest rate effects on $\hat{p}$ are offsetting, the direct effect is small. However, maintaining the monetary and fiscal impulses raises the average rates of change, $\bar{B}$ and $\bar{S}$, and in this way domestic policy contributes to $\hat{p}^a$. Further, $\hat{B}^r$ changes. The results, summarized in Table 2, show that the response of $\hat{p}^a$ to $\bar{S}$ is generally small and unreliable, but the response of $\hat{p}^a$ to $\hat{B}^r$ is most reliable.

Our results for debt finance are similar to the results reported by Stein (1976, p.211). Using quarterly data for the U.S., Stein found a small, negative effect of debt finance on the rate of price change, approximately -0.06 to -0.09. We find a coefficient of $\hat{S}$ of -0.02 for the U.S. and +0.01 for the median country, using annual data from a different sample. Moreover, Stein found

---

[9] A survey by Fase and Kuné (1975) shows a wide range of estimates for interest elasticities of money demand computed from quarterly data. Using estimates for long-term rates and a narrow definition of money (M1), the estimates of v_1 range from -0.07 to -0.86.

that the principal determinant of the current rate of price change is the anticipated rate of inflation, a finding that is entirely consistent with our results, not only for the U.S., but for all countries and blocs.

IV. COMPARISON WITH PHILLIPS CURVES

The inflation augmented Phillips curve has become a standard explanation of inflation. Our hypothesis differs from the Phillips curve hypothesis in several respects. This section discusses the differences and presents some estimates for comparison with Table 3.

Most statements of the Phillips curve make the current rate of price change depend on the anticipated rate of inflation and some measure of excess demand. Common measures of excess demand include the unemployment rate or its reciprocal, and the gap between current and full employment output. Comparable measures of unemployment or full employment output are not available for many countries. Laidler (1974), Cross and Laidler (1976), and Parkin (1977) use deviations from the trend of the logarithm of real output or income as a measure of excess demand. A typical version of equation (2) from Laidler (1974, p.536) is, using our notation,

$$(9) \quad \hat{P}_t = a_0 \, (\ell n \, y - \ell n \, y_0)_{t-1} - a_1 (\ell n \, y - \ell n \, y_0)_{t-2} + a_2 \hat{p}_{-1} \, ,$$

where $\ell n \, y$ and $\ell n \, y_0$ are natural logarithms of the levels of actual and full employment real income, respectively, and a_0, a_1, and a_2 are parameters combining the Phillips curve trade-off and adaptive adjustment of $\hat{p}$; $a_2 = 1$ for $\hat{p}_{-1}$ defined as anticipated inflation. In practice, Laidler and Parkin have used several alternatives to $\hat{p}_{-1}$ to summarize past or anticipated inflation. Their measures include the past rate of world inflation and the trend rate of domestic inflation.

One principal difference between our hypothesis, represented by (4) and (8), and a standard Phillips curve, represented by our equation (2) or (9), is in the interpretation given to past price changes. Measured rates of price change combine information about past inflation with once-and-for-all adjustments of the price level. The usual approach treats as equivalent all changes in the price level, whether they result from real shocks, tariffs, taxes, other one-time changes in government policy, or from maintained rates of monetary growth. Every increase in the current price level that contributes to the measured rate of price change becomes part of anticipated inflation.

Our hypothesis attempts to distinguish between one-time changes and maintained rates of price change. Only the latter affect the anticipated rate of inflation. The anticipated rate of inflation at the start of a period (year) depends mainly on past, maintained rates of monetary expansion, but the anticipated rate of price change for the year differs from the anticipated rate of inflation at the start of the year if, for example, money growth deviates from the maintained rate of expansion or there are real shocks.

A second main difference between our hypothesis and standard Phillips curves is the analysis of changes in demand and the effects of current policy. Equation (9) and other standard Phillips curves make no attempt to use information on current policy to alter anticipations of inflation. The only effects of current policy are on excess demand, and these effects are not often shown. The prevailing hypothesis is that the current effect of policy is on excess demand and only later on the rate of price change.

In contrast, we permit current changes in monetary and fiscal policies to affect both current spending and the current rate of price change. Changes in policy change the level of spending and the price level by shifting expenditure along the supply curve of output. Output and prices respond to changes in spending provided money wages do not instantly adjust.

Our hypothesis analyzes the effects on spending and embeds the result in an equilibrium condition, the quantity equation. Output responds to demand. The standard Phillips curve specifies the effect of excess demand on supply price. The gap between current output and full employment output is assumed to be a measure of excess demand, but rarely is there a test for the effect of policies on demand. Nor is there an attempt to explain why the response of prices to the excess demand gap is not fully anticipated. This problem arises with most force when past values of the gap affect the current rate of price change, given the anticipated rate of price change.

In this section, we compare the two approaches. First, we estimate inflation augmented Phillips curves of the type tested extensively by Laidler and Parkin and their University of Manchester colleagues. Their work has produced an impressive body of evidence for many countries, so we stay as close to their equations as our data permit. Then, we compare the results to our equation (8). There are several differences. We attempt to reduce the differences by using our measure of anticipated inflation, $\hat{p}^a$ from (4), to reestimate Phillips-type equations similar to the Cross and Laidler (1976) and Parkin (1977) equations.

To facilitate comparison, we rewrite (9) as

$$(10) \quad \hat{p}_t = a_0 \hat{y}_{t-1} - a_0 \hat{y}_{0,\,t-1} + (a_0 - a_1)(\ell n y - \ell n y_0)_{t-2} + a_2 \hat{p}_t^e ,$$

Table 4

Inflation Augmented Phillips Curves

Group or Country	Intercept	$(\hat{y}-\hat{\bar{y}})_{-1}$	$(\ell n y - \ell n \bar{y})_{-2}$	$\hat{p}_{-1}$	$\hat{\bar{p}}_{-1}$	$\hat{p}^r_{-1}$	$\bar{R}^2/DW$
EEC	- 0.004	0.13	25.80*	- 0.02	0.73*	...	0.15
Other Europe	0.07	.21	4.73	.63*	...	0.40	.50
Nordic	1.35	.22*	24.50*	.49*	...	0.08	.25
Pacific[a]	0.63	.15*	5.70	.50*	0.30	...	.52
World[a]	- 2.46*	.14	70.39*	- .69	1.72*	...	.61/2.18
Median of 17 countries	- 1.41	0.30	40.91	0.38	0.70	0.71	0.53/2.10
Germany	- 2.13	0.24*	23.54*	0.24	1.08	...	0.70/2.10
France	5.26	- 0.25	- 6.43	- 0.49	...	0.60	.00/1.87
Holland[a]	- 3.02	0.44*	55.92*	- 0.07	...	1.35	.55/2.25
Belgium	- 1.50	0.40*	68.91*	- 0.14	0.71	...	.70/2.15
Italy	- 12.73*	1.33*	222.90*	- 0.60	1.76*	...	.44/1.45
U.K.	- 0.08	0.30	- 1.51	0.43	...	0.74	.53/1.58
Switzerland	- 1.85	0.48*	40.91	0.54	...	0.38	.55/2.24
Ireland	- 0.41	0.14	19.22	0.49	...	0.73	.35/2.00
Sweden	2.18	0.35	51.84	0.52	- 0.63	...	.02/1.99
Norway	- 0.54	0.24	49.84	- 0.10	0.85	...	.00/1.88
Denmark	- 3.08	0.55*	66.38*	0.60	0.52	...	.52/2.24
Finland	6.39	0.07	12.28	0.38	- 0.62	...	.32/2.22
U.S.[a]	- 1.19	0.34*	45.67*	1.10*	...	- 0.14	.73/2.46
Canada	- 0.27	0.18*	15.91	0.42	...	0.34	.58/1.61
New Zealand	- 1.41	0.18*	0.20	- 0.14	...	1.86*	.70/2.36
Australia	- 1.58	0.30*	22.94	0.39*	...	0.71*	.65/2.29
Japan	- 1.93	0.28*	41.27*	0.02	0.68	...	0.46/1.70

[a]Indicates higher $\bar{R}^2$ than Table 3.

*Indicates $t \geqslant 2.0$.

and use measures of the expected rate of inflation $\hat{p}^e_t$, that differ from our $\hat{p}^a_t$, but are similar to the measures proposed by Cross and Laidler and Parkin.[10] Cross and Laidler argue that the world rate of inflation contributes to the anticipated rate of inflation in countries operating under fixed exchange rates. This effect is assumed to be independent of the effect on the domestic money stock and on domestic excess demand. The apparent reason is that consumers and producers believe that exchange rates will remain fixed, and therefore, domestic inflation is expected to adjust to world inflation. For the Cross and Laidler (1976) hypothesis, we use the lagged rest-of-the-world rate of price change $\hat{p}^r_{-1}$ and the three-year average rate of domestic price change, lagged one year, $\bar{\hat{p}}_{-1}$. For the Parkin (1977) hypothesis, we use the maintained three-year average and most recent rate of price change, $\bar{\hat{p}}_{-1}$ and $\hat{p}_{-1}$, as measures of anticipated inflation.

Table 4 shows the results of the test for seventeen countries, four blocs, and the world. Estimates are reported only for the better of the two regressions, judged by goodness of fit. For eight countries, we report on the Parkin version using $\bar{\hat{p}}_{-1}$, and, for nine countries, we report the Cross and Laidler version using $\hat{p}^r_{-1}$. As before, we denote with an asterisk the coefficients with a t-statistic of at least 2.0.

There are only two countries, Holland and the U.S., for which the Phillips curve explains more of the variance of $\hat{p}$ than does the hypothesis in Table 3. For the Pacific bloc and the twenty-four-country world also, the inflation augmented Phillips curve has a higher $\bar{R}^2$ than do the regressions reported in Table 3. In all other countries and blocs, the inflation augmented Phillips curve explains less, and often substantially less, of the variance of $\hat{p}$. The median $\bar{R}^2$ differs by 0.19.

Comparison of the relative effects of differences in growth rates and in levels of output or income yields mixed results. For seven countries, both differences in levels and differences in rates of growth are significant by the usual standard; in six countries, neither difference is significant. There are only four countries for which the difference between recent and maintained average rates of growth is significant, but the difference in levels is not. The evidence from the blocs is even more mixed than the evidence from the countries.

One problem with the results reported in Table 4 is that the measures of anticipated inflation often do not pass the standard test for statistical significance. Frequently, one of the coefficients is negative, and only rarely

---

[10]We use $\hat{\bar{y}}_{t-1}$ as the measure of $\hat{y}_{0,t-1}$ and $\bar{y}_{t-2}$ as the measure of $y_{0,t-2}$.

Table 5

A Test of the Phillips Curve

Group or Country	Intercept	$\hat{p}^a$	$(\hat{y} - \hat{\bar{y}})_{-1}$	$(\ell ny - \ell n\,\bar{y})_{-2}$	$\bar{R}^2$/DW
EEC	0.51	0.82*	0.005	2.41	0.10
Other Europe[b]	- .08	1.01*	.13	0.90	.56
Nordic[b]	- .33	1.12*	- .07	- 6.40	.27
Pacific	- .04	0.99*	.09	1.84	.20
World	- .12	1.01*	.07	1.89	.40/1.77
Median of 17 countries[b]	- 0.12	1.00	0.09	0.96	0.62/1.87
Germany[b]	- 0.12	1.01*	0.09*	0.96	0.89/2.38
France	- 0.52	1.11	.07	0.51	.00/2.34
Holland[a]	- 0.28	0.94*	.11	9.05	.44/2.14
Belgium[a,b]	- 0.11	0.97*	.11	4.58	.77/2.64
Italy[b]	0.83	1.12*	.09	- 22.00	.72/2.33
U.K.[a,b]	- 0.75	1.11*	.25*	13.80	.78/1.87
Switzerland[b]	0.06	0.99*	.13	- 1.38	.74/2.26
Ireland[b]	- 0.08	1.02*	.09	- 1.92	.62/1.76
Sweden[b]	0.002	1.00*	.005	- 0.37	.28/1.52
Norway[b]	- 0.09	0.98*	.08	0.04	.20/1.79
Denmark[b]	- 0.04	1.00*	.02	0.92	.89/2.74
Finland[a]	- 1.98	1.39	- .08	- 14.03	.40/1.86
U.S.[b]	- 0.13	0.98*	- .04	4.75	.62/1.29
Canada[a,b]	- 0.35	0.95*	.08*	8.42	.90/1.66
New Zealand[b]	- 0.03	1.00*	.03	1.64	.71/1.86
Australia	- 0.37	0.91*	.16	14.24	.55/1.22
Japan[b]	- 0.53	1.00*	0.11	5.88	0.58/2.47

[a]Indicates higher $\bar{R}^2$ than Table 3.

[b]Indicates higher $\bar{R}^2$ than Table 4.

*Indicates $t \geqslant 2.0$.

is the sum of the coefficients for the measures of expected inflation near unity. There is, therefore, not much evidence that the $\hat{p}$-equation is homogeneous of first degree in nominal values. This finding makes evidence drawn from Table 4 difficult to interpret. It is not clear that the results for this version of the inflation augmented Phillips curve have a valid economic interpretation.

A plausible interpretation of the findings in Table 4 is that the measures of anticipated inflation are not properly specified. Given the misspecification, it is possible to find a significant effect of the difference in levels and to accept, or fail to reject, a false hypothesis. To test for the effect of misspecification, we substitute our measure of anticipated inflation, $\hat{p}^a$ as in Table 3, for the measures of anticipated inflation proposed by Cross and Laidler and Parkin. We retain the measures of excess demand in (10). The results are shown in Table 5. Table 5 differs from Table 4 in only one way: $\hat{p}^a$ from (4) replaces $\hat{p}^e$.

The results change markedly. Anticipated inflation is generally significant, and the coefficients of $\hat{p}^a$ are similar to the results reported previously. The difference between current and maintained rates of change of output has a small effect, but the effect is significant in only a few countries. The difference in lagged levels is never significant. There is, therefore, no evidence that the full employment gap has an independent effect on $\hat{p}$.

The small number of degrees of freedom and the possible, and even likely, inaccuracies in the data suggest that the results for the countries should be used cautiously. Many of the same conclusions can be drawn, however, for the blocs, where the data are no better, but the number of degrees of freedom is larger. There is not a single bloc of countries in Table 5 that shows a significant effect of the lagged gap on the current rate of price change.

The results for countries and blocs in Table 5 are marked with superscript a or b to denote the results of comparing $\bar{R}^2$ for Tables 3, 4, and 5. We have previously compared Tables 3 and 4, so we limit current discussion to a comparison between Table 5 and Tables 3 and 4. For thirteen countries and two blocs, $\bar{R}^2$ increases when we use our measure of anticipated rate of inflation as in Table 5. But, there are only five countries, and there are no blocs, that have a higher $\bar{R}^2$ in Table 5 than in Table 3.

The comparison of the two tables is stronger evidence than may at first appear. The number of degrees of freedom is small for the countries, and Table 3 uses an extra degree of freedom. $\bar{R}^2$ would be lower by approximately 0.08, on average, if the unadjusted percentage of the variance explained by the equations is the same. The higher $\bar{R}^2$ for most countries in Table 3 shows that the hypothesis more than compensates for the extra degree of freedom. The distribution of $\bar{R}^2$ for the seventeen countries summarizes the results for the three hypotheses.

Frequency Distribution of $\bar{R}^2$ for Seventeen Countries

	Table 3	Table 4	Table 5
0.80 to 0.99	6	0	3
0.60 to 0.79	6	5	7
0.40 to 0.59	2	7	4
0.20 to 0.39	2	2	1
0 to 0.19	1	3	2

The evidence in Tables 3, 4, and 5 helps to discriminate between the equilibrium and disequilibrium theories. The hypothesis in Table 3 makes the actual rate of price change depend on the anticipated rate of inflation and on some principal determinants of the relative rate of change of current spending. Spending shifts along a supply curve of output relating prices to output or rates of price change to rates of change of output. The current rate of price change depends mainly on the stimulus provided by past domestic and world rates of growth of money through their effect on anticipated inflation and, to a limited extent, on current fiscal and monetary policies. The effects of past and current policy on the rate of price change also depend on the acceleration of output. Acceleration of output reduces the rate of price change.

The results in Table 3 were obtained from a spending equation and an equilibrium condition for the output market. Supply adjustment is treated as of secondary importance, which is to say that adjustment of supply has no important effect that is independent of its effect on anticipations.[11]

Disequilibrium theories, like the Phillips curve, assume that deviations from full employment are the result of disequilibrium in the output market. Workers and employers do not anticipate any of the real or nominal shocks that cause current output to depart from full employment, and do not adjust anticipations of prices and output simultaneously. Consequently, the current deviation from full employment--and even past deviations--causes the current rate of price change to differ from the anticipated rate of price change.

The equilibrium view as presented here and the disequilibrium view expressed in standard Phillips curves are both partial explanations. The former analyzes the adjustment of demand and presumes that the dominant influences on the anticipated rate of change of output are incorporated in the adjustment

---

[11] This does not imply that wages fully reflect the current anticipated rate of inflation. Complete adjustment of money wages would eliminate any effect of nominal or real changes in output. The absence of complete adjustment of money wages, however, does not imply disequilibrium in the output market. Workers may prefer small fluctuations in employment to changes in money wages and may knowingly enter into contracts that provide for changes in employment rather than in wages.

of anticipated rates of price change. The latter analyzes the supply response on the output market and presumes that the difference between actual and full employment output measures excess demand. At less than full employment, prices rise more slowly because there is aggregate excess supply.

The empirical evidence that we have presented discriminates between the two views. If a choice is to be made between the two explanations, the data favor the equilibrium view for the period of the dollar standard. Of course, a choice between two restricted theories is not the only choice. Many of the empirical analyses of inflation during the period of the dollar standard, however, were based on one of the partial explanations. If our findings are correct, the less relevant partial explanation has dominated discussion of the reasons for inflation and of the appropriate policies toward inflation and unemployment.

V. CONCLUSION

Many empirical studies report the results of extensive search within a given set of data to find parameter estimates that support a given hypothesis. The principal test is often a comparison with a null-hypothesis or a naive hypothesis. Our study reports on two types of tests of a theory of the rate of price change. We use the same equation to explain or predict inflation in many different countries and in groups of countries. Then, we test our hypothesis by comparison with two versions of the inflation augmented Phillips curve.

Although our tests are based on crude data that may contain more than the usual numbers of errors, the hypothesis passes both tests. The data suggest considerable uniformity for the individual countries during the period of the dollar standard. Current rates of price change depend mainly on anticipated inflation, and the latter depends mainly on maintained average rates of monetary expansion. Domestic monetary policy and foreign fiscal policy appear to have substantially larger effects on the rate of price change in several countries than does domestic fiscal policy. The effect of domestic fiscal policy is generally small.

All of our results are obtained using data from the period of the dollar standard. Our procedure is, therefore, open to the criticism that tests using the seventeen countries or four multi-country blocs are not independent experiments. Advocates of the monetary approach to the balance of payments often talk about the "law of one price" as a truth that is expected to hold always and everywhere. We find very little support for this form of the "law of one price," using annual observations. Neither rates of change of money and prices nor rates of acceleration are highly correlated.

A principal difference between our equilibrium model of spending and the Phillips curve is that the usual Phillips curve is a disequilibrium theory. In the typical version, producers or purchasers choose equilibrium prices or rates of price change only at full employment. Elsewhere, prices respond to the gap between actual and full employment output. In an equilibrium theory, the deviation from full employment affects both the anticipated rate of price change and the anticipated supply of output.

The policy implications differ for the two approaches. If the disequilibrium approach is correct, policies that increase spending change actual output without raising the anticipated rate of inflation. Reducing disequilibrium raises the actual toward the anticipated rate of price change without changing the anticipated rate. In the equilibrium model of the output market, policies that stimulate spending also affect supply. Producers and purchasers respond to stimulus by increasing inventory accumulation in anticipation of higher prices and higher rates of inflation. The full-employment equilibrium rate of inflation increases when stimulus is maintained at a higher level and falls if stimulus is reduced.

Our findings suggest that the equilibrium theory is the more relevant of the two. These findings apply, strictly, to the period of the dollar standard used for our study. Nevertheless, we believe our findings have implications for the present and future as well as for the past. The anticipated rate of inflation will be generated in a different way, but the influence of anticipation on actual rates of inflation, and the influence of the actual rate of inflation on the growth rate of spending, should not change markedly. Our finding that foreign monetary and fiscal policies were the dominant impulses on anticipations of inflation--and on inflation--in most countries is a statement about the past. The consistency of this finding with monetary theory gives reason to expect, but does not establish, that the dominant impulses are now domestic policies.

References

Brunner, K. (1976), "A Fisherian Framework for the Analysis of International Monetary Problems," in Inflation in the World Economy, eds. M. Parkin and G. Zis. Manchester: Manchester University Press.

Brunner, K., and Meltzer, A.H. (1976), "Monetary and Fiscal Policy in Open, Interdependent Economies with Fixed Exchange Rates," in Recent Issues in International Monetary Economics, eds. E. Claassen and P. Salin. Amsterdam: North-Holland.

Christ, C. (1968), "A Simple Macroeconomic Model with a Government Budget Constraint," Journal of Political Economy, 76: 53-67.

Cross, R., and Laidler, D. (1976), "Inflation, Excess Demand and Expectations in Fixed Exchange Rate Open Economies," in Inflation in the World Economy, eds. M. Parkin and G. Zis. Manchester: Manchester University Press.

Fase, M.M.G., and Kuné, J.B. (1975), "The Demand for Money in Thirteen European and Non-European Countries: A Tabular Survey," Kredit und Kapital, 3: 410-19.

Genberg, H.A. (1976), "Aspects of the Monetary Approach to Balance of Payments Theory: An Empirical Study of Sweden," in The Monetary Approach to the Balance of Payments, eds. J.A. Frenkel and H.G. Johnson. London: Allen and Unwin.

Gordon, R.A. (1976), "Recent Developments in the Theory of Inflation and Unemployment," Journal of Monetary Economics, 2: 185-220.

Hamburger, M.J., and Reisch, R. (1976), "Inflation, Unemployment and Macroeconomic Policy in Open Economies: An Empirical Analysis," Carnegie-Rochester Conference Series, 4, eds. K. Brunner and A.H. Meltzer. Amsterdam: North-Holland.

Johnson, Harry G. (1972). Inflation and the Monetarist Controversy. Professor F. de Vries Lectures, Amsterdam.

Laidler, D. (1974), "The Control of Inflation and the Future of the International Monetary System," American Economic Review, 64: 535-43.

Laidler, D., and Parkin, J.M. (1975), "Inflation: A Survey," Economic Journal, 85: 741-809.

Lucas, R.E., Jr. (1975), "An Equilibrium Model of the Business Cycle," Journal of Political Economy, 83: 1113-44.

_____(1977), "Understanding Business Cycles," Carnegie-Rochester Conference Series, 5, eds. K. Brunner and A.H. Meltzer. Amsterdam: North-Holland.

McGuire, T.W. (1976), "On Estimating the Effects of Controls," Carnegie-Rochester Conference Series, 2, eds. K. Brunner and A.H. Meltzer. Amsterdam: North-Holland.

Meltzer, A.H. (1977), "Anticipated Inflation and Unanticipated Price Change: A Test of the Price-Specie Flow Theory and the Phillips Curve," Journal of Money, Credit and Banking, 9 (2): 182-205.

Mundell, R.A. (1968). International Economics. New York: Macmillan.

Neumann, M.J.M. (1977), "Offsetting Capital Flows," multilithed, Freie Universität Berlin.

Parkin, M. (1977), "A 'Monetarist' Analysis of the Generation and Transmission of World Inflation, 1958-71," American Economic Review, 67: 164-71.

Pattison, J.C. (1976), "International Inflationary Linkages and the Recent Experience in Individual Countries," in Bank Credit, Money and Inflation in Open Economies, eds. M. Fratianni and K. Tavernier. Berlin: Duncker and Humblot.

Stein, J.L. (1976), "Inside the Monetarist Black Box," in Monetarism, ed. J.L. Stein. Amsterdam: North-Holland.

Weintraub, R. (1976). The Impact of the Federal Reserve System's Monetary Policy on the Nation's Economy, Subcommittee on Domestic Monetary Policy, U.S. House of Representatives. Washington, D.C.: U.S. Government Printing Office.

INFLATION AND STABILITY:
A COMMENT ON THE JONSON AND TAYLOR
AND KORTEWEG AND MELTZER PAPERS

Jerome L. Stein[*]

Brown University

> The principal issues, for us, are the nature of the transmission mechanism. . . , the nature of the relation between allocative adjustments and aggregative behavior, and the nature of the process generating economic fluctuations or persistent inflation. The last issue is occasionally divided into two parts. One concerns the internal stability of the private sector and the other the nature of the impulse force driving an economy (Brunner and Meltzer, 1976, p. 150).

Two subissues, in particular, are active sources of current research and controversy. First, does the change in the rate of inflation depend on the current rate of monetary expansion, or does it depend on the current state of aggregate demand (which is usually measured by the unemployment rate)?[1] Those who maintain that the change in the rate of inflation depends solely on the current state of aggregate demand (plus a random term) do not believe that a rise in the rate of monetary expansion will raise the rate of inflation if there is sufficient excess capacity. In fact, they measure this excess capacity by the difference between the current rate of unemployment and the "noninflationary rate of unemployment," estimated at 5.5 percent.

Second, will a tax cut financed by the sale of government interest-bearing debt raise excess aggregate demand and the rate of inflation?

The papers by Jonson and Taylor and by Korteweg and Meltzer are concerned with both of these issues. Both papers are lucid, sophisticated, and serious studies. Jonson and Taylor examine Australia, a small open economy; Korteweg and Meltzer examine twenty-four countries during the period 1956-72. Their techniques of analysis are different. As a discussant, my task is to evaluate what each paper says concerning the issues posed above.

Figure 1 illustrates the difficulties in interpreting recent macroeconomic research. Authors generally postulate different economic models, labeled A_1, A_2, B, C, and D. From their models, certain empirical or econometric equations

---

[*] Eastman Professor of Political Economy, Professor of Economics.

[1] This controversy is reflected in Modigliani and Papademos (1975), Stein (1978), and Tobin (1975).

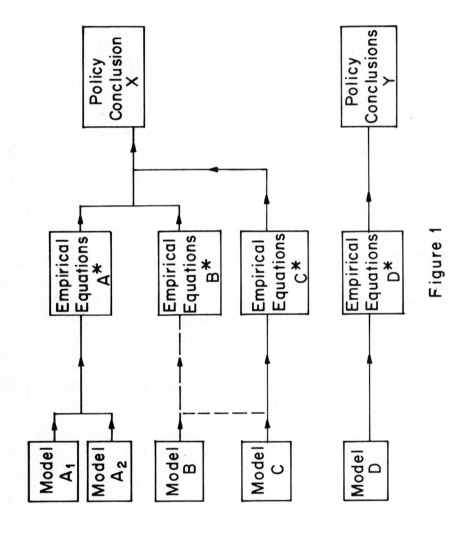

Figure 1

(labeled A^*, B^*, C^*, and D^*) are derived. On the basis of statistical analysis, certain relevant policy conclusions (labeled X and Y) are drawn.

Despite their superficial differences, models A_1 and A_2 imply the same empirical equations for the economically relevant variables and, hence, lead to the same policy conclusions. For example, model A_1 may be a twenty-two-differential equation model (as in the Jonson and Taylor work), and model A_2 may be reduced to a three-differential equation system of the relevant economic variables. For allocative detail, model A_1 is superior. If one wants to solve the system analytically and discern the essence of the transmission mechanism, model A_2 is superior. In examining a "large" model, I ask whether it can be reduced in size (to A_2) without any significant distortion.

Model B may look quite different from models A_1 and A_2 and may imply different estimating equations (B^* instead of A^*). For example, model A_2 may be "Keynesian," and model B may be based on the demand for money equation. Nevertheless, it may turn out that both imply the same policy conclusions X: e.g., that a rise in the rate of monetary expansion will raise the rate of inflation, regardless of the rate of unemployment; and that a growth in the federal interest bearing debt per se is not inflationary.

Model D, by contrast, is fundamentally different from the other models because it implies different policy conclusions. For example, model D could be the Wharton model, and model C could be that of the Federal Reserve Bank of St. Louis.

Often a model B contains nonobservable variables, e.g., the anticipated rate of price change. The author then adduces a set of assumptions, or uses some statistical transformations, which are not integral parts of model B to measure the unobservable variable. It may then turn out that the empirical equations so derived are those implied by model C and not by model B per se. When this occurs, the reader is often uncertain how to interpret the theoretical implications of the empirical equations. In my evaluation of the papers, I ask whether the authors' empirical equations permit us to confirm or disconfirm their original models.

I. THE JONSON AND TAYLOR STUDY
OF INFLATION AND ECONOMIC STABILITY IN AUSTRALIA

A. Summary

Table 1 contains the phenomena to be explained. The greatly increased inflation from 1958/68 to 1975/76 in Australia was accompanied by a low growth of real product and increased unemployment. During this period, several impulses occurred. Worldwide inflation impinged on an economy with a fixed exchange rate. Revaluation was followed by devaluation. There was a strong expansion of the government sector, a wage "explosion," and a substantial rise in the rate of monetary expansion.

Table 1

Australia: Inflation, Employment, and Growth

	1	2	3		5
	Real growth	Unemploy-ment	π Inflation (GDP)		M3 Monetary growth μ
			Actual	Predicted (Stein)	
1950/59- 1968/69 average	5.1 percent per annum	1.4 percent	2.9 percent per annum		7.7 percent per annum
1969-70	5.8	1.4	4.5	4.8 percent per annum	6.1
1970-71	4.4	1.4	5.3	5.3	6.8
1971-72	4.2	1.9	7.1	5.9	10.5
1972-73	4.6	2.1	8.9	7.8	25.8
1973-74	5.8	1.6	14.5	15.0	14.5
1974-75	-0.1	3.4	17.6	14.8	15.4
1975-76	1.5	4.3	15.3	15.0	13.8
Mean 1969/76	3.74	2.3	10.46	9.80	13.27
Standard deviation	2.22	1.12	5.27	4.89	6.64

Jonson and Taylor attempt to separate the effects of the various interrelated impulses. A twenty-two-differential equation Keynesian model is constructed and estimated with great technical skill and economic insight. This model is simulated to determine the contribution of each impulse to the rate of inflation, growth of output, unemployment rate, and international reserves.

Four simulations are reported. (i) There is a managed float with no major revaluations as in 1972 and 1973, and no devaluation as in 1974. (ii) Added to (i) is a tightening of money by raising interest rates on government securities in 1972 and 1973; at the same time, the aggregate bank liquidity ratio is not reduced from its value at the start of the simulation period. (iii) Added to (ii) is the condition that the growth rates of government spending and transfers are maintained at the rates achieved in the second half of the 1960s. (iv) Added to (iii) is the condition that real award wages grow at the rate of growth of productivity.

Their main conclusions, derived from simulations, are that: a) the removal of the various monetary, budgetary, and wage impulses, combined with a managed float, largely eliminates the domestic acceleration of inflation that occurs in the control simulation; b) a relatively steady set of policies produces a smoother output path; c) "At the most general level, it could be argued that considerable responsibility for increased inflation and economic instability be attributed to the failure of Australian economic policy to emphasize sufficiently monetary growth rates as crucial indicators of the stance of policy."

This dynamic Keynesian model implies the same policy prescriptions as do some of the monetarist models. It is also interesting to note that during the period from 1958-59 to 1968-69, the rate of inflation, $\pi = 2.9$ percent per annum, was about equal to the growth of M3, $\mu = 7.7$ percent per annum, less the growth of output, 5.1 percent per annum, equals 2.6 percent per annum.

B. Critique

Since the Jonson-Taylor (J-T) model contains twenty-two nonlinear differential equations, it is not apparent to the reader which equations are crucial and which are expendable. The reader is interested in learning what their model says about the issue posed at the beginning of this paper, namely, does the change in the rate of inflation depend on the current unemployment rate or does it depend on the rate of monetary expansion less the rate of inflation? Their model must be simulated to answer this question. In order to understand the dynamic interactions, I attempt to reduce their model (A_1) to a simpler system (model A_2).

Three of their crucial equations are (J-T6), (J-T9), and (J-T11). The first states that the rate of inflation Dlog P depends on: a) the ratio of labor costs to the value of output, and b) the ratio of real balances to the quantity demanded.[2]

$$\text{(J-T6)} \quad \text{Dlog } P = .42 \left[\log \frac{P_0 WL}{Q(t)} - \log P\right] + .23 \left(\log \frac{M}{P} - \log \hat{m}\right).$$

Their second equation states that the growth of the nominal wage, Dlog W, depends on: a) the ratio of the marginal product of labor to the real wage, b) the ratio of labor demanded to that supplied, c) the growth of award wages relative to trend, and d) the ratio of real balances to the quantity demanded.

---

[2] An important aspect of their model is that their money supply is endogenous in a small open economy.

(J-T9)   Dlog W = .2 [log (.7y/L) - log W/P'] + 1.7 log L/N

$$+ .4 \log (w_A/w^* e^{.0029t}) + .21 (\log \frac{M}{P} - \log \hat{m}) .$$

The third equation states that the growth in the demand for labor depends on: a) the ratio of the marginal product of labor to the real wage, and b) the ratio of government spending relative to trend.

(J-T11)   Dlog L = .09 [log (.7y/L) - log W/P] + .008 log g/g*e$^{.012t}$,

where P   = price level
       M/P   = real balances
       $\hat{m}$ = real balances demanded
       .7y/L = marginal product of labor
       Q(t)   = output produced
       g   = government spending
       W   = nominal wage
       L   = labor demanded
       N   = labor supplied.

Because I have been working with dynamic Keynesian-monetarist models (Stein, 1974, 1976, 1978) of order 3, I was curious to determine if our models were similar. After some estimation of the dynamic system, I arrived (Stein, 1978) at reduced form equation (1) for the change in the rate of inflation:

(1) $\pi (t) - \pi (t-1) = 0.4 [\mu (t-1) - \pi(t-1)]$,

where $\pi(t)$ is the percentage change in the GNP deflator from year t-1 to year t, and $\mu(t)$ is the percentage change in the M1 money stock from year t-1 to year t.

     I found that the current unemployment rate does not affect significantly the change in the rate of inflation. The theoretical reason is that a rise in the unemployment rate has two effects on the rate of inflation. First, it reduces the growth of the nominal wage. This is equivalent to a decline in L/N in (J-T9). The decline in the growth of the nominal wage reduces the rate of inflation, as occurs in (J-T6). Second, the rise in unemployment reduces output. Savings fall by more than investment; but the rate of price change is positively related to investment minus savings. Is this effect present in the Jonson-Taylor model, as it is in all Keynesian models?

If these two effects approximately cancel each other, then the change in the rate of inflation is independent of the current unemployment rate. That is the main reason why my equation (1) does not contain the unemployment rate.

I wonder if Jonson and Taylor obtain a similar result. As a quick check, I used my derived reduced form equation (1) based on the U.S. data in a dynamic ex ante simulation of the Australian data in Table 1. To be sure, I used their series on the M3 money stock, whereas my equations were based on M1. Nevertheless, the results are noteworthy; compare column 3 (the actual rate of inflation) with column 4 [the predicted Australian rate of inflation based on a dynamic ex ante simulation using my U.S. equation (1)]. My root mean square error is 1.25, whereas the mean inflation rate is 10.46 with a standard deviation of 5.27. The root mean square error is only 24 percent of the standard deviation of the actual rate of inflation.

These results lead me to suspect that the Jonson-Taylor model (A_1) is quite similar to my (1978) model (A_2). Both Keynesian models seem to lead to monetarist results. Moreover, during the 1969-76 period, the mean rate of inflation, 10.46 percent per annum, is very close to the mean growth of their M3 money supply, 13.27 percent per annum, less the mean growth of output, 3.74 percent per annum, equals 9.53 percent per annum. This monetarist result occurred despite the considerable external shocks that impinged on the economy.

Next, it seems that their employment rate dynamics can be simplified. The main driving force behind the employment variable L is the gap between the marginal product of labor and the real wage (J-T11). The growth of the real wage $w \equiv W/P$ is obtained by subtracting (J-T6) from (J-T9):

$$\text{Dlog } W/P \equiv \text{Dlog } w = .2 \; [\log (.7y/L) - \log W/P'] + 1.7 \log L/N$$

$$+ (.21 - .23) (\log M/P - \log \hat{m}) - .42 \; [\log \frac{W/P}{Q(t)} \; P_0 L] \; .$$

The coefficient of the excess supply of real balances .21 - .23 does not seem to be significant; each term would have been rounded to 0.2. Therefore,

361

their employment subsystem seems to be reducible to equations (2) and (3) in the employment rate L/N and real wage w:

(2)   Dlog L = .09 [log (.7y/L) - log w]

(3)   Dlog w = .2 [log (.7y/L) - log w] + 1.7 log L/N - .42 log $(\frac{wL}{P_0Q(t)})$.

When the model is simplified in this way, the transmission mechanism is seen in a different light. The excess stock of money (M/P - $\hat{m}$) no longer has a direct effect on the real wage w and, hence, on employment L. An excess stock of money affects employment only by its effect on aggregate demand.[3] This is also what happens in my model.

Those of us who share the Brunner-Meltzer view of the principal issues would like Jonson and Taylor to explain what is the basic mechanism in their model which produces "an entrenched inflation, a marked cycle in real product, and an unemployment rate that is approximately three times the average for the 1960s." In particular, what are their answers to the questions posed at the beginning of this paper? Does their Keynesian mode imply monetarist results?

II. THE KORTEWEG AND MELTZER STUDY
OF INFLATION AND PRICE CHANGES

Korteweg and Meltzer have undertaken a serious and important study of the determinants of inflation by focusing on the experiences of diverse countries. Their work is intellectually stimulating and demands careful analysis.

It is convenient to distinguish their model from their estimating equations, and to examine each separately. Then their interrelation can be considered. A major objective of their paper is to estimate the effects of monetary, fiscal, and other influences on the rate of change of prices for several countries and groups of countries.

A. Empirical Equations
First, they conclude, in discussing their Table 1, that, "Contrary to versions of the monetary approach to the balance of payments that do not distinguish short- and long-term adjustment, the data show substantial

_____

[3] The authors include the award wages effect on real wages in order to explain the high unemployment in recent years.

variability in the relation between domestic and rest-of-the-world rates of growth of monetary and fiscal variables."

The following correlations were obtained for the U.S., Denmark, and Holland with respect to: a) the growth of the domestic monetary base with the growth of the rest-of-the-world monetary base; b) the domestic rate of inflation and the rest-of-the-world rate of inflation; c) the domestic growth of government debt outstanding and the growth of the outstanding debt in the rest of the world.

Correlation Coefficients

	(a) Base	(b) Prices	(c) Debt
U.S.	0.25	0.68	0.40
Denmark	0.14	0.53	0.29
Holland	0.59	0.49	0.51

Korteweg and Meltzer conclude that, "there is not a simple, uniform mechanism linking foreign money to domestic money and then to prices through the trade account or the base." This conclusion seems to be consistent with a recent study by Borts and Hanson (1977) which examines the effects of: a) net sales of government debt to the public, and b) the government deficit, on the current and capital accounts. In the U.S., the U.K., Germany, and Japan, the creation of high-powered money by incurring a budget deficit significantly reduces the capital account. It was not significant in the Netherlands, Italy, or Australia. The effect of high-powered money creation on the current account was mixed, and no conclusions could be drawn. Both of these studies suggest that there is need for more research on this important subject.

Second, the authors' Table 2 describes the results of regressing the rate of inflation on three-year moving averages of measured rates of growth of: a) the monetary base in each country and in the rest of the world, b) the stock of outstanding government debt in each country and in the rest of the world, and c) real income. Call the vector of these five variables, X.

The regression is

(4)   rate of inflation = $(c + a \cdot X)$ + error,

and estimates are obtained of the constant c and the vector a of coefficients.

Conclusions drawn by Korteweg and Meltzer are that the response of the rate of inflation to the three-year moving average of the growth of the monetary base in the rest of the world "is the most reliable of the five responses, as measured by the t-statistics." The growth of the stock of debt does not have a significant effect on the rate of inflation, given the other variables. This is consistent with Stein (1976) that the P_5 effect[4] is nonpositive. However, the total explanatory power of these regressions is not large. For example, for the world as a whole:

(5) predicted rate of inflation = $1.7 + .46^*$ (growth of base)
$$- .28 \text{ (growth of debt)}$$
$$- .06 \text{ (growth of output)}$$
$$\equiv \text{ actual rate of inflation - error;}$$

(*) indicates $t > 2, \bar{r}^2 = .39$.

These empirical results are interesting and important.

B. The Models and Alternative Hypotheses

Korteweg and Meltzer test alternative theories of the mechanism whereby inflation is generated. Their basic model states that the price level p depends on real output y, capital or capacity output y_0, and the money wage w:

(6) $p = p (y, y_0, w)$.

In terms of rates of change, (6) implies that

(7) rate of inflation = β_1 (growth of output)
$$+ \beta_2 \text{ (growth of capacity output)}$$
$$+ \beta_3 \text{ (growth of the wage)} + \beta_0.$$

The authors never directly test this equation, which is a direct implication of their model. Using my Figure 1, if their model equation (6) is B, then econometric equation (7) is B^*. They do not go from B to B^*, even though there are data for these variables.

---

[4]This is the upward shift of the IS curve less the upward shift of the LM curve resulting from a rise in the stock of bonds, given real balances and the unemployment rate.

They go further and make the wage endogenous. The money wage depends on the anticipated price level p^a:

(8) $w = w(p^a, \ldots)$.

It follows that the actual price level p can be written as

(9) $p = P(y, y_0, p^a)$.

In terms of rates of change, (9) becomes

(10)   rate of inflation $= b_1$ (growth of output)
                    $+ b_2$ (growth of capacity)
                    $+ b_3$ (anticipated rate of price change) $+ b_0$.

Anticipations cannot be measured directly. The authors' measure of the anticipated rate of inflation is the predicted rate of inflation $c + a \cdot X$ in (4) and (5) above. Hence, (10) becomes

(11)   rate of inflation $= b_1$ (growth of output)
                    $+ b_2$ (growth of capacity output)
                    $+ b_3$ (predicted rate of inflation $= c + a \cdot X$).

From the construction of the predicted rate of inflation in (4), we derive

(12)   predicted rate of inflation $c + a \cdot X$
                $\equiv$ Korteweg-Meltzer anticipated rate of inflation
                $=$ rate of inflation - error.

In effect, therefore, their regression equation for the rate of inflation is

365

(13)   rate of inflation = b_1 (growth of output)

$+ b_2$ (growth of capacity output)

$+ b_3$ (rate of inflation - error = $c + a \cdot X$) $+ b_0$.

In their Table 3, the authors regress the rate of inflation on: a) the Korteweg-Meltzer measure of the anticipated rate of inflation, b) the growth of the base, c) the growth of the debt, and d) the change in the growth of output. What this means is that they estimate the coefficients of the following regression:

(14)   rate of inflation = b_1 (growth of base)

$+ b_2$ (growth of debt)

$+ b_3$ (rate of inflation - error = $c + a \cdot X$)

$+ b_4$ (change in growth of output) $+ b_0$.

The results for the U.S. and the Netherlands are as follows. An asterisk indicates $t \geqslant 2.0$.

(14-U.S.) rate of inflation = $.08 + .01$ (growth of base)

$- .02$ (growth of debt)

$+ .98^*$ (rate of inflation - error = $c + a \cdot X$)

$- .08$ (change in growth of output).

(14-Holland) rate of inflation = $.02 - .1$ (growth of base)

$- 0.0$ (growth of debt)

$+ 1.17^*$ (rate of inflation - error = $c + a \cdot X$)

$+ .01$ (change in growth of output).

If my understanding is correct, then, there is little additional information in the Korteweg-Meltzer Table 3 that is not already contained in their Table 2. Their "anticipated rate of price change" subsumes the major determinants of the rate of price change because it is the predicted rate of inflation derived (for example) in (5) above.

A distinguishing characteristic of "monetarism" is the importance, emphasis and attention given to the growth rate of money. . . .the growth rate of money is said to be the principal determinant of the rate of inflation (Brunner and Meltzer, 1976, pp. 154-55).

In view of this quotation, I am not sure if Korteweg and Meltzer really want to use (6) or (9) above to explain inflation.

According to (6) and (8), a rise in the growth of the money supply will not affect prices p until wages w or output y rise; and wages will not rise until the "anticipated price level" p^a rises. If the labor movement signs a "social compact" not to raise wages, then (6) states that the price level will move with the level of output, regardless of what is happening in the monetary sector. Moreover, suppose that the economy is at full employment, $y = y_0$. Then, (6) or (8) states that inflation depends exclusively on the growth of wages. If a monetary disturbance is to be inflationary, it must first raise the growth of the nominal wage. A wage freeze would then prevent inflation, according to (6). For these reasons, I wonder if the Korteweg-Meltzer model equations (6), (8) are in the spirit of the citation from Brunner and Meltzer given above.

It has been an intellectually stimulating experience to study these two papers.

References

Borts, G.H., and Hanson, J.A. (1977), "The Government Budget and the Balance of Payments," Brown University working paper.

Brunner, K., and Meltzer, A.H. (1976), "Reply--Monetarism: The Principal Issues, Areas of Agreement and the Work Remaining," in Monetarism, ed. J.L. Stein. Amsterdam: North-Holland.

Jonson, P.D., and Taylor, J.C. (1978), "Inflation and Economic Stability in a Small Open Economy: A Systems Approach," Carnegie-Rochester Conference Series, 8, eds. K. Brunner and A.H. Meltzer. Amsterdam: North-Holland.

Korteweg, P., and Meltzer, A.H. (1978), "Inflation and Price Changes: Some Preliminary Estimates and Tests of Alternative Theories," Carnegie-Rochester Conference Series, 8, eds. K. Brunner and A.H. Meltzer. Amsterdam: North-Holland.

Modigliani, F., and Papademos, L. (1975), "Targets for Monetary Policy in the Coming Year," Brookings Papers on Economic Activity, 1. Washington, D.C.: The Brookings Institution.

Stein, J.L. (1974) "Unemployment, Inflation and Monetarism," American Economic Review, 64: 867-87.

_____(1976), "Inside the Monetarist Black Box," in Monetarism, ed. J.L. Stein. Amsterdam: North-Holland.

_____(1978), "Inflation, Employment and Stagflation," Journal of Monetary Economics, in press.

Tobin, J. (1975), "Monetary Policy, Inflation, and Unemployment," Papers on Monetary Economics, Bank of Australia.

A COMMENT ON THE KORTEWEG AND MELTZER AND DUTTON PAPERS

Jeremy J. Siegel

University of Pennsylvania

An extensive comment on the paper by Jonson and Taylor on the postwar experience with inflation in Australia is provided by Jerome Stein. This discussion concentrates on the papers by Korteweg and Meltzer and by Dutton. The Korteweg and Meltzer paper analyzes the evidence for a Phillips curve in an international context as well as proposing an alternative hypothesis of inflation. The paper by Dutton analyzes Phillips theories for the U.S.

It is clear that Korteweg and Meltzer, in their attempt to formulate an alternative to the standard Phillips curve represented by their equation (1) are confronting the statistical problem of estimating such a relation in a "rational expectations" framework. If price expectations are formed rationally, i.e., if $\hat{p}^a$ is an unbiased, full information estimate of inflation $\hat{p}$, then by (1) income can only deviate from the full employment position by an uncorrelated random error. The fact that real income is a highly autocorrelated series must lead to some modification of this relationship. Many, such as Lucas (1973), Barro (1977), and others, have included a lagged income term in equation (1) or lagged errors in price expectations. One explanation for this alternative specification is that errors in expectations have persistent effects through changes in capital accumulation or some other variable in the production process. Another way of interpreting this is that the "full employment" output does change in the short run until the production process returns to its former level, which it would in the absence of future shocks.

Korteweg and Meltzer suggest an alternative hypothesis. The y_0 term in equation (1) should be interpreted as anticipated income rather than full employment income. Since (1) can be written as equation (2), the Phillips curve can be estimated on rates of change of income (rather than levels) if last period's anticipated income was equal to what was realized, and the rate of growth of anticipated income is constant. In my opinion, either the Korteweg-Meltzer refo nulation or the addition of lagged terms is a rather ad hoc attempt at eliminating the autocorrelation in the income series so that the rational expectations formulations of $\hat{p}^a$ in (1) can be empirically estimated. Of course, the standard alternative of assuming $\hat{p}^a$ is formed by some "adaptive" mechanism (which gives the series significant autocorrelation) is just as arbitrary. For this reason, it is not clear that when Korteweg and Meltzer empirically reject equation (1) it is because of the interpretation of y_0, the absence of "persistence" effects, or the assumption of a "rationally" determined $\hat{p}^a$.

The formation of price anticipations is critical to macroeconomic estimation. Both Korteweg and Meltzer and Dutton find that "sustained" changes in the monetary base are the most important determinant of anticipated inflation. Korteweg and Meltzer state that economic agents will distinguish between "maintained" and transient changes in the base when they formulate their price anticipations. Sargent and Wallace (1973) show that, as long as there is some interest elasticity to the demand for money, then a "rational" projection of next period's price level involves a projection of all future levels of the money supply and real income. Hence, a transitory blip in money should affect prices only slightly, whereas a maintained increase has a more nearly "quantity theory" effect. It is important to determine if the authors' equations improve on a simple ARIMA time series analysis of the inflation rate. Proper application of simple autoregressive estimation will automatically distinguish between "sustained" and "transient" changes in a variable.

It should be noted that, if anticipated inflation is estimated as a function of lagged values of exogenous variables, and actual inflation is then estimated from anticipated inflation and current exogenous variables, then a significant coefficient on $\hat{p}^a$ does not necessarily mean that anticipated inflation "caused" or is the primary determinant of actual inflation. Even a coefficient of 1.0 on $\hat{p}^a$ with a partial R^2 in excess of .90 may be consistent with anticipated inflation having absolutely no effect on current inflation. All these correlations mean that the stochastic structure of inflation is such that current innovations have a small effect relative to lagged values of the variables, i.e., that inflation is a sluggish process. Since the inflation series is so highly autocorrelated, it is not surprising that such strong correlations between actual and anticipated inflation were found. In fact, I found it surprising that Korteweg and Meltzer obtained such low R^2's for their price equations (given in their Tables 2 and 3), while Dutton and other seminar contributors found R^2 in the neighborhood of .85-.90. It could very well mean that the IMF data base is highly suspect, which could also explain the low correlations that Korteweg and Meltzer obtained throughout their paper.

Another interesting area explored by Korteweg and Meltzer is the relationship between the growth of the monetary base and other variables for various countries, as displayed in their Table 1. One must be extremely careful, however, in interpreting these results, primarily due to the authors' conversion of all nominal magnitudes into U.S. dollars before calculating the correlations. To understand the effect of this procedure, let us assume a trade situation in which the "law of one price" holds for traded goods among countries. Under floating exchange rates, there would be no necessary correlation between any two

370

countries' price levels and those of the rest of the world. However, the changes in the monetary aggregates adjusted to any one currency would be highly correlated. In a system of fixed exchange rates, the monetary growth rates would have to be equalized in the long run, although in the short run there would be less than perfect correlation, since the ratio of the prices of traded to nontraded goods could change. In the fixed rate regime, this partial correlation would apply whether or not the aggregates are converted into any common currency. Hence, the correlations that Korteweg and Meltzer calculate are not inconsistent with the (two-good) monetary approach to the balance of payments, as they claim. It does appear, as the authors rightly note, that a large volume of evidence has been accumulated to disprove the "one-good" (all goods traded) version of the monetary theory.

Substantially more flexibility of exchange rates exists now than prior to 1972--the period referred to by Korteweg and Meltzer as the "dollar standard." This means that the behavior of central bankers is altered, and that in all probability the estimated equations will have altered coefficients. I was disappointed that most of the Conference papers did not address this point. It is not clear, as Korteweg and Meltzer state in their conclusion, that the influence of anticipated inflation on actual inflation will not markedly change, or that the dominant impulses, while tending to be "foreign" in the pre-1972 period, are now likely to be "domestic." In fact, Dutton claims that the most significant change in the estimated equations from 1972 to 1974 is in the impact of the export sector on inflation. In my opinion, it behooves the contributors to compare the estimates of the last five-year period (with its significant structural changes) with those of the prior postwar period.

References

Barro, R.J. (1977), "Unanticipated Money Growth and Unemployment in the United States," <u>American Economic Review</u>, 67: 101-15.

Dutton, D.S (1978), "Economics of Inflation and Output Fluctuations in the United States, 1952-1974," <u>Carnegie-Rochester Conference Series</u>, 8, eds. K. Brunner and A.H. Meltzer. Amsterdam: North-Holland.

Jonson, P.D., and Taylor, J.C. (1978), "Inflation and Economic Stability in a Small Open Economy: A Systems Approach," <u>Carnegie-Rochester Conference Series</u>, 8, eds. K. Brunner and A.H. Meltzer. Amsterdam: North-Holland.

Korteweg, P., and Meltzer, A.H. (1978), "Inflation and Price Changes: Some Preliminary Estimates and Tests of Alternative Theories," <u>Carnegie-Rochester Conference Series</u>, 8, eds. K. Brunner and A.H. Meltzer. Amsterdam: North-Holland.

Lucas, R.E., Jr. (1973), "Some International Evidence on Output-Inflation Tradeoffs," <u>American Economic Review</u>, 63: 326-34.

Sargent, T.J., and Wallace, N. (1973), "The Stability of Models of Money and Growth with Perfect Foresight," <u>Econometrica</u>, 41: 1043-48.

Stein, J.L. (1978), "Inflation and Stability: A Comment on the Jonson and Taylor and Korteweg and Meltzer Papers," <u>Carnegie-Rochester Conference Series</u>, 8, eds. K. Brunner and A.H. Meltzer. Amsterdam: North-Holland.